Conflicts in a Conflict

CILE Studies

Series Editor: Ronald A. Brand

CILE Studies is a series of monographs and edited volumes dedicated to the discussion of important issues and developments in public and private international law. Each volume is selected on the basis of its contribution to the literature with the objective to provide lasting commentary and innovative analysis.

Potential authors may contact:
Center for International Legal Education
University of Pittsburgh School of Law
Barco Law Building
3900 Forbes Avenue
Pittsburgh, PA 15260
U.S.A.
Phone: 412-648-7023
fax: 412-648-2648
email: cile@law.pitt.edu

Volumes 1 and 2 are available directly from the Center for International Legal Education at the above address. Volume 3 and later volumes can be ordered from Oxford University Press by visiting their website at: www.oup.com.

The Series

Volume 1

The Draft UNCITRAL Digest and Beyond: Cases, Analysis and Unresolved Issues in the U.N. Sales Convention,
(Franco Ferrari, Harry M. Flechtner, and Ronald A. Brand, editors)

Volume 2

Private Law, Private International Law, and Judical Cooperation in the EU-US Relationship,
(Ronald A. Brand, editor)

Volume 3

Forum Non Conveniens—History, Global Practice, and Future Under the Hague Convention on Choice of Court Agreements,
(Ronald A. Brand and Scott R. Jablonski)

Volume 4

Drafting Contracts Under the CISG,
(Harry M. Flechtner, Ronald A. Brand, Mark S. Walter, editors)

Volume 5

Conflicts in a Conflict: A Conflict of Laws Case Study on Israel and the Palestinian Territories,
(Michael Karayanni)

cile
Center for International Legal Education

Conflicts in a Conflict

A Conflict of Laws Case Study on Israel and the Palestinian Territories

Michael Karayanni

OXFORD
UNIVERSITY PRESS

OXFORD
UNIVERSITY PRESS

Oxford University Press is a department of the University of Oxford. It furthers the University's objective of excellence in research, scholarship, and education by publishing worldwide.

Oxford New York
Auckland Cape Town Dar es Salaam Hong Kong Karachi Kuala Lumpur Madrid Melbourne Mexico City Nairobi New Delhi Shanghai Taipei Toronto

With offices in
Argentina Austria Brazil Chile Czech Republic France Greece Guatemala Hungary Italy Japan Poland Portugal Singapore South Korea Switzerland Thailand Turkey Ukraine Vietnam

Published in the United States of America by
Oxford University Press
198 Madison Avenue, New York, NY 10016

Library of Congress Cataloging-in-Publication Data

Karayanni, Michael Mousa, author.
Conflicts in a conflict : a conflict of laws case study on Israel and the Palestinian territories / Michael Karayanni.
pages cm — (CILE Studies ; Vol. 5)
Includes bibliographical references and index.
ISBN 978-0-19-987371-5 (hardback)
1. Conflict of laws—Israel. 2. Conflict of laws—Palestine. 3. Israel-Arab War, 1967—Occupied territories. 4. Arab-Israeli conflict—Law and legislation 5. West Bank—International status. 6. Gaza Strip—International status. I. Title.
KMK482.K37 2014
340.9095695'3—dc23

2013043372

Note to Readers

This publication is designed to provide accurate and authoritative information in regard to the subject matter covered. It is based upon sources believed to be accurate and reliable and is intended to be current as of the time it was written. It is sold with the understanding that the publisher is not engaged in rendering legal, accounting, or other professional services. If legal advice or other expert assistance is required, the services of a competent professional person should be sought. Also, to confirm that the information has not been affected or changed by recent developments, traditional legal research techniques should be used, including checking primary sources where appropriate.

(Based on the Declaration of Principles jointly adopted by a Committee of the American Bar Association and a Committee of Publishers and Associations.)

To

Mousa, Jana, and Eyas

Contents

Foreword

In 1981 a fifteen-year-old Palestinian "worker" from the West Bank city of Ramallah was injured in a work-related accident. The factory in which he was employed and where the accident occurred was also located in Ramallah, owned by Palestinian residents of that city. The parents of the Palestinian worker filed a claim for personal injuries against the Palestinian employers—in an Israeli court. In the Israeli Supreme Court's decision the justices pronounced major holdings on the doctrine of forum non conveniens and choice of law in torts.

This is the case of *Abu Attiya v. Arabtisi* (CA 300/84, 39(1) PD 365 (1985)), which I teach in my civil procedure and private international law classes at the Hebrew University. Once the facts and holdings of the case are laid out, the discussion takes a long detour into the nature of the legal system in the Occupied West Bank and Gaza Strip. The first question I pose to my students is—why did this Palestinian family chose to adjudicate its local tort against two Palestinian defendants before an Israeli court? The uninformed response is often that the family had no other choice, because the Israeli military courts operating in the West Bank do not deal with such disputes. The students are usually surprised to learn that much of the local civil court system in the West Bank, as well as the civil law that existed on the eve of the 1967 Six-Day War, is maintained by the Israel Defense Forces. So these Palestinian family members could have filed their claims before the local courts, but preferred the Israeli forum instead. This then raises a host of other questions. What does filing a Palestinian civil claim before an Israeli court say about the condition of the local legal system in the West Bank? What are the ramifications of choosing the Israeli forum for Palestinian relations with and acquiescence to Israeli rule? What are the implications of local residents not having any political recourse by which to influence the norms of the local legal system or challenge the legitimacy of the local courts? Have things changed with the establishment of the Palestinian Authority? And should any of this be of concern to Israeli courts when considering the adjudication of such a case and the application of Israeli law?

I am always bewildered by how little my students know about the Occupied Palestinian Territories—so close geographically that West Bank towns and villages are visible from the windows of our classroom at the Hebrew University on Mount Scopus in Jerusalem, yet so distant in their consciousnesses, as if they were located on another continent. It was this dislocation—territorial as well as cognitive—that brought me to write this book.

The genesis of this book is in two articles I published in 2008 and 2009. The first was titled "The Quest for Creative Jurisdiction: The Evolution of Personal Jurisdiction Doctrine of Israeli Courts Toward the Palestinian Territories" and was published in the *Michigan Journal of International Law* (volume 29, issue no. 4, 2008), and the second was "Choice of Law under Occupation: How Israeli Law Came to Serve Palestinian Plaintiffs," published in the *Journal of Private International Law* (volume 5, issue no. 1, 2009). While working on these articles I became aware that the adjudicative jurisdiction of the Israeli courts over civil disputes that are connected in one way or another to the West Bank and Gaza Strip, and the choice of law question in such disputes, is an exceptionally rich field that repays close investigation. A reworked version of the thesis offered in these two articles appears in Chapters Two and Three respectively. The chapters that follow test the compatibility of my findings with other conflict of laws spheres, such as jurisdiction in family law and real property matters; the sovereign immunity of the Palestinian Authority; the recognition and enforcement of Palestinian judgments in Israel; and the extent to which membership in the Israeli polity is based on notions of access to justice. The book thus uncovers the intimate relationship between the interests of the Israeli establishment and conflict of laws doctrines. Governmental interests are very much present, even if they are sometimes euphemistically expressed.

I owe a particular debt to a number of my colleagues. First and foremost I want to thank Celia Wasserstein Fassberg and Eyal Benvenisti. Their friendship, wisdom, academic work, and challenging observations have been instrumental in constructing this project. A substantial portion of the research and writing of the later chapters of this book was done while on sabbatical leave with a visiting professorship appointment at the Law School and the Ford Dorsey Program in International Policy Studies at Stanford University, in the fall of 2013. I would like to thank Michael Klausner, Larry Marshall, Lawerence Friedman, Larry Kramer and Amir Eshel who made my stay at Stanford both pleasant and enriching.

I owe a special thank you to Ron Brand, head of the Center for International Legal Education at the University of Pittsburg School of Law, for his patience and support throughout the process of writing this book. I am also indebted to Ehud Brosh for his valuable research assistance.

Research for this book was made possible by a grant from the Israel Science Foundation and the Bruce W. Wayne Chair in International Law.

I cannot imagine completing this project without the support of my wife, Inas, whose devotion, encouragement, and support make my work possible, and meaningful.

Introduction

The Israeli occupation of the West Bank and the Gaza Strip (the "Palestinian Territories" or "PT") is deemed the longest occupation in modern history.[1] Israel's relations with the local Palestinian population in these territories has been fraught with tensions and violence throughout the over forty-five years of occupation, enduring two major uprisings, or *intifadas*, as they are locally known.[2] These relations have also seen a major peace process,[3] the establishment of Palestinian self-rule in what has come to be known as the Palestinian Authority (PA),[4] an internal Palestinian split between the West Bank and the Gaza Strip soon after Israel's unilateral disengagement from the latter territory in 2005,[5] and more recently the PA bid for statehood before the United Nations.[6] Additionally, Israel has actively promoted civilian settlement in the PT and today maintains over one hundred Israeli settlements there.[7]

---

1 Eyal Benvenisti, The International Law of Occupation 203 (2d ed. 2012); Yoram Dinstein, The International Law of Belligerent Occupation 12–13 (2009). *See also* Ardi Imseis, *On the Fourth Geneva Convention and the Occupied Palestinian Territory*, 44 Harv. Int'l L. J. 65, 67 (2003); Adam Roberts, *Prolonged Military Occupation: The Israeli-Occupied Territories since 1967*, 84 Am. J. Int'l L. 44, 61 (1990).

2 *See* John Strawson, Partitioning Palestine: Legal Fundamentalism in the Palestinian-Israeli Conflict 168, 203 (2010); Mark Tessler, A History of the Israeli-Palestinian Conflict 677 (2d ed. 2009).

3 Nathan J. Brown, Palestinian Politics after the Oslo Accords (2003); Geoffrey R. Watson, The Oslo Accords: International Law and the Israeli-Palestinian Peace Agreements (2000).

4 Hiba I. Husseini, *Challenges and Reforms in the Palestinian Authority*, 26 Fordham Int'l L.J. 500, 503–05 (2003).

5 *See* Shane Darcy & John Reynolds, *"Otherwise Occupied": The Status of the Gaza Strip from the Perspective of International Humanitarian Law*, 15 J. Conflict & Security L. 211 (2010).

6 *See, e.g.*, Martin Wählisch, *Beyond a Seat in the United Nations: Palestine's U.N. Membership and International Law*, 53 Harv. Int'l L.J. Online 226 (2012); Khaled Elgindy, *Palestine Goes to the UN: Understanding the New Statehood Strategy*, 90 Foreign Aff. 102 (2011); William R. Slomanson, *Palestinian Statehood: A Successionist Dialogue*, 8 Miskolc J. Int'l L. 1 (2011).

7 *See* Orna Ben-Naftali, Aeyal M. Gross & Keren Michaeli, *Illegal Occupation: Framing the Occupied Palestinian Territory*, 23 Berkeley J. Int'l L. 515, 579–88 (2005). For a historical account of Israeli settlement policy, *see* Gershom Gorenberg, The Accidental Empire: Israel and the Birth of the Settlements, 1967–1977 (2006).

The extraordinary length of the occupation and this period's convulsive events may logically imply that many issues pertaining to the legal relations between the State of Israel and the PT are of a *sui generis* nature. Indeed, in many respects, Israel's relations with the PT are peculiar and unique. Yet these extraordinary conditions also provide an opportunity to examine certain norms and to learn more about their true characteristics.[8] It is a common exercise to test legal rules and standards in extreme and extraordinary conditions. Those of us who are engaged in legal education make particular use of the methodology when we have to choose the cases we want our students to read in a particular course of study. The more unusual the fact pattern of the case is, the better we are able to fathom the nature of norms. This same system of investigation is also an accepted facet of scientific procedure: hypotheses are subjected to rigorous examination, materials are tested in conditions far beyond those they are intended to function in, humans undergo stress tests to enable physicians learn more about their current state of health. Occasionally, exceptions can illuminate what norms really stand for. I relate here to the development of Israeli conflict of laws regarding the PT within this context.

Legal aspects concerning the actions taken by the State of Israel regarding the PT have drawn significant scholarly attention worldwide. Most writings focus on issues in the public eye, deemed to be of central importance to the Israeli-Palestinian conflict, particularly from the point of view of public international law.[9] These include issues such as the right of the Palestinian people to self-determination,[10] the status and nature of Israeli occupation and control over the West Bank and the

---

8 *See* Tobias Kelly, *Jurisdictional Politics in the Occupied West Bank: Territory, Community, and Economic Dependency in the Formation of Legal Subjects*, 31 LAW & SOCIAL INQ. 39, 46 (2006).

9 *See, e.g.*, INTERNATIONAL LAW AND THE ISRAELI PALESTINIAN CONFLICT: A RIGHTS-BASED APPROACH TO MIDDLE EAST PEACE (Susan M. Akram et al. eds., 2011); JOHN QUIGLEY, THE CASE FOR PALESTINE: AN INTERNATIONAL LAW PERSPECTIVE (2005); INTERNATIONAL LAW AND THE ADMINISTRATION OF OCCUPIED TERRITORIES: TWO DECADES OF ISRAELI OCCUPATION OF THE WEST BANK AND GAZA STRIP (Emma Playfair ed., 1992); JULIUS STONE, ISRAEL AND PALESTINE: ASSAULT ON THE LAW OF NATIONS (1981); HENRY CATTAN, PALESTINE AND INTERNATIONAL LAW: LEGAL ASPECTS OF THE ARAB-ISRAELI CONFLICT (1973).

10 *See, e.g.*, Eugene Rostow, *Palestinian Self-Determination: Possible Futures for the Unallocated Territories of the Palestine Mandate*, 5 YALE STUD. IN WORLD PUB. ORDER 147 (1979); John Collins, Note, *Self-Determination in International Law: The Palestinians*, 12 CASE W. RES. J. INT'L L. 137 (1980); Sally V. Mallison & W. Thomas Mallison, *The Juridical Bases for Palestinian Self-Determination*, 1 PALESTINE Y.B. INT'L L. 36 (1984); Francis A. Boyle, *The Creation of the State of Palestine*, 1 EUR. J. INT'L L. 301 (1990); James Crawford, *The Creation of the State of Palestine: Too Much Too Soon?*, 1 EUR. J. INT'L L. 307 (1990); Peter Malanczuk, *Israel: Status, Territory and Occupied Territories*, *in* 2 ENCYCLOPEDIA OF PUBLIC INTERNATIONAL LAW 1468, 1491–92 (Rudolf Bernhardt ed., 1995).

Gaza Strip,[11] and the extent to which access to human rights for the Palestinian population can be overseen and guaranteed.[12] Moreover, scholarly interest has intensified in recent years with the rise and demise of the Oslo Peace Process[13] and the international debate over the construction of the so-called separation wall/fence.[14] Interest is periodically kindled by recurring peace initiatives, in light of the Palestinian campaign for statehood, or the possible resort to international tribunals in order to address certain controversies of the conflict.[15]

Central as these questions may be, and despite the severe human cost and territorial upheavals endured by many who lived through this period, a private sphere of relations existed as well, whereby private corporations and individuals from

---

11 Yehuda Z. Blum, *The Missing Reversioner: Reflections on the Status of Judea and Samaria*, 3 ISR. L. REV. 279 (1968); Allan Gerson, *Trustee Occupant: The Legal Status of Israel's Presence in the West Bank*, 14 HARV. INT'L L. J. 1 (1973); Theodor Meron, *Applicability of Multilateral Conventions to Occupied Territories*, 72 AM. J. INT'L L. 542 (1978); ALLAN GERSON, THE WEST BANK AND INTERNATIONAL LAW (1978); Richard Falk, *Some Legal Reflection on Prolonged Israeli Occupation of Gaza and the West Bank*, 2 J. REFUGEE STUD. 40 (1989).

12 DAVID KRETZMER, THE OCCUPATION OF JUSTICE: THE SUPREME COURT OF ISRAEL AND THE OCCUPIED TERRITORIES (2002); Note, *Protection of Human Rights in Israeli-Occupied Territories*, 15 HARV. INT'L L.J. (1974); Theodor Meron, *West Bank and Gaza: Human Rights and Humanitarian Law in the Period of Transition*, 9 ISR. Y.B. HUM. RTS. 106 (1979); ESTHER R. COHEN, HUMAN RIGHTS IN THE ISRAELI-OCCUPIED TERRITORIES, 1967–1982 (1985); Wendy Olson, *UN Security Council Resolutions Regarding Deportations from Israeli Administered Territories: The Applicability of the Fourth Geneva Convention Relative to the Protection of Civilian Persons in Time of War*, 24 STAN. J. INT'L L. 611 (1988); Jordan J. Paust et al., *Report of ICJ Mission of Inquiry into the Military Court System in the Occupied West Bank and Gaza*, 14 HASTINGS INT'L & COMP. L. REV. 1 (1990); Eyal Benvenisti, *Responsibility for the Protection of Human Rights under the Interim Israeli-Palestinian Agreements*, 28 ISR. L. REV. 297 (1994).

13 THE ARAB-ISRAELI ACCORDS: LEGAL PERSPECTIVES (Eugene Cotran, Chibli Mallat & David Stott eds., 1996); Peter Malanczuk, *Some Basic Aspects of the Agreement between Israel and the PLO from the Perspective of International Law*, 7 EUR. J. INT'L L. 485 (1996); Jill Allison Weiner, Comment, *Israel, Palestine and the Oslo Accords*, 23 FORDHAM INT'L L.J. 230 (1999); WATSON, *supra* note 3.

14 Pieter H. F. Bekker, Comment, *World Court's Ruling Regarding Israel's West Bank Barrier and the Primacy of International Law: An Insider's Perspective*, 38 CORNELL INT'L L.J. 553 (2005); Robert A. Caplen, Note, *Mending the "Fence": How Treatment of Israeli Palestinian Conflict by the International Court of Justice at the Hague has Redefined the Doctrine of Self-Defense*, 57 FLA. L. REV. 717 (2005); Andrew R. Malone, Comment, *Water Now: The Impact of Israel's Security Fence on Palestinian Water Rights and Agriculture in the West Bank*, 37 CASE W. RES. J. INT'L L. 639 (2005); Barry A. Feinstein & Justus Reid Weiner, *Israel's Security Barrier: An International Comparative Analysis and Legal Evaluation*, 37 GEO. WASH. INT'L L. REV. 309 (2005); Sarah Williams, *Has International Law Hit the Wall? An Analysis of International Law in Relation to Israel's Separation Barrier*, 24 BERKELEY J. INT'L L. 192 (2006). See also a series of contributions in *Agora: ICJ Advisory Opinion on Construction of a Wall in the Occupied Palestinian Territory*, 99 AM. J. INT'L L. 1 (2005).

15 *See, e.g.*, Daniel Benoliel & Ronen Perry, *Israel, Palestine, and the ICC*, 32 MICH. J. INT'L L. 73 (2010); John Quigley, *Palestine Is a State: A Horse with Black and White Stripes Is a Zebra*, 32 MICH. J. INT'L L. 749 (2011).

both sides of the conflict interacted with each other. Occasionally, these interactions led parties to seek legal remedies to their disputes. In this context, the principles of private international law were implicated in an effort to untangle the set of conflict of laws issues that such disputes gave rise to. This particular sphere of the Israeli-Palestinian conflict has received only scant attention. In what follows, I offer an analysis of a set of Israeli conflict of laws doctrines that developed and took shape in the shadow of the conflict from 1967, when the PT were first occupied by Israel, through the present day. This body of doctrine has developed primarily as a consequence of the numerous civil actions related in one way or another to the PT that were filed before Israeli courts.

In this study, I also seek to shed light on an inter-jurisdictional dependency that has thus far also received very little attention in the conflict of laws literature: that which emerged between the belligerent occupant and the occupied territory.[16]

Conflict of laws theory and methodology has known major upheavals throughout history.[17] As a result, different rules have been offered to enable us to determine jurisdictional competency, choice of law, and the proper treatment of foreign judgments. But as the rules were modified in order to accommodate the evolving theory, another variable in the conflict of laws matrix drew attention; namely that of the jurisdictional kinship between the two or more jurisdictions that were involved. For indeed, the jurisdictions involved need not be those of two or more sovereign states;[18] such is the case, for example, in a federal scheme of government, where the separate states are united and maintained by a federal umbrella.[19]

---

16 One notable exception in the local Israeli context is Iris Canor, *Yisrael UhaShtahim: al Mishpat Binluimi Prati, Mishpat Binluimi Pumbi, uma Shibinihim [Israel and the Territories: The Interplay between Private International Law and Public International Law]*, 8 MISHPAT UMIMSHAL 551 (2005) (arguing that Israeli choice of law rules in respect of the PT developed in accordance with official Israeli public international law stands in respect of the PT).

17 *See* Friedrich K. Juenger, *A Page of History* 35 MERCER L. REV. 419 (1984); Hessel E. Yntema, *The Historic Bases of Private International Law*, 2 AM. J. COMP. L. 297 (1953).

18 Notably, at one point, A. V. Dicey defined a "country" for conflict of laws purposes as "the whole of a territory subject under one sovereign to one body of law." Later on, however, he substituted "country" with "law district," probably because not all conflict inquiries indeed involve "countries" in common parlance. *See* DICEY, MORRIS & COLLINS ON THE CONFLICT OF LAWS 30 (Lawrence Collins et al. eds., 14th ed. 2006). *See also* ARTHUR NUSSBAUM, PRINCIPLES OF PRIVATE INTERNATIONAL LAW 5–6 (1943).

19 *See, e.g.*, K. J. HOOD, CONFLICT OF LAWS WITHIN THE UK (2007); MICHAEL TILBURY ET AL., CONFLICT OF LAWS IN AUSTRALIA 9–12 (2002); J-G CASTEL, CANADIAN CONFLICT OF LAWS 2–3 (3d ed., 1994); ALBERT A. EHRENZWEIG, A TREATISE ON THE CONFLICT OF LAWS 16 (1962). Indeed, in terms of the historical development of the discipline of conflict of laws generally, intra-territorial conflicts, such as between cities, have contributed substantially to the evolution of different conflicts of laws doctrines. *See, e.g.*, Alex Mills, *The Private History of International Law*, 55 INT'L & COMP. L. Q. 1, 4–12 (2006).

And precisely because of this federal kinship among states, intra-federal choice of law inquiries, as well as others pertaining to adjudicative jurisdiction and enforcement of judgments, were made subject to certain norms designed to accommodate the needs and interests of the federal system.[20] Similarly, confederate schemes of government have also entailed the design of special bodies of norms to accommodate conflict of laws issues among the confederate states. The most notable example of this process in recent history is the European Union.[21] So as separate jurisdictions become more interdependent and connected to each other, conflict of laws principles seem to evolve alongside in order to accommodate the special inter-jurisdictional settings, all taking place in tandem with the theoretical evolution of conflicts theory itself.[22]

One form of dependency between jurisdictions that seems to influence conflict of laws doctrine is that of occupation. Since under international law, an occupied territory is presumed to form a separate jurisdictional entity from that of the occupying power but at the same time is controlled and administered by it until an international settlement is reached,[23] inter-jurisdictional conflicts between the occupier and the occupied seem also to be guided by special considerations. But unlike the extensive research devoted to the implications of the federal and confederate structure of government on conflict of laws doctrine, those of occupation

---

20 *See* RUSSELL J. WEINTRAUB, COMMENTARY ON THE CONFLICT OF LAWS 585 (4th ed. 2001); W. Müller-Freienfels, *Conflicts of Law and Constitutional Law*, 45 U. CHI. L. REV. 598 (1978). Note, however, that in American conflicts jurisprudence, it was not always clear whether a distinction is necessary between the interstate and the international context; *id.* at 599. Moreover, in historical terms, conflict rules developed in a federal context that took account of the rules developed in the international context. *See* Yntema, *supra* note 17, at 299. This amalgamated American approach has been criticized, for in some spheres courts need to distinguish between the interstate and the international context. Therefore, for other states—where the generally assumed context for conflict of laws inquiries is the international one—much of American conflict of laws doctrines are unusable because they are derived from federal concerns. *See* Mathias Reiman, *Domestic and International Conflicts in the United States and Western Europe*, in INTERNATIONAL CONFLICT OF LAWS FOR THE THIRD MILLENNIUM: ESSAYS IN HONOR OF FRIEDRICH K JUENGER 109, 113–14 (Patrick J. Borchers & Joachim Zekoll eds., 2001); Mathias Reiman, *A New Restatement—For the International Age*, 75 IND. L. J. 575, 576 (2000). *See also* Eugene F. Scoles, *Interstate and International Distinctions in Conflict of Laws in the United States*, 54 CAL. L. REV. 1599 (1966).

21 *See* PETER STONE, EU PRIVATE INTERNATIONAL LAW: HARMONIZATION OF LAWS 3–10 (2006); Bernd von Hoffmann, *The Europeanization of Private International Law*, in EUROPEAN PRIVATE INTERNATIONAL LAW 13 (Bernd von Hoffmann ed., 1998).

22 *See* ROBERT LEFLAR ET AL., AMERICAN CONFLICTS LAW 9–10 (4th ed. 1986).

23 *See* GERHARD VON GLAHN, THE OCCUPATION OF ENEMY TERRITORY 94–100 (1957).

have only rarely been examined.[24] For the most part, occupation has been the object of analysis for public international law inquiries, especially the norms pertaining to the authority possessed by the occupying power during the period of occupation, and the observance of international norms pertaining to human rights.[25]

It is easy to understand why conflicts methodology has largely disregarded the condition of occupation, which almost by definition is presumed to be a temporary state,[26] and therefore generates no significant body of conflicts proceedings worthy of analysis or theorizing. However, occupation and other abnormal inter-jurisdictional relations can become protracted.[27] Over time, interactions between private entities from the different jurisdictions begin to amass, especially if the two jurisdictions lie in geographical proximity to each other. In due course, such interactions will necessitate addressal of conflict issues that arise between these jurisdictional entities and bring courts to assess the significance of their reciprocal relationships on the conflict issues at hand, be it adjudicative jurisdiction, choice of law, enforcement and recognition of judgments or any other matter.

---

24 Conflict of laws issues in the context of international conflicts have periodically presented themselves before courts, thereby requiring judges to consider the application or the adaptation of existing rules to the new reality. *See, e.g.*, Kuwait Airways Corp. v. Iraqi Airways [1995] 3 All E.R. 694 (H.L.) (discussing the effects of the seizure and operation of civilian aircrafts owned by Kuwait Airways by Iraqi Airways after the invasion of Kuwait by Iraqi forces in 1990); Hesperides Hotels Ltd v. Aegean Turkish Holidays Ltd [1978] 1 Q.B. 205, 216–18 (C.A.) (*per* Lord Denning), appeal allowed in part, Hesperides Hotels Ltd v. Muftizade [1979] A.C. 508 (H.L.) (discussing the effect of laws enacted by the non-recognized Turkish Federated State of Cyprus in the territory that fell under its control following the 1974 invasion of the island by Turkish forces); Autocephalous Greek-Orthodox Church of Cyprus v. Goldberg and Feldman Fine Art Inc., 917 F.2d 278 (7th Cir. 1990) (recognizing the property claims of the Autocephalous Greek-Orthodox Church of Cyprus and the Republic of Cyprus over certain mosaics removed from a church that came under the territorial control of the Turkish Federated State of Cyprus following the 1974 division of the country); McDonnell Douglas Corp. v. Islamic Republic of Iran, 758 F.2d 341 (8th Cir. 1985), *cert. denied,* 474 U.S. 948 (1985) (resisting the enforcement of a forum selection clause designating Iranian courts, given the regime change in the country following the Iranian Revolution); Salimoff v. Standard Oil Co., 186 N.E. 679 (N.Y. 1933) (recognizing the effect of certain nationalization decrees on oil lands by the Soviet government, even though the USSR was not yet fully recognized by the United States). However, unlike the context of these reported decisions, this study and the methodological developments it seeks to highlight pertains to a systematic effort to develop conflict of laws rules of one party to the conflict (the occupying power) in the context of a special jurisdictional relationship that developed with the occupied territory.

25 *See generally* INTERNATIONAL LAW AND THE ISRAELI PALESTINIAN CONFLICT: A RIGHTS-BASED APPROACH TO MIDDLE EAST PEACE, *supra* note 9. .

26 DORIS A. GRABER, THE DEVELOPMENT OF THE LAW OF BELLIGERENT OCCUPATION 1863–1914—A HISTORICAL SURVEY 37 (1949).

27 Roberts, *supra* note 1, at 47.

This book is divided into five chapters. Chapter One surveys the major developments in the PT following the 1967 Six-Day War and offers a detailed analysis of the jurisdictional realities that took shape between Israel and the various territories it occupied in that war.

Chapter Two deals with the first core conflicts issue: personal jurisdiction. This chapter details how the personal jurisdiction doctrine of Israeli courts evolved over the years, reflecting the different stages of Israel's relations with the PT. This chapter also shows how personal jurisdiction doctrine accommodated Israel's policy of control over the PT. To facilitate this policy in the sphere of personal jurisdiction, some doctrinal innovations had to take place in existing conflicts law. These innovations are outlined and evaluated throughout the chapter. This chapter also shows the emergence of one important feature of Israeli conflict of laws towards the PT generally: the drawing of a legal distinction between intra-Palestinian civil disputes that are brought before Israeli courts, on the one hand, and intra-Israeli settlers or mixed Israeli-Palestinian civil disputes that are brought before the Israeli courts, on the other hand. Even though all such disputes are equally based in the PT, Israel's willingness to adjudicate such disputes on the merits has been differential. Intra-Palestinian civil dispute were kept out—but intra-settlers and mixed Israeli-Palestinian disputes were allowed in.

As I show in Chapter Four, this same reality dominated in the sphere of choice of law as well. Palestinians in their mutual civil disputes were assumed by Israeli choice of law rules to be governed by local PT law, whereas Israeli settlers in their mutual disputes and mixed Israeli-Palestinian disputes were assumed by the same rules to be governed by Israeli law. A prominent scholar, Eyal Benvenisti, labeled this state of being as that of "legal dualism."[28] I actually think of it as more than that. I posit that this state of being is a form of a modern-day civil *millet* system—analogical to the Ottoman *millet* system, in which local subjects were governed by different courts and different norms depending on their religious identity.[29] For one thing, the jurisdictional and choice of law design that Israeli conflicts law developed in respect of the PT was more than just about the existence of two systems of norms that govern two group of people. The design was also about why and how these groups were deemed to be different even if they happen to reside in the same territory and, more importantly, about who determines the rules

28 EYAL BENVENISTI, LEGAL DUALISM: THE ABSORPTION OF THE OCCUPIED TERRITORIES INTO ISRAEL (1989).

29 *See infra* Chapter Three, Section B.

that should govern. Yet the Ottomans applied their grand design primarily in the sphere of family law, whereas in the Israeli-PT context, it prevails in all spheres of private law.

Chapter Three is also concerned with jurisdiction. It deals with three forms of jurisdictional restrictions that became especially relevant in Israeli-PT relations. The first concerns whether Israeli courts could adjudicate disputes dealing with land situated in the PT; the second takes up the same question in respect to the family law matters of Palestinian residents of the PT; and the third deals with whether or not Israeli courts are willing to accord the PA foreign sovereign immunity in defending a civil action filed before an Israeli court. These issues raise some unique dilemmas in conflict of laws, and therefore they were signaled out and discussed in a dedicated chapter. One major finding in this chapter is the intimate connection between the overall political and control policies and the shape and substance of jurisdictional rules. The relationship reached a certain epic, as in the sphere of foreign sovereign immunity the question of whether the PA is entitled to sovereign immunity was deferred to the Israeli executive and legislative branches of government, leaving the judiciary with almost no say on the matter.

Chapter Four deals with choice of law. The focus of this chapter is on choice of law assessments made by Israeli organs and courts regarding PT-related disputes, with a special emphasis on the torts and contracts of employment. Here as well, we encounter a dominating civil *millet* conception. Yet, this chapter also points to a new trend. In two landmark Israeli Supreme Court decisions that dealt with a mixed Israeli-Palestinian dispute, the Court justified the application of Israeli law by reference to the equal treatment of Palestinians. This resolution was by no means to the detriment of the Palestinian plaintiffs; on the contrary—it was these plaintiffs who argued and fought their way up to Israel's highest court in order to have Israeli law apply, while the Israeli defendants, most of whom were part of the Israeli settlement project in the PT, argued against the application of Israeli law and sought the application of West Bank Jordanian law instead. These two decisions are critically evaluated in this chapter, exposing their anchor in the principle of equality as fictitious—even if well-intended—given the overall design of law and legal institutions in the PT over the years. Ultimately, however, I think that the result in both these cases is justified in reference to the principles of choice of law fairness, as they have developed under a modern choice of law theory.

The last chapter, Chapter Five, deals with PT judgments and access to justice rights of Palestinian plaintiffs as constitutionally protected rights under Israeli law. The thread that binds these two topics is the effort to design conflicts doctrines that take the entire proceeding into consideration rather than this or that particular aspect of it—be it jurisdiction, choice of law, or any other topic. As for the enforcement and recognition of PT judgments in Israel, the evolution of Israeli conflict of laws rules on this are found to be in a state of disorder. The primary reason for this situation is the general conflicts rules in Israel on the enforcement and recognition of judgments. It seems that this law, at least in the context of PT judgments, is guided by ad hoc teleology more than anything else, i.e., whether in the particular circumstance of the case it would be just to grant enforcement or recognition.

The question of whether Israel is willing to provide the Palestinian plaintiff with constitutional protections guaranteeing access to justice rights in Israeli courts was until recently a non-issue. The rules of jurisdiction, especially the doctrine of forum non conveniens, governed in this respect, providing the Palestinian plaintiff with no such rights when the defendant was another Palestinian and only limited protection when the defendant was an Israeli. In terms of Israeli settlers or Israelis generally who sought litigation in an Israeli court for a PT-related civil action, the general perception was that they were indeed entitled to access Israeli courts. Given the current state of relations between Israel and the PA, the restrictions imposed on Palestinian plaintiff are increasing, especially when the cause of action for damages results from an IDF military operation. Moreover, conditioning litigation by Palestinian plaintiffs in such and other actions on the providing of a security bond is also a common practice today.

However, a recent Israeli Supreme Court judgment seems to configure the availability of access to justice rights differently.[30] According to this holding, these rights also depend on choice of law rules, especially when pointing to Israeli law as the governing law. In such cases, the norm deserves to be litigated by an Israeli court. Resultantly, access is made possible to the plaintiff even if he or she is from the PA. If this holding is taken one step further, it can yield some substantial implications on the access to justice rights of Palestinian plaintiffs and maybe on those of foreign plaintiffs in general.

30 HCJ 8276/05 Adalah, The Legal Center for Arab Minority Rights in Israel v. Minister of Defense (December 12, 2006), Nevo Legal Database (by subscription).

The main focus of the analysis offered here is Israeli conflict of laws. I regard this to be the proper focus given that conflict of laws is basically a discipline governed by the municipal law of each and every state. I gather that much could also be said about the development of Palestinian conflict of laws in the shadow of Israeli occupation and control.[31] Moreover, it will also be interesting to look into the evolution of conflict of laws doctrine in the contexts of other conflicts. It is my hope that this study will offer some assistance in facilitating such research.

31 The major commentary on Palestinian conflict of laws is, however, general and comparative in nature. *See* AMIN R. DAWWAS, TANAZO' AL-QAWANIN FI FALASTIN [CONFLICT OF LAWS IN PALESTINE] (2001) (in Arabic).

CHAPTER 1

Jurisdictional Designs

Contents

A. The 1967 Six-Day War and Its Aftermath

The Six-Day War of June 5 to 10, 1967 was a watershed event in the Middle East.[1] When the war ended, Israel had occupied territories that were three times larger than its own. The West Bank (including East Jerusalem) was captured from Jordan, the Golan Heights were captured from Syria, and the Sinai Peninsula and Gaza Strip were captured from Egypt. No wonder that in Israel, this war was considered the Great Victory (*Ha-Nitzahon ha-Gadol*) and in the Arab world, the Setback (*Al-Naksa*).

In spite of its decisive outcome, the 1967 Six-Day War was by no means the end of the Arab-Israeli conflict, but only a prelude to additional conflicts. Six years later, another major war followed: the 1973 Arab-Israeli War (known in Israel as the Yom Kippur War and in the Arab world as the October War). Eventually, a new front of conflict was established between Israel and Lebanon, or specifically between Israel and certain factions operating from Lebanon. These factions began as various Palestinian organizations and ultimately became the Hezbollah. Two major Palestinian uprisings, *intifidas* (singular: *intifada*), took place in the West Bank and the Gaza Strip, the first from 1987 to 1993 and the second from 2000 to 2005 (although the latter still continues to some extent).

Some significant peace processes also form a part of the region's history. The first was between Israel and Egypt, culminating in the Camp David Accords. The second, between Israel and the Palestinians, is known as the Oslo Peace Process, and the third involved Israel and Jordan. Each of these conflicts and peace processes has left its mark. Ultimately, none of the regions that Israel occupied in 1967 maintained its initial status. Each was transformed into a different entity, either as a result of unilateral Israeli acts or on the basis of accords reached between Israel and various parties to the conflict. This chapter describes these transformations, with special emphases on the jurisdictional characteristics of each of the occupied regions. As we shall observe, these characteristics will become instrumental when analyzing the conflict of laws issues that evolved over the years.

In dealing with the jurisdictional design of the areas occupied by Israel in the 1967 Six-Day War, I will focus on the Israeli position. Not that the other positions are irrelevant or unimportant, but simply because this position is the relevant

1 Mark Tessler, A History of the Israeli-Palestinian Conflict 399 (2d ed. 2009). As soon as the war ended, a number of legal issues arose, mainly in the domain of public international law. *See, e.g.*, Quincy Wright, *The Middle East Problem*, 64 Am. J. Int'l L. 270 (1970); Yoram Dinstein, *The Legal Issues of "Para-War" and Peace in the Middle East*, 44 St. John's L. Rev. 466 (1970); Shabtai Rosenne, *Directions for a Middle East Settlement—Some Underlying Legal Problems*, 33 Law & Contemp. Probs. 44 (1968).

one for Israeli notions of conflict of laws. However, given the particular interest of public international law in international belligerent conflicts and belligerent occupation, it becomes essential to refer to the relevant public international law norms—for as we shall see, these also played a critical role in determining the jurisdictional characteristics of the occupied regions.[2]

B. East Jerusalem

On June 27, 1967, the Knesset (the Israeli parliament) amended the Law and Administration Ordinance, 1948, empowering the Israeli government to issue an order that extends "the law, jurisdiction and administration" of the State of Israel to any other territory of what was once Mandatory Palestine (referred to in the amendment in Hebrew as *Eretz Israel* "Land of Israel").[3] The next day, on June 28, 1967, the Israeli government issued an order in which it extended "the law, jurisdiction and administration" to the area of East Jerusalem.[4] Interestingly, this jurisdictional expansion did not refer to the area of East Jerusalem by name, but rather indicated the relevant geographic coordinates of this area. These acts were supplemented by an order issued by the Israeli Minister of Interior by which the municipal boundaries of the City of Jerusalem were now expanded to include the area of East Jerusalem.[5]

Some doubts were cast at first as to whether these acts by the Israeli government amounted to an official annexation of East Jerusalem.[6] Note that none of the enactments mentioned above used the term "annexation" or explicitly apply Israeli "sovereignty" to East Jerusalem.[7] Moreover, in a letter to the United Nations secretary-general, the Israeli Ministry of Foreign Affairs explained these measures as

---

2 For a recent study on the interplay between public and private international law, *see* Alex Mills, The Confluence of Public and Private International Law (2009). However, this study does not touch upon the interaction between international norms governing belligerent occupation and conflict of laws.

3 Law and Administration Ordinance (Amendment no.11), 5727-1967, 21 LSI 75 (1966–67).

4 Law and Administration Order (No. 1), 1967, KT 2064, 2690.

5 The Jerusalem Declaration (Extension of Municipal Boundaries), 1967, KT 2065. The power to issue such an order was possible under a specific amendment of the Knesset enacted in tandem with the amendment to the Administration Ordinance. *See* Municipalities Ordinance (Amendment No. 6) Law, 5727-1967, 21 LSI 75 (1966–67). Indeed, like the government order itself, this enactment also referred to the East Jerusalem area by means of geographical coordinates (identical to those set by the government order) rather than by name.

6 *See* Yoram Dinstein, The International Law of Belligerent Occupation 18 (2009) [hereinafter Dinstein, Belligerent Occupation]; Ian S. Lustick, *Has Israel Annexed East Jerusalem?* 5 Middle East Pol'y 34 (1997); Nathan Feinberg, Studies in International Law with Specific Reference to the Arab-Israeli Conflict 511–12 (1979).

7 Elihu Lauterpacht, Jerusalem and the Holy Places 50 (1968).

administrative in nature, aimed at ensuring the availability of municipal services to the residents of East Jerusalem and the Holy Places.[8] The international community was not appeased.[9] A special United Nations Security Council Resolution declared that all the actions taken by the State of Israel in respect of Jerusalem are "invalid."[10] Foreign states reacted by relocating their embassies from Jerusalem to Tel-Aviv.[11]

In terms of internal Israeli politics, local leaders were not shy to admit that as a result of these enactments, East Jerusalem was now fully integrated within Israel. Asher Maoz aptly summarized this policy as follows: "while the leaders of the state were making it clear both within and without the Knesset that East Jerusalem had been annexed to Israel, the representatives of the state in international forums fervently denied that this was the result."[12]

Yet beyond any significant doubt, as a result of these enactments, East Jerusalem became part of Israel under Israeli law—no different from any other Israeli territory.[13] This situation was clarified by Israeli case law developed by courts that were required by the specific litigation to take a definite position on the jurisdictional identity now acquired by East Jerusalem. One of the first important cases in this respect was *Ruidi v. Military Court of Hebron*.[14] Two antique dealers were cited before an Israel Defense Forces (IDF) military court sitting in the West Bank city of Hebron for the unauthorized export of antiques "outside the country," as they transported antiques from the West Bank to their antique shop in East Jerusalem. The law under which they were cited was a Jordanian law kept in effect by the IDF in the West Bank that deemed it a crime to export antiques without first obtaining a proper permit. But is East Jerusalem "outside the country" vis-à-vis the West Bank?

---

8 Eyal Benvenisti & Eyal Zamir, *Private Claims to Property Rights in the Future Israeli-Palestinian Settlement*, 89 Am. J. Int'l L. 295, 307 (1995).

9 Adam Roberts, *Prolonged Military Occupation: The Israeli Occupied Territories since 1967*, 84 Am. J. Int'l L. 44, 60 (1990) [hereinafter Roberts, *Prolonged Military Occupation*].

10 S.C. Res. 252, U.N. Doc. S/RES/252 (May 21, 1968).

11 Leon Sheleff, *Application of Israeli Law to the Golan Heights Is Not Annexation*, 20 Brook. J. Int'l L. 333, 344 n.42 (1994).

12 Asher Maoz, *Application of Israeli Law to the Golan Heights Is Annexation*, 20 Brook. J. Int'l L. 355, 366 (1994).

13 *See* Yoram Dinstein, *The Israel Supreme Court and the Law of Belligerent Occupation: Reunification of Families*, 18 Isr. Y.B. Hum. Rts. 173, 173 (1988) ("East Jerusalem is treated by Israel as if it were part of its own domain") [hereinafter Dinstein, *Reunification of Families*]; Alan Levine, *The Status of Sovereignty in East Jerusalem and the West Bank*, 5 N.Y.U. J. Int'l L. & Pol. 485, 499, 500 (1972) (commenting that the Israeli government "has assumed the attributes of a sovereign in East Jerusalem" and that "Jerusalem now effectively exists as one unified city").

14 HCJ 283/69, 24(2) PD 419 (1970).

The defendants' lawyer argued that although East Jerusalem was effectively annexed to Israel, they committed no crime because when Jordan outlawed the unauthorized export of antiques, East Jerusalem was still part of the West Bank and of Jordan. The IDF military court in Hebron rejected this argument. The two defendants then filed a petition before the Israeli Supreme Court in its capacity as the High Court of Justice, seeking an order instructing the IDF military officers to dismiss the charges against them. The petition was denied. Two of the justices held that given the admission of petitioners' attorney that East Jerusalem was effectively annexed to Israel, it was necessary to conclude that following the 1967 order, this part of the West Bank had now become a foreign territory thereto and therefore was deemed as located "outside the country." These two justices, however, did not decide the question whether the extension of Israeli law, jurisdiction, and administration to a certain territory necessarily means that territory had been annexed to the state.[15] The third justice, on the other hand, had no trouble making this deduction from the specific Israeli legislation in respect of East Jerusalem that was enacted following the Six-Day War.[16]

Another decision that more authoritatively categorized East Jerusalem as part of Israel for conflict of law purposes is *Gertz v. Dajani*.[17] The plaintiff, a German corporation, filed a claim based on a bill of exchange drawn in 1966 in East Jerusalem on an East Jerusalem debtor who signed the bill there as acceptor. The German corporation presented the bill in May 1967, but the bill was not discharged. Two years afterwards, in 1969, the German corporation filed this claim before the Israeli District Court of Jerusalem. This court dismissed the claim reasoning, inter alia, that it lacked the jurisdictional capacity to enforce this bill, since the bill had no connection to Israel. The bill, the court reasoned, was drawn, accepted and not discharged between foreign entities and in a foreign jurisdiction, i.e., East Jerusalem when it was under Jordanian rule. On appeal, the Israeli Supreme Court reversed. The Court held that since the defendants were properly served with process in East Jerusalem, an Israeli court is considered to have proper personal jurisdiction.[18] This decision implies that the transient rule of personal jurisdiction, which conditions the establishment of personal jurisdiction upon service of process to the defendant while present in the sovereign territory of the forum state, and which has been imported into Israeli law from English law,[19] is fully

15 *Id.* at 422 (*per* A. Witkon, J.); *id.* at 423 (*per* H. Cohn, J.).

16 *Id.* at 424 (*per* Y. Kahan, J.).

17 CA 434/79, 35(2) 351 (1981).

18 *Id.* at 354–55.

19 *See infra* Chapter Two.

applicable to service of process in East Jerusalem. For this purpose, it is irrelevant whether the claim or any of the parties have any connection to Israel, as long as the defendant is served while present on what Israel considers to be part of its territory.[20] This holding unequivocally means that in light of the 1967 Order, East Jerusalem has essentially become part of the State of Israel.

Absorbing East Jerusalem into the Israeli legal system was also facilitated by special legislation enacted to secure the recognition of judgments rendered by East Jerusalem courts on the eve of its occupation. In light of the Israeli establishment's assumption that this part of the city has become part of Israel for jurisdictional and administrative purposes, special rules were enacted by the Israeli Minister of Justice providing that litigation that was pending on June 7, 1967 in Jerusalem courts is to be continued in equivalent courts of the State of Israel.[21] In one case where Israeli courts were required to enforce a judgment given by the Jerusalem Court of Appeals rendered when Jordan governed the region, it was argued that the Israeli courts should refrain from enforcement since before the 1967 Six-Day War, parties to an appeal before this court had recourse to the Court of Cassation in Amman—recourse that was now abolished.[22] This in turn raised the question of whether Israel had any obligation to establish a new court of cassation in order to compensate for the lack of recourse to the Amman court. In *Al Qottob v. Shaheen*,[23] the Israeli Supreme Court answered this question in the negative. Referring to international law precedents on state succession, the Court found no definite authority on this matter, and furthermore reasoned that subjects of the captured territory are also expected to adjust to the new legal order, and in any case cannot expect to be accommodated in terms of appellate procedure beyond the procedures provided by Israeli law. So in light of the fact that Israel has no court of cassation sitting as a court of final appeal, East Jerusalem subjects should not expect to be afforded with such recourse.

Much doubt regarding East Jerusalem's status as an integral part of the State of Israel was eliminated in 1979, when the Knesset passed the Basic Law: Jerusalem,

---

20 LCA 9810/05 Martin J. Hecke v. Pimcapco Ltd. (Aug. 30, 2009), Nevo Legal database (by subscription).

21 Legal and Administrative Matters (Regulation) Rules (Continuity of Civil Proceedings, Enforcement of Judgments and Recognition of Documents), 1968, KT 2314, 356. The rules were enacted on the basis of Legal and Administrative Matters (Regulation) Law [Consolidated Version], 5730-1970, 24 LSI 144 (1969–70). *See also* MP (Miscellaneous Petitions) 110/73 Al Alami v. Al Alami, 29(1) PD 17 (1974) (the Israeli Supreme Court ordered the continuation of the litigation in a local dispute first litigated before a Jordanian court operating in East Jerusalem in the Israeli District Court of Jerusalem).

22 *See infra* Section E(4).

23 25(2) PD 77, 82–83 (1971).

Capital of Israel.[24] This law stipulated that a complete and united Jerusalem is the capital of the State of Israel. As a result, "there cannot be a shred of doubt that the Knesset considered East Jerusalem annexed."[25] This law has received strong condemnations from the international community, with the UN Security Council characterizing it as a "violation of international law"[26] and maintaining that Israel's status vis-à-vis East Jerusalem continues to be that of an occupant.[27] Although Israel has challenged these contentions, the international community overwhelmingly stood by the assertion that Israeli actions regarding East Jerusalem were contradictory to international law.[28] Yet again, this stance had no bearing on Israel's conflict of laws, as Israeli courts continued to regard East Jerusalem as an integral part of the State of Israel. The Israeli Supreme Court explicitly held that even if extending Israeli municipal law to East Jerusalem is contrary to international law, the law of the Knesset remains superior and binding upon Israeli courts.[29]

Another crucial fact relevant for the status of East Jerusalem after the 1967 Six-Day War concerns it municipal boarders. Following the 1967 Order, East Jerusalem became part of the existing Jerusalem municipality. At that time, East Jerusalem was 6.5 square kilometers in size—a territory that included the Old City and some of its immediate surrounding areas. However, the municipal boarders of

---

24 34 LSI 209 (1979–80).

25 DINSTEIN, BELLIGERENT OCCUPATION, *supra* note 6, at 18. However, some scholars maintain that even after the enactment of this law, East Jerusalem remained in a legal limbo as this law, like the Order of 1967, did not explicitly speak of annexation or the extension of Israeli sovereignty. *See* Lustick, *supra* note 6.

26 Benvenisti & Zamir, *supra* note 8, at 307.

27 *Id.*

28 *See* Michael Dumper, *Constructive Ambiguities? Jerusalem, International Law, and the Peace process, in* INTERNATIONAL LAW AND THE ISRAELI-PALESTINIAN CONFLICT: A RIGHTS-BASED APPROACH TO MIDDLE EAST PEACE, 113, 113 (Susan M. Akram et al. eds., 2011); Ardi Imseis, *Facts on the Ground: An Examination of Israeli Municipal Policy in East Jerusalem*, 15 AM. U. INT'L L. REV. 1039, 1042 (2000) [hereinafter Imseis, *Facts on the Ground*]; David Herling, *The Court, the Ministry and the Law: Awad and the Withdrawal of East Jerusalem Residence Rights*, 33 ISR. L. REV. 67, 69–70 (1999). As to the general discussion concerning the contentions put forward by the different parties, *see, e.g.*, Jordie Saperia, *Jerusalem: Legal Status, Condominium and Middle East Peace*, 3 J. E. ASIA & INT'L L. 175 (2010); Moshe Hirsch, *The Legal Status of Jerusalem Following the ICJ Advisory Opinion on the Separation Barrier*, 38 ISR. L. REV. 298 (2005); Charles Bryan Baron, *The International Legal Status of Jerusalem*, 8 TOURO INT'L L. REV. 1 (1998); John Quigley, *Sovereignty in Jerusalem*, 45 CATHOLIC U. L. REV. 765 (1996); Michael Eisner, *Jerusalem: An Analysis of Legal Claims and Political Realities*, 12 WIS. INT'L L.J. 221 (1993–94); John Quigley, *Old Jerusalem: Whose to Govern*, 20 DENV. J. INT'L L. & POL'Y 145 (1991); Larry Kletter, Note, *The Sovereignty of Jerusalem in International Law*, 20 COLUM J. TRANSNAT'L L. 319 (1981); Mark I. Gruhin, *Jerusalem: Legal & Political Dimensions in a Search for Peace*, 12 CASE W. RES. J. INT'L L. 169 (1980); Joseph B. Tulman, *The International Legal Status of Jerusalem*, 3 ASILS INT'L L.J. 39 (1979).

29 HCJ 256/01 Rabah v. Jerusalem Court for Local Matters, 56(2) PD 930 (2002), reprinted in 32 ISR. Y.B. HUM. RGTS 356 (2002).

Jerusalem gradually began to expand, taking in additional regions from the West Bank, effectively annexing these parts to the State of Israel. The present territory of these regions is 71 square kilometers.[30] As a result of concentrated governmental efforts, different regions in East Jerusalem became heavily populated with Israeli citizens. Hence in 1972, the Jewish population of East Jerusalem was about 9,200.[31] It reached 50,000 in 1977,[32] 103,900 in 1986,[33] and at the end of 2005 it was estimated at 175,000.[34] The jurisdictional identity of this expanded region of the West Bank was identical with that of East Jerusalem itself after 1967; i.e., it became considered part of Israel for all jurisdictional purposes.

While the status of East Jerusalem under Israeli conflict of laws is fairly settled, this by no means implies the absence of frictions regarding private law matters between the local Palestinian population and the Israeli authorities. One major issue of friction concerns Israel's unaccommodating policies regarding the needs of the local Palestinian population in matters of housing under local government zoning and planning regulations.[35] Another issue involves Palestinian residents' quest to maintain their residency status in East Jerusalem. The majority of the Palestinian population of East Jerusalem resisted acquiring Israeli citizenship. Their residence rights in the city as well as their entitlement to social benefits and services were thus solely dependent on their status as legal residents. However, through various Israeli legal mechanisms that became applicable in East Jerusalem, many Palestinian Jerusalemites have been denied this residency status, thereby making them subject to deportations.[36]

As the preceding discussion indicates, Israel's official policy towards East Jerusalem is intimately intertwined with deep political currents. This became apparent in the November 2010 amendment to the Law and Administration Ordinance as

---

30 Imseis, *Facts on the Ground*, *supra* note 28, at 1044; Orna Ben-Naftali, Aeyal M. Gross & Keren Michaeli, *Illegal Occupation: Framing the Occupied Palestinian Territory*, 23 BERKELEY J. INT'L L. 515, 573 (2005).

31 GERSHON SHAFIR & YOAV PELED, BEING ISRAELI: THE DYNAMICS OF MULTIPLE CITIZENSHIP 181 (2002).

32 Robert H. Mnookin, Ehud Eiran & Sreemat Mitter, *Barriers to Progress at the Negotiating Table: Internal Conflicts among Israelis and among Palestinians*, 6 NEV. L. J. 299, 311 (2006).

33 SHAFIR & PELED, *supra* note 31, at 181.

34 Mnookin, Eiran & Mitter, *supra* note 32, at 311.

35 *See* Irus Braverman, *Powers of Illegality: House Demolition and Resistance in East Jerusalem*, 32 LAW & SOC. INQUIRY 333 (2007).

36 *See* Herling, *supra* note 28. *See also* CHERYL RUBENBERG, THE PALESTINIANS: IN SEARCH OF A JUST PEACE 203–09 (2003); Usama Halabi, *Revoking Permanent Residency: A Legal Review of Israeli Policy*, 9 JERUSALEM Q. FILE 40 (2000); YAEL STEIN, THE QUIET DEPORTATION: REVOCATION OF RESIDENCY OF EAST JERUSALEM PALESTINIANS (1997).

adopted by the Knesset.[37] Under this amendment, the Israeli government cannot sign or ratify an agreement by which Israeli law, jurisdiction and administration becomes inapplicable in a region where it is currently applicable, unless that agreement is first ratified by the absolute majority of the Knesset (i.e., 61 of the 120 members) and by a simple majority in a national referendum (to be held following the vote by the Knesset that approved the agreement). As we shall see in the following discussion, this law applies to the Golan Heights as well—for this region has also become intimately connected to Israeli political ideologies.

C. The Golan Heights

The Golan Heights were long considered of special strategic value for both Israel and Syria, given their elevated location and water resources.[38] This region was relatively well populated before the 1967 Six-Day War, with a population of 120,000 to 130,000 living on a plateau of 70 kilometers.[39] The population that lived in the Golan Heights was very diverse—the vast majority was Muslim Sunnis, and minorities included Alawites, Druze, Circassians, Turcomans, Armenians, Kurds, Christians, and some 8,000 Palestinian refugees that moved there following the 1948 War.[40] Within a month of the 1967 Six-Day War, the Golan Heights became almost empty.[41] Of the 130 villages in the area Israel occupied, only six predominantly Druze villages remained.[42] The Syrian population of the Golan Heights at present is about 17,000.[43]

---

37 Law and Administration Matters Law (Revocation of Application of Law, Jurisdiction and Administration), 5759-1999, SH No. 1703 p. 86, as amended in November 2010: SH No. 2263, p. 58.

38 *See* Jerome Slater, *Lost Opportunities for Peace in the Arab Israeli Conflict: Israel and Syria (1948–2001)*, 27 INT'L SECURITY 79 (2002).

39 TESSLER, *supra* note 1, at 404. For a detailed account of the circumstances leading to Israel's occupation of the Golan Heights, *see* Eyal Zisser, *June 1967: Israel's Capture of the Golan Heights*, 7 ISR. STUD. 168 (2002).

40 Sakr Abu Fakhr, *Voices from the Golan*, 29 J. PALESTINE STUD. 5, 5–6 (2000).

41 Tayseer Mara'i & Usama R. Halabi, *Life under Occupation in the Golan Heights*, 22 J. PALESTINE STUD. 78, 78 (1992).

42 These were Majdal Shams, Buqa'ata, Masada, Ayn Qinye, Shita (destroyed in 1970), and Ghajar (Alawite). *Id.* at 79. Tayseer Mara'i and Usama Halabi state three main reasons why the Druze stayed put following Israeli occupation. First, this population was mostly concentrated in villages located on a rugged terrain at the foothills of Mount Hermon—a region that witnessed almost no fighting during the 1967 Six-Day War. Second, in the Great Syrian Revolt against the French in 1925–1927, local residents that fled their homes lost their property. Afraid that the same would happen this time around, the local population preferred to stay put. Third, Israeli authorities had traditionally taken a more conciliatory attitude towards the Druze, given the fact that the Druze community inside of Israel was generally cooperative with the Israeli establishment. Israeli authorities had reason to believe that the Syrian Druze would take a similar position to that taken by their kin inside of Israel and refrain from coming into direct conflict with them. *Id.* at 80.

43 Abu Fakhr, *supra* note 40, at 7.

As the years went by, a number of Israeli settlements were established in the Golan Heights. Today, this region has 33 such settlements with a total of some 18,000 Israeli settlers.[44]

The Golan Heights were effectively annexed to Israel shortly after the 1967 Six-Day War and absorbed into the Israeli economy.[45] The application of Syrian law was discontinued a short time after the war,[46] and local disputes were handled by Israeli judges or local community leaders.[47] Israeli authorities explained these measures by the fact that in the wake of the war, all local judges had fled and there were no local law books from which local law could be ascertained.[48] So shortly after the war the Israeli legal system effectively repealed the Syrian legal system.[49]

The incorporation of the Golan Heights into Israel was completed with the enactment of the Golan Heights Law, 1981.[50] The legislative process that culminated in the enactment of this law began and ended in less than one day! The Prime Minister at the time, Menachem Begin, contemplated the bill on the morning of December 14, 1981. By the early evening hours, the bill was submitted to the Knesset, and just before midnight it managed to pass the necessary three readings and became law.[51] This enactment has one major provision, Section 1, prescribing that "the law, jurisdiction and administration of the state shall apply to the Golan Heights." Like in the case of East Jerusalem, this wording drew some discussion as

---

44 *Israel Is Selling Lands in the Occupied Territories: Adalah Position Paper on the Privatization of the Lands of the Settlements on the Golan Heights and in East Jerusalem*, 63 Adalah's Newsletter (2009), *available at* http://www.adalah.org/features/land/Position_Paper_on_Land_Reform_and_EJ_and_GH_settlements_English_Final%5B1%5D.pdf.

45 R. Scott Kennedy, *The Druze of the Golan Heights: A Case of Non-Violent Resistance*, 13 J. Palestine Stud. 48, 50–51 (1984).

46 Thomas S. Kuttner, *Israel and the West Bank: Aspects of the Law of Belligerent Occupation*, 7 Isr. Y.B. Hum. Rts. 166, 191 n.86 (1977); Mara'i & Halabi, *supra* note 41, at 80.

47 Sheleff, *supra* note 11, at 338.

48 Meir Shamgar, *The Observance of International Law in the Administered Territories*, 1 Isr. Y.B. Hum. Rts. 262, 269 (1971) [hereinafter Shamgar, *The Observance of International Law*].

49 Eyal Benvenisti, The International Law of Occupation 212 (2d ed. 2012) [hereinafter Benvenisti, International Law of Occupation].

50 36 LSI 7 (1981–82).

51 For the exact chronicles of the enactment, *see* Sheleff, *supra* note 11, at 334 n.6. The vote on the law was 63 in favor, 21 against. Yael Yishai, *Israeli Annexation of East Jerusalem and the Golan Heights: Factors and Processes*, 21 Middle Eastern Stud. 45, 56 (1985). It is also worth noting that the polls showed a majority in the Israeli public in favor of annexation. *Id.* at 55.

to whether it constituted annexation of the Golan Heights to Israel.[52] Leon Sheleff has argued that in the absence of express language favoring annexation, the Golan Heights Law should be construed as narrowly as possible: it merely applies Israeli law there, but does not change the status of the region as an occupied territory.[53] In his opinion, the enactment was deemed necessary in light of the legal vacuum that existed in the Golan Heights, mentioned previously.[54] Since the annexation of a territory governed by a belligerently occupying regime is repugnant to international law,[55] Sheleff's stand is also justified as consistent with the well-established prism according to which national laws should not be interpreted in a manner inconsistent with international law.[56]

Asher Maoz, on the other hand, maintained that the application of Israeli law to the Golan Heights indeed must imply the annexation of the region,[57] since this was the explicit intent of the Israeli Knesset and because the legislation at hand overrides the international law norm.[58]

The international community regarded the Golan Heights Law as an act of annexation and responded accordingly.[59] Immediately following the enactment of the Golan Heights Law, the United Nations Security Council adopted Resolution 497, which declared that "the Israeli decision to impose its laws, jurisdiction and administration in the occupied Syrian Golan Heights is null and void and without international legal effect."[60] The most severe response to the enactment of the law came from Syria, which regarded the law as a declaration of war and the annulment of the state of cease fire agreement.[61]

Beyond doubt, the Golan Heights Law incorporated this region as an integral part of Israel under Israeli law. This perspective was abundantly clear in the Israeli

---

52 DINSTEIN, BELLIGERENT OCCUPATION, *supra* note 6, at 19–20.

53 Sheleff, *supra* note 11, at 335–36.

54 *Id.* at 337–38.

55 *See* support of this statement by Yehuda Z. Blum, who in 1981 was Israel's ambassador to the United Nations, regarding Jordan's annexation of the West Bank in 1950—a subject we will return to later on. Yehuda Z. Blum, *The Missing Reversioner: Reflections on the Status of Judea and Samaria*, 3 ISR. L. REV. 279, 289 (1968).

56 Sheleff, *supra* note 11, at 336.

57 Maoz, *supra* note 12, at 363.

58 *Id.* at 357.

59 *Id.* at 384.

60 S.C. Res. 497, U.N. DOC. S/RES/497 (Dec. 17, 1981).

61 Maoz, *supra* note 12, at 386.

Supreme Court case of *Abu Saleh v. Minister of Interior*.[62] Following the enactment of the Golan Heights Law, Israeli authorities tried to effectuate it by imposing the duty to carry official Israeli ID cards on the local Syrian population. In protest, this population vehemently resisted this initiative.[63] In *Abu Saleh*, a number of Syrian residents petitioned the Israeli Supreme Court, arguing that the standing obligation under which all those legally present in Israel must carry an ID card does not apply to them since they cannot be regarded as being present in Israel. Aharon Barak, then an Associate Justice, delivered the majority opinion of the Court by first stating that the question posed by the petition is not one of public international law, nor one of international relations, but rather one that requires the assessment of the implications of the Golan Heights Law's enactment. According to Barak, the Golan Heights Law makes it necessary to include the Golan Heights in the term "Israel," whenever any reference by any other law is made to Israel. Therefore, if all those legally present in Israel of the age 17 and above are required to carry an Israeli ID card, then under that law so are all residents of the Golan Heights of the same age.[64] Accordingly, under Israeli municipal law, the Golan Heights have now become part of Israel, certainly for conflict of laws purposes.

Israel's grip on the Golan Heights was tightened yet further as a result of the November 2010 amendment to the Law and Administration Ordinance, 1948—an amendment mentioned earlier in the discussion on East Jerusalem. Consequently, if Israel is to withdraw from the Golan Heights in any future peace agreement with Syria, the Knesset will first need to approve of the agreement with an absolute majority vote and then have the Israeli public also approve of it in a national referendum.

D. The Sinai Peninsula

On the eve of the 1967 Six-Day War, the Sinai Peninsula was under full Egyptian sovereignty.[65] Moreover, Israel had fully conceded that following the war, its status regarding the Sinai Peninsula was that of a belligerent occupant.[66]

---

62 HCJ 205/82, 37(2) PD 718 (1983).

63 *See* Jonathan Molony, Michelle Stewart & Nancy Touhy-Hamill, From Settlement to Shelf: The Economic Occupation of the Syrian Golan 19 (2009); Kennedy, *supra* note 45, at 53–55.

64 *Abu Saleh*, 37(2) PD at 720.

65 Dinstein, Belligerent Occupation, *supra* note 6, at 13.

66 *See* Meir Rosenne, *Development of Oil Resources in Sinai*, in 1 Military Government in the Territories Administered by Israel 1967–1980: Legal Aspects 335, 335–36 (Meir Shamgar ed., 1982).

One major issue of friction between Israel and Egypt as to Israel's status as a belligerent occupant, however, was whether this status enabled Israel to exploit the Sinai Peninsula's oil resources.[67] This friction, as well as all other issues concerning the Sinai Peninsula, was eventually resolved as Israel and Egypt signed the Camp David Accords (1978)[68] and the Israeli-Egyptian Peace Treaty (1979).[69] Under these accords, Israel agreed to withdraw from the Sinai Peninsula over a period of three years, and indeed completed this undertaking in 1982.[70]

During Israeli occupation, the Sinai Peninsula maintained the jurisdictional status of a foreign region held by Israel as a belligerent occupant. Therefore, Israeli laws had no direct application in the Sinai Peninsula. The laws in effect in the region were the existing Egyptian laws, which Israeli courts could determine to be the governing law for specific instances under Israel's choice of law rules.[71]

A different outlook was devised, though, regarding the Israeli courts' *in personam* jurisdiction towards defendants present in the Sinai Peninsula when this region was under Israel's belligerent occupation. According to an Israeli set of civil procedure rules that will be discussed in detail in Chapter Two, a defendant present in the Sinai Peninsula was to be treated as if present on Israeli sovereign soil for the purpose of effectuating service of process. In turn, this made it possible to establish personal jurisdiction over anyone present in the Sinai Peninsula during Israel's occupation through direct personal service of process—given Israel's long adherence to the English common law rule of transient jurisdiction.

---

67 *Id. See also* Brice M. Clagett & O. Thomas Johnson, *May Israel as a Belligerent Occupant Lawfully Exploit Previously Unexploited Oil Resources of the Gulf of Suez?*, 72 AM. J. INT'L L. 558 (1978); Antonio Crivellaro, *Oil Operations by a Belligerent Occupant: The Israel—Egypt Dispute*, 3 ITALIAN Y.B. INT'L L. 171 (1977); Allan Gerson, *Off-Shore Oil Exploration by a Belligerent Occupant: The Gulf of Suez Dispute*, 71 AM. J. INT'L L. 725 (1977).

68 Israel-Egypt, Camp David Agreements: A Framework for Peace in the Middle East, Sept. 17, 1978, 17 ILM 1466 (1978) [hereinafter Camp David Agreements].

69 Israel-Egypt, Treaty of Peace, Mar. 26, 1979, 18 ILM 362 (1979).

70 DINSTEIN, BELLIGERENT OCCUPATION, *supra* note 6, at 14. Controversy emerged over the Taba region and was ultimately settled in 1988 by means of international arbitration. *Id.*

71 *See* CC (BS) 151/80 Kaplan v. Gabbay, PM 5742(2) 290 (1982).

E. The Palestinian Territories of the West Bank and the Gaza Strip

1. The West Bank, 1948–1967

Prior to the 1967 Six-Day War, the West Bank was part of Jordan;[72] but this was not always the case. Until 1948, the West Bank—or to be exact, what was known at the time as Central or Eastern Palestine[73]—was part of Mandatory Palestine no different in status at the time from any other part of what became Israel. Immediately after the 1948 War, Central Palestine fell under the control of the Hashemite Kingdom of Transjordan (the Hashemite Kingdom of Jordan since 1949).[74] Its king, Abdullah, had greater ambitions than just controlling this region: he sought to merge it with his kingdom. In a number of administrative actions culminating in a special parliamentary resolution issued in April 1950, Central Palestine, or the West Bank as it had already came to be called,[75] was annexed to Jordan.[76] In an effort to appease the aspirations of the Palestinian people and to counter mounting criticism in the Arab world over Jordanian annexation of the West Bank, the Jordanian parliament also stated that "Arab rights in Palestine shall be protected" and that the unity of the West Bank with Jordan "shall in no way be connected with the final settlement of Palestine's just case within the limits of national hopes, Arab cooperation and international justice."[77] Questions loomed as to whether these actions amounted to a full and permanent annexation of the West Bank to Jordan or whether they only constituted provisional measures.[78] In any case, only two states—Britain and Pakistan—were prepared to recognize the merger of the West Bank with Jordan.[79]

As a result of this unity with Jordan, many of the Palestinians living in the West Bank became Jordanian citizens.[80] As of 1950, representatives from the West Bank were appointed to the Jordanian parliament.[81]

---

72 *See* DINSTEIN, BELLIGERENT OCCUPATION, *supra* note 6, at 15.

73 *See* JOHN QUIGLEY, THE STATEHOOD OF PALESTINE: INTERNATIONAL LAW IN THE MIDDLE EAST CONFLICT 107 (2010) [hereinafter QUIGLEY, THE STATEHOOD OF PALESTINE].

74 *Id.*

75 *Id.* at 118.

76 *Id.* at 109–10.

77 *Id.* at 119.

78 *Id.*

79 *Id.*

80 DINSTEIN, BELLIGERENT OCCUPATION, *supra* note 6, at 15.

81 John Quigley, *Judicial Autonomy in Palestine: Problems and Prospects*, 21 U. DAYTON L. REV. 697, 706 (1996) [hereinafter Quigley, *Judicial Autonomy in Palestine*].

In terms of its municipal legal order, the West Bank maintained its laws as they existed on May, 15, 1948—the day it fell under Jordanian control.[82] Yet in light of its annexation, the West Bank was made subject to newly enacted Jordanian legislation.[83] This in turn created some problems in identifying the applicable legal norms—which led to a process of unifying the laws of the two banks.[84] However, since this unification process was not complete when the West Bank fell under Israeli occupation in 1967, this region maintained a distinct legal order: in addition to the laws of the British Mandate (that included Ottoman influence), a tier of Jordanian law was involved as well.

Any official Jordanian ties that remained with the West Bank after the 1967 Six-Day War formally ended in July of 1988, when King Hussein gave an address to the nation in which he declared Jordan's disengagement from the West Bank.[85] This disengagement was justified as an act complying with a resolution of an Arab Summit held in Rabat, Morocco, back in 1974, that recognized the Palestinian Liberation Organization as the sole representative of the Palestinian people.[86] Following this disengagement, Jordan amended its election law and cancelled the seats allocated to representatives from the West Bank in the Jordanian House of Representatives.

2. The Gaza Strip, 1948–1967

The Gaza Strip came under Egyptian control in the course of the 1948 Arab-Israeli war.[87] Egypt did not purport to annex the Gaza Strip and actually has never claimed this region as part of its territory—neither before 1948 nor afterwards.[88] In administering the Gaza Strip, Egypt followed the law of belligerent occupation.[89] Accordingly, the law that was in force in the Gaza Strip on the

82 QUIGLEY, THE STATEHOOD OF PALESTINE, *supra* note 73, at 118.

83 Benvenisti & Zamir, *supra* note 8, at 302.

84 Shamgar, *The Observance of International Law*, *supra* note 48, at 264.

85 An English translation of King Hussein's address can be found at http://www.kinghussein.gov.jo/88_july31.html.

86 *See* Abd El-Mahdi Massadeh, *The Structure of Public Administration in Jordan: A Constitutional and Administrative Law Perspective*, 14 ARAB L.Q. 91, 91 (1999).

87 TESSLER, *supra* note 1, at 275.

88 *See* Mahnoush H. Arsanjani, *United Nations Competence in the West Bank and the Gaza Strip*, 31 INT'L & COMP. L.Q. 426, 441 (1982); Carol Farhi, *On the Legal Status of the Gaza Strip*, *in* 1 MILITARY GOVERNMENT IN THE TERRITORIES ADMINISTERED BY ISRAEL 1967–1980: LEGAL ASPECTS, *supra* note 66, at 61, 74, 79–80.

89 Quigley, *Judicial Autonomy in Palestine*, *supra* note 81, at 704–05 (1996).

eve of Egyptian control—a combination of British Mandate and Ottoman law—remained in effect.[90] In due course, the Egyptian administration did enact its own decrees, but these came to supplement the existing body of law.[91] The Egyptian administration also maintained the local judiciary that included at the time a number of Magistrate Courts and a District Court that sat in Gaza.[92] One other important ingredient of Egyptian control over the Gaza Strip was the Egyptian effort to stress this region's Palestinian-Arab identity. For example, when the Egyptian governor-general issued local orders, he did so "in the name of the Palestinian people."[93] The 1962 constitution promulgated for the Gaza Strip by Jamal Abd al-Nassir as president of the United Arab Republic stated in Section I, Article 1: "The Gaza Strip is an indivisible part of the land of Palestine and its people are part of the Arab Nation."[94] This constitutional document, which included guarantees for basic human rights and liberties (Section II), envisioned local governmental bodies, the Executive Council and the Legislative Assembly, in which local Palestinian residents of the Gaza Strip would take part. However, little of this vision has been realized, and control over the Gaza Strip remained in the hands of the Egyptian governor-general until 1967. Notably, however, this Egyptian control over the Gaza Strip was briefly interrupted between October 29, 1956, and March 8, 1957—a period in which the Gaza Strip was occupied by Israel as a result of the 1956 Suez War.[95]

3. The Status of the West Bank and the Gaza Strip under International Law

Following the Israeli occupation of the West Bank and the Gaza Strip, the status of these regions became the subject of a public international law controversy.[96] Important as this topic is, it is somewhat beyond the subject matter at hand. The level

---

90 Bob Labes, Note, *The Law of Belligerent Occupation and the Legal Status of the Gaza Strip*, 9 MICH. Y.B. INT'L LEGAL STUD. 383, 391 (1988).

91 *Id.*

92 Farhi, *supra* note 88, at 76.

93 Quigley, *Judicial Autonomy in Palestine, supra* note 81, at 705.

94 *Republican Decree Announcing Constitutional System of Gaza Sector, March 9, 1962*, 17 MIDDLE EAST J. 156 (1963).

95 Labes, *supra* note 90, at 393–97.

96 This was not the case regarding the Sinai Peninsula and the Golan Heights. No doubt existed regarding the status of both of these regions as occupied territories that should be governed by the international law of belligerent occupation. Yoram Dinstein, *The International Law of Belligerent Occupation and Human Rights*, 8 ISR. Y.B. HUM. RGTS 104, 108 (1978) [hereinafter Dinstein, *The International Law of Belligerent Occupation and Human Rights*].

of compliance with public international law norms by parties to the Israeli-Arab (Palestinian) conflict is not a primary concern here. The primary interest of this study is the evolution of Israeli conflict of laws doctrines that are municipal in character and as such are not governed by international law norms or standards. Nonetheless, in some spheres, the close connection between conflict of laws and public international law cannot be disregarded. One such sphere is the subject of sovereignty—specifically, the type of sovereignty that exists in an occupied territory in light of a state of belligerent occupation. As will become evident in the coming chapters, sovereignty is a guiding notion when articulating the reach of adjudicative, prescriptive, and enforcement jurisdiction. This in turn makes it imperative to understand the nature and limits of sovereignty in occupied territories.

In principle, two major international conventions govern in a state of belligerent occupation.[97] The first is the 1907 Hague Convention Respecting the Laws and Customs of War on Land and its annexed Regulations (Hague Regulations),[98] and the second is the 1949 Geneva Convention IV Relative to the Protection of Civilian Persons in Time of War (Fourth Geneva Convention).[99] Subsequently, a third document was added: the 1977 Geneva Protocol I.[100]

Initially, Israel considered its status in the West Bank and the Gaza Strip as that of a belligerent occupant, thereby accepting the application of the relevant public international norms.[101] However, it soon (at least partially) retracted this position. The Israeli position focused on the Fourth Geneva Convention.[102] Article 2,

---

97 *See* Gerhard von Glahn, The Occupation of Enemy Territory: A Commentary on the Law and Practice of Belligerent Occupation 27 (1957).

98 Regulations Concerning the Laws and Customs of War on Land, annexed to Convention Respecting the Laws and Customs of War on Land, Oct. 18, 1907, 36 Stat. 2277, 1 Bevans 631.

99 Convention (Fourth) Relative to the Protection of Civilian Persons in Time of War, Aug. 12, 1949, 6 U.S.T. 3516, 75 U.N.T.S. 287.

100 Adam Roberts, *What Is a Military Occupation*, 55 Brit. Y.B. Int'l L. 249, 251 (1985) [hereinafter Roberts, *What Is a Military Occupation*].

101 Raja Shehadeh, Occupier's Law: Israel and the West Bank xi-xii (revised ed. 1985) [hereinafter Shehadeh, Occupier's Law].

102 *See* Benvenisti, International Law of Occupation, *supra* note 49, at 206–09; Richard Ober, *Current Israeli Practices and Policies in the West Bank and the Gaza Strip: A Historical and Legal Analysis*, 10 B.C. Third World L.J. 91, 100–05 (1990); Joseph H. H. Weiler, *Israel, the Territories and International Law: When Doves Are Hawks, in* Israel Among the Nations: International and Comparative Law Perspectives on Israel's 50th Anniversary 381, 384–88 (Alfred E. Kellermann et al. eds., 1998); Alan Levine, *The Status of Sovereignty in East Jerusalem and the West Bank*, 5 N.Y.U. J. Int'l L. & Pol. 485 (1972); Peter Malanczuk, *Israel: Status, Territory and Occupied Territories, in* 2 Encyclopedia of Public International Law 1468, 1495–96 (Rudolf Bernhardt ed., 1995); Peter J. Morgan III, Note, *Recent Israeli Security Measures under the Fourth Geneva Convention*, 3 Conn. J. Int'l L. 485, 485–87 (1988).

paragraph 2 of this convention states that "[t]he convention shall also apply to all cases of partial or total occupation of the territory of a High Contracting Party." Though Israel, Jordan, and Egypt were all High Contracting Parties to the Fourth Geneva Convention, Israel maintained that on the eve of the 1967 Six-Day War, or any time before that, the West Bank was not considered to be a territory of Jordan and the Gaza Strip was not a territory of Egypt. Neither had lawfully extended their sovereignty over any of these regions. Egypt has never annexed the Gaza Strip and explicitly maintained its status as a foreign jurisdiction, and Jordan's annexation of the West Bank in 1950 was not internationally recognized.[103] This position was characterized as "territory oriented," since it bases the primary emphasis of the law of belligerent occupation on preserving the reversionary interests of the legitimate sovereign ousted by the occupant.[104]

Indeed, the Israeli position was motivated by political and strategic concerns. If Israel were to officially recognize its status as a belligerent occupant under the Fourth Geneva Convention, it would have implicitly recognized the sovereignty of Jordan and Egypt in the West Bank and the Gaza Strip respectively in the period preceding the 1967 Six-Day War. Israel was not prepared to do that.[105]

From the Israeli positive law perspective, another argument was offered to explain why the Fourth Geneva Convention is not binding. Israel has maintained that the provisions of this convention are conventional (as opposed to customary) international law and as such do not form part of domestic law, unless incorporated by Knesset legislation.[106] Since no such legislation exists, then the Fourth Geneva Convention is not binding on Israeli courts and other governmental institutions.

Israel took a somewhat more hesitant position regarding the Hague Regulations.[107] At first glance, Article 42 of the Hague Regulations seems to rather clearly classify

---

103 Shamgar, *The Observance of International Law, supra* note 48, at 263–64; Meir Shamgar, *Legal Concepts and Problems of the Israeli Military Government—The Initial Stage, in* 1 MILITARY GOVERNMENT IN THE TERRITORIES ADMINISTERED BY ISRAEL 1967–1980: LEGAL ASPECTS, *supra* note 66, at 13, 31–43 [hereinafter Shamgar, *Legal Concepts and Problems of the Israeli Military Government*]. *See also* Blum, *supra* note 55.

104 Kuttner, *supra* note 46, at 170.

105 MOSHE DRORI, HA-HAKIKA BE-EZOR YEHUDA VE-HA-SHOMRON [THE LEGISLATION IN THE AREA OF JUDEA AND SAMARIA] 27 (1975) (Hebrew) [hereinafter DRORI, THE LEGISLATION IN THE AREA OF JUDEA AND SAMARIA]; Kuttner, *supra* note 46, at 170; Yaron Butovsky, *Law of Belligerent Occupation: Israeli Practice and Judicial Decisions Affecting the West Bank*, 21 CAN. Y.B. INT'L L. 217, 219 (1983).

106 Ober, *supra* note 102, at 102.

107 *See* Nissim Bar-Yaacov, *The Applicability of the Laws of War to Judea and Samaria (The West Bank) and the Gaza Strip*, 24 ISR. L. REV. 485, 486 (1990).

both the West Bank and the Gaza Strip as occupied territories.[108] The article prescribes: "Territory is considered occupied when it is actually placed under the authority of the hostile army." However, this article is part of a section (Section III of Chapter V) titled "Military Authority over the Territory of the Hostile State."[109] This title further makes the application of the Hague Regulations contingent upon the territories occupied being those of an enemy—a precondition that Israel denied on the grounds that neither Jordan nor Egypt had sovereignty over the West Bank and the Gaza Strip.[110] However, Israel's efforts in promoting this position were not as forceful as those it applied regarding its reading of the Fourth Geneva Convention.[111] To a large extent, this was due to the fact that the Hague Regulations are declaratory in nature; i.e., they are part of customary international law and as such become domestically applicable without the need for incorporating legislation.[112]

The Israeli government's position regarding the Fourth Geneva Convention, aptly characterized as "excessively legalistic,"[113] was widely rejected by prominent international organizations such as the International Committee of the Red Cross (ICRC), the United Nations, and leading international law experts both within Israel and beyond its borders.[114] This rejection was not grounded in the formal status of the West Bank and the Gaza Strip on the eve of the 1967 Six-Day War, but rather was based on the fact that the army of a foreign state captured these

---

108 *See* Kuttner, *supra* note 46, at 171–72.

109 In the original text in French: "*Territoire de l'État Ennemi.*"

110 Bar-Yaacov, *supra* note 107, at 492–93.

111 *See* Kuttner, *supra* note 46, at 171–72.

112 *See* Ruth Lapidoth, *International Law within the Israel Legal System*, 24 ISR. L. REV. 451, 452, 458, 475 (1990).

113 Roberts, *What Is a Military Occupation*, *supra* note 100, at 282.

114 *Id.*; Dinstein, *The International Law of Belligerent Occupation and Human Rights*, *supra* note 96, at 107; Richard A. Falk & Burns H. Weston, *The Relevance of International Law to Israeli and Palestinian Rights in the West Bank and Gaza*, *in* INTERNATIONAL LAW AND THE ADMINISTRATION OF OCCUPIED TERRITORIES: TWO DECADES OF ISRAELI OCCUPATION OF THE WEST BANK AND GAZA STRIP 125, 132–33 (Emma Playfair ed., 1992); Ben-Naftali, Gross & Michaeli, *supra* note 30, at 567; DAVID KRETZMER, THE OCCUPATION OF JUSTICE: THE SUPREME COURT OF ISRAEL AND THE OCCUPIED TERRITORIES 32, 34 (2002); BENVENISTI, INTERNATIONAL LAW OF OCCUPATION, *supra* note 49, at 207; Ardi Imseis, *On the Fourth Geneva Convention and the Occupied Palestinian Territory*, 44 HARV. INT'L L. J. 65, 97–100 (2003) [hereinafter Imseis, *On the Fourth Geneva Convention and the Occupied Palestinian Territory*]. Additionally, some experts argued against the Israeli formalistic approach while referring to other formalistic considerations that Israel had not taken into due consideration. *See* Joseph H. Weiler, *Israel and the Creation of a Palestinian State: The Art of the Impossible and the Possible*, 17 TEX. INT'L L.J. 287, 315–18 (1982) [hereinafter Weiler, *Israel and the Creation of a Palestinian State*].

territories as a result of a war between "High Contracting Parties."[115] Indeed, Article 1 of the Fourth Geneva Convention provides: "The High Contracting Parties undertake to respect and to ensure respect for the present Convention in all circumstances." Moreover, Article 4 of the same Convention provides that "persons protected by the Convention are those who, at any given moment and in any manner whatsoever, find themselves, in a case of conflict or occupation, in the hands of a Party to the conflict or Occupying Power of which they are not nationals." This approach was depicted as the "people oriented approach," given that it puts greater emphasis on the rights of the inhabitants of the territory, rather than on the territories' previous formal status.[116] Since Palestinians in the West Bank and the Gaza Strip are living under Israeli occupation and Israel as well as Jordan and Egypt are parties to the Convention, it has been argued that the Convention applies irrespective of the pre-1967 status of the West Bank and Gaza Strip.[117]

An accurate depiction of the Israeli position on whether international belligerent law applies to the West Bank and Gaza Strip requires consideration of the Israeli Supreme Court's position on the matter.[118] Throughout the years, numerous petitions were filed with the Israeli Supreme Court by Palestinian residents and organizations contesting Israeli actions and policies in the Palestinian Territories (PT).[119] The principal point of reference in these petitions was the international law of belligerent occupation as embodied in the Hague Regulations and the Fourth Geneva Convention. The Israeli Supreme Court, in its capacity as the High Court of Justice, has judicial review authority over the actions of the state organs, including the Israeli government and the IDF.[120] Additionally, local courts in the West Bank and the Gaza Strip had no jurisdictional authority over the military government or any member of the occupying army.[121] For this reason,

115 *See* Samirah Shah, *On the Road to Apartheid: The Bypass Road Network in the West Bank*, 29 Colum. Hum. Rghts L. Rev. 221, 245 (1997); Roberts, *Prolonged Military Occupation*, *supra* note 9, at 64–65.

116 *See* Kuttner, *supra* note 46, at 170.

117 *See* Roberts, *What Is a Military Occupation*, *supra* note 100, at 250, 282; Ober, *supra* note 102, at 104.

118 Mazen Qupty, *The Application of International Law in the Occupied Territories as Reflected in the Judgments of the High Court of Justice in Israel*, *in* International Law and the Administration of Occupied Territories: Two Decades of Israeli Occupation of the West Bank and Gaza Strip, *supra* note 114, at 124.

119 Dinstein, *Reunification of Families*, *supra* note 13, at 174.

120 *Id.*

121 Dinstein, *The International Law of Belligerent Occupation and Human Rights*, *supra* note 96, at 115; Moshe Drori, *The Legal System in Judea and Samaria: A Review of the Previous Decade with a Glance at the Future*, 8 Isr. Y.B. Hum. Rts. 144, 151 (1978) [hereinafter Drori, *The Legal System in Judea and Samaria*].

Palestinians have often sought after the Israeli Supreme Court in their efforts to challenge Israeli actions and policies. But are such actions justiciable, and if so are they to be judged according to the international law of belligerent occupation as embodied in both of these conventions? When responding to these petitions, the Israeli government raised no objection to the Court's jurisdiction,[122] nor did it fully object to the application of the international law of belligerent occupation.[123] In fact, the government submitted that it undertakes—though only voluntarily—to abide by the humanitarian (as opposed to political) norms detailed in these conventions.[124]

Another important factor that attested to the Israeli commitment to abide by the international law of belligerent occupation were the orders issued by the IDF to its commanders. A number of authorities have indicated that IDF commanders serving in the West Bank and the Gaza Strip were ordered to follow the Hague Regulations and the Fourth Geneva Convention.[125]

So, in spite of its official position, Israeli did commit itself to observing both the conventional and the customary international law of belligerent occupation; whether in fact it did live up to this commitment, as it has argued but others dispute vehemently,[126] is beyond the scope of this study.

One important residue from the official Israeli position against the *de jure* application of the international law of belligerent occupation involved semantics. The

---

122 *See* Ben-Zion Farhy, *Current Legal Trends in the Area Administered by Israel*, 113 MIL. L. REV. 47, 49 (1986); Cheryl V. Reicin, *Preventive Detention, Curfews, Demolition of Houses, and Deportations: An Analysis of Measures Employed by Israel in the Administered Territories*, 8 CARDOZO L. REV. 515, 532–33 (1987); Esther Rosalind Cohen, *Justice for the Occupied Territory? The Israeli High Court of Justice Paradigm*, 24 COLUM. J. TRANSNAT'L L. 471, 471 (1986); Butovsky, *supra* note 105, at 219.

123 Dinstein, *The International Law of Belligerent Occupation and Human Rights, supra* note 96, at 108.

124 *See* Haim H. Cohn, *Foreword, in* ISRAEL NATIONAL SECTION OF THE INTERNATIONAL COMMISSION OF JURISTS, THE RULE OF LAW IN THE AREA ADMINISTERED BY ISRAEL vii–viii (1981); Shamgar, *The Observance of International Law, supra* note 48; Shamgar, *Legal Concepts and Problems of the Israeli Military Government, supra* note 103, at 15; Roberts, *Prolonged Military Occupation, supra* note 9, at 62–66; Lapidoth, *supra* note 112, at 478; Imseis, *On the Fourth Geneva Convention and the Occupied Palestinian Territory, supra* note 114, at 93. At a later stage, however, the Court did hold positively that the Hague Regulations do apply as a matter of customary international law. BENVENISTI, INTERNATIONAL LAW OF OCCUPATION, *supra* note 49, at 208–09; Dinstein, *Reunification of Families, supra* note 13, at 175–78. The distinction between "humanitarian" and "political" has not always been clear. Bar-Yaacov, *supra* note 107, at 493–94; Roberts, *What Is a Military Occupation, supra* note 100, at 283.

125 Farhy, *supra* note 122, at 50; Shamgar, *The Observance of International Law, supra* note 48, at 271; Lapidoth, *supra* note 112, at 478; Butovsky, *supra* note 105, at 219.

126 Ober, *supra* note 102, at 100–01.

Israeli Knesset and courts no longer referred to the West Bank and the Gaza Strip by the term "occupied territories" but rather applied the terms "Administered Territories" (*Shtahim Moukhzakim* in Hebrew),[127] merely "Territories" (*Shtahim*),[128] or "Region" or "Area" (*Ezor*).[129] The West Bank in particular became referred to by the biblical name of "Judea and Samaria."[130]

4. Establishing Military Government

Once Israel took control of the West Bank and the Gaza Strip, it placed each of these territories under a so-called Military Government. This body was run by the IDF, and its primary function was to ensure effective control.[131] A most elaborate legal design established and subsequently maintained authority by the Military Government. This plan was significantly aided by the early preparations of the military advocate general at the time, Mier Shamgar.[132] In fact, years before the 1967 Six-Day War, Shamgar prepared a manual with instructions on how to handle territories that Israel might occupy.[133] Even during the actual fighting, Shamgar ordered that military advocate units be deployed with the

127 Reicin, *supra* note 122.

128 Shlomo Gazit, *Policy in the Administered Territories*, 1 ISR. Y.B. HUM. RTS. 278, 281 (1971).

129 This is the term used in Emergency Regulations (Offences Committed in Israel-Held Areas—Jurisdiction and Legal Assistance) (Extension of Validity) Law, 5728-1967, 22 LSI 20 (1967–68).

130 Amnon Rubinstein, *The Changing Status of the "Territories" (West Bank and Gaza): From Escrow to Legal Mongrel*, 8 TEL-AVIV U. STUD. IN L. 59, 61–62 (1988). On how "Judea and Samaria" terminology is connected to this region's biblical status, *see* Malvina Halberstem, *The Myth that Israel's Presence in Judea and Samaria Is Comparable to Iraq's Presence in Kuwait*, 19 SYRACUSE J. INT'L L. & COM. 1, 4–5 (1993).

131 *See* ISRAEL NATIONAL SECTION OF THE INTERNATIONAL COMMISSION OF JURISTS, *supra* note 124, at 1–2; Raja Shehadeh, *The Legislative Stages of the Israeli Military Occupation, in* INTERNATIONAL LAW AND THE ADMINISTRATION OF OCCUPIED TERRITORIES: TWO DECADES OF ISRAELI OCCUPATION OF THE WEST BANK AND GAZA STRIP, *supra* note 114, at 151, 152 [hereinafter Shehadeh, *The Legislative Stages*]. This was also true for the Sinai Peninsula and the Golan Heights until the eventual change of status of these two regions in the early 1980s. *See* Roberts, *Prolonged Military Occupation, supra* note 9, at 58–59.

132 Meir Shamgar was appointed to the post of the Military Advocate General in 1961 and went on to hold this office until 1968. Immediately afterwards, Shamgar served as the attorney general of the State of Israel (1968–1975), a Justice of the Supreme Court (from 1975) and the Court's president (1983–1995). This long service in key legal positions helped Shamgar influence Israel's legal outlook regarding the West Bank and the Gaza Strip.

133 MICHAL SHAKED, MOSHE LANDAU, SHOFET [MOSHE LANDAU, JUDGE] 387–88 (2012) (Hebrew); Shamgar, *Legal Concepts and Problems of the Israeli Military Government, supra* note 103, at 24–25, 25 n.27, 28–31. In due course, Shlomo Gazit, an IDF general who became the "Coordinator of Government Authorities in the Administered Territories," admitted that the Military Advocate General office was the most prepared of all IDF units for the 1967 Six-Day War. *See* Shlomo Gazit, *Policy in the Administered Territories*, 1 ISR. Y.B. HUM. RTS. 278, 278 (1971).

various forces to instruct IDF commanders.[134] Hence, it is no wonder that the Israeli occupation was labeled as a "legalistic occupation," given the effort to base each and every action of the Military Government on a preconceived legal order.[135]

The first important legal instrument issued by the IDF commander in the West Bank was Proclamation No. 1, which stated that the IDF had now "assumed responsibility for security and maintenance of public order."[136] Immediately afterwards came Proclamation No. 2, which established two additional constitutive norms.[137] First, the proclamation established that law in existence in these territories on June 7, 1967 "shall remain in force so far as there is nothing therein repugnant to this proclamation."[138] Second, it ordered that "all powers of government, legislation, appointment and administration in relation to the Region or its inhabitants shall henceforth vest" in the military commander.[139] An equivalent set of proclamations was also issued by the military commander for the Gaza Strip.[140]

Beyond doubt, these proclamations were issued in accordance with the international law of belligerent occupation, and more specifically Article 43 of the Hague Regulations.[141] That article provides:

> The authority of the legitimate power having in fact passed into the hands of the occupant, the latter shall take all the measures in his power to restore, and ensure, as far as possible, public order and safety, while respecting, unless absolutely prevented, the laws in force in the country.

---

134 Shamgar, *Legal Concepts and Problems of the Israeli Military Government, supra* note 103, at 24–25, 25 n.27.

135 Shehadeh, *The Legislative Stages, supra* note 131, at 167.

136 Shamgar, *Legal Concepts and Problems of the Israeli Military Government, supra* note 103, at 13.

137 *Id.* at 52.

138 *Id.*

139 *Id.* at 52–53.

140 *Id.* at 13, n.1.

141 *See* Farhy, *supra* note 122, at 48; Shamgar, *The Observance of International Law, supra* note 48, at 262, 267; Mahnoush H. Arsanjani, *United Nations Competence in the West Bank and the Gaza Strip*, 31 INT'L & COMP. L.Q. 426, 440–41 (1982); Reicin, *supra* note 122, at 518, 531; Shehadeh, *The Legislative Stages, supra* note 131, at 155; Arie Pach, *Human Rights in the West Bank Military Courts*, 7 ISR. Y.B. HUM. RTS. 222, 226, 252 (1977). For a more detailed discussion on the international law norm of maintaining the local legal order in the occupied territory, *see* Davis P. Goodman, Note, *The Need for Fundamental Change in the Law of Belligerent Occupation*, 37 STAN. L. REV. 1573, 1585–89 (1985).

In a nutshell, this article prescribes that authority over the occupied area passes to the hands of the occupant, who executes this authority through its armed forces[142]—and so Israel acted.

These proclamations led to three basic legal axioms regarding the West Bank and the Gaza Strip. These axioms defined the nature of sovereignty in both of these regions, both domestically in terms of what the IDF military commander was authorized to do, and internationally in terms of the extent to which other sovereign entities such as Israel, Jordan, and Egypt could apply their sovereign powers there.

Axiom I: *The Existing Legal Systems Should Be Preserved.* Preserving the existing laws in both the West Bank and the Gaza Strip enabled each of these two regions to preserve its own legal identity, in terms of both the applicable law and, to a great extent, the existing court system.[143] Hence, the West Bank and the Gaza Strip were preserved as separate jurisdictional entities from each other[144]—a situation akin to that of sister states. As already indicated, in the interim period between 1948 and 1967, each of these regions were governed by different entities and subject to different rules—so maintaining the existing law in each implied maintaining their differences.

As the office of the IDF military commander assumed its status as the ultimate sovereign in the PT, it issued thousands of orders,[145] effectively displacing much of the existing law.[146] The need to adjust the existing legal system to the evolving needs, so the argument went, made it necessary to continuously amend and add to the existing legal system.[147]

---

142 Roberts, *What Is a Military Occupation*, *supra* note 100, at, 252.

143 Pach, *supra* note 141, at 225–26; Kuttner, *supra* note 46, at 191; Reicin, *supra* note 122, at 530–31.

144 *See* Anis F. Kassim, *Legal Systems and Developments in Palestine* 1 Palestine Y.B Int'l L. 19, 27–29 (1984); The International Commission of Jurists, The Civilian Judicial System in the West Bank and Gaza: Present and Future 14–15 (The Center for the Independence of Judges and Lawyers, 1994) [hereinafter Civilian Judicial System in the West Bank]; Shehadeh, *The Legislative Stages*, supra note 131, at 155.

145 Drori, The Legislation in the Area of Judea and Samaria, *supra* note 105, at 34–39, 114; Drori, *The Legal System in Judea and Samaria, supra* note 121, at 163–64.

146 Quigley, *Judicial Autonomy in Palestine, supra* note 81, at 707. However, the contents of these orders were not always known to the public as many of them, at least in the first decade of occupation, were not published. Shehadeh, *The Legislative Stages, supra* note 131, at 151. For a different account *see* Shamgar, *The Observance of International Law, supra* note 48, at 269.

147 Drori, The Legislation in the Area of Judea and Samaria, *supra* note 105, at 81. *See also* Goodman, *supra* note 141, at 1606 n.133 (recognizing the difficulties in adjusting the rules of belligerent occupations that presume occupation to be temporary to a state where occupation takes on a prolonged and even permanent state).

This rather large amount of military orders and what they entailed in terms of the transformation of the local legal system and thereby life itself throughout the PT raised once again the question of compliance with international law norms. At the heart of the matter was the proper interpretation of Article 43 of the Hague Regulations.[148] As noted before, the Hague Regulations were taken to represent customary international law, and therefore Israel was generally more committed to observing their enforcement in the PT than it was to conventional norms of the law of belligerent occupation such as the Fourth Geneva Convention. It would seem that the occupying power has very little leeway in changing the existing legal order in the occupied territory. This is true given the wording of the Hague Regulations' Article 43—particularly the restriction pertaining to the subject matter of legislation conducted by the occupying power, permitting legislation that is intended to "restore and ensure…public order and safety"—and the restriction pertaining to the circumstances in which such legislation is to be made, and given the fact that the occupying power must respect the laws in force "unless absolutely prevented."

Notwithstanding the strong wording of Article 43 of the Hague Regulations, there was a long-standing view that the article in fact allows for greater latitude of legislation by the occupying power than a simple reading would suggest.[149] First, it was noted that the French version of the article, which is the more authoritative version, in pertaining to the permitted scope of subject matter of legislation by the occupying power, does not speak merely about ensuring "public order and safety" but rather of "*l'ordre et la vie publique*," i.e., "public order and civil life."[150] This broader definition of the subject matter of permitted legislation under Article 43 of the Hague Regulations was adopted by the Israeli Supreme Court in its decision in 1971 in *Christian Society for the Holy Places v. Minister of Defence*.[151] The Court determined that the military commander in the PT could apply its legislative powers as long as the motivation behind the measures it introduced was to promote the good of the local population, even when such measures are innovative relative to the existing legal system.

148 It has been noted that this article represents "the gist of the law of occupation." BENVENISTI, INTERNATIONAL LAW OF OCCUPATION, *supra* note 49, at 68.

149 *See* Edmund H. Schwenk, *Legislative Power of the Military Occupant under Article 43, Hague Regulations*, 54 YALE L.J. 393 (1945).

150 *Id.* at 398. *See also* Shah, *supra* note 115, at 270.

151 HCJ 337/71 Christian Society for the Holy Places v. Minister of Defense, 26(1) PD 574 (1971).

The more intriguing aspect of the interpretive course taken by the Court concerned the circumstantial limitation of Article 43 of the Hague Regulations, whereby the occupying power should respect the laws in force, unless it is "absolutely prevented" from doing so. The Court held that this limitation should permit legislation by the IDF military commander whenever such legislation is deemed necessary in the fulfillment of duty towards the residents of the territory.[152] The concern for the welfare of local PT residents voiced by the Court in this decision earned the Israeli occupation its characterization as a form of "benevolent occupation."[153]

The Israeli Supreme Court seems to have abandoned this initial attitude in later judgments, by enabling the military commander to legislate in order to accommodate the political agenda of the government of Israel instead of the welfare of the indigenous Palestinian population.[154] As a result, the Court proceeded to hold as legal under Article 43 of the Hague Regulations legislative measures such as restrictions on the freedom of press, refusal to allow local government elections, imposition of new taxes, and other such orders.[155] Hence, clearly, that major transformations to the law applicable in the PT did take place—notwithstanding Israel's initial commitment to maintain the local legal system.

Regarding the local judiciary, Israel made two major modifications in the West Bank. The first involved abolishing recourse from West Bank courts to the Court of Cassation in Amman, which operated as the highest court in Jordan.[156] The second was dissolving the Court of Appeals for the West Bank that operated in East Jerusalem and transferring its powers to the District Court of Ramallah.[157]

In terms of their civil jurisdiction, the local courts in both the West Bank and the Gaza Strip continued to operate in accordance with the existing rules. In principle, these courts had jurisdiction over the indigenous Palestinian population in various local civil disputes. Perhaps surprisingly, these courts were also jurisdictionally competent to handle civil actions filed against Israeli citizens,

---

152 *Id.* at 584.

153 KRETZMER, *supra* note 114, at 59.

154 *Id.* at 64.

155 *Id.* at 60.

156 *See* RAJA SHEHADEH & JONATHAN KUTTAB, THE WEST BANK AND THE RULE OF LAW 18–19 (1980).

157 Shamgar, *The Observance of International Law*, *supra* note 48, at 269; Kuttner, *supra* note 46, at 192.

including settlers.[158] International law of belligerent occupation restricts the civil jurisdiction authority of the local courts of an occupied territory over ordinary citizens of the occupying power.[159] A case on point is that of *Tsfania v. Minister of Defense*,[160] in which an Israeli citizen tried to revoke an eviction order given by a local Ramallah court. In doing so, he did not contest the jurisdictional capacity of this local court to grant the eviction order. Presumably, the fact that the real property in question was located in the West Bank was sufficient to authorize the court to issue the order. The petition centered on the plaintiff's right to submit his pleadings and briefs in Hebrew instead of the usual Arabic. According to a newly issued set of orders by the military commander, the plaintiff argued that he had such a right, and was referred by the Supreme Court to the appropriate authorities within the military government to raise his complaint. The one major restriction that exists involves a civil or administrative action filed before the local courts of the occupied territory against the occupying power itself or members of its army.[161] This restriction was indeed maintained in the West Bank and Gaza. As already noted, this was the major reason why Palestinian residents turned to the Israeli courts, especially the Supreme Court in its capacity as the High Court of Justice, in an effort to contest IDF actions.

Axiom II: *The IDF Military Commander Is the Ultimate Sovereign Authority*. The military commander of the West Bank and the Gaza Strip became the exclusive sovereign in these regions.[162] Any sovereignty that previously existed in the West Bank and the Gaza Strip was now suspended and its powers transferred to the IDF military commander.[163] Therefore, any newly enacted law in Jordan henceforth had no application in the West Bank, unless otherwise provided by the IDF military commander.[164]

---

158 This jurisdictional authority was an antithesis to the dominant perception that Israeli settlers in the PT should remain governed by Israeli law. *See* NEVE GORDON, ISRAEL'S OCCUPATION 28 (2008).

159 Dinstein, *The International Law of Belligerent Occupation and Human Rights, supra* note 96, at 116.

160 HCJ 138/75 Tsfania v. Minister of Defense, 29(2) PD 197 (1975).

161 Dinstein, *The International Law of Belligerent Occupation and Human Rights, supra* note 96, at 115.

162 Drori, *The Legal System in Judea and Samaria, supra* note 121, at 148; Pach, *supra* note 141, at 227; Kuttner, *supra* note 46, 183; HCJ 94/75 Nassar v. Gregorian Armenian Court, 30(2) PD 44, 48 (1975).

163 HCJ 337/71 Aljamiyah Almassehia v. Minister of Defense, 26(1) PD 574 (1972); HCJ 302/72 Abu Hilo v. Government of Israel, 27(2) PD 169 (1973); HCJ 663/78 Kiryat Arba Administration v. National Labor Court, 33(2) PD 398 (1979).

164 Dinstein, *The International Law of Belligerent Occupation and Human Rights, supra* note 96, at 113–14.

As the effective sovereign, the military commander is empowered to amend, suspend, or repeal any existing norm and enact new orders that attain the status of primary laws,[165] or form a "basic norm" of the land.[166]

Moreover, the maintenance of the West Bank and the Gaza Strip as separate jurisdictional entities in no way means that they were also maintained as viable political entities as well. Until the establishment of the Palestinian Authority (PA) in the mid-1990s, no central political process existed whereby the local population could vote and elect a governing body.[167] The military commander of each region was "a one man parliament"[168] that "assumed unchallenged control over all aspects of Palestinian life."[169] The military commander had no obligation to consult with representatives of the local population before issuing military orders.[170] Even civilian assemblies and the publication of material that had a political content required the permission of the Israeli military authorities.[171] Such procedures correspond with the international law of belligerent occupation. The military government in the PT has no obligation to administer democratic governance[172] or to place the welfare of the local population as its primary objective.[173]

The sovereign powers now invested in the IDF military commander meant complete control over the local judiciary. The military commander assumed the power to appoint judges.[174] A new network of military courts was established in which Israeli judges, lawyers, university lecturers, and government attorneys were appointed as judges.[175] The main business of these courts was to handle criminal proceedings concerned with "security offences."[176]

165 Shamgar, *The Observance of International Law, supra* note 48, at 268.

166 Pach, *supra* note 141, at 228.

167 At the beginning there were elections to local government authorities. DRORI, THE LEGISLATION IN THE AREA OF JUDEA AND SAMARIA, *supra* note 105, at 123; Kuttner, *supra* note 46, at 184.

168 Shehadeh, *The Legislative Stages, supra* note 131, at 151, 166.

169 *Id.* at 153.

170 *Id.* at 152.

171 DRORI, THE LEGISLATION IN THE AREA OF JUDEA AND SAMARIA, *supra* note 105, at 147–48.

172 Dinstein, *The International Law of Belligerent Occupation and Human Rights, supra* note 96, at 116.

173 *Id.*

174 Quigley, *Judicial Autonomy in Palestine, supra* note 81, at 707.

175 Drori, *The Legal System in Judea and Samaria, supra* note 121, at 154.

176 *Id.*

These measures were not well received by the local Palestinian population. Several civilian protests emerged immediately after the establishment of the military government.[177] Lawyers in the West Bank (but not in the Gaza Strip) announced a general strike of their own and refrained from representing clients before the local courts. The vast majority of Palestinian judges (31 of 39) serving in local West Bank courts resigned their posts.[178] The military government was not indifferent to this defiance. It appointed new judges and issued an order authorizing members of the Israeli Bar to appear before the local courts.[179] As Mier Shamgar explained himself, the order was issued so as "to facilitate the enforcement of the law and the activity of the local courts and to enable the inhabitants to receive the service of lawyers to this end."[180]

Another important amendment was an IDF order issued in 1969, providing that documents written in Hebrew or actions processed in Hebrew will not be inadmissible in a legal proceeding.[181] Evidently, this order was important to facilitate the authorization now provided to Israel lawyers. Additionally, it also made it possible for Israeli citizens who came under the jurisdiction of local courts in the West Bank and the Gaza Strip to also conduct litigation in Hebrew.[182]

In the realm of civil law, two important judicial bodies were established. The first is the Appeals Committee that reviewed the military government's handlings of absentee real property and an array of other administrative decisions.[183] Another judicial body was the Appeals Claim Committee, which had jurisdiction over claims filed by local residents based on damages suffered from IDF operations.[184]

This axiom by which sovereign powers were now invested in the IDF military commander underlay the abolishment of recourse to the Court of Cassation in Amman. In a report published by the Israel National Section of the International Commission of Jurists, this act was justified by the proposition that the court's

---

177 *Id.* at 150.

178 *See* Israel National Section of the International Commission of Jurists, *supra* note 124, at 23. A less significant number is reported in Kuttner, *supra* note 46, at 192.

179 Shamgar, *The Observance of International Law, supra* note 48, at 269. No strike took place in the Gaza Strip and thus no parallel order was issued there. *Id.*

180 *Id.*

181 *See* HCJ 138/75 Tsfania v. Minister of Defense, 29(2) PD 197, 198 (1975).

182 Drori, *The Legal System in Judea and Samaria, supra* note 121, at 152.

183 *Id.* at 154–55.

184 *Id.* at 155–56.

venue in Amman "became inaccessible to the local population after 1967."[185] Yet that same report, as well as other writings, complemented Israeli policy of freedom of movement, especially from the West Bank across the Jordan River—a policy that came to be known as the "open bridges" policy.[186] Hence, the abolition of recourse to the Court of Cassation in Amman due to restrictions on transportation imposed on West Bank residents does not correspond well with Israel's pride in affording these same residents an "open bridge" into Jordan! I think the more convincing argument is that when the West Bank came under the effective sovereignty of the IDF military commander, it was no longer possible to tolerate the jurisdictional capacity of a court sitting in Amman, Jordan—particularly if that court happens to head the judiciary.

Axiom III: *The State of Israel Has No Sovereignty over the West Bank and the Gaza Strip.* Israel's sovereignty does not extend to the West Bank and the Gaza Strip, notwithstanding total military control.[187] This truth follows from the international law on belligerent occupation, which prescribes that an occupying state cannot acquire sovereignty through military conquest,[188] even if the occupied territory was conquered from a state with no legitimate sovereignty over it.[189] Therefore, no law enacted in Israel is directly applicable in the West Bank and the Gaza Strip, unless it is incorporated by the military commander and made part of local law.[190]

In my opinion, this axiom explains why the Court of Appeals for the West Bank was dissolved in East Jerusalem and relocated to Ramallah. It was inconceivable that a court serving the West Bank would now sit in Israel—given the fact that East Jerusalem had come under Israeli jurisdiction.[191]

---

185 Israel National Section of the International Commission of Jurists, *supra* note 124, at 22

186 *Id.* at 85–86; Kuttner, *supra* note 46, at 183; Dinstein, *Reunification of Families, supra* note 13, at 178; Drori, *The Legal System in Judea and Samaria, supra* note 121, at 168. Writing as the Israeli government coordinator in the West Bank and the Gaza Strip, Shlomo Gazit, a brigadier general in the IDF, further argued, "We hope that the people in the Territories will use the open bridges with the Arab world as a corridor for transmitting messages about what Israel really is." Gazit, *supra* note 128, at 281.

187 Dinstein, *The International Law of Belligerent Occupation and Human Rights, supra* note 96, at 117.

188 Iain Scobbie, *Natural Resources and Belligerent Occupation: Perspectives from International Humanitarian and Human Rights Law, in* International Law and the Israeli-Palestinian Conflict: A Rights-Based Approach to Middle East Peace, *supra* note 28, at 229.

189 Antonio Cassese, *Legal Considerations on the International Status of Jerusalem*, 3 Palestine Y.B. Int'l L. 13, 23 (1986). *See also* Michael Akehurst, *The Arab-Israeli Conflict and International Law*, 5 New Zealand Universities L. Rev. 231, 242 (1973).

190 Dinstein, *The International Law of Belligerent Occupation and Human Rights, supra* note 96, at 113–14.

191 Drori, *The Legal System in Judea and Samaria, supra* note 121, at 150. *See also* Butovsky, *supra* note 105, at 225.

Yet the West Bank and the Gaza Strip cannot accurately be depicted as totally independent from the State of Israel. After all, the IDF military commander—the supreme sovereign in the region—is part of an organization that is subordinated to the Israeli government and obliged to follow its dictates.[192] Already in September 1968, a special Israeli government committee that included senior members of the government was established in order to articulate policies in Israel's Occupied Territories.[193] The Israeli Ministry of Defense then channeled the decisions of these governmental bodies to the IDF military commanders.[194] In reality, indeed, policies and public actions in the West Bank and the Gaza Strip have been influenced more by internal Israeli politics than by the will of the local Palestinian population.

Another important element that functioned to blur the divide between Israel and the PT was Israel's total dominance over the local Palestinian economy. The pre-1967 international border (the "Green Line") became virtually absent in this domain,[195] ultimately making the West Bank and the Gaza Strip's work forces totally dependent on the Israeli economy.[196]

5. The Camp David Accords and the Establishment of the Civil Administration

The 1978 Camp David Accords signed by Israel and Egypt were intended to establish a path for the solution of the Israeli-Palestinian conflict.[197] The agreements contained extensive provisions for a self-governing authority in the West Bank and Gaza,[198] to be realized by the granting of "full autonomy to the inhabitants" and the free election of a "self-governing authority."[199]

192 *See* CA 6860/01 Hamadah v. Israeli Pool for Vehicle Insurance, 57(3) PD 8 15–17 (2003); Shehadeh, *The Legislative Stages, supra* note 131, at 155; Pach, *supra* note 141, at 227–28.

193 *See* GEORGE E. BISHARAT, PALESTINIAN LAWYERS AND ISRAELI RULE: LAW AND DISORDER IN THE WEST BANK 51 (1989).

194 Kuttner, *supra* note 46, at 182–83.

195 Drori, *The Legal System in Judea and Samaria, supra* note 121, at 168.

196 Kuttner, *supra* note 46, at 185.

197 *Supra* note 68.

198 Roberts, *Prolonged Military Occupation, supra* note 9, at 59.

199 *See* Mayer Gabay, *Legal Aspects of the Camp David Framework for Peace in Relation to the Autonomy Proposal, in* MODELS OF AUTONOMY 255, 255–56 (Yoram Dinstein ed., 1981).

The Israeli-Egyptian Camp David Accords successfully established peace between Israel and Egypt—albeit a cold and fragile one. But these same accords ultimately failed to foster peace between Israelis and Palestinians and have been heavily criticized by Palestinians within and beyond the West Bank and Gaza Strip.[200] In addition, a number of key provisions of the accords turned out to be extremely vague, leading to conflicting interpretations by Israeli and Egyptian officials. For example, while Israel interpreted the proposition "full autonomy for the inhabitants" as meaning "personal autonomy," Egypt took this proposition to mean "territorial autonomy" in the West Bank, Gaza Strip, and even East Jerusalem.[201] These and other major differences led one scholar to comment that in the context of Israeli-Palestinian relations, "the Camp David agreements loosely amalgamated two different 'models' that in actual fact were poles apart."[202]

However, the major modification that the Camp David Accords brought about in Israeli-Palestinian relations was the reorganization of the military government in the West Bank and the Gaza Strip through the creation of a civil administration in November 1981.[203] The Camp David Accords were designed in a way that this civil administration "would gradually be taken over by civilians... [and] that local Palestinians would assume the administrative tasks, including senior positions."[204] Yet in reality they did not imply that the civil administration was to become independent of the military government.[205] On the contrary, the military orders were drawn out so that the civil administration would remain under the ultimate control of the military government.[206] Hence, it is not surprising that the Palestinian leadership resented and boycotted the civil administration, accusing the scheme of being "an introductory step to Israeli annexation" or at best, "a perpetuation of the existing occupation."[207]

200 Roberts, *Prolonged Military Occupation*, *supra* note 9, at 59.

201 Gabay, *supra* note 199, at 256.

202 Antonio Cassese, *The Israel-PLO Agreement and Self-Determination*, 4 Eur. J. Int'l L. 564, 570 (1993).

203 *See* Joel Singer, *The Establishment of a Civil Administration in the Areas Administered by Israel*, 12 Isr. Y.B. Hum. Rts. 259 (1982); Jonathan Kuttab & Raja Shehadeh, Civilian Administration in the Occupied West Bank: Analysis of Israeli Military Government Order No. 947 7 (1982).

204 Singer, *supra* note 203, at 278.

205 *See* Menachem Hofnung, Democracy, Law and National Security in Israel 224 (1996).

206 *Id.* at 280.

207 *Id.* at 259.

F. The Israeli Settlement Project

The first articulated policy concerning the settlements was in fact drawn up immediately after the 1967 Six-Day War in what came to be known as the Allon Plan, named after its principal architect, Yigal Allon, a long-time Israeli Labor Party government and cabinet member.[208] The plan (which Allon presented as a peace plan) aimed to have Israel annex "the minimal defensible borders that are indispensable without impairing, to any meaningful effect, the basic interests of the other side, including those of the Palestinian Community."[209] The Allon Plan envisioned settlements only in areas essential to Israel's strategic military interests,[210] whereby the rest of the PT was not to be held "as an end in itself."[211] The plan had substantial influence on the Labor Party's political objectives, effectively becoming the policy of the Israeli government in the first decade after the 1967 Six-Day War, during which the Labor Party led the government coalition.[212] As per this plan, Israeli settlements were built in the Jordan Valley, which was intended to become Israel's eastern border, so as to prevent forces from crossing the Jordan River and amassing in the West Bank. Settlements were also constructed in the area surrounding Jerusalem. Relatively modest settlement construction took place during this first decade in comparison to the ultimate scope of the settlement project. In 1973, there were only 17 settlements in the West Bank, with a total population of 1,514 Jewish Israeli citizens.[213] Four years later, in 1977, when the Labor Party was defeated in the general elections the PT had 36 settlements, 31 in the West Bank and 5 in the Gaza Strip, with a total population of 4,500 Jewish Israeli settlers.[214]

A dramatic shift in settlement policy came in 1977, with the rise to power of the Likud Party, led by Menachem Begin.[215] This party, and the right-wing coalition

---

208 Much of the plan became public in an article authored by Allon himself. *See* Yigal Allon, *Israel: The Case for Defensible Borders*, 55 FOREIGN AFF. 38 (1976).

209 *Id.* at 44.

210 *Id.* at 49–50.

211 *Id.* at 51.

212 Though the plan was never officially approved by the government. *See* HOFNUNG, *supra* note 205, at 217.

213 RAJA SHEHADEH, FROM OCCUPATION TO INTERIM ACCORDS: ISRAEL AND THE PALESTINIAN TERRITORIES 5 (1997) [hereinafter SHEHADEH, FROM OCCUPATION TO INTERIM ACCORDS].

214 Robert H. Mnookin & Ehud Eiran, *Discord "Behind the Table": The Internal Conflict Among Israeli Jews Concerning the Future of Settlements in the West Bank and Gaza*, 1 J. DISPUTE RESOLUTION 11, 21 (2005).

215 MERON BENVENISTI, THE WEST BANK DATA PROJECT: A SURVEY OF ISRAEL'S POLICIES 52–53, 59 (1984) [hereinafter BENVENISTI, THE WEST BANK DATA PROJECT]; Yadin Kaufmann, *Israel's Flexible Voters*, 61 FOREIGN POL'Y 109, 111–12 (1985–86); HOFNUNG, *supra* note 205, at 235–36; BISHARAT, *supra* note 193, at 63.

governments it formed over the years, was much more ambitious in terms of retaining control and eventually extending Israeli sovereignty over territories occupied in the 1967 Six-Day War.[216] Ideologically, the Likud Party considered the PT (and in effect the Golan Heights) as part of "Greater Israel" into which pre-1967 Israel could expand,[217] and it actively encouraged Israeli civilians to move to these regions by presenting settlement as a fulfillment of Zionist ideology.[218] The Allon Plan was now replaced by the Drobles Plan, officially submitted in 1978 by Matityahu Drobles, who was at the time the head of the Rural Settlement Division of the World Zionist Organization.[219] This plan called for the establishment of settlement blocs in populated areas in the West Bank, in an effort to prevent the creation of a future Arab state in the area.[220] Drobles's plan was supplemented by a number of other initiatives that shared the same ambition of establishing a massive and irreversible Israeli civilian presence in the PT.[221] The Drobles Plan was updated in 1980 and 1983,[222] and then supplemented by the One-Hundred Thousand Plan that facilitated settlement of an additional 80,000 Jews in the West Bank by the end of 1985.[223] In 1991 Ariel Sharon, who served as Minister of Housing at the time, announced the "Seven Star" Plan, which initiated seven new towns right on the Green Line, "with the declared intention of its consequent eradication."[224] The aforementioned plans provided economic incentives for settlers, including special grants, government-backed mortgages, and tax breaks.[225]

---

216 WILLIAM W. HARRIS, TAKING ROOT: ISRAELI SETTLEMENT IN THE WEST BANK, THE GOLAN AND GAZA-SINAI, 1967–1980 138 (1980); KRETZMER, *supra* note 114, at 8.

217 *See* W. THOMAS MALLISON & SALLY V. MALLISON, THE PALESTINIAN PROBLEM IN INTERNATIONAL LAW AND WORLD ORDER 244–52 (1986).

218 SHEHADEH, FROM OCCUPATION TO INTERIM ACCORDS, *supra* note 213, at 117. John Quigley, *Living in Legal Limbo: Israel's Settlers in Occupied Palestinian Territory*, 10 PACE INT'L L. REV. 1, 6 (1998). *See also* Daphne Barak-Erez, *Israel: The Security Barrier—Between International Law, Constitutional Law, and Domestic Judicial Review*, 4 INT'L J. CONST. L. 540, 548 (2006). This ideology materialized into a political program also as a consequence of the Gush Emunim (Bloc of the Faithful) movement founded in 1974, which advocated the expansion of Greater Israel into "Judea and Samaria." *See* Weiler, *Israel and the Creation of a Palestinian State, supra* note 114, at 304; Marilyn J. Berliner, *Palestinian Arab Self-Determination and Israeli Settlements on the West Bank: An Analysis of Their Legality Under International Law*, 8 LOY. L.A. INT'L & COMP. L.J. 551, 582–83 (1986).

219 KRETZMER, *supra* note 114, at 76.

220 *Id.*

221 Indeed, this is how a leading Israeli authority perceived the settlement project very early on, warranting the conclusion that the settlement project is a *de facto* annexation of the PT. *See* BENVENISTI, THE WEST BANK DATA PROJECT, *supra* note 215, at 60.

222 *Id.*

223 SHAFIR & PELED, *supra* note 31, at 172.

224 KRETZMER, *supra* note 114, at 76.

225 SHAFIR & PELED, *supra* note 31, at 173.

Indeed, the settlement population grew dramatically as a result of these initiatives. In 1980, the Jewish population in the West Bank was 12,000.[226] By 1992, it had reached 101,100; in 1996, it stood at 142,000; and in 2000, it reached a total of 195,000.[227] At the end of 2005, an estimated 250,000 Israeli settlers were living in the West Bank, even after the disengagement from the Gaza Strip and the evacuation of four settlements in the northern part of the West Bank (that in total comprised some 8,000 settlers) in August of that year.[228]

These statistics exclude East Jerusalem. As indicated earlier, Jerusalem's municipal borders were significantly expanded over the same period, taking in regions from the West Bank, which as a result of concentrated governmental efforts also became heavily populated by Israeli citizens.[229] Please refer to "Map 1: Settlements Established and Evacuated 1967–2008" that is located between pages 36 and 37.

Israel has maintained that the settlement project in the PT is legal.[230] First, it conceived of the PT as not "occupied" and therefore not subject to the international law of belligerent occupation. Second, Israel has contended that the norm contained in Article 49 of the Fourth Geneva Convention prohibiting the occupying power from transferring its own civilian population to the occupied territory applies only in cases of forced transfer but not, as is the case with Israeli settlements in the PT, of voluntary relocation of residence.[231] Third, Israel has also contended that settlements fulfill vital Israeli security needs.[232]

However, these contentions received negligible support in the international community.[233] Indeed, the more dominant view, including that held by the U.S. State Department, is that the Israeli settlements in the PT are illegal under

226 *Id.* at 171.

227 *Id.* at 180–81.

228 *See* Mnookin, Eiran & Mitter, *supra* note 32, at 310, 317. In fact, the number of Jewish settlers in the PT increased after the Israeli disengagement in August 2005. *Id.* at 317.

229 Ben-Naftali, Gross & Michaeli, *supra* note 30, at 573.

230 *See* Berliner, *supra* note 218, at 578–79.

231 *Id.*; Dinstein, *The International Law of Belligerent Occupation and Human Rights*, *supra* note 96, at 124.

232 DRORI, THE LEGISLATION IN THE AREA OF JUDEA AND SAMARIA, *supra* note 105, at 89.

233 Adam Roberts, *The Palestinians, the Uprising and International Law*, 2 J. REFUGEE STUD. 26, 34 (1989); Berliner, *supra* note 218, at 576 ("The United States, the United Nations and others have pointed out that the Israeli settlements contravene international law").

international law.[234] It was also asserted that the settlements alone have a very limited military-security function, if any at all.[235]

Interestingly, the Israeli Supreme Court, which over the years has come to provide some form of judicial review over the actions of the Israeli government and IDF authorities in the PT, has generally refrained from intervening in government decisions regarding settlements in the PT.[236] An important and exceptional decision in this respect was that of *Dweikat v. Government of Israel*,[237] or as it is more commonly known, the Elon Moreh Case.[238] Here, the Court took a more activist stance, holding that Israeli civilian settlement in the PT on private lands owned by Palestinian residents is unlawful when it is found to be unjustified in terms of security needs. Since in this case disagreement existed among various government and IDF officials as to whether the proposed settlement was indeed necessary on security grounds, the Court was willing to hold the government decision to settle the particular location under dispute as invalid.[239] In practice, however, this decision had very limited impact.[240] The settlement itself was eventually constructed on a nearby plot of land.[241] But more importantly, the Court refrained from holding the settlement project itself was illegal. To circumvent the legal issue, the Israeli government began labeling major strips of land in the PT as public rather than private land,[242] thus freeing itself to establish settlements there without legal hindrance.[243]

Intriguingly, during the period of settlement expansion, Israel was involved in two major peace processes with sovereign powers, to which the Israeli settlements in the PT were anathema: first with Egypt in the late 1970s, and second, the Oslo Peace Process with the Palestinians. From 1977 to 1981, when Egyptian-Israeli

---

234 *See* Ghada Talhami, *The Palestinian Perception of the Human Rights Issue*, 13 SYRACUSE J. INT'L L. & COM. 475, 486–87 (1987).

235 Weiler, *Israel and the Creation of a Palestinian State, supra* note 114, at 365.

236 KRETZMER, *supra* note 114, at 78.

237 HCJ 390/79, 34(1) PD 1 (1979).

238 *See* Israel: Supreme Court Judgment with respect to the Elon Moreh Settlement in the Occupied West Bank (Oct. 22, 1979), 19 ILM 148 (1980).

239 KRETZMER, *supra* note 114, at 85–89.

240 Although at least one scholar had predicted that the decision will seriously impede government support for settlements in the PT. *See* Weiler, *Israel and the Creation of a Palestinian State, supra* note 114, at 363.

241 Roberts, *Prolonged Military Occupation, supra* note 9, at 91.

242 KRETZMER, *supra* note 114, at 90–91.

243 Kaufmann, *supra* note 215, at 112.

Map 1: Settlements Established and Evacuated 1967–2008

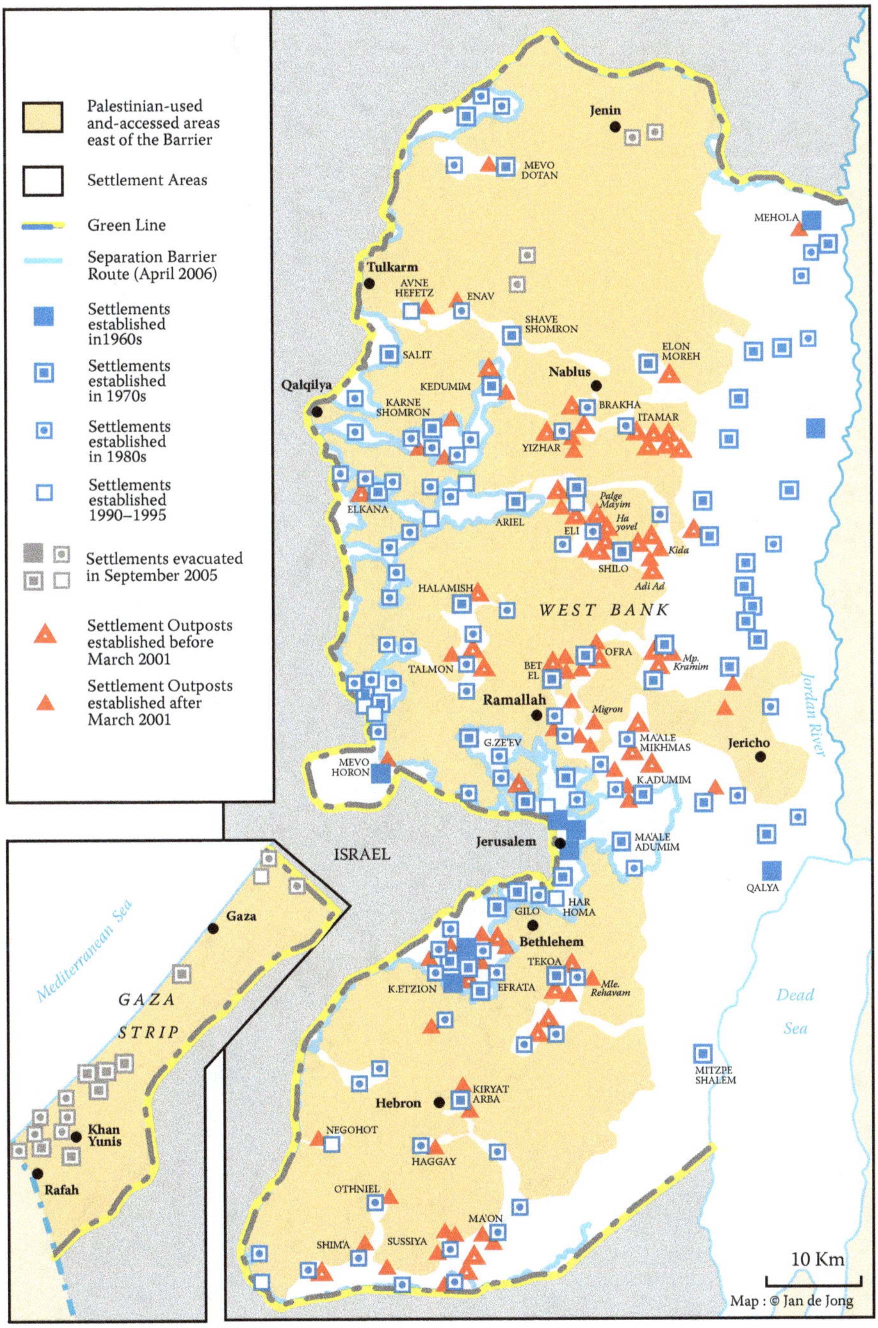

peace negotiations took place, the number of settlers in the West Bank almost quadrupled, from 4,500 to over 16,000.[244] Additionally, in this same period, the Golan Heights were annexed to Israel.[245] In the 1990s, the decade dominated by the Oslo Peace Process, the number of West Bank settlers grew from 78,000 to nearly 200,000.[246] According to Raja Shehadeh, a prominent Palestinian lawyer who has closely monitored Israeli legal measures in the West Bank, by 1993, Israeli settlers comprising a 6% minority of the West Bank population had taken over more than 60% of the land.[247]

G. Legally Accommodating the Settlements

Legally accommodating the Israeli settler population was an integral part of the whole settlement project.[248] The objective of this accommodation was to make settlers' residence beyond the sovereign borders of the State of Israel as legally insignificant as possible.[249] Israel has largely realized this objective, as both the settlers and their local government units were made subject to Israeli law and excluded from the application of local PT law.[250] In other words, the Israeli settlements in the PT and the population that lives therein were virtually annexed to Israel,[251] eventually leading the Israeli Supreme Court to depict an Israeli industrial zone in the PT as an "Israeli enclave."[252] What Eyal Benvenisti called a reality of legal dualism evolved—one system of law governed the Jewish settlers and another governed the Palestinians, all notwithstanding the fact that both happen to inhibit the same jurisdictional entity.[253] This legal dualism was also present in the civil administration system—separate offices handled the affairs of Jewish settlers and the local Palestinian population. So in effect, Israeli sovereignty followed

244 Mnookin & Eiran, *supra* note 214, at 22.

245 *See supra* Section C.

246 Mnookin & Eiran, *supra* note 214, at 23.

247 Raja Shihadeh, *Can the Declaration of Principles Bring About a "Just and Lasting Peace"?*, 4 EUR. J. INT'L L. 555, 559 (1993).

248 EYAL BENVENISTI, LEGAL DUALISM: THE ABSORPTION OF THE OCCUPIED TERRITORIES INTO ISRAEL 58 (1989) [hereinafter BENVENISTI, LEGAL DUALISM].

249 Ben-Naftali, Gross & Michaeli, *supra* note 30, at 584–85; HOFNUNG, *supra* note 205, at 229–32.

250 BENVENISTI, LEGAL DUALISM, *supra* note 248, at 3–4, 58; Shehadeh, *The Legislative Stages, supra* note 131, at 158–60.

251 SHEHADEH, OCCUPIER'S LAW, *supra* note 101, at 11, 13, 63, 212; SHAFIR & PELED, *supra* note 31, at 197.

252 CA 1432/03 Yanon Manufacturing and Marketing of Foodstuffs Ltd. v. Qara'an, 59(1) PD 345, 379 (2004) (*per* E. Rivlin, J.).

253 BENVENISTI, LEGAL DUALISM, *supra* note 248, at 3–4.

the Israeli Jewish settlers into the PT, to the exclusion of the local Palestinian population.[254]

The legal accommodation of the Israeli settler population in the PT was achieved by using one of the following two methods: (1) defining the scope of Israeli legislation in a manner that made it applicable to the Israeli settler population in the PT; and (2) issuing military orders in the PT, under which special legal arrangements are made to accommodate the Israeli settler population.[255] Through the combined effect of both these methods, Israeli enactments pertaining to income tax, social security, health care, local government and Knesset elections laws, and municipal and rabbinical courts, to name just a few, were made selectively applicable only to the Israeli settler population in the PT.[256] In addition, according to a special Knesset enactment, the Minister of Justice, with the approval of the Knesset's Constitution, Law and Justice Committee, could introduce the entire body of Israeli statutes to the PT and apply it only to the Israeli settlers that reside there.[257]

The driving force behind these legal arrangements was the Israeli government.[258] In 1979, Prime Minister Menachem Begin proclaimed that "the Jewish inhabitants of Judea and Samaria and Gaza will be subject to the laws of Israel."[259] In conjunction, legislation in the PT takes the form of military orders issued by the military commander, who under international law is presumed to be the sovereign power in an occupied territory. As Amnon Rubinstein has noted, regarding the legal accommodation of Israeli settlers, this presumed distinct sovereign authority over the PT was a mere fiction.[260]

The indigenous Palestinian population, on the other hand, was meant to remain subject to a different and distinct legal system that existed in the PT under Jordanian rule before the 1967 Six-Day War—primarily in the sphere of private

---

254 Talhami, *supra* note 234, at 486.

255 Rubinstein, *supra* note 130, at 69–73; Ben-Naftali, Gross & Michaeli, *supra* note 30, at 585.

256 *See* BENVENISTI, LEGAL DUALISM, *supra* note 248, at 15; SHEHADEH, OCCUPIER'S LAW, *supra* note 101, at 65–67.

257 HOFNUNG, *supra* note 205, at 232.

258 *Id.* at 224.

259 BENVENISTI, THE WEST BANK DATA PROJECT, *supra* note 215, at 39. For additional remarks made at the time by Prime Minister Begin, *see* W. Thomas Mallison, Jr. & Sally V. Mallison, *A Juridical Analysis of the Israeli Settlements in the Occupied Territories*, 10 PALESTINE Y.B. INT'L L. 1, 7–9 (1998/99).

260 Rubinstein, *supra* note 130, at 73.

law. In the West Bank, this system of law was for the most part the Jordanian legal system, and in the Gaza Strip it was the British Mandate system as preserved by the Egyptian military government between 1948 and 1967.[261] Over the years, some changes were introduced to this body of norms to benefit the local population.[262] For example, one military order increased employees' entitlement under Jordanian labor law to include sick leave[263] and increased the sums due for workman's compensation.[264] Broadly, however, these changes were insignificant and did not alter the general design of distinct legal systems for the settler population and the local Palestinian population.[265] In matters pertaining to security, the Palestinian population of the PT was made subject to yet another legal system, namely that of military law and military courts.[266]

This reality of a dual system of law that evolved in the PT did not develop accidentally or out of a negligently articulated policy.[267] As already noted, official Israeli government agencies "were deeply involved in planning and implementing the creation and expansion of settlements."[268] Within the confines of what was called "jurisdictional politics," repeated attempts were made to categorize Palestinian and Israeli settlers of the PT differently.[269] "Israeli citizens living and working in the West Bank were made to integrate into the protective orbit of Israeli law, while effectively treating the Palestinian residents of the West Bank as 'foreign non-residents.' "[270]

In due course, the Israeli Supreme Court held that actions taken by the IDF military commander in the PT that are designed to accommodate the Israeli settlements can be justified under international law. This approach became apparent

---

261 Civilian Judicial System in the West Bank, *supra* note 144, at 13–14.

262 Bisharat, *supra* note 193, at 137.

263 Shehadeh, Occupier's Law, *supra* note 101, at 221. *See also* Lisa Hajjar, Courting Conflict: The Israeli Military Court System in the West Bank and Gaza (2005).

264 Shafir & Peled, *supra* note 31, at 197.

265 *Id.*

266 Shehadeh, Occupier's Law, *supra* note 101, at 221–22.

267 Rubinstein, *supra* note 130, at 69, 72.

268 Mnookin & Eiran, *supra* note 214, at 22. *See also* Michael Galchinsky, *The Jewish Settlements in the West Bank: International Law and Israeli Jurisprudence*, (2004) 9 Isr. Stud. 115 116 ("Since 1967, successive Israeli governments have, directly or indirectly, participated in the transfer of some 230,000 civilians into 145 West Bank and Gaza Settlements and approximately 110 outposts").

269 Tobias Kelly, *Jurisdictional Politics in the Occupied West Bank: Territory, Community, and Economic Dependency in the Formation of Legal Subjects*, 31 Law & Social Inq. 39, 46 (2006).

270 *Id.*

in the Court's decision in *Electricity Company for Jerusalem District v. Minister of Defense.*[271]

The petitioner, a Palestinian corporation based in East Jerusalem that supplies electricity to the West Bank and East Jerusalem, sought to challenge the orders of the IDF military commander, under which the supply of electricity for the city of Hebron and the adjacent Israeli settlement of Kiryat Arba (one of the first Israeli settlements in the West Bank) would henceforth be provided by the Israel Electricity Company. The petitioner argued that it had been granted a concession for the supply of electricity in the West Bank, including in Hebron, under the existing law of the West Bank. Therefore, it argued, inter alia, the said military orders are incompatible with Article 43 of the Hague Regulations. The petition was ultimately dismissed. The Court reasoned that the military orders in this case were fully within the scope of Article 43 as articulated in the *Christian Society* case, and determined that under the article, Israeli settlers are included in the local population whose interests the military commander is to take into consideration when taking legislative measures in the PT.[272]

This broad policy of legal dualism largely corresponded with Israel's grand vision regarding the West Bank, certainly in the 1970s and 1980s. Israel's quest at the time was to fully integrate into Israel all Israeli settlements and strategic areas in the West Bank, while allowing some kind of Jordanian control or local Palestinian autonomy regarding the heavily populated Palestinian areas.[273]

H. The Oslo Peace Accords and the Establishment of the Palestinian Authority

Israeli-Palestinian relations entered a new phase with the outburst of the Palestinian uprising in December of 1987, commonly known today as the First *Intifadah*.[274] Besides raising global attention to the Palestinian cause and the Israeli occupation of the West Bank and the Gaza Strip, the First *Intifada* proved to be a major catalyst for the Israeli-Palestinian peace process. Both sides apparently became aware

---

271 HCJ 256/72, 27(1) PD 124 (1972).

272 *Id.* at 138-39.

273 *See* Noam Chomsky, *The Intifada and the Peace Process*, 14 Fletcher F. World. Aff. 345, 346 (1990).

274 *See* Eitan Y. Alimi, Israeli Politics and the First Palestinian Intifada: Political Opportunities, Framing Processes and Contentious Politics (2007).

of the fact that without a directly negotiated political resolution to the conflict, the situation would only get worse. The first major step in this direction was the Madrid Summit of 1991.[275] The public process initiated by this summit was eventually overtaken by the secret negotiations held in Oslo, Norway between Israeli and Palestinian officials—a process that led to the Oslo Peace Accords signed by Israel and the Palestine Liberation Organization (PLO).[276]

In the preamble of the first of the Oslo Peace Accords, the Declaration of Principles on Interim Self-Government Arrangements of September 13, 1993 (also referred to as Oslo I) ceremonially announced:

> It is time to put an end to decades of confrontation and conflict, recognize... mutual and political rights, and strive to live in peaceful coexistence and mutual dignity and security and achieve a just, lasting and comprehensive peace settlement and historic reconciliation through the agreed political process.[277]

In addition to the mutual recognition between Israel and the PLO,[278] the Declaration of Principles established a framework for a series of additional interim agreements,[279] and set May of 1999 as the date for reaching a permanent status agreement.[280]

---

275 *See* F. ROBERT HUNTER, THE PALESTINIAN UPRISING: A WAR BY OTHER MEANS 232–33 (1991).

276 GEOFFREY R. WATSON, THE OSLO ACCORDS: INTERNATIONAL LAW AND THE ISRAELI-PALESTINIAN PEACE AGREEMENTS (2000).

277 Declaration of Principles on Interim Self-Government Arrangments, Isr.-P.L.O., Sept. 13, 1993, 32 I.L.M. 1525 (1993) [hereinafter Declaration of Principles].

278 *See* David L. Schulman, *The Israel-PLO Accords on the Declaration of Principles on Interim Self-Government Arrangements: The First Step Toward Palestinian Self-Determination*, 7 EMORY INT'L L. REV. 793 (1993).

279 *See* Eyal Benvenisti, *The Israeli-Palestinian Declaration of Principles: A Framework for Future Settlement*, 4 EUR. J. INT'L L. 542 (1993).

280 Declaration of Principles, *supra* note 277, arts. I, IV, V. *See also* Justus R. Weiner, *Hard Facts Meet Soft Law—The Israel-PLO Declaration of Principles and the Prospects for Peace: A Response to Katherine W. Meigham*, 35 VA. J. INT'L L. 931, 948–52 (1995); Katherine Meighan, Note, *The Israel-PLO Declaration of Principles: Prelude to Peace?*, 34 VA. J. INT'L L. 435 (1994). This phased process by which interim agreements are to be concluded was first envisioned within the confines of the Egyptian-Israeli Camp David Agreements as the appropriate track to follow in order to reach peace between Israel and the Palestinians. The Oslo Peace Accords adopted this strategy. *See* SHEHADEH, FROM OCCUPATION TO INTERIM ACCORDS, *supra* note 213, at 14. *See also* Yehuda Z. Blum, *From Camp David to Oslo*, 28 ISR. L. REV. 211 (1994) (discussing the differences between the two processes in spite of the shared vision of a phased peace process). However, the initial Israeli position in the Camp David negotiations was that only autonomy over persons will be shared and that this will also be the permanent solution. Gabay, *supra* note 199, at 258.

Although the Oslo Peace Process was intended to relieve both sides of their anxieties and bring them to realize the actual meaning of peace, the end result was the contrary.[281] Since the signing of the Declaration of Principles, relations between Israel and Palestinians went from bad to worse,[282] as violence escalated and many innocent lives were lost; 1999 has long passed and a permanent status agreement is nowhere on the horizon. Nonetheless, the two sides did manage to conclude additional interim agreements that have had some impact on their future relations.[283] The second of the Oslo Accords was the Agreement on the Gaza Strip and the Jericho Area of May 4, 1994[284] (also known as the Cairo Agreement or the Gaza-Jericho Agreement). This Agreement provided for the partial redeployment of the Israeli administration and military in the Gaza Strip and in the West Bank territory in and around the ancient city of Jericho and the transfer of administrative and judicial powers to the PA.[285] Next came the Agreement on Preparatory Powers and Responsibilities of August 29, 1994 (the Erez Agreement),[286] which transferred to the PA responsibility for spheres such as health, social welfare, direct taxation, tourism, education, and culture in additional parts of the West Bank populated by Palestinians, beyond Jericho.

Yet the most important legal document of the Oslo Accords, certainly the most elaborate, is the Israeli-Palestinian Interim Agreement on the West Bank and the Gaza Strip, signed on September 28, 1995,[287] more commonly known as the "Interim Agreement." This agreement provided and designed an election process for the selection of a legislative council and an executive body in the PA (formally known as the "Palestinian Council"), scheduled a phased reduction of Israeli forces in populated Palestinian areas, and regulated judicial assistance between Israel and the PA, while also establishing the PA courts' jurisdiction in criminal and civil matters. The

281 Orde F. Kittrie, *More Process than Peace: Legitimacy, Compliance, and the Oslo Accords*, 101 Mich. L. Rev. 1661, 1668 (2003) ("The Oslo Accords were largely, if not entirely, a failure"). *See also* George Ivezaj, *Oslo Breakdown: The Failing Israeli and Palestinian Peace Process*, 7 J. Int'l L. Prac. 275 (1998).

282 Joseph W. Dellapenna, *Exploring the Oslo Accords: Recipe for Peace or Footnote to History?*, 40 Alberta L. Rev. 525, 526 (2002) (noting how the Declaration of Principles began to unravel almost immediately after it was signed).

283 *See* Justus R. Weiner, *Co-Existence without Conflict: The Implementation of Legal Structure for Israeli-Palestinian Cooperation Pursuant to the Interim Peace Agreement*, 26 Brook. J. Int'l L. 591 (2000).

284 Agreement on the Gaza Strip and the Jericho Area, May 4, 1994, 33 I.L.M. 626 (1994).

285 This body of the "Palestinian Authority" as envisioned in this agreement was to be composed of 24 members and was to assume both legislative and executive powers. *Id.* art. IV.

286 Agreement on Preparatory Powers and Responsibilities, Aug. 29, 1994, 34 I.L.M. 457.

287 Israeli-Palestinian Interim Agreement on the West Bank and the Gaza Strip, Sept. 28, 1995, 36 I.L.M. 557 (1995).

Interim Agreement also divided the West Bank into three areas: A, B, and C.[288] Area A initially comprised some 4% of the West Bank and 19% of the Palestinian population, and included the major cities of the West Bank (other than Hebron, regarding which a special arrangement was drawn).[289] In Area A, the PA was to have control over internal security and municipal matters. Area B included populated Palestinian areas outside the major cities, comprising 23% of the West Bank and 68% of the Palestinian population. In area B, the PA was to control municipal matters while the IDF remained in charge of overall security. Area C, containing Israeli settlements and military installations, remained under IDF control, thereby preserving its jurisdictional identity as formulated in the wake of the 1967 Six-Day War. Today, Areas A and B include over 90% of the Palestinian population of the West Bank but only 41% of West Bank land.[290] Area C, which covers 59% of the West Bank, includes all the Israeli settlements and a small portion of the Palestinian population.[291]

In due course, additional agreements were reached within the confine of the Oslo Peace Process, but none was as important as those indicated above. Among these additional agreements was the Wye River Memorandum that dealt with issues pertaining to security measures and economic and civil cooperation,[292] and the Sharm el-Sheikh Memorandum that tried to get the Israeli-Palestinian peace process back on track.[293]

The PA emerged from the Oslo Accords as a body with substantial governing powers in the territories under its control. It gained legislative powers in areas that came under its jurisdiction and authority over the local judiciary, including the appointment of judges.[294] The PA has also worked to establish new courts: the

---

288 *See* Omar M. Dajani, *Stalled Between Seasons: The International Legal Status of Palestine During the Interim Period*, 26 DENV. J. INT'L L. & POL'Y 27, 63 (1997) (explaining the structure of Areas A, B and C). It should be noted that the Gaza Strip was not subject to this territorial classification. In practice, from the signing of the Cairo Agreement until the unilateral disengagement of Israel from the Gaza Strip in 2005, the Gaza Strip was divided into two areas—one under PA control and the other under IDF control. *Id.*

289 Protocol Concerning the Redeployment in Hebron, Jan. 17, 1997, 36 I.L.M. 653 (1997).

290 *See* http://www.fmep.org/settlement_info/settlement-info-and-tables/stats-data/territorial-division-of-the-west-bank-according-to-the-wye-memorandum.

291 *Id.*

292 Wye River Memorandum, Oct. 23, 1998, 37 I.L.M. 1251 (1998).

293 Sharm el-Sheikh Memorandum on Implementation Timeline of Outstanding Commitments of Agreements Signed and the Resumption of Permanent Status Negotiations (Sept. 4, 1999), *reprinted in* WATSON, *supra* note 276, at 385–89.

294 *See* Hiba I. Husseini, *Challenges and Reforms in the Palestinian Authority*, 26 FORDHAM INT'L L.J. 500, 512, 539 (2003)

Map 2: Staged Israeli Transfers of West Bank Territory to Palestinian Self-Rule During the Interim Period, 1994–2000

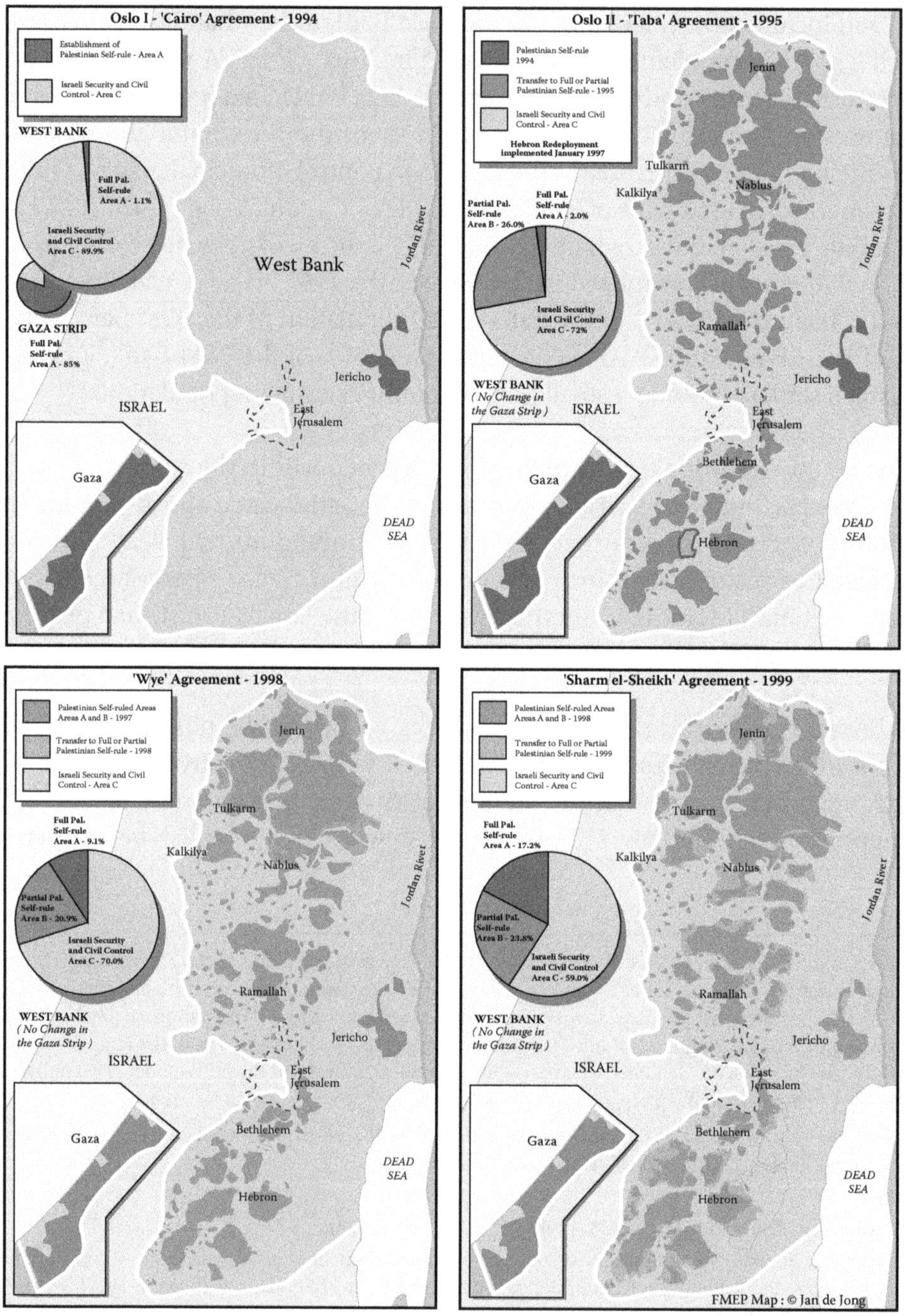

Constitutional Court, the Supreme Court, and three levels of lower courts with different subject matter jurisdiction emerged, in addition to the existing religious courts with jurisdiction over issues of family law.[295] Another important act of legal independence was the enactment of the Basic Law in May 29, 2002. This piece of legislation was in practice a constitutional document that regulated the operation of the different branches of government. It prescribed the principle of separation of powers among them, the independence of the judiciary, and the overriding effect of the rule of law, while also guaranteeing basic freedoms such as the freedom of speech, of religion, and others.[296] Much discussion has emerged regarding whether these basic constitutional principles have been realized and the reasons why the PA was not successful in living up to these basic norms.[297] Yet the failed application of one basic norm of the entire Oslo Accords needs to be highlighted: the PA is not a self-sustained government body, nor does it have the government powers that it deems appropriate. The Oslo Accords' design is premised on the notion that the PA only has the authorities and jurisdiction that are ascribed to it by the agreements. The source of authority is Israel as the occupying power, and the military government maintained the residual government powers in those spheres of government that were not transferred to the PA.[298] Therefore, in spheres such as agriculture, archeology, planning and zoning, international telecommunications and others, the authorities transferred to the PA were not complete.[299] For example, navigational waters in the Mediterranean Sea that border the Gaza Strip form the West were also divided into different territories (this time K, L, and M), with fishing restricted to one area only.[300] More important issues involved controlling the movements of people and goods from and into PA territories—a sphere that remains fully under Israeli control.[301] Similarly, Israel has maintained total control over foreign relations and matters of external security.[302] PA courts lacked jurisdictional powers over Israeli citizens in criminal proceedings and, as will be outlined in Chapter Two, received only some limited jurisdiction in civil matters.

295 *Id.* at 544.

296 *Id.* at 539–42.

297 *Id.* at 543.

298 *Id.* at 506.

299 *Id.* at 512.

300 *Id.* at 511.

301 *Id.* at 506.

302 *See* Joel Singer, *Aspects of Foreign Relations under the Israeli-Palestinian Agreements on Interim Self-Government Arrangements for the West Bank and Gaza*, 28 ISR. L. REV. 268, 277–78 (1994).

I. Post-Oslo Developments

Three important developments took place since the signing of the Oslo Peace Accords that impacted the jurisdictional identity of the PT: (1) the construction of the Israeli separation wall/fence; (2) the unilateral disengagement of Israel from the Gaza Strip; and the internal split of the PA between the West Bank and the Gaza Strip; and (3) the PA's declaration of statehood before the United Nations. As with all of the previous stages since the 1967 Six-Day War, these developments have also attracted wide attention of the international community as well as public international law and international relations scholars. In the following, I will relate to the major attributes of each of these developments, with particular emphasis on the implications each initiative yielded on the jurisdictional identity of the PT.

1. The Israeli Separation Wall/Fence

Towards the end of September 2000, the Second *Intifada* or the *Al-Aqsa Intifada* broke out.[303] What sparked this uprising was the visit of Ariel Sharon, then leader of the Likud opposition party, to the grounds of the *Al-Aqsa* Mosque. In the clashes that followed, which spread all over the West Bank and the Gaza Strip, dozens of Palestinians were killed and hundreds were injured. As the violence spread, certain Palestinian fractions—mainly from among Islamic fundamentalist movements such as Hamas and the Islamic Jihad—renewed the practice of suicide bombings. Many Israeli civilians were killed and injured.[304] Israel, with Ariel Sharon now as prime minster, reacted by initiating the construction of the separation wall/fence in 2002.

The separation wall/fence is intended to literally contain the West Bank, making it physically impossible to cross from the West Bank into Israel without passing through a controlled check-point. At some points, this physical impediment takes the form of a concrete wall that is 8 meters (26.2 feet) high and in other areas it consists of a complex structure of chain link fencing, electronic sensors, a strip of sand intended to detect footprints, and barbed wire.[305] Ultimately, this separation

---

303 Richard Falk, *International Law and the al-Aqsa Intifada*, 217 Middle East Rep. 16 (2000).

304 *See* Alberto De Puy, *Bringing Down the Barrier: A Comparative Analysis of the ICJ Advisory Opinion and the High Court of Justice of Israel's Ruling on Israel's Construction of a Barrier in the Occupied Territories*, 13 Tul. J. Int'l & Com. L. 275, 278 (2005).

305 Geoffrey R. Watson, *The "Wall" Decision in Legal and Political Context*, 99 Am. J. Int'l L. 6, 7 (2005) [hereinafter Watson, *The "Wall" Decision*].

wall/fence is intended to comprise some 700 kilometers—of which 439.7 had been constructed as of July 2012.[306]

Israel would have been within its sovereign powers were it to build this separation barrier on the Green Line. But this was not the case. Many portions of the separation wall/fence were pushed across these international borders and in some places well into the West Bank territory.[307] As observed by Geoffrey Watson: "Eventually, about 15 percent of the territory of the West Bank, home to several hundred thousand Palestinians, will lie between the wall/fence and the Green Line."[308] The end result was very harsh on many Palestinians, who because of the barrier were cut off from their farmed land[309] or had to travel around the area now engulfed by the separation wall/fence and go through additional checkpoints in order to reach close-by towns to visit relatives and friend, to obtain social services, to attend school, or to receive medical care. Israel justified the existing route on the basis of its security needs (which included securing the settlements) and argued that the separation barrier is a temporary measure—it is not intended to form a new international border but will be brought down when Israel's security interests no longer require the barrier's continued existence.

The separation wall/fence did not change the jurisdictional status of the West Bank, including its various divisions according to the Oslo Peace Accords. The wall/fence's significance lies in the legal battles it produced and in particular, the pronouncements found in the judgments regarding some of the outstanding controversies noted above. First and foremost among these judgments is the advisory opinion in *Legal Consequences of the Construction of a Wall in the Occupied Palestinian Territory*, rendered by the International Court of Justice (ICJ) on July 9, 2004.[310] After the General Assembly of the United Nations requested an opinion

306 http://www.btselem.org/separation_barrier/statistics.

307 Charles F. Martel, *Give Peace a Chance: How Considering Peace Process Obligations Would Have Improved the Rulings of the International Court of Justice and the Israeli Supreme Court on the Israeli Security Barrier*, 17 Duke J. Comp. & Int'l L. 305, 308 (2007); Aeyal M. Gross, *The* Construction of a Wall *Between The Hague and Jerusaelm: The Enforcement and Limits of Humanitarian Law and the Structure of Occupation*, 19 Leiden J. Int'l L. 393 (2006); Barak-Erez, *supra* note 218, at 540.

308 Watson, *The "Wall" Decision, supra* note 305, at 6–7.

309 *See, e.g.*, http://www.btselem.org/separation_barrier.

310 Advisory Opinion, Legal Consequences of the Construction of a Wall in the Occupied Palestinian Territory, 2004, I.C.J. 131 (July 9), 43 I.L.M. 1009 (2004). For a detailed discussion on the proceedings that lead to the ICJ advisory opinion and those that took place before it, *see* Michelle Burgis, *Discourses of Division: Law, Politics and the ICJ Advisory Opinion on the Legal Consequences of the Construction of a Wall in the Occupied Palestinian Territory*, 7 Chinese J. Int'l L. 33 (2008).

from the ICJ on the separation barrier,[311] the ICJ declared, in an overwhelming majority, that the sections of the separation barrier built in the West Bank violate international law. In the process, the ICJ determined that Israel is a belligerent occupant in the West Bank and thus governed not only by the Hague Regulations but also by the Fourth Geneva Convention. Additionally, with the apparent consent of all judges, the ICJ determined that Israeli settlements in the West Bank are an illegal act and that the Palestinians have a right to self-determination.[312] If Israel is to comply with international law, it should cease the construction of the separation barrier, dismantle the existing structure, and pay reparations for damages caused as a result of the construction of those segments built across the Green Line in West Bank territory.[313] Notably, in its opinion the ICJ assumes that the entire West Bank, even those areas that are controlled by the PA, should still be considered an occupied territory.[314]

In parallel, individual Palestinians sought to challenge the construction of the separation wall/fence before the Israeli Supreme Court in its capacity as the High Court of Justice.[315] This in turn made it possible for Israel's highest court to also

311 The wording of General Assembly resolution ES—10/14 was: "What are the legal consequences arising from the construction of the wall being built by Israel, the occupying Power, in the Occupied Palestinian Territory, including in and around East Jerusalem, as described in the report of the Secretary-General, considering the rules and principles of international law, including the Fourth Geneva Convention of 1949, and relevant Security Council and General Assembly resolutions?" Illegal Israeli Actions in Occupied East Jerusalem and the Rest of the Occupied Palestinian Territory, U.N.GAOR, 10th Sess., U.N.Doc.A/RES/ES-10/14 (2003). For a background of the UN proceedings, *see* Adam M. Smith, *Good Fences Make Good Neighbors?: The "Wall Decision" and the Troubling Rise of the ICJ as a Human Rights Court*, 18 HARV. HUM. RTS. J. 251, 252–53 (2005). On the subject matter jurisdiction of the ICJ to render advisory opinions, *see* Mark Angehr, Comment, *The International Court of Justice's Advisory Jurisdiction and the Review of Security Council and General Assembly Resolutions*, 103 NW. U. L. REV. 1007 (2009); David L. Breau, *The World Court's Advisory Function: "Not Legally Well-Founded,"* 14 U. MIAMI INT'L & COMP. L. REV. 185 (2006); Fr. Robert J. Araujo, S. J., *Implementation of the ICJ Advisory Opinion—Legal Consequences of the Construction of a Wall in the Occupied Palestinian Territory: Fences [Do Not] Make Good Neighbors?*, 22 B.U. INT'L L.J. 349 (2004).

312 The ICJ was unanimous in this holding. *See* Susan Akram & Michael Lynck, *The Wall and the Law: A Tale of Two Judgments*, 24 NETH. Q. HUM. RTS. 61, 77 (2006); Ruth Wedgwood, *The ICJ Advisory Opinion on the Israeli Security Fence and the Limits of Self-Defense*, 99 AM. J. INT'L L. 52, 60 (2005).

313 The ICJ advisory opinion attracted much scholarly attention, both regarding the ICJ's jurisdiction to take on issues referred to it by the UN General Assembly and to the opinion's actual reasoning. *See Agora: ICJ Advisory Opinion on Construction of a Wall in the Occupied Territory*, 99 AM. J. INT'L, L. 6 (2005); Arie M. Kacowicz, *The Normative Dimension of International Relations and the Advisory Opinion of the ICJ on the Separation Barrier*, 38 ISR. L. REV. 348 (2005).

314 *See* Robbie Sabel, *The International Court of Justice Decision on the Separation Barrier and the Green Line*, 38 ISR. L. REV. 316, 321 (2005).

315 *See* Ron Dudai, *The Wall, the Law and the Court: Reflections on the Beit Sourik Case in the Israeli Supreme Court*, 10 Y.B. ISLAMIC & MIDDLE E. L. 471, 472 (2003–2004).

have its say on the subject and in due course respond to the ICJ's advisory opinion. In the first major judgment *Beit Sourik Village Council v. Government of Israel*,[316] rendered on June 30, 2004—nine days before the ICJ's advisory opinion—the Israeli Supreme Court (lead by its President Aharon Barak) ordered that certain sections of the separation barrier under consideration be rerouted. However, this holding was not based on the total illegality of the separation barrier belt on West Bank land. Actually, the Court held as valid Israel's security interests demanding that the separation barrier be belt across the Green Line.[317] The holding of the Court rested on its evaluation that certain sections of the separation barrier as chosen by the IDF did not properly balance Israel's security interests with the interests of the local Palestinian population, but rather unproportionately inflicted harm on Palestinians. Interestingly, in the process of making this pronouncement, the Court held that Israel is obliged to follow the Hague Regulations because these form part of customary international law and the humanitarian provisions of the Fourth Geneva Convention, given that both parties (including the State of Israel) agree to that effect.

The second important case rendered in respect of the separation barrier was that of *Mara'abe v. Prime Minster of Israel*.[318] The Israeli Supreme Court, sitting this time in a special panel of nine Justices instead of the usual three, once again ordered the IDF to reroute the separation barrier, while affirming Israel's status in the West Bank as that of a belligerent occupant and thus governed by the international law of belligerent occupation as set forth in the Hague Regulations and the humanitarian provisions of the Fourth Geneva Convention (the latter by its admission). The decision's importance lies in its reference to the ICJ advisory opinion—which by now had already been rendered. The Israeli Supreme Court was highly critical of the advisory opinion, mainly, it said, because the opinion was rendered without properly relating to the facts and the context that lead to the construction of the separation barrier.[319] It also held that Israel acted within the confines of international law on belligerent occupation, and that the interest of protecting the settlements' population, which happens to hold Israeli citizenship, is a viable security interest, irrespective of whether the settlements are legal or illegal under international law.[320]

---

316 HCJ 2056/04, 68(5) PD 807 (2004), reprinted in 43 ILM 1099 (2004).

317 *Beit Sourik Village Council*, 68(5) PD at 830.

318 HCJ 7957/04, 60(2) PD 477 (2005); 45 ILM 202 (2006)

319 *Mara'abe*, 60(2) PD at 524–35 (*per* A. Barak, C.J.), 557–58 (*per* M. Cheshin, J.).

320 *Mara'abe*, 60(2) PD at 498–99.

As a result of the ICJ advisory opinion and the rerouting of the separation barrier as ordered by the Israeli Supreme Court, the West Bank territory trapped within the Israeli side of the barrier was reportedly narrowed to 7%.[321]

2. Israel's Unilateral Disengagement from the Gaza Strip and the Internal Palestinian Split

Another major initiative by Israel that came in the wake of the *Al-Aqsa Intifada* (though talk on the subject was present even before) was the decision to unilaterally disengage from the Gaza Strip.[322] Prime Minister Ariel Sharon announced the plan in December 2003, the Israeli government (cabinet) approved it in June 2004, and the disengagement was carried out in August 2005 and formally concluded that September. The disengagement entailed the evacuation of the IDF, the dismantling of all 21 settlements and the evacuation of some 8,500 Israeli settlers.[323] The IDF military order that established the military government in the Gaza Strip was also officially revoked.[324] As a result, all responsibilities in the Gaza Strip were transferred to the PA—at least from the Israeli point of view.[325] On September 21, 2005, Israel defined the Gaza Strip as "foreign territory."[326]

One important debate that evolved after Israel's unilateral disengagement was whether the Gaza Strip should still be considered as "occupied" under international law.[327] Those who argued in favor of Gaza's "occupied" status have stressed

---

321 Moshe Hirsch, *The Impact of the Advisory Opinion on Israel's Future Policy: International Relations Perspective*, 1 J. INT'L L. & INT'L REL. 319, 327 (2004–2005).

322 Yaacov Bar-Siman-Tov & Kobi Michael, *The Israeli Disengagement Plan as a Conflict Management Strategy*, *in* THE ISRAELI-PALESTINIAN CONFLICT: FROM CONFLICT RESOLUTION TO CONFLICT MANAGEMENT 261 (Yaacov Bar-Siman-Tov ed., 2007).

323 The Israeli cabinet decision included the dismantling of four settlements in the northern West Bank, which were also evacuated during the same period. *See* Benjamin Rubin, *Disengagement from the Gaza Strip and Post Occupation Duties*, 42 ISR. L. REV. 528, 532 (2009).

324 Solon Solomon, *Occupied or Not: The Question of Gaza's Legal Status after the Israeli Disengagement*, 19 CARDOZO J. INT'L & COMP. L. 59, 65 (2011).

325 *Id.* at 76.

326 Robert A. Caplan, *Rule of "Disengagement": Relating the Establishment of Palestinian Gaza to Israel's Right of Exercise Self-Defense as Interpreted by the International Court of Justice at the Hague*, 18 FLA. J. INT'L L. 679, 710 (2006).

327 Shane Darcy & John Reynolds, *"Otherwise Occupied": The Status of the Gaza Strip from the Perspective of International Humanitarian Law*, 15 J. CONFLICT & SECURITY L. 211 (2010); Susan Power, *War, Invasion, Occupation? A Problem of Status on the Gaza Strip*, 12 TRINITY COLLEGE L. REV. 25 (2009); Carey James, *Mere Words: The "Enemy Entity" Designation of the Gaza Strip*, 32 HASTINGS INT'L & COMP. L. REV. 643 (2009); Marc S. Kaliser, *A Modern Day Exodus: International Human Rights Law and International Humanitarian Law Implications of Israel's withdrawal from the Gaza Strip*, 17 IND. INT'L & COMP. L. REV. 187, 219–27 (2007).

Israel's broad control of many facets of life in Gaza, despite the IDF's evacuation and the dismantling of settlements.[328] For example, Israel still maintains control over Gaza's air space, coast, electricity (60%), telecommunications network, and sewage system. Israel supplies Gaza with fuel and gas, conducts military operations there whenever it deems them necessary, and controls most of its borders with considerable power over the movement of goods and people into and from the Strip. Indeed, leading international human rights organizations as well as some important foreign institutions still maintain that the Gaza Strip is still an "occupied territory".[329]

On the other hand, some have argued that in order to establish the necessary "effective control," for a territory to be "occupied" a hostile military force must be present in the territory that replaces any existing local government—a state of being that no longer exists in the Gaza Strip.[330] However, after the Israeli disengagement, the Gaza Strip is controlled by an organized government and has a locally organized military force.[331]

The Israeli Supreme Court took a stand on the matter in *Al-Bassiouni v. Prime Minister*.[332] The case challenged Israel's reaction to the firing of rockets from Gaza on an Israeli civilian population, whereby the Israeli government decided to reduce the supply of electricity by 5% (of the 60% Israel provides—the rest being provided by Egypt and a local plant), as well the supply of fuel. In its judgment, the Court accepted the government's basic argument that the Gaza Strip is no longer governed by the international law of belligerent occupation and thus Israel is relieved from attending to the welfare of the local residents or from maintaining public order there. Israel is not to be held accountable due to its lack of

328 *See* Raja Shehadeh, *The Gaza Occupation: Beginnings and Endings*, 14 PAL. Y.B. INT'L L. 13, 25 (2006–2007); Mustafa Mari, *The Israeli Disengagement from the Gaza Strip: An End of Occupation?*, 8 Y.B. INT'L HUM. L. 356 (2005); Iain Scobbie, *An Intimate Disengagement: Israel's Withdrawal from Gaza, the Law of Occupation and of Self-Determination*, 11 Y.B. ISLAMIC & MIDDLE E.L. 3 (2003–2005) (also stressing the invalidity of Israel's unilateral action, arguing that it encroaches on the Palestinian right of self-determination).

329 *See* Solomon, *supra* note 324, at 69.

330 *See* Elizabeth Samson, *Is Gaza Occupied?: Redefining the Status of Gaza under International Law*, 25 AM. U. INT'L L. REV. 915, 934–36 (2010); Rubin, *supra* note 323, at 537; Yuval Shany, *Faraway So Close: The Legal Status of Gaza after Israel's Disengagement*, 8 Y.B. HUMANITARIAN L. 369, 380 (2005).

331 *See* Yuval Shany, *The Law Applicable to the Non-Occupied Gaza: A Comment on* Bassiouni v. The Prime Minister of Israel, 42 ISR. L. REV. 101, 105 (2009).

332 HCJ 9132/07 (Jan. 30, 2008), Nevo Legal Database (by subscription), available in English at http://elyon1.court.gov.il/Files_ENG/07/320/091/n25/07091320.n25.pdf.

"effective control" over the Gaza Strip that resulted from the disengagement and the termination of IDF presence and administration there. This does not mean, however, that Israel is absolved from any duty towards the Gaza Strip. Based on the international law of armed conflict, the Court accepted once again the government's position that it needs to attend to the local population's "basic humanitarian needs." Through this standard, the Court found no need to intervene and invalidate the actions taken by the government.

Clearly, the discussion regarding the status of the Gaza Strip does not merely relate to its formal status under international law, but mostly focuses on what its status entails in terms of Israel's obligations towards the local Palestinian population. The Court's reasoning in *Al-Bassouni,* as well as the Israeli government's position as depicted by the Court, clearly indicates that the level of duty Israel owes the local Palestinian population is derived from whether the Gaza Strip continues to be governed by the international law of belligerent occupation—if considered to be under Israel's effective control—or by another lenient set of standards if not considered to be an occupied territory. Apparently, moreover, the discussion over the status of the Gaza Strip relates not only to this area but also to the West Bank—or, more specifically, to those areas that are presently controlled by the PA, principally Area A. Were the Gaza Strip, with its border with Egypt, to be considered as occupied, then certainly Areas A and B that are absolutely contained within IDF checkpoints are to also be considered as occupied.[333] If so, this would also entail a higher level of duties by Israeli towards the West Bank Palestinian population, which Israel is not that ready to recognize.

Another important development that took place in the Gaza Strip was the internal Palestinian divide between Fatah and Hamas that ultimately lead to the administrative and political separation of the Gaza Strip from the West Bank. This split originated with the Palestinian national elections of January 2006. Amidst accusations of corruption and improper handlings made by Hamas—an Islamist movement with a political division—Fatah lost its parliamentary majority. Hamas won 74 seats in the 132-member parliament.[334] When Hamas was assigned to form the new government, its tension grew with the Fatah movement—the long-dominating fraction of the PLO. Pressure exerted by the United States and

333 For an initial examination as to whether the West Bank is to be considered as occupied, *see* Sabel, *supra* note 314, at 321.

334 *See* Carey James, *Mere Words: The "Enemy Entity" Designation of the Gaza Strip*, 32 HASTINGS INT'L & COMP. L. REV. 643, 647 (2009).

Israel, which were disappointed with Hamas's success, no doubt intensified these tensions. Ultimately, these tensions led to a bloody week of fighting between the two factions in June of 2007, with Hamas emerging victorious in the Gaza Strip.[335] In reaction, the Palestinian president, Mahmoud Abbas, dismissed the Hamas-run government and appointed a caretaker government in its place. But Hamas continued to run the Gaza Strip, and thus two different Palestinian governments have now come to run the PA.[336]

As violence between Israel and the Gaza Strip escalated, the Israeli cabinet declared in September of 2007 that the Gaza Strip is to be designated as a hostile territory.[337] Since then, thousands of rockets were sent into Israeli towns, and numerous Israeli military operations were conducted in the Gaza Strip, including major ones such as Operation Cast Lead at the end of 2008.[338] The human suffering dimension of this violence is the subject of much attention and debate and even international investigations.[339]

Of special interest in the legal context, though, is the jurisdictional identity of the Gaza Strip in the wake of these developments. As far as Israeli law is concerned, two major implications are worth highlighting. First, the designation of the Gaza Strip as a "hostile territory" made it extremely difficult for Palestinian plaintiffs who are residents of Gaza to file civil suits before Israeli courts. In some instances they have been prevented from filing such actions based on the enemy alien exception, and in other instances they were simply not granted a permit to enter Israel in order to conduct the actual litigation. Second, given the "hostile territory" definition, there was no hope for the execution of any civil order or judgment granted by an Israeli court in the Gaza Strip.

3. Palestinian Statehood

Palestinian institutions have constantly sought international recognition. In the post-1967 Six-Day War era, towards the mid-1970s, the PLO was the first to seek

---

335 *Id.* at 647–48.

336 *Id.* at 648–49.

337 *See* HCJ 9132/07 *Al Bassiouni*, Nevo Legal Database (by subscription).

338 Milena Sterio, *The Gaza Strip: Israel, Its Foreign Policy, and the Goldstone Report*, 43 CASE W. RES. J. INT'L L. 229, 231 (2010–2011).

339 *See, e.g.*, Yaël Ronen, *ICC Jurisdiction over Acts Committed in the Gaza Strip*, 8 J. INT'L CRIM. JUST. 3 (2010).

an international law status as a form of government in exile.[340] Later on, the claim was made for Palestinian statehood. This claim was initiated with the Palestinian Declaration of Statehood in November 1988[341] and became more persistent as a result of the Oslo Peace Accords,[342] with the PA's call on the International Criminal Court (ICC) to apply its jurisdiction to war crimes committed during Israel's Cast Lead Operation (in late 2008 and early 2009).[343] The statehood claim was raised again in the context of qualifying for financial assistance from the World Bank,[344] and more recently in the wake of the PA's bid for statehood before the United Nations General Assembly.[345]

No general agreement has been reached yet as to whether the PA has attained statehood—mainly because of the lucid and vague nature of the conditions set by international law for statehood. There are four such conditions: (1) a permanent population; (2) a defined territory; (3) a government in control; and (4) capacity to enter into relations with other states. So, given the fact that a large Palestinian diaspora still lives outside the West Bank and the Gaza Strip, including many refugees, some question whether there is a permanent Palestinian population now living in the area claimed by the PA; in light of the fact that the final status agreement as to the territories that will come under Palestinian control is yet to take place, doubts are sounded as to whether Palestine has a defined territory; and as a result of the intra-Palestinian split, uncertainty exists as to whether there is a government in control.

---

340 *See* discussion in William V. O'Brien, *The PLO in International Law*, 2 B.U. INT'L L.J. 349 (1984); Evyatar Levine, *A Landmark on the Road to Legal Chaos: Recognition of the PLO as a Menace to World Public Order*, 10 DENV. J. INT'L L. & POL'Y 243 (1981); Anis F. Kassim, *The Palestine Liberation Organization's Claim to Status: A Juridical Analysis under International Law*, 9 DENV. J. INT'L L. & POL'Y 1 (1980); Leo Gross, *Voting in the Security Council and the PLO*, 70 AM. J. INT'L L. 470 (1976).

341 *See* James L. Prince, *The International Legal Implication of the November 1988 Palestinian Declaration of Statehood*, 25 STAN. J. INT'L L. 681 (1988–1989).

342 *See* Kathryn M. McKinney, *The Legal Effects of the Israeli-PLO Declaration of Principles: Steps Toward Statehood for Palestine*, 18 SEATTLE U. L. REV. 93 (1994).

343 Daniel Benoliel & Ronen Perry, *Israel, Palestine, and the ICC*, 32 MICH. J. INT'L L. 73 (2010); John Quigley, *Palestine Is a State: A Horse with Black and White Stripes Is a Zebra*, 32 MICH. J. INT'L L. 749 (2011).

344 *See* Ibrahim F.I. Shihata, I. Hadi Abushakra & Hans-Jürgen Gruss, *Legal Aspects of the World Bank's Assistance to the West Bank and the Gaza Strip*, 7 PAL. Y.B. INT'L L. 19 (1992–1994).

345 Martin Wählisch, *Beyond a Seat in the United Nations: Palestine's U.N. Membership and International Law*, 53 HARV. INT'L L.J. ONLINE 226 (2012); Khaled Elgindy, *Palestine Goes to the UN: Understanding the New Statehood Strategy*, 90 FOREIGN AFF. 102 (2011); William R. Slomanson, *Palestinian Statehood: A Successionist Dialogue*, 8 MISKOLC J. INT'L L. 1 (2011).

At times, the indecisiveness of these qualifications is aggrieved yet further by the actions taken by the direct parties to the conflict. For example, though the Palestinian side has been pressing for more recognition for statehood and in the process establishing embassies not different in status from those of independent states, this move has nonetheless undermined the independence of the local Palestinian government by pressing the point that the Palestinian territories of the West Bank and the Gaza Strip are still "occupied territories." This argument involves a number of facts (noted above) stressing how Israel, rather than the PA, is still controlling various aspect of Palestinian life. In turn, it undermines the third condition pertaining to the existence of a government in control in the PA. Yet Israel is no more consistent in its messages on this matter. While Israel has been undermining Palestinian statehood, it has entered into bilateral agreements with the PLO and has been holding the PA accountable for violence exerted from its territory, as if it was a fully independent state.

I suspect that the debate regarding whether the exiting Palestinian entity can be considered a state will attract further attention and political battles. At times, John Quigley's most expressive title, *Palestine is a State: A Horse with Black and White Stripes is a Zebra*, seems to adequately describe the situation.[346] Yet upon closer inspection of the "horse," the stripes are not perfectly aligned, nor are they in black and white; and from afar or from very close, depending on the circumstances, the horse does not seem to be a horse at all.

The question of the PA's statehood has major implications on a number of conflict of laws matters. First and foremost is the question of whether the PA is entitled to sovereign immunity when named as a defendant in a civil action filed before an Israeli court—or any other court for that matter. Another important issue is the extent to which Israeli courts should defer to the PA's national sovereign interests when assessing their adjudicative jurisdiction capacity regarding claims related to the PA. The same assessment must be made in the sphere of choice of law—in ascertaining whether the PA should be accorded a particular interest in applying its laws to the pending controversy—and in the sphere of judgments—when determining whether a Palestinian court judgment should be enforced or recognized by an Israeli court. The international standing of the PA is no doubt an important factor when approaching these questions. Given the indefinite nature

346 *Supra* note 343.

of Palestinian statehood, certainly from Israel's perspective, a trend of imprecision has emerged regarding issues relating to sovereign immunity, choice of law, and judgment that are intimately attached to the statehood question. This situation has led to indefinite legal structures that apply to neither private entities nor independent states.

CHAPTER 2

Personal Jurisdiction

Contents

A. On the Jurisdiction of Courts to Adjudicate Civil Disputes—General Remarks

Each country has a separate body of rules that help judges to determine whether the national courts possess adequate power to adjudicate a civil dispute. This power is usually examined when the pending dispute is tied to another country or countries and hence the propriety of having it adjudicated by local courts is questioned. The rules that are meant to guide courts in this respect are referred to by a score of terms, such as those of "international jurisdiction,"[1] "territorial jurisdiction or competence,"[2] and "municipal jurisdiction."[3] At times, this same jurisdictional power is referred to by reference to the type of proceedings involved. If these proceedings happen to be of a personal nature and their object is to bestow a personal obligation on the defendant, then judicial capacity is identified as pertaining to the court's *in personam* or personal jurisdiction.[4] If, on the other hand, the object of the proceeding is a *res*, like a ship,[5] a certain property,[6] or the status of a person (traditionally considered a *res*),[7] then *in rem* jurisdiction is implicated.[8]

In Israel, it is common to refer to all rules pertaining to the judicial power of courts to deal with disputes that have a foreign element as rules of "international

---

1 Arthur Nussbaum, *Jurisdiction and Foreign Judgments*, 41 COLUM. L. REV. 221, 221–22, 225–26 (1941).

2 Christof von Dryander, *Jurisdiction in Civil and Commercial Matters under the German Code of Civil Procedure*, 16 INT'L LAW. 671, 674 (1982).

3 Nussbaum, *supra* note 1, at 225–26.

4 *See* CHESHIRE, NORTH & FAWCETT, PRIVATE INTERNATIONAL LAW 353 (James Fawcett & Janeen M. Carruthers eds, 14th ed. 2008).

5 In fact, in English common law only actions in admiralty against a ship and its cargo are considered to be actions *in rem*. *See id.* at 414–15.

6 This is more in accordance with American common law; *see* EUGENE F. SCOLES ET AL., CONFLICT OF LAWS 295–96 (4th ed. 2004).

7 Restatement (Second) of Conflict of Laws §21, Comment d (1971); JEFFREY A. SCHOENBLUM, MULTISTATE AND MULTINATIONAL ESTATE PLANNING § 7-29 (2009).

8 CHESHIRE, NORTH & FAWCETT, *supra* note 4, at 532.

jurisdiction."[9] However, this terminology is too crude, even if it adequately depicts the context in which a court's judicial capacity is called into question, because these rules of international jurisdiction can substantially differ depending on the type of action involved. Generally, one set of rules applies to personal actions,[10] and another set—or even sets—of rules apply to *in rem* actions. This chapter will relate only to personal jurisdiction of Israeli courts towards the Palestinian Territories (PT). The next chapter, Chapter Three, will deal with *in rem* jurisdiction, as well as additional rules of jurisdiction that operate in a similar way.

But before proceeding further and describing personal jurisdiction principles of Israeli courts, one caveat is in order. It is important to dispel the impression that rules of international jurisdiction of Israeli courts (or any other country for that matter) are derived or mandated from a body of international law. It is generally accepted that no international norms exist regulating the municipal power of national courts to adjudicate international civil disputes,[11] leaving each and every country free to devise its own rules.[12] This situation in turn enables states to devise their rules on international jurisdiction (both *in personam* and *in rem*) in accordance with their own national interests. Hence, the discussion of Israeli rules of personal jurisdiction regarding the PT is particularly interesting, since these rules have developed within the context of a peculiar international relationship—that of occupation. To what extent do Israeli personal jurisdiction rules that are primarily concerned with private disputes accommodate Israel's institutional interests regarding the PT? The answer is, to a great extent—as will be revealed in this chapter.

---

9 *See* TALIA EINHORN, PRIVATE INTERNATIONAL LAW IN ISRAEL 339 (2d ed. 2012); Stephen Goldstein & Elisheva HaCohen, *Israel*, *in* 3 INTERNATIONAL ENCYCLOPEDIA OF LAWS: CIVIL PROCEDURE 67 (Piet Taelman ed., 1994).

10 *See* William W. Blume, *Place of Trial of Civil Cases*, 48 MICH. L. REV. 1 (1949); William H. Wicker, *The Development of the Distinction Between Local and Transitory Action*, 4 TENN. L. REV. 55 (1925).

11 *See* O. KAHN-FREUND, GENERAL PROBLEMS OF PRIVATE INTERNATIONAL LAW 24 (1976); Michael Akehurst, *Jurisdiction in International Law*, 46 BRIT. Y.B. INT'L L. 145, 170 (1972–73); Kurt Lipstein, *The General Principles of Private International Law* 135 RECUEIL DES COURS 97, 167 (1972-I). *See also* Andrew L. Strauss, *Beyond National Law: International Law of Personal Jurisdiction in Domestic Courts*, 36 HARV. INT'L L.J. 373 (1995). However, some have maintained that international law can and in fact does limit national courts' exercise of international jurisdiction in civil disputes. *See* F. A. Mann, *The Doctrine of Jurisdiction in International Law*, 111 RECUEIL DES COURS 1, 10–11 (1964-I).

12 This is not the case regarding the international jurisdiction of national courts to deal with criminal proceedings. Over the years, a body of binding international law norms was formed in this respect. *See* MALCOLM N. SHAW, INTERNATIONAL LAW 652–87 (6th ed. 2008).

B. The International Jurisdiction of Israeli Courts in Actions in Personam

1. The English Common Law Heritage

The basic rules and principles that guide Israeli courts when determining their personal jurisdiction are firmly embedded in English common law.[13] Therefore, it is essential to outline the British rules and principles before analyzing the Israeli rules and their application regarding the PT.

The traditional English common law rules on personal jurisdiction are highly procedural. A court's power depended on whether the defendant was properly served with the claim form.[14] This practice made the defendant the focus of the jurisdictional inquiry. The identity of the plaintiff was irrelevant to the assessment of whether a court had personal jurisdiction,[15] and to a great extent this is still the case today.[16]

Notwithstanding their procedural character, the rules on personal jurisdiction were highly influenced by substantive concerns related to the sovereignty and comity of nations.[17] The power to serve the claim on the defendant depended on whether the defendant was physically present within the sovereign territorial borders of the forum state.[18] This notion of territorial sovereignty[19] was

13 Amos Shapira, *Private International Law*, in INTRODUCTION TO THE LAW OF ISRAEL 361, 366 (Amos Shapira & Karen C. DeWitt-Arar eds., 1995).

14 CHESHIRE, NORTH & FAWCETT, *supra* note 4, at 353.

15 As we shall see later on, the plaintiff's identity and interests can be of relevance to a court's discretion to stay the pending proceedings on grounds of forum non conveniens or when considering whether it is proper to grant leave for service outside the jurisdiction. However, in both cases, the orientation that defines the overall course of the jurisdictional inquiry is that of the defendant, rather than the plaintiff.

16 The principal exception in this respect is when the plaintiff is considered to be an alien enemy. CHESHIRE, NORTH & FAWCETT, *supra* note 4, at 490–91.

17 *Cookney v. Anderson*, 46 Eng. Rep. 146, 151 (1863) ("If... one sovereign causes process to be served in the country of another, and summons a foreign subject to this Court of Justice, it is in fact an invasion of sovereignty, and would be unjustifiable, unless done with consent"). *See also* Grant v. Anderson & Co., [1892] 1 Q.B. 108 (C.A.).

18 CHESHIRE, NORTH & FAWCETT, *supra* note 4, at 354.

19 One notable figure that had substantial influence on disseminating the notion of territorial sovereignty in common law jurisdictions was the American scholar and United States Supreme Court Justice Joseph Story. Among Story's most notable observations in this respect was that:

> ... jurisdiction, to be rightfully exercised, must be founded either upon the person being within the territory, or the thing being within the territory; for, otherwise, there can be no sovereignty exerted, upon the known maxim, *Extra territorial jus decent impune non paretur*... on the other

the governing theory of jurisdiction in both English law[20] and American law.[21] United States Supreme Court Justice Oliver Wendell Holmes, Jr. succinctly echoed this notion when he observed that "[t]he foundation of jurisdiction is physical power...."[22] This rule was derived from the long-abandoned practice of physically arresting the defendant being sued in a civil action. Indeed, in order for a court to be able to adjudicate a personal action against the defendant, the defendant had to be present before the court.[23] This arrest was conducted by a special writ called *capias ad respondendum*.[24] If the defendant proved to be evasive, a whole set of additional measures were made available in order to secure his or her appearance before the court. These measures came to be known as *mesne* processes, and they included attachment, distringas, and even outlawry.[25] These old practices established a Gordian knot between personal jurisdiction and service of process on the defendant's person while present in the sovereign's territory. Since personal jurisdiction was contingent on the defendant's presence before the court and such presence was only possible if the defendant was subject to the court's execution powers of service of the different writs—powers limited to the sovereign's realm—personal jurisdiction was thus conditioned on the defendant's presence within the forum's sovereign territory at the time service of process was sought.

In due course, the defendant's arrest was abolished and so was the procedural rule that mandated the defendant's actual appearance before the court. However, the basic contingency between personal jurisdiction and service of process within

---

> hand no sovereignty can extend its process beyond its own territorial limits, to subject either persons or property to its judicial decisions. Every exertion of authority of this sort, beyond this limit, is a mere nullity, and incapable of binding such persons or property in any other tribunals.

See JOSEPH STORY, COMMENTARIES ON THE CONFLICT OF LAWS, FOREIGN AND DOMESTIC 450–51 (Boston, Hilliard, Gray, and Co., 1834).

It should be noted, however, that the notion of territorial sovereignty as a guiding theory in the conflict of laws was present in English and American common law long before the writings of Joseph Story. *See* KURT H. NADELMANN, CONFLICT OF LAWS: INTERNATIONAL AND INTERSTATE, SELECTED ESSAYS 1–48 (1972).

20 *See, e.g.*, Sirdar Gurddyal Singh v. Rajah of Faridkote, [1894] A.C. 670, 683 (P.C.) ("All jurisdiction is necessarily territorial...").

21 *See* Pennoyer v. Neff, 95 U.S. 714, 722–23 (1877).

22 McDonald v. Mabee, 243 U.S. 90, 91 (1917).

23 *See* Robert W. Miller, *The Formative Principles of Civil Procedure—I*, 18 ILL. L. REV. 1, 4 (1923).

24 *See* International Shoe Co. v. Washington, 326 U.S. 310, 316 (1945).

25 Nathan Levy, Jr., *Mesne Process in Personal Action at Common Law and the Power Doctrine*, 78 YALE L.J. 52 (1968).

the sovereign territory of the forum state prevailed.[26] Under the current English practice of personal jurisdiction, if a defendant who is not domiciled in any of the European Union states is served with process while present in England, even if temporarily, an English court is considered to have sufficient personal jurisdiction to adjudicate the personal action filed against the defendant.[27] Additionally, since this form of establishing personal jurisdiction aligns with notions of territorial sovereignty, the jurisdictional capacity that resulted was considered to be bestowed on local courts as a matter of "right."[28]

Another important development in the English doctrine of personal jurisdiction was the realization that English courts must also at times acquire judicial power over defendants who were physically absent from England.[29] This situation was particularly poignant when the defendant committed a tort in England or accrued debts while domiciled there but succeeded in leaving the country before the plaintiff managed to serve process. Under the guiding notions of territorial sovereignty, an absent defendant was assumed to be beyond the jurisdiction of English courts.[30] However, during the nineteenth century, a number of statutory enactments were introduced, enabling English courts to attain sufficient jurisdiction over absent defendants. These enactments initially related to courts of equity[31] and later applied to the courts of common law.[32] When these two court systems were united following reforms in the English judiciary in the second half of the nineteenth century,[33] one united mechanism was also introduced for

---

26 *See* Robert C. Cassad, *Jurisdiction in Civil Actions at the End of the Twentieth Century:* Forum Conveniens *and* Forum Non Conveniens, 7 Tul. J. Int'l & Comp. L. 91, 93 (1999) ("Historically, Anglo-American common law has considered jurisdiction over the person of a defendant to be primarily a function of the court's coercive power. If a court can physically arrest a person, that person is subject to the court's jurisdiction.").

27 *See* David McClean & Kisch Beevers, Morris on the Conflict of Laws 114 (7th ed. 2009).

28 *See* C. G. J. Morse, *Not in the Public Interest?* Lubbe v. Cape Plc, 37 Tex. Int'l L.J. 541, 544 (2002).

29 Cheshire, North & Fawcett, *supra* note 4, at 490–91.

30 *See, e.g.*, Berkley v. Thompson, 10 A.C. 45, 49 (1885) (H.L.) (*per* Earl of Selborne) ("[A] person resident abroad, still more, ordinarily resident and domiciled abroad and not brought by any special statute or legislation within the jurisdiction, is prima facie not subject to the process of a foreign court, he must be found within the jurisdiction to be bound by it"); Drummond v. Drummond, (1866) L.R. 2 Ch. App. 32, 37 ("It may justly be considered to be an invasion of the jurisdiction of a country whenever an attempt is made to force one of its subjects, or any one under its protection and temporary allegiance, before a foreign tribunal. But the Legislature of every country has power to regulate the course of proceeding in its own Courts.")

31 *See* 2 Will. 4, c. 33 (1832); 4 & 5 Will. 4 c. 82 (1834).

32 Common Law Procedure Act, 1852, 15 & 16 Vict. Ch. 76 (1852).

33 *See* Supreme Court of Judicature Act, 1873, 36 & 37 Vict. Ch.66 (1873) (hereinafter SCJ, 1873); Supreme Court of Judicature Act, 1875, 38 & 39 Vict. Ch. 77 (1875) (hereinafter SCJ, 1875).

bringing an absent defendant into the jurisdiction of English courts. Through this mechanism, upon the plaintiff's request, a leave of the court can be granted to serve the claim to the absent defendant. This leave is to be granted if, among other factors, the court is reasonably satisfied that the defendant or the underlying cause of action are sufficiently connected to England by one of the contacts specified in the English rules. For example, the Supreme Court of Judicature Act, 1873, provided:

> Whenever it appears fit to the court or to a judge in a case in which the cause of action has arisen within the jurisdiction, or is properly cognizable against a defendant within the jurisdiction, that any person out of the jurisdiction of the court should be served with the writ or other process of the court, the court of judge may order such service, or such notice in lieu of service, to be made or given in such manner and on such terms as may seem just.[34]

Two years afterwards, the Supreme Court of Judicature Act, 1875 afforded power to the courts to grant leave out of the jurisdiction:

> [1] Whenever the whole or any part of the subject-matter of the action is land or stock, or other property situated within the jurisdiction... [2] any act, deed, will or thing affecting such land, stock, or property... [3] whenever the contract which is sought to be enforced or rescinded, dissolved, annulled, or otherwise affected in any such action, or for the breach whereof damages or other relief are or is demanded in such actions, was made or entered into within the jurisdiction... [4] whenever there has been a breach within the jurisdiction of any contract wherever made... [5] whenever any act or thing sought to be restrained or removed, or for which damages are sought to be recovered, was or is to be done or is situate within the jurisdiction.[35]

As cross-border interactions became more common and sophisticated, the list of causes permitting leave for service outside the jurisdiction was also expanded. In each round of expansion, the English rules tried to identify cases in which England is regarded as having a substantial connection with the underlying legal relationship and to permit service outside of the jurisdiction accordingly.[36] This

---

34 SCJ, 1873, Schedule, Rules of Procedure, Rule 6.

35 SCJ, 1875, Rules of Court, Order 11.

36 *See* Michael Pryles, *The Basis of Adjudicatory Competence in Private International Law*, 21 INT'L & COMP. L.Q. 61 (1972).

list exists today in Civil Procedure Rules, 1998, Rule 6.20, which includes some 19 different causes for service outside of the English jurisdiction.[37]

Personal jurisdiction created by virtue of service outside of jurisdiction is a genuine divergence from the dictates of the original notion of territorial sovereignty.[38] Jurisdiction is no longer restricted to defendants that are present on English soil. However, the English rules could not completely escape the grip of territorial sovereignty. Moreover, conscious of the fact that service outside of England stands against notions of territorial sovereignty and undermines the comity towards the state in which the defendant is present at time of service, English law perceived such jurisdictional authority as one of an "assumed" nature and thus handled its operation with care.[39] A number of procedural implications followed. As already mentioned, service on an absent defendant is contingent on the plaintiff first acquiring the leave of the court seized with the claim[40]—a leave that is contingent on the existence of a recognized contact between the forum and the underlying dispute or defendant.[41] Additionally, it has been determined that the list of causes permitting service outside the jurisdiction is a *numerus clausus* list that courts cannot expand on,[42] that there must be a serious issue implicated to be tried on the merits,[43] and that the English forum is a forum conveniens.[44]

The English common law jurisprudence on personal jurisdiction had far-reaching influence on other common law jurisdictions, such as those of Australia, Canada, the United States, and New Zealand. These countries also make a basic distinction between present and absent defendants. Although rules for acquiring personal jurisdiction tend to vary between these countries, in the case of an absent defendant, all require that a contact be established between the defendant or the underlying cause of action and the forum state in order make jurisdiction possible.

---

37 *See* ADRIAN ZUCKERMAN, ZUCKERMAN ON CIVIL PROCEDURE 217–18 (2d ed. 2006).

38 LAWRENCE COLLINS, ESSAYS IN INTERNATIONAL LITIGATION AND THE CONFLICT OF LAWS 226 (1994).

39 CHESHIRE, NORTH & FAWCETT, *supra* note 4, at 372; Ellen L. Hayes, Forum Non Conveniens in *England, Australia and Japan: The Allocation of Jurisdiction in Transnational Litigation*, 1992 U. BRIT. COLUM. L. REV. 41, 44.

40 CHESHIRE, NORTH & FAWCETT, *supra* note 4, at 372.

41 Seaconsar Far East Ltd. v. Bank Markazi Jomhouri Islami Iran, [1994] 1 A.C. 438, 453–54, 456–57 (H.L.).

42 *See* Siskina v. Distos Compania Naviera S.A., [1979] A.C. 210 (C.A.).

43 *See* Seaconsar Far East Ltd. v. Bank Markazi Jomhouri Islami Iran, [1994] 1 A.C. 438, 452.

44 *See* Berezovsky v. Michaels, [2000] 1 W.L.R. 1004 (H.L.); Spiliada Maritime Corp. v. Cansulex Ltd., [1987] A.C. 460, 481; Amin Rasheed Corp. v. Kuwait Insurance Co., [1984] A.C. 50, 72.

2. The Israeli Personal Jurisdiction Doctrine—A Faithful Disciple

The Israeli personal jurisdiction doctrine was highly influenced by the English common law doctrine as just described.[45] Therefore, the first question an Israeli court inquiring into its personal jurisdiction capacity will resort to is whether the defendant is present on Israeli soil or absent therefrom. If the defendant is present in Israel, even temporarily, and is served with the claim while present, then Israeli courts are considered to have sufficient general personal jurisdiction.[46]

Personal jurisdiction against an absent defendant was also recognized in cases where the defendant had a representative who is present in the country and the Rules of Civil Procedure, 1984, deem that representative qualified to receive service on the defendant's behalf, as would be an attorney[47] or a business agent.[48] However, in such cases, the jurisdiction acquired by the Israeli court is specific rather than general in nature—the action filed needs to be related to the subject matter of the representation in Israel.[49]

Submission to Israeli jurisdiction by the defendant, even if implicit, is also recognized as sufficient for the establishment of *in personam* jurisdiction.[50] The scope of this jurisdictional authority as general or specific depends on the interpretation of the act of submission.

In the case of a defendant who is absent from Israel at the time service is sought, the plaintiff must petition the court seized with the action to grant a special leave for service outside of the jurisdiction. This procedure exists today in RCP, 1984, Rule 500 (hereinafter Rule 500) and includes a list of some eleven contacts with Israel that may allow such a leave being granted. This list is considered to be of a *numerus clausus* nature,[51] and for consideration of international comity, leave is to be handled with care.[52] Therefore, the plaintiff bears the burden of providing

---

45 CA 74/83 Ra'ad v. Chai, 40(2) PD 141, 146 (1986); Summons 420/63 Abramovsky v. Gleitmann, 17 PD 2605, 2607 (1963).

46 LCA 9810/05 Martin J. Hecke v. Pimcapco Ltd. (Aug. 30, 2009), Nevo Legal database (by subscription).

47 LCA 2610/73 Uniroyal v. Zion Insurance Co., 28(1) PD 229 (1973).

48 LCA 11822/05 Philip Morris Corp. v. Al-Roi (May 8, 2006), Nevo Legal Database (by subscription); LCA 39/89 General Electric Corp. v. Migdal Insurance Co., 42(4) PD 762 (1987).

49 CA 23/83 Youhamik v. Kedem, 38(4) PD 309 (1984).

50 *See* CA 4601/02 Rada Electronic Industries Ltd. v. Bodstray Company Ltd., 58(2) PD 465, 471 (2004).

51 CA 613/70 Gdomsky v. Rozmayati, 25(1) PD 798, 800 (1971).

52 CA 481/84 Atlantic Shipping and Fishing Corp. Ltd. v. Stiller's Y. Talleres Del Noroeste S.A., 42(3) PD 102, 109–10 (1988); CA 565/77 Mizrahi v. Nobel's Explosives Ltd., 32(2) PD 115, 117 (1978); CA 98/67 Liebherr v. Gazit and Shaham Construction Corp. Ltd., 21(2) PD 243, 250 (1968).

that an arguable case exists, that one of the grounds in the list of causes indicated in Rule 500 exists,[53] that a serious issue to be tried on the merits exists,[54] and that the Israeli forum is a forum conveniens.[55]

Moreover, Israeli courts recognize their power to decline jurisdiction in cases where a forum-selection clause might favor a foreign forum, if litigation between the parties is already pending before a foreign court (*lis alibi pendens*) and if it finds itself as an inappropriate forum for litigation under the forum non conveniens doctrine.[56] In practice, this power to decline jurisdiction is relevant only when service of process is performed in Israel on the defendant's person or a representative thereof. In such cases, the defendant bears the burden of justifying why jurisdiction of the Israeli court already established by virtue of service is to be declined. When jurisdiction is assessed against an absent defendant according to Rule 500, these same considerations become relevant when the plaintiff applies for service outside of jurisdiction. Therefore, in the context of Rule 500, the plaintiff bears the burden of providing adequate evidence satisfying the pre-conditions for granting the leave.

With this context in mind, we can now proceed to evaluate Israeli personal jurisdiction doctrine in PT-related civil actions.

C. Designing International Jurisdiction of Israeli Courts towards the PT

The strong territorial underpinnings of Israeli international jurisdiction doctrine created extraordinary challenges for Israeli courts when needing to assess the country's personal jurisdiction authority in PT-related civil disputes, first and foremost toward defendants present in the PT. On the one hand, the West Bank and the Gaza Strip have been under Israeli control, albeit to varying degrees of intensity, from 1967 through the present day. A major organ of the state, the IDF, has worked to control much of the activities and much of the movement into and outside of both these regions. No other state had any sovereign authority in the PT. On the other hand, the PT were never annexed to Israel but rather

53 CA 9725/04 Ashbourne Company for Agencies and Commerce Ltd. v. CAE Electronics Ltd. (Sept. 4, 2007), Nevo Legal Database (by subscription).

54 *Id.*

55 *Rada*, 58(2) PD at 471–72.

56 *See* Stephen Goldstein, *Israel, in* DECLINING JURISDICTION IN PRIVATE INTERNATIONAL LAW 259 (James J. Fawcett ed., 1995) [hereinafter Goldstein, *Israel*].

remained beyond its sovereign military boarders. This uncertain nature of the PT, at least from the perspective of Israeli law, became even more extreme as time went by. While dozens of Israeli settlements were established with the clear intent of becoming Israeli enclaves in all sense of the term, a semi-sovereign Palestinian entity was established—the Palestinian Authority (PA)—which was ascribed extensive jurisdictional powers in the territories that came under its control as a result of the Oslo Accords. No doubt, designing international jurisdiction under such conditions while still adhering to territorial orthodoxy required significant efforts and maneuvering on the part of Israeli courts. From a conflict of laws perspective, particularly in the context of an international conflict, this experience offers researchers interested in the field with an opportunity to closely examine the kind of considerations that guided the courts throughout.

My central thesis here contends that the construction of the Israeli personal jurisdiction doctrine is characterized by three different stages. The first one spanned from 1967 until the early 1980s, during which personal jurisdiction doctrine expanded. In this period, the West Bank and Gaza Strip were in many respects regarded as Israeli territory for personal jurisdiction purposes. The second stage spanned from the early 1980s until the signing of the Oslo Peace Accords in the mid-1990s, during which the personal jurisdiction doctrine became more instrumental. With the establishment of a relatively firm grip of personal jurisdiction doctrine towards the West Bank and Gaza Strip, courts in Israel began to employ discretionary jurisdictional tools, principally the forum non conveniens doctrine, in order to filter in only those cases that had a substantial tie with the State of Israel. The examination of the forum non conveniens doctrine in this setting is very revealing, as it discloses the issues that really matter to Israeli courts when deciding to keep or decline their personal jurisdiction authority. The start of the third stage is marked by the initiation of the Oslo Peace Process in the mid-1990s. The creation of the PA and the newly attained status of the West Bank and Gaza Strip as entities over which the PA has effective territorial jurisdiction required the personal jurisdiction doctrine of Israeli courts to adjust to the new developments. However, since the jurisdiction accorded to the PA under the Oslo Peace Accords did not reach the level generally accorded to an independent sovereign state and at the same time Israel maintained its control over the PT, personal jurisdiction of Israeli courts reflected this reality as well. While special rules for the service of process were enacted so as to accommodate the judicial assistance mechanism designed by the Oslo Accords, courts in Israel applied these rules in a manner that permitted direct service of process as if the PT were still under total Israeli occupation.

1. Stage One: Personal Jurisdiction Doctrine as a Means of Control over the PT

a. The *Sandoka* Case

The first legal pronouncement on how Israeli personal jurisdiction doctrine should relate to the PT, and more accurately a civil action filed against an PT resident defendant, came in October 1967 in the District Court of Tel Aviv judgment of *Sandoka v. Sandoka*.[57] The case dealt with an alimony and maintenance action filed by a Gaza wife and her children against their husband and father, also a resident of Gaza. The case was filed before the Israeli court soon after the 1967 Six-Day War ended, when the wife together with her children moved to Jaffa. Importantly, service on the husband/father-defendant was effectuated by the IDF military police stationed in Gaza. No leave for service outside the jurisdiction was sought or granted. Given the absence of such leave, the defendant moved to dismiss the action for lack of personal jurisdiction, and his motion proved successful. A lengthy judgment delivered by Judge Shlomo Asher, later to become an Israeli Supreme Court Justice, stated that "everyone knows, and no proof is needed on this issue, that the City of Gaza is located in a territory that was occupied by the IDF in the Six-Day War—and the question is whether this Court (or any other district court in Israel) has jurisdiction over the mentioned occupied territory."[58] Since Israeli sovereignty, as the court explained, had not been extended over the Gaza Strip, the area was to be regarded as foreign to the State of Israel, making it essential to obtain leave for service to the defendant outside the state's jurisdiction.[59] One Israeli scholar recognized this case as drawing a clear border between Israel and the West Bank and Gaza Strip, despite Israel's military control of the Strip.[60]

Shortly afterwards, the Israeli Minister of Justice issued a special set of rules: The Rules of Procedure (Service of Documents in the Administered Territories), 1969, (SDAT, 1969).[61] These rules made three important provisions. The first pertains

---

57 Summons (TA) 1163/67, 59 PM 356 (1967).

58 *Id.* at 357. Note the ease with which the court characterized Gaza as an "occupied territory"—a terminology that soon afterwards vanishes from court decisions as Israel's official policy regarding the status of the West Bank and the Gaza Strip materializes.

59 *Id.* at 357–59.

60 Amnon Rubinstein, *Yisra'el ve-ha-Shtakhim: Samkhuyot Shiput [Israel and the Territories: Judicial Powers]*, 14 IYUNEI MISHPAT 415, 444 (1989) (Hebrew).

61 KT 2482, 458. The rules were supplemented by an order issued by the military commander in the PT authorizing the service of documents originating in Israeli proceedings in the PT. *See* EYAL BENVENISTI, LEGAL DUALISM: THE ABSORPTION OF THE OCCUPIED TERRITORIES INTO ISRAEL 25 (1989) [hereinafter BENVENISTI, LEGAL DUALISM].

to the definition of "Region" (*ezor* in Hebrew), defined in Rule 1 as being "each of the territories held by the Israel Defense Forces." The second and most important provision is contained in Rule 2(a), under which service of any official documents generated by a civil claim filed before an Israeli court is to be effectuated in accordance with the ordinary set of civil procedure rules relevant to the service of documents inside of Israel. These later rules, as shown earlier, provide for service on any present defendant without the need for any form of leave. The third provision worthy of notice is the code added in Rule 2(b), providing that all documents served in accordance with Rule 2(a) must be accompanied by an Arabic translation.

It is interesting to note that the rules refrain from use of the term "occupied" (*kvushim* in Hebrew), applying instead the term "held" (*mukhzakim*) in relation to the PT. This latter word corresponds more with the English adjective "administered." In addition, the need to translate all served documents into Arabic is a provision most certainly implying that the perceived potential receivers of service of documents are the indigenous Arabic-speaking Palestinian residents of the PT.

All this now seems to entail that service of process inside the PT, a territory "held" by the IDF and thus qualifying as a "Region," does not require a grant of leave for service outside the Israeli jurisdiction. This was the conclusion the Israeli Supreme Court eventually reached in *Al-Khir & Sons Co. v. Van Der Hurst Fruit Import.*[62] The proceedings dealt with an action filed by a Dutch company against a Gaza defendant before the District Court of Jerusalem. The cause of action involved a contract made in Rotterdam for the export of a certain amount of oranges from Gaza to Holland. The contract stipulated that if the quantity of putrid oranges in the received shipment exceeded 4%, then the Dutch importer would be entitled to sell the oranges and claim the loss from the Gaza exporter. When such a situation ensued, the Dutch company initiated a monetary claim against the Gaza exporter. Interestingly, the action was initiated in the Israeli court, despite the lack of any connection between the case or the parties to the State of Israel. Furthermore, the Dutch plaintiff served the defendant with process directly, without obtaining a leave from the court. The defendant moved to dismiss the action for lack of personal jurisdiction, arguing that if personal jurisdiction were to be recognized in the present case then Israel would be considered to have annexed the Gaza Strip—a step the government of Israel explicitly chose not to undertake. The deputy president of the Israeli Supreme Court at the time, Justice Yoel Sussmann, rejected these arguments. Though he recognized the basic legal principal that

62 LCA 55/71, 25(2) PD 13 (1971).

service of process outside the jurisdiction usually necessitates the leave of court, he held that no such leave is required when service is effectuated in the PT. In light of SDAT, 1969 Justice Sussmann went on to proclaim, service can be made directly to a defendant that happens to be present in the PT, since the ordinary rule of service to a defendant present in Israel has been extended to these "Regions." The Court dismissed the annexation argument explaining that at issue in the case is the extent of Israeli personal jurisdiction authority over a defendant that happens to be present in what was defined to be the "Region," and nothing more.[63]

The *Al-Khir* decision was severely criticized in an article published soon after it was rendered.[64] The author argued that the Court in *Al-Khir* strayed from the guiding principles of the personal jurisdiction doctrine regarding foreign defendants previously established in Israeli Supreme Court judgments. These judgments, heavily influenced by English law, stipulate that when personal jurisdiction is assessed against an absent defendant, the assessment must be cautious and guarantee the existence of a sufficient nexus (one that is explicitly specified in the rules for service outside the jurisdiction) before personal jurisdiction is established. The *Al-Khir* judgment effectively obviates these requirements, making it possible to establish personal jurisdiction in an extra-territorial manner without the need to take these rules into consideration, while downplaying the function of service of process as a rule of personal jurisdiction. Ultimately, the *Al-Khir* decision implies that a defendant present in the PT has a similar status as one present in Israel.[65] The note suggested that the SDAT 1969 rules should have been interpreted only as offering the method of serving the documents on the defendant, after leave had been sought by the plaintiff and granted by the court.[66]

The Israeli Supreme Court was not swayed by this criticism. A short time after rendering its judgment in *Al-Khir*, it rendered another decision in which it went out of its way to offer a doctrinal rationale for service of process in the PT without need for recourse to the procedure for service outside the jurisdiction. This took place in the case of *Shourafa v. Wechsler*,[67] in which an Israeli resident brought

---

63 *Id.* at 15.

64 Baruch Bracha, *Hamtsa'at Mismakhim la-Shtakhim ha-Mukhzakim*, [*Service of Documents to the Administered Territories*], 4 MISHPATIM 119 (1972) (Hebrew).

65 Goldstein & HaCohen, *supra* note 9, at 67 ("It should be noted that due to special regulations in this regard [supposedly referring to SDAT, 1969 – M.K.], for purposes of service of process the territorial limits of Israel include the territories administered by Israel since the 1967 Six Day War").

66 Bracha, *supra* note 64, at 126, 129; *see also* BENVENISTI, LEGAL DUALISM, *supra* note 61, at 24, 67, n.134.

67 CA 211/73, 28(1) PD 512 (1974).

summary proceedings in Israel against a resident of Gaza to collect a dishonored check. The court concluded that the proceedings should be dismissed on grounds of both the plaintiff's defective articulation of the cause of action and the fact that the court seized with the proceedings lacked proper venue (local jurisdiction).[68] Nonetheless, the Court added that in light of *Al-Khir*, no lack of personal jurisdiction existed, since the defendant was properly served under SDAT, 1969. As to the doctrinal reason why no leave for service outside the jurisdiction is required when SDAT, 1969 rules are applicable, the Court explained this as "simple." According to the Court, leave for service outside the jurisdiction is required because of the potential infringement on the sovereign powers of the foreign state in which the defendant is present when he or she is brought under the personal jurisdiction authority of local courts by virtue of being served with the opening summons. But given the current status of the "Administered Territories," the court explained, all sovereign powers that existed over them are suspended under international law. In light of the fact that these territories were captured by the IDF, the sovereign entity that effectively controls them is the State of Israel. It follows, therefore, that when residents of the PT are served with the opening summons of an Israeli court in a direct fashion, no powers of foreign sovereignty are undermined, and thus no need exists to condition service upon obtaining a leave for service outside the jurisdiction.[69]

In spite of its marginal effect on the outcome of the case at hand, this rationale had a profound doctrinal influence on affirming the personal jurisdiction grip of Israeli courts over defendants present in the PT.[70] The far-reaching significance of this process emerged a few years later in a judgment concerning the jurisdictional capacity of Israeli courts to issue interim injunctions regarding property located in the PT. The relevant case is that of *Bank Leumi le-Yisrael Ltd. v. Hirschberg*.[71] The District Court of Jerusalem issued a provisional attachment order for a bank account held by the Bethlehem branch of Bank Leumi, an Israeli incorporated bank that operated at the time a number of branches in the PT—including the respondent's branch in Bethlehem. The bank account was apparently owned by a local Palestinian resident who was the defendant in an action filed by an Israeli plaintiff before the Israeli court. According to Israeli civil procedure, such

---

68 *Id.* at 515–18.

69 *Id.* at 517.

70 CA 318/81 Cohen v. Mantsura, 36(1) PD 222 (1981); CC (BS) 151/80 Kaplan v. Gabbay, PM 5742(2) 290 (1982).

71 CA 179/77, 32(1) PD 617 (1978).

attachment orders can be issued as part of the enforcement of a monetary judgment. The Israel Supreme Court affirmed the grant of this attachment order, while acknowledging the well-established international law principle under which one sovereign state cannot undertake enforcement actions in the territory of another sovereign state without the express consent of the latter.[72] The court once again reasoned that in the case of the "Administered Territories," no foreign power exists, and that these territories are effectively controlled by the State of Israel. Therefore, when such a provisional attachment order is effectuated in Bethlehem, no foreign sovereignty is undermined, and thus there should be no concern about transgressing established norms of international law.[73]

However, the doctrinal innovation of the *Al-Khir* decision was not enough to achieve the jurisdictional expansion it sought, for another hurdle still had to be overcome.

b. The Missing Link: Venue

According to established principles of Israeli civil procedure, a civil court needs to possess proper venue, or as Israeli terminology has it, proper "local jurisdiction,"[74] even when the court is otherwise competent to deal with the action.[75] This requirement effectively prevented Israeli courts from entertaining most PT-related actions. For unlike the doctrine developed in *Al-Khir*, local jurisdiction under Israeli rules of civil procedure requires that the judicial district seized with the action have a specific contact with either the defendant or the underlying cause of action to be able to adjudicate the case. The fact that service of the claim was made in some particular judicial district during the defendant's presence there is irrelevant. So although an Israeli court may have personal jurisdiction over a defendant resident in the PT, it would still be unable to adjudicate the case on the merits for lack of local jurisdiction.

Presently, Israel is divided into six different judicial districts for venue purposes. Each of these districts has one district court and a number of other magistrate

---

72 On this principle *see generally* IAN BROWNLIE, PRINCIPLES OF PUBLIC INTERNATIONAL LAW 306–08 (6th ed. 2003).

73 *Hirschberg*, 32(1) PD at 620–21.

74 At times, this term is interchangeable with "territorial jurisdiction." *See* Goldstein & HaCohen, *supra* note 9, at 6.

75 *Abramovsky*, 17 PD 2507.

courts.[76] The District Court serves both as an appellate court on judgments rendered by the intra-district Magistrate Courts and as a court of first instance in certain civil and criminal matters. RCP, 1984 provide a detailed set of provisions for litigants for choosing between the courts of the different local jurisdiction districts.[77] In general, in actions not wholly limited to immovable property (when they *are* limited to real property, venue lies in the district where the property is situated),[78] and where no forum selection clause exists designating the forum of a certain district (since a forum selection clause overrides the rule),[79] the action can be brought in any of the districts depending on the nexus. The latter is determined by the defendant's place of residence or place of business, the place where the obligation was created, the place assigned or intended for fulfilling the obligation, the place of delivery of the goods concerning which the action is brought, or the place of the act or omission concerning which the action is brought.[80] Therefore, if the defendant is properly served with the opening summons, but none of the recognized nexuses for the establishment of venue can be established with any of the local Israeli judicial districts, the case must be dismissed. This happened in *Shourafa v. Wechsler*, where dismissal was based on the finding that the Jerusalem district did not have any local jurisdiction nexuses for adjudicating the case.[81]

The missing nexus or venue link, when the defendant is properly served with process, was seen as a jurisdictional deficit. It created a strange anomaly whereby Israel qualifies as a single geographical unit in terms of dealing with an action, yet no court in the country has proper venue to adjudicate the case.

The military commander for the West Bank took the first step to fill in this jurisdictional void. A special military order issued in 1968 provided that Israeli citizens

76 Goldstein & HaCohen, *supra* note 9, at 61.

77 *Id.* at 62–63.

78 RCP 1984, Rule 4.

79 RCP 1984, Rule 5.

80 RCP 1984, Rule 3.

81 The Supreme Court's ruling in *Shourafa v. Wechsler* was preceded by a district court decision in Summons (Jer) 1149/68 Hamdan v. Shaheen, 64 PM 91 (1968), which also found that the seized court lacked local jurisdiction authority, notwithstanding that the defendant, a resident of Bethlehem, was properly served with the opening summons. Interestingly, it seems that the court first seized with the action in *Al Khir*, the District Court of Jerusalem, also lacked local jurisdiction to adjudicate the case. However, the defendant had not raised this issue. According to accepted civil procedure principles, the court is not allowed to raise the issue of local jurisdiction on its own motion (*sue sponte*), and the defendant, once failing to raise an objection to the court's supposed local jurisdiction authority early in the proceedings, is deemed to have waived any argument on the issue. *See* Goldstein & HaCohen, *supra* note 9, at 64.

injured in motor vehicle accidents in the West Bank could bring their claims before an Israeli court, in a jurisdiction in which the Israeli insurance agency overseeing the activities of local West Bank insurance companies has its principal place of business. But this order was found to be invalid by the District Court of Haifa. The court reasoned that the office of the military commander of the West Bank had no administrative power over the Israeli civil courts and therefore could not prescribe for such courts when and under what circumstance they can have local jurisdiction.[82] The real change took place only after the Israeli Supreme Court decided to voice its dissatisfaction with this anomalous jurisdictional reality in *Mantsura v. Cohen*.[83] The action was brought by an Israeli settler and resident of Kiryat Arba (one of the first Israeli settlements in the West Bank), against another Kiryat Arba Israeli settler, in which the plaintiff claimed compensation for an alleged tort that was also committed in Kiryat Arba. The District Court of Jerusalem dismissed the action after finding that it lacked local jurisdiction. The Supreme Court affirmed the decision, clarifying once again that while service of process establishes personal jurisdiction when served on the defendant present in the PT, it does not necessarily establish local jurisdiction. Justice Sussmann, at that time president of the Supreme Court, ended his judgment by sending a clear message to the legislative branch. In the current state of affairs, he cautioned, there is a "void in the rules of jurisdiction in respect of Jewish settlements in the Administered Territories, but it is the legislature's duty to provide a solution."[84] Importantly, the Court noted this void only in regard to the Israeli settlers but not in regard to PT residents at large. If this observation was implicit at this stage, it would soon become explicit in the Court's first chance to relate to the amendment passed regarding the local jurisdiction rules.

Indeed, the call made by President Sussmann was soon answered. In 1979, the Israeli Minister of Justice amended the Israeli rules on local jurisdiction, providing that when an action is within the jurisdiction of Israeli courts but venue does not lie in any of the existing judicial districts, the action may be filed in a court sitting in Jerusalem with proper subject matter jurisdiction.[85] With this

82 Summons (Hi) 3650/74 Amr v. Mana'a, PM 5736(1) 156 (1975).

83 CA 301/77, 32(3) PD 405 (1978).

84 *Id.* at 407.

85 At present, the relevant provision is contained in CPR 1984, Rule 6, which reads as follows: "An action that is not within the proper jurisdiction of a court under these rules or any other law, is to be brought before a court in Jerusalem that has proper subject matter jurisdiction, but the court in Jerusalem may order otherwise should it believe that under the circumstances trial in another forum would be more convenient for the parties."

amendment, the Israeli courts effectively consolidated their jurisdictional authority over defendants present in the PT. Any action filed against a defendant resident in the PT who happens to be served with the opening summons while present in the PT, even temporarily, is within the territorial jurisdiction of Israeli courts, both in terms of personal jurisdiction and in terms of venue. Interestingly, the 1979 amendment to local jurisdiction rules did not distinguish between Israeli and non-Israeli plaintiffs; it effectively offered recourse to the Jerusalem courts for all plaintiffs that managed to establish personal jurisdiction. So in practice, the 1979 amendment went far beyond what Sussmann's remark in *Mantsura* had envisioned. And as subsequent developments amply showed, Palestinian plaintiffs took advantage of this amendment to the same extent as Israeli settler plaintiffs, even when their adversaries were other Palestinian litigants.[86]

The common understanding regarding this amendment was, however, that its primary purpose was to serve PT Israeli settlers. This became abundantly clear shortly after the enactment of the amendment in *Cohen v. Mantsura*.[87] The action here was initiated once again before the District Court of Jerusalem for the affirmation of an arbitration award rendered as a result of an arbitration proceeding that took place in Kiryat Arba between two settlers who were local residents. Finding no specific contact to the district of Jerusalem as specified in the then-applicable rules of arbitration, the District Court of Jerusalem dismissed the action for lack of local jurisdiction. The Supreme Court reversed, holding that the 1979 amendment granting the District of Jerusalem proper local jurisdiction applies to arbitration proceedings, including the one taken here.[88] Justice Yitzhak Kahan, who at the time was the deputy president of the Israeli Supreme Court, later to become the Court's president, with the concurrence of two other Justices (Aharon Barak and Yitzhak Shilo), wrote that the application of this venue amendment may prove to be challenging in other cases in which it will not be appropriate to conduct adjudication in Israel. An example for this, he writes, would be "when an Arab resident of Gaza files a claim against another resident of this region in a Jerusalem court...."[89] In such cases, he says, the court can overcome the problem by invoking the court's power to decline jurisdiction.[90] Indeed, while the wording of the law left the issue vague, the general understanding was that the 1979 amendment

86 *See infra* Part C(2).

87 CA 318/81, 36(1) PD 222 (1981).

88 *Id.* at 224–25.

89 *Id.* at 226.

90 *Id.*

to local jurisdiction rules was made to serve Israeli settlers of the PT.[91] But how exactly could Israeli courts decline their jurisdiction when seized by a Palestinian plaintiff in a totally local PT cause of action filed against a Palestinian defendant? The jurisdictional fine-tuning enabling a court to decline its power to litigate such an action was achieved by the forum non conveniens doctrine. The only problem was that at the time, the doctrine was quite underdeveloped, enabling local courts to decline jurisdiction only in exceptional circumstances. But courts in Israel were determined to filter in only those PT related cases that implicated Israelis, and thus worked to liberalize this doctrine, as discussed in the next section. Before proceeding to that discussion, however, I would like to make two observations in evaluating this first stage of development.

c. Evaluation of the First Stage

Question 1: Is the *Al-Khir* decision equivalent to the jurisdictional annexation of the PT to the State of Israel?

On a number of occasions it has been generally stated that the end result of the *Al-Khir* decision was to "simply wipe out, for purposes of personal jurisdiction, the pre-1967 [Israeli] borders."[92] Indeed, in terms of the transient rule of personal jurisdiction, especially after the 1979 amendment of the rules on venue, this assessment is accurate.[93] However, at the end of this stage the PT cannot categorically be characterized as part of Israel for purposes of personal jurisdiction. Notwithstanding the developments described above, one material distinction in the sphere of personal jurisdiction between Israel and the PT still remained. The distinction becomes apparent when an Israeli court is asked to establish personal jurisdiction against a defendant that is not present in Israel or in the PT, and that has substantial ties and contacts with the PT but none with Israel. In such a hypothetical case, the plaintiff would need to seek permission for service on the defendant under the civil procedure rules for service of process outside the jurisdiction—a procedure stipulated primarily in Rule 500.[94] As mentioned earlier, this procedure conditions the grant of leave for service outside the jurisdiction

91 Rubinstein, *supra* note 90, at 449–50.

92 BENVENISTI, LEGAL DUALISM, *supra* note 61, at 24.

93 *See* Goldstein & HaCohen, *supra* note 9, at 67.

94 However, the plaintiff might not need to take this route for acquiring personal jurisdiction against the absent defendant if service can be made on another person present in Israel or the PT who is related to or operates on behalf of (represents) the defendant. Such circumstances are detailed in a special section of the RCP 1984.

upon establishing the existence of a nexus from a list stipulated in Rule 500, such as the fact that the defendant happens to maintain regular residence in Israel, or that the contract was made in Israel, etc. . But these provisions specifically refer to the State of Israel and as such disregard any and all connections to the PT. The *Al-Khir* decision brought with it a substantial expansion of Israeli personal jurisdiction regarding the PT, but only in circumstances when service of process is sought in the PT. When the defendant happens to be absent from the PT and the plaintiff seeks to obtain leave for service outside the jurisdiction, a nexus with the PT is not considered to be equivalent to a nexus with Israel's sovereign territory. Yet were the PT to be considered as having been annexed to Israel for personal jurisdiction purposes, the conclusion would have necessarily been just the opposite. In this respect, neither *Al-Khir* nor any other enactment could overcome the international obligations implicit in the pre-1967 borders.

Question 2: Presence or service, which comes first?

In assessing the meaning and significance of *Al-Khir*, one point seems to have escaped the scrutiny of both the courts and the scholars who have discussed the decision. This involves the functional relationship between the power to serve process on the defendant and the assessment of whether personal jurisdiction exists. The *Al-Khir* analysis pre-supposes the existence of a legal axiom according to which if procedural power to serve the defendant with process is said to exist, then upon service, personal jurisdiction is established. But the history of personal jurisdiction under the power theory demonstrates that the axiom seems to be the other way around. The initial inquiry involves whether the forum state has territorial power over the defendant's person, a power that exists if the defendant happens to be present in the sovereign territory of said state, and does not exist if the defendant happens to be absent from this territory.[95]

95 *See* J. G. COLLIER, CONFLICT OF LAWS 71 (3d ed. 2001). The United States Supreme Court made this very clear in its landmark decision on personal jurisdiction in Pennoyer v. Neff, 95 U.S. 714 (1878). Discussing the boundaries of states' personal jurisdiction, the Court observed:

> The several States of the Union are not, it is true, in every respect independent, many of the rights and powers which originally belonged to them now vested in the government created by the Constitution. But, except as restrained and limited by that instrument, they possess and exercise the authority of independent States, and the principles of public law to which we have referred are applicable to them. One of the principles is, that every State possesses exclusive jurisdiction and sovereignty over persons and property within its territory. As a consequence, every State has the power to determine for itself the civil *status* and capacities of its inhabitants... The other principles of public law referred to follow from the one mentioned; that is, that no State can exercise direct jurisdiction and authority over persons or property without its territory. The several States are of equal dignity and authority, and the independence of one implies the exclusion of power from all

Only after undertaking this initial inquiry can courts determine whether the defendant can be served with process or not.[96] Under the notion of the power theory, therefore, the matter at hand was not the procedural power to serve process, but rather the whereabouts of the defendant. The mode of service was simply the corollary of this inquiry. Indeed, the fact that acquiring personal jurisdiction required actual service on the defendant, and such service was pre-conditioned by different requirements depending on the whereabouts of the defendant, leads to the impression that personal jurisdiction depended on whether a mode for service of process exists. This, however, is not the rule. Had the Israeli Supreme Court in *Al-Khir* first asked whether the defendant was present on Israeli sovereign territory and could thus be served directly, it would have been much harder for it to reach a positive finding on personal jurisdiction. Even if the PT were not under the control of some foreign sovereign, they were not considered to be part of Israel or under Israeli sovereignty either. So the facts of the case would not have passed the first leg of the inquiry under the power theory of personal jurisdiction—a theory that supposedly guided the Court in its legal maneuverings in *Al-Khir* and thereafter. What is interesting is that in spite of this theoretical shortcoming of the *Al-Khir* holding, the axiomatic relationship it drew between service of process and jurisdiction became deeply embedded within Israeli legal interpretation and reverberated in other decisions in which personal jurisdiction was assessed in contexts not connected to the PT.[97]

The flawed nature of the *Al-Khir* holding becomes even more apparent through the prism of general jurisdiction. American jurisprudence on the law of personal jurisdiction offers a very useful distinction between general jurisdiction

> others. And so it is laid down by jurists, as an elementary principle, that the laws of one State have no operation outside of its territory, except so far as is followed by comity; and that no tribunal established by it can extend its process beyond that territory so as to subject either persons or property to its decisions. (*Id.* at 722)

This same notion of presence in the sovereign territory of the forum state as the initial qualifying factor for deciding jurisdiction also characterizes the English doctrine. Presence within the forum state under the English view was taken to mean allegiance to the forum state and thus made the defendant amenable to the process of the forum state. *See* Zelman Cowen, *Transient Jurisdiction: A British View*, 9 J. PUB. L. 303 (1960).

96 The Australian High Court highlighted this point in its decision Laurie v. Carroll, (1958) 98 C.L.R. 310, 322–23: "The defendant must be amenable or answerable to the command of the writ. His amenability depended and still depends upon nothing but presence within the jurisdiction."

97 *See, e.g.*, *General Electric Corp.*, 42(4) PD at 767.

and specific jurisdiction.[98] General jurisdiction exists when there is a relationship between the forum state and the defendant that enables the courts in that forum state to adjudicate any personal action against the defendant, irrespective of whether the underlying controversy is related to the defendants' relationship or not.[99] Thus, Mary Twitchell has observed that general jurisdiction is "dispute-blind."[100] This basic relationship can take the form of the defendant being domiciled in the forum state,[101] but can also include other circumstances such as performing service of process on the defendant's person while he or she happens to present in the forum state.[102] Specific jurisdiction exists when jurisdiction is based on a connection between the forum state and the underlying controversy. In such a case, that connection can give rise to personal jurisdiction; but if it does, personal jurisdiction is limited only to resolving that specific controversy and nothing more. Specific jurisdiction is functional in nature, since it seeks to carve out state jurisdictional authority in relation to the specific underlying dispute. On the other hand, and as already indicated, if general jurisdiction exists then it is all-encompassing, since it justifies personal jurisdiction in the forum state for all personal action against the defendant. Therefore, much discussion exists regarding the nature of the personal relationship between the defendant and the forum state that can give rise to general jurisdiction. Seemingly, however, all take for granted that if general jurisdiction is premised on the existence of a certain relationship, that relationship is between the forum state and the defendant.[103] Yet the *Al-Khir* holding created general jurisdiction capacity in Israeli courts based on a relationship with a foreign jurisdiction, that of the PT. As a result, anyone present in the PT and served with the process of Israeli courts comes under the general jurisdiction of Israeli courts. This is truly one great leap forward in personal jurisdiction practice.

98 The distinction was first offered in Arthur T. von Mehren & Donald Trautman, *Jurisdiction to Adjudicate: A Suggested Analysis*, 79 HARV. L. REV. 1121 (1966). Since then, the distinction became common-place in the law of personal jurisdiction and accepted by the United States Supreme Court. *See, e.g.*, Burger Kink Corp. v. Rudzewicz, 471 U.S. 462, 473 n.15 (1985); Helicopteros Nacionales de Colombia, S.A. v. Hall (Helicol), 466 U.S. 408, 414 (1984).

99 *See* LEA BRILMAYER, CONFLICT OF LAWS 281–82 (2d ed. 1995).

100 Mary Twitchell, *The Myth of General Jurisdiction*, 101 HARV. L. REV. 610, 612 (1988).

101 *See* Goodyear Dunlop Tires Operations, S.A. v. Brown, 564 U.S. ____, 131 S. Ct. 2846 (2011).

102 *See* Lea Brilmayer et al., *A General Look at General Jurisdiction*, 66 TEX. L. REV. 721, 747–55 (1988) [hereinafter Brilmayer et al., *A General Look*]. *See also* Burnham v. Superior Court of California, 495 U.S. 604 (1990).

103 Brilmayer et al., *A General Look*, *supra* note 102, at 727 ("General jurisdiction rests upon a direct relationship between the defendant and the forum").

2. Stage Two: The Forum Non Conveniens Doctrine Dominating the Jurisdictional Inquiry

a. General Remarks

From the early 1980s onwards, a growing number of civil actions originating in the PT found their way into Israeli courts. From the legal-positivistic point of view, this recourse was facilitated by the combined effect of the SDAT, 1969—establishing personal jurisdiction in Israeli courts whenever the defendant is served with process while present in the PT—and the 1979 venue amendment, which establishes local jurisdiction in Jerusalem courts if and when such jurisdiction is lacking in any other local jurisdiction district in Israel. Interestingly, a noticeable portion of such cases was comprised of civil actions filed by Palestinian plaintiffs against Palestinian defendants concerning incidents that took place entirely in the PT. In addition, Israeli settlers in the PT—a steadily-increasing population at the same period—also filed civil actions. It is obvious why the latter group of litigants should seek adjudication in Israeli courts. Like settlers in other countries, both ideologically and practically, Israeli settlers in the PT wanted to maintain their ties to Israeli civil institutions in spite of their physical relocation to the PT.[104] It is less clear, however, why Palestinian plaintiffs should seek adjudication of their PT-based actions against Palestinian defendants before Israeli courts.

One explanation lies in the already established practice of filing petitions before the Israeli Supreme Court in its capacity as the High Court of Justice (HCJ) in an effort to challenge the legality of IDF action in the PT. As these petitions became common-place, it was natural that Palestinians, this time as plaintiffs, will come to seek civil adjudication before Israeli courts.

But there is one basic difference between administrative petitions before the HCJ and the filing of civil claims before ordinary Israeli courts. No effective recourse to local PT institutions existed when Palestinian litigants asked to contest the legality of the IDF measure taken there. Under the accepted norms of belligerent occupation, the IDF military government in the PT was effectively immune from the jurisdiction of local PT courts. On occasion, certain committees were established to handle petitions by local residents, but these were run by the IDF military

104 *See* Catherine Cook & Adam Hanieh, *The Separation Barrier: Walling in People, Walling out Sovereignty*, *in* THE STRUGGLE FOR SOVEREIGNTY: PALESTINE AND ISRAEL, 1993–2005 338, 339 (Joel Beinin & Rebecca L. Stein eds., 2006).

government and had limited judicial review authorities.[105] Hence, turning to the Israeli Supreme Court in its capacity as the ultimate administrative court was the only effective judicial recourse available. On the other hand, PT residents did have recourse to the PT's local civil courts, which as already described in Chapter One, were maintained under Israel's belligerent occupation. As described in one Palestinian study, the local PT judiciary was the only national institution in the PT that continued to function after Israeli occupation.[106] This supposedly made the local PT courts the natural forum for civil litigation among Palestinians.

Yet as it turned out, local PT civil courts were not that attractive to local Palestinian plaintiffs—at least to those who sought to maximize their interests by having recourse to an effective and efficient legal process. The local PT courts had limited subpoena powers (especially towards government officials),[107] and were charged with corruption.[108] They operated under very poor conditions:[109] understaffed,[110] poorly equipped,[111] and operated by judges whose judicial pronouncements were less than inspiring.[112] In light of these conditions, as two Palestinian attorneys have observed, "a lawyer cannot hope to help his client obtain justice or get a fair trial. . . ."[113] It is no wonder, therefore, that plaintiffs strove to have their claims litigated before Israeli civil courts, which were reputed to be relatively efficient (though less so in recent years), well equipped, and free of corruption.[114]

Additionally, it is questionable whether local PT courts under Israeli occupation were actually held to be a true local and autonomous institution. More realistically, since these courts were under the complete control of the IDF military

---

105 *See supra* Chapter One.

106 RAJA SHEHADEH & JONATHAN KUTTAB, THE WEST BANK AND THE RULE OF LAW 11 (1980).

107 *Id.* at 36.

108 *See* George E. Bisharat, *Peace and the Political Imperative of Legal Reform in Palestine*, 31 CASE W. RES. J. INT'L L. 253, 266 (1999).

109 *See* BENVENISTI, LEGAL DUALISM, *supra* note 61, at 23, 28.

110 SHEHADEH & KUTTAB, *supra* note 106, at 37 (noting the problem of having to suspend proceedings because of the unavailability of a clerk to take record).

111 *Id.* at 38 (noting the unavailability of even a coin-operated photocopier in PT courts, making it necessary for "an attorney wishing to photocopy the official court record in a case, or any documents that have been entered in the file" to ask for "a special permit and then persuade on [*sic*] the bus clerks at the court to accompany him to a commercial photocopying center").

112 *Id.* at 43, 44.

113 SHEHADEH & KUTTAB, *supra* note 106, at 41.

114 *See* TOBIAS KELLY, LAW, VIOLENCE AND SOVEREIGNTY AMONG WEST BANK PALESTINIANS 15, 116–18 (2006); RAJAH SHEHADEH, STRANGERS IN THE HOUSE: COMING OF AGE IN OCCUPIED PALESTINE 138 (2002).

government,[115] at least up until the Oslo Peace Accords, they were identified more as an Israeli institution than an indigenous one. In this respect, it is important to stress once again that of the 39 judges employed by Jordan prior to 1967, only 8 continued their judicial functions past 1967.[116] A substantial number of practicing lawyers in the PT, especially in the West Bank, went on strike and refused to represent clients before these local courts.[117] According to the prevalent view, such representation would legitimize Israeli actions,[118] thereby implying a close link between the local judiciary and Israeli occupation. So while the local PT judiciary was maintained by the IDF military government as a functioning local institution, one cannot say that it was actually regarded as such by the local Palestinians.[119] Palestinian plaintiffs who sought some form of reliable legal process and were aware of the conditions in local PT courts realized that they might as well turn to Israeli courts.

The rising tide of PT-related civil actions aroused discomfort among the Israeli courts. First, as it will become apparent from the holdings on the forum non conveniens doctrine, Israeli courts did not consider themselves as an appropriate forum for local disputes among Palestinians—an adjudication that made it necessary to deal with a legal system and legal standards that were in large part foreign to their own.[120] Second, in the early 1980s, courts in Israel became overburdened with litigation—as indicated by the re-appointment of public committees to study

---

115 SHEHADEH & KUTTAB, *supra* note 106, at 28.

116 ISRAEL NATIONAL SECTION OF THE INTERNATIONAL COMMISSION OF JURISTS, THE RULE OF LAW OF THE AREA ADMINISTERED BY ISRAEL 23 (1981) (explaining that "a number of local judges had left the Region. Several refused to resume their duties and others chose to retire.").

117 *Id.*

118 SHEHADEH & KUTTAB, *supra* note 106, at 45–46. For similar considerations, local Palestinian leaders of the PT were reluctant to lobby the military government for legislative reforms. *See* Bisharat, *supra* note 108, at 265.

119 *See* SHEHADEH & KUTTAB, *supra* note 106, at 25–26; ISRAEL NATIONAL SECTION OF THE INTERNATIONAL COMMISSION OF JURISTS, *supra* note 116, at ix-x, 35–42; Eli Nathan, *The Power of Supervision of the High Court of Justice over military government, in* 1 MILITARY GOVERNMENT IN THE TERRITORIES ADMINISTERED BY ISRAEL 1967–1980: LEGAL ASPECTS 109 (Meir Shamgar ed., 1982); Adam Roberts, *Prolonged Military Occupation: The Israeli Occupied Territories since 1967*, 84 AM. J.INT'L. L. 44, 88–95 (1990); Mazen Qupty, *The Application of International Law in the Occupied Territories as Reflected in the Judgments of the High Court of Justice in Israel, in* INTERNATIONAL LAW AND THE ADMINISTRATION OF OCCUPIED TERRITORIES: TWO DECADES OF ISRAELI OCCUPATION OF THE WEST BANK AND GAZA STRIP 124 (Emma Playfair ed., 1992).

120 Notably, however, the Supreme Court was not equally disturbed by petitions asking it to review the actions taken by the IDF and the military government officials operating in the PT. Apparently, this open-door policy towards judicial review petitions was motivated, inter alia, by the desire to promote faith in the Israeli legal system. *See* Eyal Benvenisti, *Judicial Review of Administrative Action in the Territories Occupied in 1967, in* PUBLIC LAW IN ISRAEL 371, 372 (Itzhak Zamir & Allen Zysblat eds., 1996).

the legal structure and propose reforms to make it more efficient.[121] Third, a growing realization of the need to resist the forum shopping phenomenon emerged within the discipline of international civil litigation.[122] Courts and scholars alike began to realize that a plaintiff's drive to seek litigation in a certain forum only because of the procedural or substantive advantages of law available within the forum can be burdensome and unfair to the defendant, even if courts have adequate jurisdiction to adjudicate the case on the merits.[123] Unlike the plaintiff, the defendant is usually a passive party in terms of the forum in which litigation is initiated. So if the forum seized by the plaintiff lacks any meaningful connection to the controversy other than the fact that its process was properly served on the defendant—as the case is in PT-related disputes among Palestinians[124]—then such cases presented themselves as being an act of forum shopping on part of the plaintiff.

However, when Israeli courts began realizing the burden of PT-related civil litigation, they found themselves ill-equipped in terms of a legal doctrine that enabled them to decline a duly conferred judicial authority. At the time, Israeli courts had at their disposal only limited discretion authorizing them to abstain from entertaining proceedings that amounted to an abuse of process by the plaintiff. To control more effectively the flow of litigation into Israeli courts, Israeli courts eventually adopted the forum non conveniens doctrine, which was a much more efficient filtering device. At the end of this process, PT-related civil litigation among Palestinian litigants was kept out of Israeli courts, while PT-based civil litigation among Israeli settlers or any other proceeding implicating an Israeli party was kept in.

---

121 On the problem of docket congestion in the Israeli court system, *see generally* DIN VE-HESHBON HA-VA'ADA LE-BDIKAT HA-MIVNE VE-HA-SAMKHUYOT SHEL BATEI HA-MISHPAT [REPORT OF THE COMMITTEE TO OVERVIEW THE STRUCTURE AND THE POWERS OF THE COURTS] (1980) (Hebrew); DIN VE-HESHBON HA-VA'ADA LE-BDIKAT MIVNE BATEI HA-MISHPAT HA-REGILIM BE-YISRAEL [REPORT OF THE COMMITTEE TO OVERVIEW THE STRUCTURE OF GENERAL COURTS IN ISRAEL] (1997) (Hebrew). *See generally* Forum, *Al ha-Reforma be-Ma'arekhet Batei ha-Mishpat* [*On the Reform in the Court System*], 8 MEHKAREY MISHPAT 9 (1990) (Hebrew).

122 *See* MICHAEL KARAYANNI, FORUM NON CONVENIENS IN THE MODERN AGE 132–45 (2004).

123 *Id.*

124 Indeed, the rule of transient jurisdiction has been traditionally perceived as being exorbitant because it lacks the guarantee of any meaningful connection with the underlying cause of action. *See* Kevin M. Clermont & John R. B. Palmer, *Exorbitant Jurisdiction*, 58 ME. L. REV. 474 (2006); Kurt H. Nadelmann, *Jurisdictionally Improper Fora, in* XXTH CENTURY COMPARATIVE AND CONFLICTS LAW 321, 328–29 (Kurt H. Nadelmann et al. eds., 1961). Some scholars, however, defined "exorbitant jurisdiction" as a function of whether the specific judgment rendered on the basis of a certain jurisdictional rule will be recognized and enforced in other jurisdictions or not; *see* L. I. De Winter, *Excessive Jurisdiction in Private International Law*, 17 INT'L & COMP. L.Q. 706, 712–13 (1968).

b. Forum non Conveniens and the Traditional Constraints Against Declining Jurisdiction

Initially, courts were apprehensive towards motions intended to bring them to decline a jurisdictional power they considered rightly theirs. The existence of jurisdictional power was taken to imply the existence of a duty to adjudicate the case on the merits. This notion was enshrined in a frequently quoted Latin maxim: *judex tenetur impertiri judicium suum* (a judge with jurisdiction over a case must render a final decision).[125] Nonetheless, English law recognized some room for discretion to decline a duly conferred jurisdiction under exceptional circumstances.[126] The traditional approach is found in Lord Scott's opinion in the English Court of Appeal case of *St. Pierre v. South American Stores Ltd.*[127] According to this holding, a mere balance of convenience is not sufficient to stay the pending proceedings. To cause the stay, the defendant needs to satisfy the court that the continuance of the action in the original forum "would be oppressive or vexatious to him" and that the stay will not "cause injustice to the plaintiff."[128] This standard essentially requires that the choice of the English forum as the original forum for adjudication be essentially an act of abuse of process in order for adjudication to be denied. If, for example, the plaintiff had chosen the original English forum in order to take advantage of a particular legal advantage that this forum is willing to grant—a classic circumstance of forum shopping—this in itself would not offer just cause for declining jurisdiction. Such an act would "cause injustice to the plaintiff" and not satisfy the second limb of the *St. Pierre* prong.

Until the late 1970s, this English approach guided Israeli courts.[129] It is important to note, however, that when the Israeli courts first came to apply these standards, they allowed themselves more latitude to decline jurisdiction than the traditional English approach suggested. The first Israeli case to articulate a local forum discretional power to decline jurisdiction was *Hakhamov v. Schmidt.*[130] The defendant moved to have the proceedings in Israel stayed, given the fact that litigation on the same matter was pending elsewhere. Since a *lis alibi pendens*

125 David W. Robertson & Paula K. Speck, *Access to State Courts in Transnational Personal Injury Cases: Forum Non Conveniens and Antisuit Injunctions*, 68 TEX. L. REV. 937, 949 (1990). *See also* John Bies, Comment, *Conditioning Forum Non Conveniens*, 67 U. CHI. L. REV. 498, 508 n.93 (2000).

126 *See* RONALD A. BRAND & SCOTT R. JABLONSKI, FORUM NON CONVENIENS 11–12 (2007).

127 [1936] 1 K.B. 382 (C.A.).

128 *Id.* at 398.

129 Goldstein, *Israel*, *supra* note 56, at 261.

130 Summons 280/57, 12 PD 59 (1958).

argument has traditionally been treated as a specific cause for a stay of proceedings,[131] the Israeli Supreme Court stated that the governing principles were those of *St. Pierre*, and ultimately stayed the action. However, had the Court followed the *St. Pierre* standard fully, it is doubtful whether it would have rendered the stay. The plaintiffs in the *Hakhamov* case could not be said to have brought the action in Israel to vex and oppress the defendant—the underlying cause of action (construction of a hotel resort in Israel) was reasonably connected to the original forum, Israel, and justifies why the plaintiff sought to litigate the action there.[132] The same liberal approach in terms of *St. Pierre* was displayed some 20 years later in *Perlmutter v. Perlmutter*, where the action was stayed also based on *lis alibi pendens* grounds.[133] Here, the Court once again upheld the *St. Pierre* standard to stay proceedings as the guiding principle but in fact applied it in a less restrictive manner by including other considerations as well.[134] In spite of the Israeli courts' somewhat more liberal approach towards declining jurisdiction, at no time before the early 1980s did they reach the level of discretion permitted under the American doctrine of forum non conveniens. .

In the 1970s, English law began to change.[135] The first step was taken in 1973 in *Atlantic Star*,[136] and the second in 1978 in *MacShannon v. Rockware Glass Ltd.*[137] By the end of this process, scholars observed that a reformulation of the English standard to decline jurisdiction had taken place, making the English law inquiry now turn on whether there is another clearly more appropriate forum for litigation in which justice can be sought.[138] This new English development was ultimately noted in an Israeli law review article published in 1980 by Professor

---

131 Goldstein, *Israel, supra* note 56, at 261.

132 Stephen Goldstein, *Samkhut Shipput Beinle'umit Mevuseset al Tfisat ha-Nitba—Halakha le-Ma'ase ka-Yom [International Jurisdiction Based Solely on Service of Process—In Practice Today]*, 10 Mishpatim 409, 429–30 (1980) (Hebrew) [hereinafter Goldstein, *International Jurisdiction*].

133 CA 100/76, 30(3) PD 355 (1976).

134 *Id.* at 358–60. The case dealt with the custody of a child born and raised in Israel by an Israeli couple. After the dissolution of the marriage but before the divorce, the mother traveled with the couple's child to Germany, telling the father that her stay in Germany would be only temporary. While in Germany, the mother initiated custody proceedings before a German court. After learning of this, the father initiated proceedings in Israel, which the mother asked the Israeli court to stay in light of the already ongoing proceeding in the German court. *Id.* at 357–58.

135 *See* Brand & Jablonski, *supra* note 126, at 14.

136 The Atlantic Star, [1974] A.C. 436 (H.L.).

137 [1978] A.C. 795 (H.L.).

138 *See* Collier, *supra* note 95, at 84–85; Rhona Schuz, *Controlling Forum-Shopping: The Impact of* MacShannon v. Rockware Glass Ltd., 35 Int'l & Comp. L.Q. 374, 376 (1986). Ultimately, the House of Lords acknowledged this development in Spiliada Maritime Corp. v. Cansulex Ltd., [1987] A.C. 460 (H.L.).

Stephen Goldstein. He suggested that the present English law standard for staying proceedings where personal jurisdiction has been established on the basis of service of process on a present defendant is not much different from the already elastic American doctrine of forum non conveniens.[139] Professor Goldstein welcomed this development and hoped for its adoption by Israeli courts, particularly in light of the 1979 amendment on venue that effectively guaranteed the availability of an Israeli forum for any case in which process can be served on a present defendant.[140]

Fusing these developments with the need to control the flow of litigation from the PT into Israel inevitably led Israeli courts to adopt the American forum non conveniens doctrine.[141] The flexible criteria of this doctrine proved to be most efficient for accommodating Israel's institutional interests.[142] I now turn to describe how exactly this doctrine was adopted.

c. Paving the Way Back to the PT: *Jabour* and *Abu Attiya*

Judge Eli Nathan, in the District Court of Jerusalem case *Jabbour v. Hanitan*,[143] provided the first thorough articulation of an Israeli court's discretional power to decline its duly acquired jurisdiction in a PT-related civil action. The action was brought by a Palestinian resident of the PT injured in a motor-vehicle accident that occurred between Hebron and Bethlehem in the West Bank. The two named defendants were also Palestinian: the first was the alleged tortfeasor and the second was his insurance company. Within the confines of a motion filed by the defendants to dismiss the action for lack of local jurisdiction, Judge Nathan decided that although the court had both local and personal jurisdiction to adjudicate the case, it should decline its jurisdictional authority—and so he ordered. The Israeli forum, Judge Nathan pronounced, is not the "natural forum," since neither the parties nor the underlying cause of action have any substantial connection to Israel.[144] In reaching this conclusion, Judge Nathan took into consideration the fact that all parties were residents of the PT; witnesses as to the damages incurred by the plaintiff would also be from the PT; and it will more appropriate that a forum more familiar with the social and economic reality of life in the PT assess

139 Goldstein, *International Jurisdiction*, *supra* note 132, at 427.

140 *Id.* at 411–12. *See also* Goldstein & HaCohen, *supra* note 9, at 67.

141 *See* Goldstein, *Israel*, *supra* note 56, at 260–61.

142 *See* Benvenisti, Legal Dualism, *supra* note 61, at 28 (noting the flexible criteria adopted by Israeli courts in identifying the natural forum in PT-related civil actions).

143 Originating Summons (Jer) 748/82, PM 5743(1) 499 (1982).

144 *Id.* at 503, 506–07.

the damages.[145] This move towards identifying the natural forum for litigation by looking into the context of the case is a major advance relative to the "abuse of process" standard initially adopted in *St. Pierre*. In fact, Judge Nathan noted that the *St. Pierre* standard was applied rather liberally in the Israeli Supreme Court decisions, but his decision was the first to take the extra step of offering an alternative standard. Since Judge Nathan himself made clear his dissatisfaction with the rule that establishes personal jurisdiction by Israeli courts upon service in the PT in an article he published very close to the rendering of this decision,[146] it was not surprising that he would work to limit the personal jurisdiction of Israeli courts toward the PT, especially after the 1979 amendment on venue. Judge Nathan was explicit in this respect, explaining that it was "inconceivable" that by introducing the 1979 amendment, Israel sought to indiscriminately apply its jurisdiction to all residents of the "Administered Territories"—effectively annexing these territories without the issuance of an explicit order in this respect as required by law.[147] Judge Nathan added that it was similarly inconceivable that by making the amendment, Israel meant to undermine the working of the local courts in the "Administered Territories," especially involving their status as the natural forum of local citizens regarding PT-based civil litigation.[148]

Judge Nathan dismissed the plaintiff's arguments depicting the local West Bank courts as inefficient and as adhering to a rigid and sometimes arbitrary civil process.[149] These issues, Judge Nathan held, do not form "a true grave wrong to the plaintiff" but might only cause some inconvenience that could be overcome.[150] The only factor that Judge Nathan was willing to consider involved the fact that medical experts, apparently from Israel, might be called upon to give testimony before the local PT court, which might prove impracticable. He held that should this prove to be the case, he would be willing to renew the adjudication of the case before the Jerusalem court.[151]

Judge Nathan's decision in *Jabbour* can be considered another watershed in the development of the personal jurisdiction doctrine of Israeli courts towards the PT. It essentially furnished the doctrinal mechanism that Israeli courts (soon afterwards

145 *Id.* at 507.

146 *See* Eli Nathan, *Israeli Civil Jurisdiction in the Administered Territories*, 13 Isr. Y.B. Hum. Rts. 90 (1983).

147 *Jabbour*, PM 5743(1) at 505.

148 *Id.*

149 *Id.*at 506–07.

150 *Id.* at 507.

151 *Id.*

with the blessing of the Supreme Court) came to use in order to "filter" PT-related civil actions. The technique is to look into the various contacts of the case, in order to identify the natural forum for the litigation. When all litigants were Palestinian residents of the PT, and the underlying cause of action was also based in the PT, then the natural forum was identified to be that of the local PT courts.[152]

The first major decision by the Israeli Supreme Court to endorse Judge Nathan's course of analysis was *Abu Attiya v. Arabtisi*.[153] The plaintiff, a minor, was injured in a work-related accident in the Ramallah factory where he was employed. The named defendants were the employer, also a resident of Ramallah, and Prudential—a foreign insurance company that issued a policy covering the employer's liability through its West Bank branch, which also had an office in Jerusalem. The plaintiff filed his action before the District Court of Jerusalem. The court dismissed the action after it identified the natural forum for the present litigation to be in what the court termed as the litigants' "backyard," i.e., Ramallah. On appeal, the Supreme Court affirmed the decision.

In its holding, the Court explicitly ruled that a need no longer exists to adhere to the *St. Pierre* standard. Instead, an Israeli forum can decline its jurisdiction when it identifies the natural forum for the pending litigation as lying elsewhere. In making this assessment, the court is to take into consideration the nexus of the parties and the underlying cause of action to the contending forum, as well as the reasonable pre-litigation expectations of the parties as to where the prospected litigation among them is to take place. In practice, this standard has become the Israeli version of the forum non conveniens doctrine.[154]

Two observations the Supreme Court made regarding the PT in this context are of particular importance. First, the court validated the conception already set forth in *Jabbour* about the existence of an Israeli official policy whereby local residents

---

152 BENVENISTI, LEGAL DUALISM, *supra* note 61, at 28; Rubinstein, *supra* note 60, at 456–57.

153 CA 300/84, 39(1) PD 365 (1985). However, a short published decision of the Supreme Court clearly indicates that regarding claims filed by a Palestinian resident of the PT against another Palestinian resident of the PT as a result of a cause of action originating in the PT, the applicable standard demands a stay and the relegation of the parties to the local PT courts, without the need to apply the pre-modern standard of *St. Pierre*. CA 588/83 Al-Rayis v. The Arab Insurance Company, 38(3) PD 495 (1984).

154 It should be noted that some disagreement existed among the judges as to whether all the factors that are relevant to the US version of the doctrine would also be relevant in the Israeli practice. While Justice Tova Strassberg-Cohen opined that Israeli courts, like their American counterparts, should take into consideration public interest factors and choice of law evaluations, Justice Aharon Barak seemed to have some reservations about these factors. *Abu Attiya*, 39(1) PD at 377–79, 386.

of the PT should presumably litigate their claims in the PT. The Court found support for this policy in the fact that the IDF worked to maintain the operation of the local court system in the PT. Justice Tova Strassberg-Cohen wrote:

> [O]ne needs to consider that on the one hand, the relations between the Region and Israel are not identical to the relations between two independent sovereigns, and on the other hand, that the Israeli legislature made it explicit that residents of the Region, who are not Israeli citizens and whose relation under all circumstances is to the law applicable in the Region and to the court there, are to be judged in the courts there and according to the applicable law there.[155]

The second observation involved cases that included what was termed as a "significant Israeli element," in which case the forum non conveniens analysis is to lead the Israeli court to adjudicate the case on its merits.[156] As to what could constitute such a significant factor, the court gave as an example a case where "one of the parties was an Israeli citizen or resident."[157] This approach effectively protects Israeli settlers of the PT from being denied recourse to Israeli courts, since they usually embody such a personal connection by virtue of being Israeli citizens.[158]

The *Abu-Attiya* decision supplied the guidance sought by the Israeli courts in limiting the flow of cases from the PT. From that point on, in cases where all the litigants were Palestinians from the PT and the underlying cause of action was based in the PT, the forum non conveniens doctrine would be routinely applied, enabling courts to decline their jurisdictional powers.[159]

d. One Additional Leap in Liberalizing Discretion under the Forum non Conveniens Doctrine: *Abu Jahla*

The liberal standard for declining jurisdiction was pushed one step further in another Supreme Court case, *Abu Jahla v. The East Jerusalem Electric Company*.[160]

155 *Id.* at 382.

156 *Id.* at 386.

157 *Id.*

158 Yet, as a result of this standard, courts refrained from declining jurisdiction when the Israeli resident was a Palestinian from East Jerusalem. See CA 5118/92 Al-Tarifi v. Salaymeh, 50(5) PD 407, 413 (1997).

159 *See* CA 489/85 Salahat v. Municipality of Nablus, 42(1) PD 497 (1988); LCA 4716/93 The Arab Insurance Company v. Zarikat, 48(3) PD 265 (1994); Summons (Jer) 1410/83 The Arab Insurance Company v. Khader, PM 5744(2) 172 (1984).

160 CA 2705/91, 48(1) PD 554 (1993).

This case concerned a Palestinian plaintiff residing in the PT, who within the confines of a civil action sought compensation for an accident that took place in the PT. The difference between this case and those described above was the fact that the action was filed against the East Jerusalem Electric Company, commonly known as the Jerusalem District Electric Company (JDEC). The JDEC is a Palestinian-run corporation with headquarters in East Jerusalem. Following the Extension of Israeli law to East Jerusalem in 1967, the JDEC was required to register as an Israeli corporation but continued to supply electricity solely to East Jerusalem and the West Bank.[161] Given the JDEC's services to the general public, its Palestinian-dominated board of directors, its headquarters in East Jerusalem, the company became "a symbol of Palestinian independence in East Jerusalem"[162] and even a microcosm of the conflict between Israel and the two main Palestinian factions at the time, namely pro-Jordanians and Palestinian nationalists.[163] Upon filing the claim before an Israeli court in Jerusalem, the JDEC asked that the proceedings be stayed on forum non conveniens grounds. This was a tricky case. As far as Israeli law was concerned, the JDEC was an Israeli corporation with headquarters in Jerusalem. Hence, the case was one with a "significant Israeli element," making it necessary under existing standards to keep the case before Israeli courts; any other conclusion would undermine Israel's annexation of East Jerusalem, especially in light of JDEC's history. On the other hand, willingness to entertain this action would produce an additional burden on Israeli courts, forcing them to adjudicate claims against East Jerusalem entities which like JDEC operate in the West Bank. This latter concern proved to be more dominant, as the Israeli Supreme Court ultimately applied the forum non conveniens doctrine and stayed the proceedings. A decision authored by Meir Shamgar, at that time the president of the Supreme Court, noted that JDEC's relation with Israel is of a "formal" nature.[164] In this respect, Shamgar stressed the fact that JDEC was incorporated under Israeli law a short time after the 1967 Six-Day War in order to comply with a specific military order obliging all East Jerusalem corporations to re-register under Israeli law, and did not actually do so of its own free will. Given the fact that the bulk of the company's operations were in the West Bank, and the accident took place there, the Court determined

161 *Id.* at 557.

162 Bill Hutman & Amir Cheshin, *Living Together and Apart in Jerusalem: Lessons Learned*, *in* JERUSALEM: A CITY AND ITS FUTURE 401, 417 (Marshal J. Breger & Ora Ahimeir eds., 2002).

163 JEHUDA LUKACS, ISRAEL, JORDAN AND THE PEACE PROCESS 84 (1997).

164 *Abu Jahla*, 48(1) PD at 576.

that the parties' pre-litigation expectations as to where a mutual action was to be brought also pointed to the PT. Additionally it held that a PT forum is better situated than the Israeli forum to assess and determine the relevant standard of care.[165]

In an effort to keep adjudication of his claims before the Israeli courts, the Palestinian plaintiff in *Abu Jahla* argued against referral to PT courts, claiming that as a result of the events of the First *Intifada* (uprising), adjudication there is so inefficient that it has become unjust.[166] The Court dismissed this argument, holding that "it is of little weight, relatively, when it is raised between the parties who are before us in this matter, even if we ignore the fact that it has not been proven."[167] The Court thereby implied that since both litigants are Palestinian entities, their arguments against appearing before the PT judiciary do not carry much weight,[168] for the First *Intifada* and what ensued is a result of their own actions.[169]

The great doctrinal leap that took place in the evolution of the discretional power of Israeli courts to decline jurisdiction is apparent, especially after *Abu Jahla*, in comparison with the point of departure set by the *St. Pierre* standard. In the past, it would have been inconceivable for a defendant sued in the forum of its place of its residence to convince the court that the adjudication of the action in this particular venue is vexatious or oppressive. It is no wonder, then, that one of the most common personal jurisdiction rules internationally is the one that grants the courts of the defendant's domicile jurisdiction over civil claims filed against it.[170] Ultimately, at the end of this stage, Israeli courts were able to adopt broad discretional powers that helped them to filter out the bulk of civil litigation among Palestinians that involved PT-based causes of action, while maintaining their capacity to filter in PT-related civil litigation against Israeli settlers.

---

165 *Id.*

166 *Id.* at 577–78.

167 *Id.* at 578.

168 *Id.*

169 Goldstein, *Israel, supra* note 56, at 272.

170 For a detailed critical assessment of the defendants' domicile as the basis of jurisdiction, *see* Arthur Taylor von Mehren, *Must Plaintiffs Seek out Defendants? The Contemporary Standing of Actor Sequitur Forum Rei*, 8 KING'S COLLEGE L.J. 23 (1997).

e. Evaluation of the Second Stage

Question 1: The PT through the lens of the forum non conveniens doctrine: Is it "Israeli" or "Palestinian"?

Israeli courts considered the fact that the IDF military government maintained the local PT judiciary and legal system after the 1967 Six-Day War to demonstrate an active policy on part of the State of Israel to keep PT-based civil litigation among Palestinian litigants under the jurisdiction of PT courts.[171] Israeli courts felt compelled to observe this policy by applying the forum non conveniens doctrine in a rather liberal manner when such PT-related civil litigation found its way to an Israeli court. What is interesting about this trend was the ease with which the Israeli courts aligned themselves with this IDF military government policy. Consider once again Justice Strassburg-Cohen's holding in *Abu Attiya*, where she spoke about how

> ...the Israeli legislature made it explicit that residents of the Region, who are not Israeli citizens and whose relation under all circumstances is to the law applicable in the Region and to the court there, are to be judged in the courts there and according to the applicable law there.[172]

This Israeli legislature Justice Strassburg-Cohen that refers to is not the Israeli Knesset, who in fact enacted no law to this effect. What she identifies as the Israeli legislature is the IDF military commander, which indeed maintained the operation of the local PT legal system, including the judiciary.

Yet when Palestinian plaintiffs came before Israeli courts and tried to prevent the case from being referred back to the inadequate PT courts, the sentiment, as became apparent in *Abu Jahla*, was one of distancing the Israeli establishment from the PT. If PT courts are inefficient, it is not "us" Israelis to blame but "you," the Palestinians. What emerges is a Janus-headed Israeli policy: regarding issues of control and dictating policy—the PT are drawn closer to Israeli establishment and dictates; yet in the context of the burden of handling the local population and of political unrest, the PT become less Israeli and more Palestinian.

Question 2: The PT Forum: Is it just one step away but a whole standard apart?

The Israeli forum non conveniens decisions in PT-related civil litigation were not singled out as dealing with a special legal situation, but rather were cited and

---

171 *See Jabbour*, PM 5743(1) at 505.

172 *Abu Attiya*, 39(1) PD at 382.

followed when courts were asked to stay Israeli proceedings in favor of foreign forums generally.[173] This was the case until the Israeli Supreme Court decided to change course and refashion the standard for staying actions under the forum non conveniens doctrine, in *Ha-Geves A. Sinai Ltd. v. The Lockformer Co.*[174] The underlying dispute was between a corporate Israeli plaintiff, Ha-Geves, who ordered a sophisticated and expensive manufacturing machine for its factory in Israel from an American corporation, The Lockformer, which works out of Illinois. The negotiations between the parties all took place in the United States and upon agreement, representatives of Ha-Geves traveled to Illinois in order to sign the contract. Interestingly, the contract had a choice of law clause in favor of the laws of the state of Illinois as governing, but no choice of forum clause. When the machine arrived in Israel, Ha-Geves found that it did not meet the specifications of the agreement. Eventually, Ha-Geves filed an action against The Lockformer before an Israeli court. The Lockformer argued that the Israeli forum is not the proper forum for litigation and therefore the action should be dismissed. The Israeli Supreme Court disagreed. One main reason why the Court found the Israeli forum to be proper for adjudication involved contemporary advancement in the sphere of communications and transportations, which the Court said made the defendant's argument about the difficulties of litigating a case in a faraway forum less credible and less convincing. In the Court's own words:

> In the past, the hardships endured by the defendants, who needed to litigate a case before a foreign forum, were many and genuine. These were caused by difficulties in communication and their high cost. In our era of jet airplanes, cellular phones, the facsimile and the Internet, these hardships have lost much of their meaning. The whole world is becoming "one big village" in which the distance between two different locations does not have the same meaning it used to have before. Therefore, one should not exaggerate in weighing the difficulties associated with the need of the defendant and his witnesses to come to another country, and from this it is also necessary to conclude that the willingness to accept a forum non conveniens motion will diminish in time.[175]

173 *See, e.g.*, CA 45/90 Abbada v. Abbada, 48(2) PD 77 (1994).

174 CA 2705/97, 52(1) PD 109 (1998).

175 *Id.* at 114.

Ha-Geves has had a substantial impact on the application of the forum non conveniens doctrine in Israel.[176] Elsewhere, I have attempted to show that the deduction the Court makes in *Ha-Geves* from advancements in modern transportation and communications to the standard of the forum non conveniens doctrine is methodologically faulty and represents poor legal policy design.[177] First, the very same reasons mentioned by the Court could equally be used to argue that a plaintiff today can more conveniently engage in forum shopping than ever before, given the possibilities afforded by modern means of communication and transportation to undertake and manage litigation in a distant forum. Second, today it is easier for the plaintiff to establish personal jurisdiction in a fortuitous nexus. The required jurisdictional contact still largely hinges on a territorial relation with the forum, but increasingly, this contact is shown as weak and attenuated precisely because of modern means of communications and transportation. For example, is the forum where a computer server is located most relevant to the contractual relationship concluded by an exchange of emails facilitated by that particular server, if and when the "place" of contracting is considered to be an appropriate nexus for establishing personal jurisdiction?

So in essence, the limitation of the forum non conveniens doctrine in the modern age is a recipe for more forum shopping and a larger volume of cases where personal jurisdiction can be accidentally established.[178] But more importantly for our discussion, the course taken in *Ha-Geves* is remarkable given the geographical context in which Israeli courts developed their elastic and liberal standard of the forum non conveniens doctrine to begin with—PT-related civil actions among Palestinian litigants who lived at most only tens of kilometers away from the Israeli forum. Needless to say that in such a setting, modest rather than modern means of transportation and communication would suffice to make litigation before an Israeli forum conveniently possible. In fact, in the *Abu Jahla* case, the defendant, JDEC, held its headquarters in East Jerusalem, just a few blocks away from the Jerusalem courthouse where the action was originally filed. As shown earlier, this did not prevent the Israeli Supreme Court

---

176 For decisions applying *Ha-Geves, see, e.g.*, LCA 2903/96 Masika v. Dolens, 52(1) PD 817, 821 (1998); LCA 2736/98 Habboub Bros. Co. v. Nike International Ltd., 54(1) PD 614, 621 (2000); LCA 9141/00 Lang v. Marx, 56(1) PD 118, 123 (2001); LCA 749/05 Insight Venture Partners IV L.P. v. Techno Hold Ekhad Ltd. (Apr. 11, 2005), Nevo Legal Database (by subscription); LCA 4501/05 Deluxe Laboratories Inc. v. De Luxe Hollywood/Israel Film and Video Processing Ltd. (Oct. 10, 2005), Nevo Legal Database (by subscription).

177 *See* KARAYANNI, *supra* note 122, at 103–08.

178 *Id.* at 153–54.

from staying the proceedings on forum non conveniens grounds. In fact, the case served to allow the court to make the forum non conveniens doctrine even more elastic and considerate of the normative interests of both Israel and the PT.

Comparing the development in *Ha-Geves* with that in *Abu Jahla* makes it rather obvious that the forum non conveniens doctrine practiced in Israel is now based on a dual standard: a liberal standard ready to consider alternatives when the context of litigation is PT-related; and a restrictive standard allowing a forum non conveniens stay only in limited circumstances in non-PT-related international civil litigation. From the forum shopping perspective, such a dual standard can be regarded as somewhat creative. If forum shopping is particularly attractive in one context, as in the case of PT-related civil actions in Israeli courts, then the forum non conveniens standard can be adjusted in order to filter incoming litigation more rigorously, and the liberal standard makes such an adjustment possible. When forum shopping is not a plausible alternative, however, then courts can afford to maintain a more restrictive standard. This normative ontology is not at all foreign to the doctrine of forum non conveniens. It resembles to a great extent the position taken by the US Supreme Court in *Piper Aircraft Co. v. Reyno*,[179] which pronounced that a foreign plaintiff's recourse to an American court deserves less deference than would the recourse of an American plaintiff.[180] For an underlying presumption exists that in the case of a foreign plaintiff, it is more likely that filing the action in an American court can turn out to be a case of forum shopping than in the case of a domestic plaintiff.[181] However, the dual standard developed in Israel seems to take this notion of *Piper Aircraft* one step further by distinguishing between foreign plaintiffs from one group of countries relative to which the Israeli forum is regarded as particularly attractive, and plaintiffs from another group of countries relative to which the Israeli forum is not particularly attractive. If this assessment is correct, I gather that Israeli courts will need to face the argument raised against the *Piper Aircraft* holding, primarily the argument that by limiting access of foreign plaintiffs to American courts, American courts are turning their backs on actions conducted by American corporations or their subsidiaries

179 454 U.S. 235 (1981).

180 *Id.* at 266 ("When the home forum has been chosen, it is reasonable to assume that this choice is convenient. When the plaintiff is foreign, however, this assumption is much less reasonable. Because the central purpose of any forum non conveniens inquiry is to ensure that the trial is convenient, a foreign plaintiff's choice deserves less deference.").

181 *See* Laurel E. Miller, Comment, *Forum Non Conveniens and State Control of Foreign Plaintiff Access to U.S. Courts in International Tort Actions*, 58 U. CHI. L. REV. 1369 (1991).

outside the United States.[182] And in the context of relations between Israel and the PT, such an argument becomes particularly forceful in light of the fact that the IDF controls the PT's government, which further implicates Israeli responsibility for jurisdiction over the PT. For if local Palestinian plaintiffs are relentlessly "forum shopping" in Israeli courts in their efforts to have their civil actions adjudicated, this no doubt also stems from the fact that local courts, which are under direct control of the IDF, do not have much to offer. However, as the status of the PT has changed in the aftermath of the Oslo Accords, it is possible that this duality in the standard of the forum non conveniens doctrine will not be further scrutinized or refined.

3. Stage Three: Personal Jurisdiction according to the Oslo Peace Accords and beyond

a. The Interim Agreement on Personal Jurisdiction

The most relevant document of the Oslo Accords on adjudicative jurisdiction in civil actions, as well as for many other matters dealing with institutional interactions between Israel and the PA, is the Interim Agreement signed in 1995. The Protocol Concerning Legal Matters contained in Annex IV, Article III of the Interim Agreement contains a whole section dedicated to the issue of "Civil Jurisdiction." However, this article is blatantly one-sided. It only deals with the civil jurisdiction of PA courts when an Israeli is a party to the pending litigation. Regarding such circumstances, Annex IV, Article III of the Interim Agreement is valid when: (1) the subject matter of litigation is an "ongoing Israeli business situated in the Territory"; (2) the claim regards "real property located in the Territory"; or (3) the Israeli party has consented in writing to the jurisdiction of the PA court. Apparently, the common thread in all three circumstances is to guarantee that the Israeli party has in one way or another anticipated the actual litigation before the PA court.

What then governs the personal jurisdiction of Israeli courts when a Palestinian is a party? One might think that nothing has changed and that the *Al-Khir* holding by which personal jurisdiction on every one present in the PT is still the law, given the simple fact that the rules on which this holding is based, i.e., SDAT, 1969, have not been abolished but continue to be in effect. One might further assume that notwithstanding all the developments of the Oslo Peace Accords

182 *See* Stephen L. Cummings, *International Mass Tort Litigation:* Forum Non Conveniens *and the Adequate Alternative Forum in Light of the Bhopal Disaster*, 16 Ga. J. Int'l & Comp. L. 109 (1986).

and the establishment of the PA, the West Bank and the Gaza Strip could still be regarded as a "Region" within the meaning of these rules. Despite the establishment of the PA, still one can reasonably argue that Israel, or rather the IDF, significantly controls movement into and from these regions, and therefore they are to be regarded as controlled by the IDF and thus a "Region" within the meaning of SDAT, 1969. However, this rendering is doubtful at least as far as Areas A and B of the West Bank and the Gaza Strip are concerned. The only part of the West Bank that can still be regarded as a "Region" for *Al-Khir* purposes is Area C. Hence, if at all, SDAT, 1969 will still apply only to Area C of the West Bank. I note this in light of two major Israeli enactments that came about as a result of the Interim Agreement, which established a new definition for the term "Region" and more importantly, provided some special procedures on judicial assistance between Israel and the PA that explicitly excluded the applicability of SDAT, 1969 and resultantly also the *Al-Khir* holding. In the following section, I will examine these new enactments and assess the present state of Israeli personal jurisdiction authority in respect to Palestinian litigants.

b. Service of Process in the PT in the Wake of the Interim Agreement

The Interim Agreement imposes an equal obligation on the Israeli and Palestinian sides for mutual cooperation regarding the service of official court documents. Annex IV, Article IV, which deals with the service of documents, provides that "Israel and the Council [i.e. the PA] will be responsible for the service of legal documents including subpoenas, issued by the judicial organs under the responsibility of the other state." Accordingly, service of process to a Palestinian defendant in an action brought before an Israeli court now falls under the responsibility of the PA. Yet this accord did not suffice for the purpose of making this norm part of Israeli municipal law. In Israel, special legislation needs to be enacted in order for an international treaty that was signed and ratified by the Israeli government to become part of Israeli law.[183] Such special legislation was enacted in 1996, in the form of an amendment to an existing law, and was called the Law for the Extension of Emergency Regulations (Judea and Samaria—Jurisdiction over Criminal Offences and Legal Assistance), 1967 (LEER, 1996).[184] This law

183 *See* HCJ 2717/96 Ali v. Minister of Defense, 50(2) PD 848, 851–52 (1996).

184 The law was originally titled, in a translation authorized by the Israeli Ministry of Justice, Emergency Regulations (Offences Committed in Israel-Held Areas—Jurisdiction and Legal Assistance) (Extension of Validity) Law, 5728-1967, 22 LSI 20 (1967–68). The relevant 1996 amendments were published in SH No. 1556, 34 (1996).

provided a new definition of the term "Region," which explicitly excluded those areas of "Judea and Samaria and the Gaza Strip" that are under the jurisdiction of the PA.[185] Accordingly, one can argue that in light of this new definition, the areas of the PT that are controlled by the PA—Areas A and B of the West Bank and the Gaza Strip—should no longer be regarded as a "Region" also for the purpose of SDAT, 1969 and the *Al-Khir* holding.

Another enactment that substantiates this conclusion is a special set of rules enacted by the Israeli Minister of Justice that provided the actual mechanism for judicial assistance between Israel and the PA. Pursuant to a special authorization in LEER, 1996,[186] the Israeli Minister of Justice enacted a set of regulations outlining the procedures for Israeli-Palestinian mutual judicial assistance. These regulations were laid out in the Emergency Order (Judea and Samaria and the Gaza Strip—Jurisdiction over Criminal Offences and Legal Assistance) (the Territories of the Palestinian Council—Judicial Assistance in Civil Matters), 1999 ("1999 Emergency Order").[187] According to the elaborate mechanism set out in Section 3 of these regulations, when service of official court documents is needed in the PA territories, these documents are to be handed to the Israeli Judicial Assistance Officer, who will deliver them to his Palestinian counterpart, who in turn will make the actual service in the PA. This same Section 3 then makes it clear that when service of process is conducted according to the mechanism of judicial assistance provided therein, SDAT, 1969 becomes inapplicable.

Interestingly, this exclusion of SDAT, 1969 creates some confusion. Supposedly, it can be taken as supporting the assertion made earlier that all of the West Bank and the Gaza Strip should be considered as a "Region" even under SDAT, 1969 for the following reason: if according to the primary legislation by virtue of which this 1999 Emergency Order was enacted, those sections of the PT that are controlled by the PA are no longer regarded as a "Region," then why was it necessary to make the extra effort and exclude the application of SDAT, 1969? Logically, one need not exclude the application of an enactment when that enactment is no longer applicable. So this very exclusion, therefore, lends support to the original proposition that the West Bank and the Gaza Strip should still be regarded as "Regions," at least for the specific purpose of service of process.

185 LEER, 1996, Section 1.

186 *Id.* Section 7.

187 KT 5947, 278.

Notwithstanding this, it would be hard to maintain that those sections of the PT that are controlled by the PA are to be regarded as a "Region". LEER, 1996 is the primary legislation, and what emanates from it explicitly regarding which parts of the PT are still to be regarded as a "Region" must override an implicit conclusion of secondary legislation, i.e., the 1999 Emergency Order. Additionally, it is reasonable to assume that the free and direct mode of service in the PT as provided for by SDAT, 1969 was authorized given the control that Israel had through the IDF over all spheres of life—including the civil, judicial, and administrative elements—and not necessarily just the movement into and from these regions. As a result of the Oslo Accords, Israel has given up such total control with the clear intention of passing civil responsibilities to the PA, at least in Areas B and A, as well as in the Gaza Strip. So what counts is not whether the IDF controls the PT from beyond, but rather the fact that it has stopped controlling the PT (at least in the areas mentioned) from within. Indeed, lower courts in Israel have already held that neither Area A[188] nor Area B[189] is to be considered today as a "Region" under SDAT, 1969.

To conclude this discussion, one can say that the PT areas that in the wake of the Oslo Accords came under the control of the PA should no longer be considered as a "Region" under SDAT, 1969 and therefore are not subject to the *Al-Khir* holding. The only part of the PT that is still to be considered as a "Region" and thus subject to SDAT, 1969 and the *Al-Khir* holding is Area C, which as indicated earlier is still fully controlled by the IDF.[190] This in turn leaves open the question about the nature and reach of Israel's personal jurisdiction capacity regarding Palestinian litigants. So far, we know what does not apply but still not much about what does.

Before I provide an evaluation in this regard, I would like to note one strange anomaly that resulted from the existing rules regarding Area C. As just discussed, SDAT, 1969 and the *Al-Khir* holding are still binding in this part of the West Bank. In order to fulfill the instructions of SDAT, 1969, documents served in accordance must be translated into Arabic. This provision was a natural one back in 1969, since these rules were intended to apply to the Palestinian Arabic-speaking

188 CC (Jer. Magistrate Ct.) 1558/98 Shaheen v. The National Insurance Co., Ramallah (Aug. 1, 1999), Nevo Legal Database (by subscription).

189 MPC (Jer. Magistrate Ct.) 1421/01 Abd El-Hamid v. Far'un (June 24, 2001), Nevo Legal Database (by subscription).

190 *See* MPC (Jer. Regional Lab. Ct.) 2061/00 Shirlin v. Youssef (Apr. 28, 2003), Nevo Legal Database (by subscription) (recognizing the effect of establishing personal jurisdiction when service of process was effectuated under the SDAT, 1969 on a defendant resident in Ma'aleh Adumim—an Israeli settlement east of Jerusalem, located in Area C).

population of the West Bank. But as noted in Chapter One, Area C—the largest of all West Bank Areas—is mostly populated by Israeli settlers. So as things stand today, it will be necessary to translate all documents served to these settlers into Arabic, even when litigation only involves the settlers themselves!

c. Two Approaches to the Governing Rules of Personal Jurisdiction

So if SDAT, 1969 no longer governs regarding PA-held territories and the 1999 Emergency Order does, then what does this mean regarding the body of norms that governs personal jurisdiction in PT-related civil disputes, especially when the defendant is a Palestinian resident of the PT? There are two legal outlooks in this respect. The first regards the 1999 Emergency Order as only a mechanism for judicial assistance. Accordingly, personal jurisdiction against Palestinian defendants present in PA-controlled territories will need to be established according to the rules of service out of jurisdiction relevant for defendants present in foreign countries, as set forth in RCP, 1984, Rule 500. The second approach deems the 1999 Emergency Order as offering the exclusive mechanism for service of process in PA-held territories, making it unnecessary to resort to any special procedure for service of process outside the jurisdiction. According to this view, the 1999 Emergency Order simply replaced SDAT, 1969.

The first approach is represented by the District Court of Haifa's decision in *Makhoul v. The Arab Bank.*[191] The plaintiff, a citizen and resident of Israel, filed this action before the Haifa court, seeking recovery of the current value of 1,000 Palestinian pounds deposited in 1947 in the Arab Bank's branch office in Jaffa. The plaintiff based his claim on being the heir of an intestate (his father-in-law), who originally deposited the sum, and asked the court to have the claim certified as a class action, supposedly in an effort to bind the defendant bank by the prospective judgment in future similar adjudications. The defendant bank was established in Mandatory Palestine back in 1930, and after 1948 relocated its activities to Jordan. The plaintiff tried to claim the sum on three different occasions in the 1950s and 1960s, but to no avail. The bank argued that in accordance with the instructions of the Jordanian government, it froze all assets belonging to residents and citizens of Israel, then an enemy state. After the creation of the PA, the Arab Bank established a number of branches in the PT, including in Ramallah,

191 MPC (Hi) 3475/00, PM 5770(1) 913 (2001).

which, according to the claim made by the plaintiff, received all of the original deposits and documents of the Jaffa branch. In filing the claim, the plaintiff was all the more confident about his chances of recovering the money, given that by then Israel and Jordan had signed a peace treaty ending the state of hostility that existed between them.[192]

However, despite repeated attempts, the plaintiff failed to establish personal jurisdiction against the bank. At first, his attorney had an intern from his office personally effectuate service on the Ramallah branch. The intern served the documents to the bank guard. On advice of the bank's attorney, the documents were returned to the plaintiff's attorney by registered mail. Then the documents were sent to the Israeli Judicial Assistance Officer acting on the authority of the 1999 Emergency Order. For reasons that remain unclear from the decision, the Israeli Judicial Assistance Officer, instead of having the documents sent to his Palestinian counterpart who then was supposed to have the documents served on the defendant bank, had the documents sent by mail to the bank branch in Ramallah. Shortly afterwards, the envelope was returned to the Israeli officer, stamped "addressee rejected delivery."

The case presented the court with two important questions as to the rules now governing personal jurisdiction of Israeli courts towards PT-based defendants: (1) is service of process in a PA-held territory sufficient to establish personal jurisdiction in absence of the plaintiff having first secured leave of the court seized with the action? And (2) can the Israeli Judicial Assistance Officer effectuate service of process in a manner that does not coincide with the framework established in the 1999 Emergency Order? The court answered both of these questions in the negative.

On the first question, the court held that since service was effectuated in this case outside of Israel, it was necessary to obtain a leave of court according to RCP, 1984, Rule 500. The court went on to add that service of process outside the jurisdiction is not merely a technical issue, but rather a substantive one, and in granting the leave the court is supposed to be sensitive to values pertaining to the sovereignty of foreign courts and comity.[193] In this context, the court attached

192 Treaty of Peace Between the State of Israel and the Hashemite Kingdom of Jordan, Oct. 26, 1994, Isr.-Jordan, 34 I.L.M. 43 (1995).

193 *Makhoul*, PM 5770(1) at 916–17.

particular importance to the fact that the Arab Bank's headquarters are based in Amman, Jordan.[194]

Turning to the second question regarding the applicability of the 1999 Emergency Order, the court stated that the existence of this order did not obviate the need to obtain a leave of court in accordance with RCP, 1984, Rule 500.[195] In any case, in the court's perspective, the provisions of the 1999 Order itself were not implemented. As mentioned before, the Israeli Judicial Assistance Officer sent the statement of claim directly to the defendant bank instead of first sending it to his Palestinian counterpart.[196] Ultimately, since leave for service outside of jurisdiction was not requested, and since service was not carried out in accordance with the 1999 Emergency Order—conditions that the court regarded as supplementary and cumulative—the court deemed itself as lacking personal jurisdiction to deal with the action.[197]

The position taken by the District Court of Haifa is a genuine leap forward in the ontology of Israeli personal jurisdiction doctrine regarding the PT. For the purpose of personal jurisdiction, the PA was now treated on par with independent sovereign states, and its courts were considered worthy of deference and comity—notions commonly reserved for courts of foreign states. Moreover, the decision suggests that the PA deserves an even more robust form of reverence compared to other foreign states, since effectuating service to PA-governed territories requires use of the judicial assistance channel as prescribed in the Emergency 1999 Order. Such a restriction does not exist in Israeli law regarding service in any other foreign jurisdiction.

The second approach is that represented by the Israeli National Labor Court's judgment in *Mahajneh v. Amutat Merkaz Ha-Demokratiya ve-Zekhuyott ha-Ovdim*.[198] The plaintiff was an Israeli lawyer who was employed by the defendant, a Ramallah-based organization that offers legal services in the domain of human rights and employment entitlements. The parties signed a contract written in Arabic in Ramallah that detailed the terms and conditions of employment. After two years, a dispute erupted between the parties concerning the plaintiff's

194 *Id.* at 917.

195 *Id.*

196 *Id.*

197 *Id.* at 918.

198 LabApp 723/07 (July 6, 2009), Nevo Legal Database (by subscription).

own entitlements under the contract. Eventually, the defendant terminated the employment relation, and the plaintiff sought compensation by filing this action with an Israeli district labor court. This court dismissed the action, based on the forum non conveniens doctrine. On appeal to the National Labor Court, this judgment was reversed. What is interesting about the National Labor Court's holding is the court's rather expansive discussion of the personal jurisdiction rules that now govern when an action is brought against a PA-based entity such as the defendant in this case. The court held that the 1999 Emergency Order, with its special procedure for service of process, is operative without any need to first obtain a leave for service outside of the jurisdiction according to RCP, 1984, Rule 500. The court takes this position based on an explicit provision in the 1999 Emergency Order providing that when service is performed according to this order, the ordinary rules for service of process in RCP, 1984—including Rule 500—are inapplicable.[199] In light of this decision, the *Makhoul* holding is clearly erroneous, as it misread the 1999 Emergency Order. I will discuss later whether the spirit that motivated this holding in *Makhoul* is also mistaken.

Another interesting facet of the *Mahajneh* decision is the court's reference to a major amendment made to the 1999 Emergency Order adding alternative methods for service of process in the PA. The *Al-Aqsa Intifada* that erupted in September of 2000 led to the deterioration of relations between Israel and the PA, including in the sphere of judicial assistance.[200] Resultantly, an amendment was made to the 1999 Emergency Order in 2004, authorizing the Israeli Judicial Assistance Officer to allow for substitute service when service is deemed unavailable through the ordinary channel—that is, through the Palestinian Judicial Assistance Officer. Such alternative means include direct service through a person specifically authorized to effectuate service by registered mail, by facsimile or even by publication in a local Arabic newspaper that is widely circulated in the PT.

Despite this extremely accommodating mechanism that was now installed in the 1999 Emergency Order, the plaintiff in *Mahajneh* was unsuccessful in proving adequate service, since he did not first seek the authorization of the Israeli Judicial Assistance Officer before placing the claim document at the door of the defendant's offices in Ramallah. Ultimately, however, the court concluded that it had sufficient personal jurisdiction over the defendant, since the lawyer representing

199 *Id.* para. 13.

200 MPC (TA) 3069/03 Merck Frosst Canada & Co. v. Birzeit Palestinian Pharmaceutical Company (Apr. 29, 2003), Nevo Legal Database (by subscription).

it in the proceeding made an unconditional appearance and even filed a motion, which indicated voluntary submission to the court's jurisdiction.

The decisions of other courts in Israel that dealt with this same question reveal that the course taken by the *Mahajneh* decision predominates.[201] The end result under this second approach is really not different from that under the *Al-Khir* decision and its progeny. As before the Oslo Peace Accords, service of process in PA-held territories can be conducted without the need to obtain any special leave, and given the current state of relations between Israel and the PA, service can be as simple as a facsimile transmission. The only difference is that this alternative method needs to be approved by the Israeli Judicial Assistance Officer. Since the 1999 Emergency Order, this approval is not contingent on a finding that there is any meaningful contact between the State of Israel and the underlying controversy, but rather on the premise that effectuating service through the usual channel of cooperation—which is itself unconditioned on the finding of any such connection—is impossible. Effectively, this means that in principle, Israeli courts' general personal jurisdiction authority over whoever is present in the PT has not changed since the *Al-Khir* holding, and this wide form of jurisdictional authority is still applicable despite the Oslo Accords. The only change is the mode in which actual service is to be effectuated. Whereas before, service could have been conducted directly by the plaintiff, now it must take place through the office of the Israeli Judicial Assistance Officer (who is also free to authorize a direct method of service).

d. The Discretion to Stay PT-Related Civil Actions

Another issue regarding the Israeli doctrine of personal jurisdiction in PT-related civil actions concerns the power of Israeli courts to decline jurisdiction in such actions. Unlike the subject of establishing personal jurisdiction, the Israeli enactments implementing the Interim Agreement directly address this issue. Section 2B(a) of the LEER, 1996 states as a general rule that an Israeli court may not abstain from exercising its duly acquired jurisdiction over a civil matter brought by an Israeli when the cause of action is based on an act or an omission committed in the PT under the jurisdiction of the PA solely on the grounds that an

201 *See, e.g.*, LA (Jer) 3384/07 Ha-Le'umit—Insurance Co. v. Hamdan (Jan. 21, 2008), Nevo Legal Database (by subscription); CC (Jer) 3913/00 Ararat Insurance Co. Ltd. v. Abed (Apr. 9, 2001), Nevo Legal Database (by subscription); MPC (Jer. Magistrate Ct.) 5074/06 National Insurance Company v. Abu Shihadeh (Sept. 26, 2006), Nevo Legal Database (by subscription); MPC (Jer. Magistrate Ct.) 1421/01 *Abd El-Hamid*, Nevo Legal Database (by subscription).

PT resident is the defendant or party to the action. This provision is unusual. Instead of first providing when it would be appropriate for an Israeli court to decline jurisdiction over PT-related civil actions, it regulates instances in which the Israeli court is expected not to decline its jurisdictional powers. Such a mode of regulation strongly implies that in PT-based actions filed by an Israeli against a Palestinian, the Israeli court is expected to deal with the action rather than to decline jurisdiction. This implication becomes stronger in light of the fact that Section 2B(b) of the same enactment specifies those instances where the court, in spite of the foregoing, can decide to decline its jurisdictional powers. This can happen when one of the following circumstance is present: (1) the action's subject involves the ongoing business of an Israeli in the PA; (2) the action's subject is land situated in the PA; (3) the action's subject is a contract that includes a forum selection clause in favor of a jurisdiction outside of Israel; or (4) a pending action exists elsewhere between the parties.

Such provisions, especially when considered in light of the one-sided focus of the Interim Agreement on limiting and restricting the power of Palestinian courts to litigate actions in which Israelis are parties, are clear manifestations of Israel's strong mistrust towards the Palestinian Judiciary. The provisions have been designed in particular to accommodate cases in which the civil action implicates Israeli interests and to preempt the option that an Israeli party will face litigation in a Palestinian court.

e. Evaluation of the Third Stage

Question 1: Why is the the Interim Agreement one-sided?

The overall design of personal jurisdiction under the Interim Agreement and the Israeli enactments that were made to enforce it beg investigation into the reasons behind such one-sidedness.[202] No doubt, this outcome is to be partially attributed to poor negotiation skills on the part of the Palestinian delegation.[203] Likely, however, it also involved the working assumption of the Oslo Peace Accords, acquiesced to by the Palestinian side, that the established Palestinian entity is to only have such jurisdictional authority as is delegated to it by the Israeli side.[204]

202 Raja Shehadeh, *Can the Declaration of Principles Bring About a "Just and Lasting Peace?,"* 4 EUR. J. INT'L L. 555, 558 (1993) [hereinafter Shehadeh, *Declaration of Principles*].

203 *See* RAJA SHEHADEH, FROM OCCUPATION TO INTERIM ACCORDS: ISRAEL AND THE PALESTINIAN TERRITORIES 29, 30, 71, 72 (1997).

204 Raja Shehadeh, *Questions of Jurisdiction: A Legal Analysis of the Gaza-Jericho Agreement*, 23 J. PALESTINE STUD. 18, 22–23 (1994).

When such authority is not transferred, residual power is to lie in the hands of the IDF;[205] this is the "delegation paradigm." The rationale of this paradigm involves the status of authority in the PT prior to the agreements. Since such authority was fully within the hands of Israeli organs, any change thus necessitated the transfer of such authority from the Israeli side to the Palestinian side. In such a setting, specific arrangements are bound to be unbalanced and one-sided, for the underlying assumption is unbalanced where one side is taken to possess the "whole" and the other side is to possess only what is given.[206]

The breakdown of the Oslo Peace Process and its fitful revival provided food for thought. It might be helpful to realize that in the interest of establishing a lasting future settlement, the aim should not necessarily be to maximize to the utmost whatever negotiation power and legal paradigms each party can marshal, but rather to reach an arrangement that could qualify as balanced and just. For if negotiations are designed to produce a sustainable relationship under which the other side is expected to act as an equal, it is reasonably likely that this side is to be treated from the start as an equal.

Question 2: What is the exact nature of the Palestinian Authority?

As already alluded to in the introductory remarks to this chapter, the rules governing service of process under traditional common law are a function of the power of sovereign power over the defendant's person. If the defendant is present on the sovereign territory of the forum state then service can be direct and unmediated by any other connection with the underlying dispute. If the defendant is absent, however, and present in some foreign jurisdiction, then a court-mediated approach needs to take place guaranteeing some kind of a meaningful nexus with the controversy that makes litigation before the local forum reasonable. Comity

205 Shehadeh, *Declaration of Principles, supra* note 202, at 558.

206 This also explains why it was agreed to maintain the existing legal system in both the West Bank and the Gaza Strip even after areas in both places were transferred to the PA. In practice, this implied the existence of a formal obligation on the part of the PA to implement existing military order in the laws of the West Bank and Gaza Strip, as well as to maintain two separate legal systems in these two jurisdictions. This latter point is a consequence of the historical fact that when Israel occupied the West Bank in 1967, the law there already included a substantial amount of Jordanian law, whereas the law of the Gaza Strip, which was never under Jordanian rule, simply remained dependent on British Mandatory law. *See* Celia Wasserstein Fassberg, *Israel and the Palestinian Authority: Jurisdiction and Legal Assistance*, 28 ISR. L. REV. 318, 320 n.8 (1994); Keith C. Molkner, *Legal and Structural Hurdles to Achieving Political Stability and Economic Development in the Palestinian Territories*, 19 FORDHAM INT'L L.J. 1419, 1429–31 (1996); Bisharat, *supra* note 108, at 263.

concerns are also involved here—making defendants present in a foreign country answerable to a local litigation was deemed infringement on the foreign state considered to have exclusive control over the defendant's person. An appraisal of the dominant approach represented by the *Mahajneh* decision deems that following the Oslo Peace Accord, the PA's status was no different than it was earlier, when the PT was under total occupation of the IDF. The 1999 Emergency Order—like SDAT, 1969—makes personal jurisdiction over a defendant present in PA territory possible irrespective of whether the underlying controversy has any connection to Israel. Indeed, the Israeli Judicial Assistance Officer simply has to deem cooperation with the Palestinian counterpart as ineffective, as indeed it is today, and then authorize a substitute mode of service—which seems to be a matter of course. By this process, no special comity considerations are accorded to the PA. A defendant present there is not much different from a defendant present in Israel.

Hence, the *Makhoul* holding that represented the initial approach is particularly interesting. Although the holding itself is obviously erroneous, it still embodies a spirit of unusual accommodation toward the PA. Although Israel did not (and in fact still does not) recognize the PA as an independent state, the court nonetheless was willing to treat it as such. Service of process in PA territory was subject to RCP, 1984, Rule 500, which requires the operation of a rather complex mechanism designed to guarantee a reasonable connection between the dispute or the defendant and the State of Israel, cognizant of comity considerations regarding the foreign jurisdiction. I emphasize this position because, if embraced by other governmental bodies, it might very well point the way to some kind of peaceful coexistence. In the fragile and delicate relationship between Israel and the PA, it seems advisable for the courts of one side to take extra precautions in the application of legal doctrine that courts of other jurisdictions are not prepared to apply. In other words, in the context of the conflicting entities that seemingly conduct their actions as two international entities, there might be special value in having the courts of one side accord the courts of the other side special considerations of comity. Such a stance will create a proper legal environment that will undoubtedly help to stabilize the overall relationship.

D. The Evolution of Personal Jurisdiction Doctrine in Context

Examination of the different development stages of the personal jurisdiction doctrine as applied by Israeli courts towards the PT reveals a close connection between these different stages and the basic policies of the State of Israel toward the PT. When Israel first sought full territorial control over the PT, its personal jurisdiction doctrine was expansionist and regarded the PT as part of Israel; any person present in the PT was no different from anyone present on Israeli sovereign territory. To the extent that the latter could be brought under an Israeli court's jurisdictional authority, so could the former. Israel's consolidation of control over the PT, which meant total dominance of life and government in the PT, involved also the Israeli courts' articulation of their personal jurisdiction authority over the PT. When Israel began to realize the burden of ruling the PT—at least regarding the indigenous Palestinian population—the personal jurisdiction doctrine produced an elastic form of the forum non conveniens doctrine in order to relieve Israeli courts from PT-related civil litigation. On first impression, the doctrine's application regarding the PT seems to be odd. If Israeli courts realized that PT-related civil litigation was particularly burdensome, then why not simply do away with the rules that formed its proximate cause: SDAT, 1969 and the *Al-Khir* holding? Yet on further reflection, nothing would have served better Israel's interests than an elastic forum non conveniens doctrine. By the early 1980s when the doctrine was reformulated, a considerable presence of Israeli settlers existed in the PT. Israel's interest regarding which courts should resolve disputes among this population or in actions implicating any of them, as well as the interest of the settler population itself, was to stream such litigation to an Israeli forum. The only population in the PT that was supposed to be governed by local PT courts and local PT law was the Palestinian one. This separate status conformed with the general policy of the civil *millet* system where by the local Palestinian population was subject to one legal system and the Israeli settler population was subject to another, i.e., Israeli law.[207] As Ghada Talhami observed, Israeli sovereignty moved wherever Israelis moved, "and the land was virtually annexed to Israel but without the Arabs living in those areas."[208] When there was a mixed Israeli-Palestinian dispute, Israeli interests dominated and all doctrines were constructed so as to offer unhindered access to the Israeli forum. The policy that best comports with this general design is to keep SDAT, 1969 and *Al-Khir* in place, thereby guaranteeing personal jurisdiction over all those present in the PT, in addition to an elastic forum non conveniens doctrine that will keep PT-related litigation among Palestinians out. Rejecting jurisdiction of all PT-related civil litigation was not an option, but neither was accepting jurisdiction over all such litigation.

---

207 For more on the *millet* system, *see infra* Chapter Three.

208 Ghada Talhami, *The Palestinian Perception of the Human Rights Issue*, 13 Syracuse J. Int'l L.& Com. 475, 486 (1987).

The establishment of the PA, marking the third stage, was also accommodated by a personal jurisdiction doctrine suited to Israel's control policy. When determining whether under the Oslo Accords any significant change has emerged in the prevailing doctrine, one court took the bold step and answered this question in the affirmative—at least for litigation related to PA-controlled areas (Areas A and B). According to this initial stand, courts treated the PA as a foreign sovereign state, although it had not attained this status—certainly not as far as Israel was concerned. While the court's analysis was wrong as far as the black letter of the law was concerned, it was obviously motivated by the spirit of the evolving and fragile peace process. When this process was in total collapse and cooperation between Israel and the PA failed, Israel strived once again to take control over the PA. Ultimately, therefore, the personal jurisdiction doctrine adapted provides Israeli courts with the same power they had during the era of the *Al-Khir* holding.

Given that Israeli personal jurisdiction doctrine towards the PT is still largely based on this notion of control, it also strongly resembles the traditional notion of territorial sovereignty as a guiding principle. A sovereign's control over a territory—even if that forum's sovereignty does not extend over that territory—is what makes the exertion of judicial power legitimate.

However, there seems to be a deeper principle at play regarding the personal jurisdiction doctrine as it developed beyond the existential stage of deciding whether the authority to adjudicate exists or not and when examined from a perspective including the discretional power to decline jurisdiction under the forum non conveniens doctrine as well. Such examination implicates the principle of "jurisdictional politics."[209] Under this framework, jurisdictional powers come to reproduce the existing political boundaries—in this context those between Israel and the PT, and between Israelis and Palestinians. Since the conventions required that the two groups be separated by status and norms, even though both are ultimately controlled by the same sovereign power, Israeli courts went along with these conventions and designed their jurisdictional rules accordingly. The courts hence established an all-encompassing jurisdictional authority for Israel, which suits Israel's institutional political interests but in practice differentiates (according to the same interests) between the two populations on the basis of their national affinity. This reality also confirms Richard Ford's view of jurisdiction as a concept that transcends lines on a map to play an important role in producing

209 *See* Tobias Kelly, *Jurisdictional Politics in the Occupied West Bank: Territory, Community, and Economic Dependency in the Formation of Legal Subjects*, 31 LAW & SOC. INQUIRY 39, 41 (2006).

status differences.[210] As the discussion throughout this chapter demonstrates, this is essentially the story of Israel's personal jurisdiction doctrine regarding the PT.

The thesis offered here explaining the nature of Israeli personal jurisdiction as a political construct is enforced by yet another argument. Were we to examine the present reality of Israel's personal jurisdiction towards the PT in the context of contemporary theories that legitimize this form of adjudicative power over claims brought against defendants, we would find the existing Israeli practice to be hollow and senseless.

Contemporary writings on general jurisdiction have advocated a significantly limited form of general jurisdiction.[211] The main reason for this perspective implicates what is conceived today as general jurisdiction's main rationale. Writings on the topic offer a political notion based on John Locke's work on political compact theory as the principle guiding idea behind general jurisdiction.[212] Since the jurisdictional power of courts is a form of governmental power, scholars have resorted to political thought in order to justify forms of personal jurisdiction, namely the idea of government based on the consent of the governed.[213] We the people, so the argument goes, give up our naturally given rights and freedoms in order to obtain the benefits of an ordered society and "the hazards found in a natural state."[214] Yet who should we assume forms this body of people in a modern society? The common answer might be those whose lives are centered in the particular political unit—i.e., local residents. Thus, it is widely accepted that if the defendant is domiciled in the local forum, then it is perfectly legitimate for that forum to have general jurisdiction over the defendant's person.[215] As Lea Brilmayer explained, like other strong relations with the forum such as location of a company's incorporation or systematic business in the forum, domicile "suggests that a person of corporate entity is enough of an 'insider' that he may safely be relegated to the State's

210 Richard Ford, *Law's Territory (A History of Jurisdiction)*, 97 Mich. L. Rev. 843, 844 (1999).

211 Allan R. Stein, *The Meaning of "Essentially ay Home" in* Goodyear Dunlop, 63 S. Car. L. Rev. 527, 532 (2012).

212 *See* Richard B. Cappalli, *Locke as the Key: A Unifying and Coherent Theory of* In Personam *Jurisdiction*, 43 Case W. Res. L. Rev. 97, 106–09 (1992) (proposing an argument regarding specific jurisdiction as well).

213 *See* Lea Brilmayer, *Consent, Contract, and Territory*, 74 Minn. L. Rev. 1, 5–10 (1989).

214 Cappalli, *supra* note 212, at 102.

215 *See* Patrick J. Borchers, *The Problem with General Jurisdiction*, 2001 U. Chi. Legal F. 119, 122–23 (2001); Friedrich K. Juenger, *The American Law of General Jurisdiction*, 2001 U. Chi. Legal F. 141, 143 (2001); Twitchell, *supra* note 100, at 667.

political process."[216] A special relationship exists between the state and those who have the right to influence the local political process. This capacity makes it legitimate for the state to exert judicial power over the defendant's person.[217]

In examining Israel's general personal jurisdiction power over Palestinians present in the PT, it becomes rather clear that Israel lacks such authority from the perspective of this contemporary theory of personal jurisdiction. Neither in the pre-Oslo period when the Palestinian population of the PT was under total Israeli occupation nor afterwards did this population have any recourse to the Israeli political process so as to influence local decision making. At best, Palestinians had recourse to the Israeli Supreme Court siting as the High Court of Justice, who ideally held Israeli authorities responsible in accordance with the international law of belligerent occupation—but certainly not by enlightened norms of a vibrant democracy. So to hold this population as being under the Israeli court's general personal jurisdiction powers stands against the very essence of these commonly accepted justifications. In contrast, from the perspective of Lockean theory, subjecting the Israeli settler population to Israeli courts does make sense, given their power to influence Israel's political process. The theory that best explains the reality of personal jurisdiction within Israeli courts is that of control and more fundamentally, personal jurisdiction as a political construct designed to maintain that control.

216 Lea Brilmayer, *How Contacts Count: Due Process Limitations on State Court Jurisdiction*, 1980 SUP. CT. REV. 77, 87.

217 Brilmayer et al., *A General Look*, *supra* note 102, at 742.

CHAPTER 3

Jurisdictional Restrictions in Actions Pertaining to Land, Personal Status, and the Palestinian Authority

Contents

A. International Jurisdiction over Subject Matter

This chapter will discuss three jurisdictional issues pertaining to Israeli courts' competence to deal with Palestinian Territories (PT)-related litigation: (1) jurisdiction over real property situated in the PT; (2) jurisdiction over personal status issues relating to Palestinians; and (3) jurisdiction regarding civil actions filed against the Palestinian Authority (PA).

A common thread weaves through these three jurisdictional topics: in each of them, the jurisdictional capacity of local Israeli courts is directly connected with the subject matter of the litigation. As opposed to the issues discussed in the previous chapter, the procedural power to serve the defendant with process is of no significance to the jurisdictional assessment regarding these topics. The particular subject matter of adjudication is the first issue raised here and determines the jurisdictional evaluation altogether.

B. Jurisdiction over PT Land

1. The Common Law Rule Restricting Jurisdiction over Foreign Land

Common law has always maintained a basic restriction on local courts' capacity to deal with disputes that relate to real property located in a foreign jurisdiction.[1] The origin of this restriction is in a rule of venue dictating the filing of actions in the locality where the cause of action arose.[2] In the fifteenth and sixteenth centuries, and possibly before, juries were supposed to be knowledgeable of the facts of the case. In order to make sure that the proper jury is convened, actions needed to be litigated in the locality of the events.[3] As time went by, the qualifications of jurors changed dramatically and so did the existing

1 Cheshire, North & Fawcett, Private International Law 478 (James Fawcett & Janeen M. Carruthers eds., 14th ed. 2008).

2 2 Dicey, Morris & Collins, The Conflict of Laws 1320 (Lord Collins of Mapesbury ed., 15th ed. 2012).

3 *Id.*

venue rules. However, part of the tradition managed to survive: disputes that are necessarily local, such as those connected to real property,[4] were regarded as pertaining to the exclusive jurisdiction of the state in which the real property is situated.[5] These local actions were distinguished from transitory actions in which the facts giving rise to the cause of action could have happened anywhere and thus could also be litigated in any locality with proper jurisdiction over the parties.[6]

In contrast, the modern rationale of the local action rule regarding real property is intertwined with notions of sovereignty and convenience.[7] States are assumed to have exclusive sovereignty over real property located within their borders.[8] Comity and reciprocity considerations require that other states refrain from dealing with actions pertaining to local land; such foreign interventions would necessarily undermine sovereign powers of the local state.[9] Moreover, in terms of convenience, the inability of one state to actually affect the status of land located in another state also militates against such cross-national jurisdiction; why take on the effort of adjudication when ultimately, the judgment cannot be enforced?[10] Another concern pertaining to litigation convenience that has been mentioned in support of the local action rule pertains to choice of law concerns and the location of evidence.[11] Generally, disputes over land are governed by the law of their location (*lex situs*). Therefore, all states are expected to benefit from the local action rule, which guarantees adjudication in the locality that is most familiar with the governing law.[12] Additionally, it is assumed that the most direct evidence connected with the dispute is to be found in this locality.

---

4 William W. Blume, *Place of Trial of Civil Cases*, 48 MICH. L. REV. 1 (1949).

5 June F. Entman, *Abolishing Local Action Rules: A First Step toward Modernizing Jurisdiction and Venue in Tennessee*, 34 U. MEM. L. REV. 251, 254 (2004).

6 *See* William H. Wicker, The Development of the Distinction between Local and Transitory Actions, 4 TENN. L. REV. 55, 58–62 (1926).

7 W. Ruport Johnson, *The Mozambique Rule and the (Non) Jurisdiction of the Supreme Court of Western Australia over Foreign Land*, 31 U.W. AUST. L. REV. 266, 268 (2003).

8 Stephen Lee, *Jurisdiction over Foreign Land: A Reappraisal*, 26 ANGLO-AM. L. REV. 273, 283–84 (1997) [hereinafter Lee, *Jurisdiction over Foreign Land*]; Stephen Lee, *Title to Foreign Real Property in Transnational Money Claims*, 32 COLUM. J. TRANSNAT'L L. 607, 629 (1995).

9 *See* Lucasfilm Ltd. v. Ainsworth, [2011] 3 W.L.R. 487, 508, 518 (H.L.).

10 CHESHIRE, NORTH & FAWCETT, *supra* note 1, at 479. For a critical analysis of this justification for the rule, *see* Michael J. Whincop, *Conflicts in the Cathedral: Towards a Theory of Property Rights in Private International Law*, 50 U. TORONTO L.J. 41, 57–61 (2000).

11 *See* Entman, *supra* note 5, at 261.

12 JOSEPH STORY, COMMENTARIES ON THE CONFLICT OF LAWS, FOREIGN AND DOMESTIC 807 (Boston, Hilliard, Gray & Co., 2d ed. 1841).

One major question that accompanied the local action rule since its modern application in the nineteenth century involved its breadth: is the rule restricted only to *in rem* claims that address the determination of property rights regarding the foreign land? Or rather, can the rule include *in personam* actions oriented only towards having the defendant (who can very well be under the court's personal jurisdiction) perform a certain act—such as the payment of damages—that is somehow connected to the land? The original distinction between local and transitory actions was not very helpful. A local action can still be regarded as local even if it is personal—what matters is whether it relates to the land. A personal action regarded as local, for example, might be an action for trespass where the plaintiff only seeks compensation.[13]

In the nineteenth century and well into the twentieth, both American and English law precedents have applied the rule restricting jurisdiction to foreign land also in personal actions.[14] What mattered for the local action rule was whether the adjudication deals, even incidentally, with the issue of rights in real property.[15] At times, this broad application of the local action rule had very severe consequences. Take, for example, the American case of *Livingston v. Jefferson*,[16] which dealt with a claim alleging trespass by the defendant, no other than former United States President Thomas Jefferson, to land situated in Louisiana. The claim for damages was filed before a Virginia court.[17] The Virginia court had personal jurisdiction over the defendant, since he was duly served with process while present in this forum state. However, the court ultimately dismissed the claim given that it dealt with a local action pertaining to foreign land. This outcome was extremely harsh on the plaintiff. Were he to now resort to a Louisiana court seeking damages from the defendant—an out-of-state resident—that court would not have jurisdiction either, at least not to the extent of having its judgment enforced, given that at the time, service of process sufficient for establishing personal jurisdiction was only possible in the forum state.[18]

---

13 *See* Entman, *supra* note 5, at 267.

14 Livingston v. Jefferson, 15 F. Cas. 660 (C.C.D. Va. 1811) (No. 8411); The British South Africa Company v. Companhia de Moçambique, [1893] A.C. 602 (H.L.); Hesperides Hotels Ltd. v. Augean Turkish Holidays Ltd., [1978] 3 W.L.R. 379 (H.L.).

15 *See* Fall v. Eastin, 215 U.S. 1 (1909); Clarke v. Clarke, 178 U.S. 186 (1900).

16 15 F. Cas. 660 (C.C.D. Va. 1811) (No. 8411).

17 For a historical account of the case, *see* Ronan E. Degnan, Livingston v. Jefferson—*A Freestanding Footnote*, 75 Cal. L. Rev. 115 (1987).

18 It is exactly because of this quandary that some state courts decided to break free from the traditional rule. *See, e.g.*, Reasor-Hill Corp. v. Harrison, 249 S.W.2d 994 (Ark. 1952).

The wide dissatisfaction with the original rule led to the creation of a whole list of exceptions to its application.[19] For example, jurisdiction over an action dealing with foreign land is recognized when the action seeks to "rescind contracts or deeds for sale of foreign land on the ground of mistake or fraud, undue influence, or incapacity";[20] and when the action asks the court to "grant injunctions to prevent the acquisition of foreign land in the breach of trust or fiduciary duty."[21] In short, many personal actions were exempted from the local action rule. In due course, England enacted a special provision that makes it possible for English courts "to entertain proceedings for trespass to, or any other tort affecting immovable property" even when such property is located outside of England, "unless the proceedings are principally concerned with a question of the title to, or right to possession of, that property."[22]

2. The Israeli Rule Restricting Jurisdiction over Foreign and PT Land

As in other spheres of conflicts, the initial Israeli approach regarding jurisdiction over real property corresponded with English common law. The House of Lords' decision in *British South Africa Company v. Companhia de Moçambique*,[23] which was the primary English precedent barring a local forum from dealing with local actions dealing with foreign lands, even those seeking damages for trespass, was considered guiding in Israel as well.[24] It is also notable that the primary Israeli cases referring to this rule were all concerned with land located in the PT rather than in some foreign sovereign state.

19 *See* Lee, *Jurisdiction over Foreign Land, supra* note 8, at 294–95. *See also* Antonin I. Pritetic, *Staking Claims against Foreign Defendants in Canada: Choice of Law and Jurisdictional Issues Arising from the In Personam Exception to the Mocambique Rule for Foreign Immovables*, 25 Advoc. Q. 230 (2009); B. Welling & E. A. Heakes, *Tort and Foreign Immovables Jurisdiction in Conflict of Laws*, 18 U. W. Ontario L. Rev. 295 (1979–1980).

20 Lee, *Jurisdiction over Foreign Land, supra* note 8, at 294.

21 *Id.* at 295.

22 Civil Jurisdiction and Judgments Act 1982, ch. 27, section 30(1). Likewise, under the various schemes of jurisdiction within the European Union (EU), members states' courts are prevented from taking jurisdiction in claims dealing with foreign land only in proceedings that have as their object rights in rem, or tenancies of, immovable property situated in another EU state. *See* Article 16(1) of the Brussels Convention, Article 22(1) of the Brussels I Regulation, Article 22(1) of the Lugano Convention. A similar approach has also been developed in the United States. *See* Eugene F. Scoles et al., Conflict of Laws 328, 375–76 (4th ed. 2004).

23 [1893] A.C. 602 (H.L.)

24 Talia Einhorn, Private International Law in Israel 380 (2d ed. 2012).

The first Israeli court to consider the application of the *Moçambique* rule in respect of PT land was the District Court of Jerusalem in *Levy v. Baruch*.[25] At issue was a contract for the sale of a piece of land located in the West Bank village of Beit-Anan. The original owner was a local Palestinian. The action was for the enforcement of the contract, so that ownership would pass to an Israeli Jewish resident of Jerusalem who was the plaintiff. Such a transaction, given the political context of the conflict, is usually conducted in complete secrecy. In order to avoid embarrassment on the part of the Palestinian owner, an apparently Palestinian middle-man served as a representative. The property was supposed to pass to this middle-man first and then onward. After signing a number of documents to make the transaction possible, the Palestinian owner defaulted, arguing that the agreement was invalid. In this action, the plaintiff sought a declaration that he was the sole owner of the land, as well as an order instructing that ownership be transferred to him. One of the preliminary issues raised was whether the Israeli court had jurisdiction over the action, given that the claim is concerned with foreign land. Although the court recognized the applicability of the *Moçambique* rule as already established in English common law, it did not adhere to it, citing three main reasons. First, the court noted that the relations between the State of Israel and the "Administered Territories" are not as between two sovereign states. Given Israel's total control of this region, no foreign sovereign exists there and therefore, no sovereignty would be undermined if jurisdiction is taken over persons and property present there.[26] So if the *Moçambique* rule is motivated by concerns of comity towards the foreign sovereign, in the absence of a foreign sovereign in the area to which any comity is due, no comity considerations weigh in favor of applying the rule.

Second, the court noted a special order issued by the IDF military commander in the PT, enabling enforcement of an Israeli judgment in the PT as if this judgment were rendered by a local PT court.[27] The court also noted the fact that this approach is reciprocal; local PT court judgments are enforced in Israel as if they were local Israeli judgments—so was the practice at least until the Oslo Peace Accords.[28] So if the *Moçambique* rule was also motivated by the will to guarantee the effectiveness of pending judgments, no concern emerges when an Israeli court seeks to adjudicate a case dealing with land situated in the PT. Given the aforementioned military order, such effectiveness is guaranteed.

25 Summons (Jer) 438/83, PM 5744(3) 45 (1984).

26 *Id.* at 52 (citing CA 179/77 Bank Leumi le-Yisra'el Ltd. v. Hirschberg, 32(1) PD 617 (1978)).

27 *Levy*, PM 5744(3) at 54.

28 Regarding the enforcement of PT judgments in Israel, *see infra* Chapter Five.

Just to be on the safe side, the court also noted that since this case involved the enforcement of a contract, then as already established by the list of exceptions to the *Moçambique* rule, it could be adjudicated by an Israeli court[29] that has proper personal jurisdiction over the defendants—which the court in this case indeed had, given that service was duly performed.[30]

These basic holdings were all eventually approved by the Israeli Supreme Court in another case decided some six years later, in 1990. In *Bassilious—The Coptic Bishop of the Holy Seat of Jerusalem and the Near East v. Adila*.[31] The Coptic Bishop had the option to purchase certain land located in near the West Bank city of Jericho. Though the Court does not disclose the identity of the registered owner of the land, the procedures indicate that the owner is a local Palestinian resident of the PT. This owner resisted the Coptic Bishop's move to execute the option, which made it necessary to instigate legal proceedings against him before the local PT court in Ramallah. Ultimately, the Ramallah Court of Appeal issued a judgment in favor of the Coptic Bishop. However, before ownership was conveyed to the Coptic Bishop in the official registrar, the disputed land was attached as collateral in a financial dispute between the owner and a creditor of his. The Coptic Bishop, who became a party to this later proceeding, argued that the action is a scam intended to yield the foreclosure of the disputed land, thereby hindering the Coptic Bishop's attempts to acquire ownership over the property. But the argument was to no avail. The Ramallah court dismissed the Coptic Bishop's arguments and ordered that the land be foreclosed on. At this point, the Coptic Bishop filed a civil action before an Israeli court seeking an order granting him ownership of the PT land. The Israeli Supreme Court dismissed this claim on the grounds that the Ramallah court's decision in the creditor-owner action in which the Coptic Bishop also took part was res judicata. But before arriving at this conclusion, the Court addressed the preliminary jurisdictional issue of whether it had jurisdiction over this foreign land case. Basing its judgment on the same considerations afforded in *Levy v. Baruch*,[32] the Court decided that Israeli courts do have proper jurisdiction over the case. Moreover, it held that an exception to

29 *Levy*, PM 5744(3) at 55–56.

30 *Id.* at 56. In a short passage towards the end of its judgment, the court also addressed the question whether it should decline jurisdiction based on the forum non conveniens doctrine. The court decided not to, given that three of the four parties were Israeli residents and that the contract was signed in Jerusalem. *Id.* at 57.

31 CA 490/88, 54(4) PD 397 (1990).

32 *Id.* at 403.

the *Moçambique* rule was also applicable here: the action seeks to rescind a transaction regarding foreign land that was conceived by fraud.[33]

As noted in the legal literature, in light of the numerous exceptions to the rule restricting jurisdiction to foreign land, the rule itself has become irrelevant.[34] The two cases discussed above also demonstrate that Israeli courts could not find any solid justifications for the application of the rule to PT land in the first place. The end result was that PT land, like any person present there, came under Israeli adjudicative jurisdiction. Based on *Bassilious*, lower courts understood that the *Moçambique* rule was inapplicable to the PT,[35] at least in the pre-Oslo period when the PT was under full Israeli occupation—and thereafter in regards to Area C of the West Bank. This understanding optimized even further Israeli judicial control over the PT, in conformity with the state's general control policy. For the large part this, the jurisdictional capacity over PT land, was concurrent in nature; it was not meant to exclude local PT courts from dealing with land disputes. I might also venture to say that if two Palestinian residents of the PT tried to litigate a PT land dispute before an Israeli court, then this court would probably decline its jurisdiction based on the forum non conveniens doctrine. However, if a local PT land dispute implicated an important Israeli interest, it is reasonable to assume that the Israeli court would seek to exert control through jurisdiction. I posit that this is how we should also read the judgment in *Levy v. Baruch*.

Another Jerusalem District Court judgment provides further testament to jurisdiction serving as an instrument of control in PT land-related disputes. In *Hijalah v. Judea and Samaria Company (JSC)*, for the sake of securing its jurisdiction, the court issued an anti-suit injunction preventing the local PT court from handling the adjudication altogether.[36] Here, a large area of the West Bank Palestinian village of Masha was allegedly purchased by JSC from Hijalah for the purpose of establishing a Jewish settlement in the West Bank.[37]

33 *Id.*

34 *See* Lee, *Jurisdiction over Foreign Land*, *supra* note 8, at 288 n.64 (commenting that the local action rule "is so riddled with exceptions and prone to circumvention that it has become irrelevant").

35 *See* CC (Jer) 1456/98 Abu Sa'an v. Abu Hamdah, paras. 71, 73 (Oct. 19, 2006), Nevo Legal Database (by subscription); CC (Jer) 2416/00 Kfar Gil'adi Quarries v. State of Israel, para. 30 (Apr. 30, 2006), Nevo Legal Database (by subscription).

36 Summons (Jer.) 2967/87 (1988, unreported).

37 Regarding private Israeli land acquisitions in the West Bank after 1967, *see generally* Eyal Benvenisti & Eyal Zamir, *Private Claims to Property Rights in the Future Israeli-Palestinian Settlement*, 89 AM. J. INT'L L. 295, 314–16 (1995).

After Jewish settlers began construction on the land, but before ownership was officially transferred, Hijalah together with a number of other Palestinian residents claiming title to the land sought relief before a local PT court: the District Court of Nablus, to declare the transaction void and to prevent the respondent from pursuing land registration in its name in the land registry. The respondent claimed that the action taken by the claimant and other local residents regarding the unbinding nature of the transaction is a conspiracy on their part, designed to evade the consequences of a valid sale agreement. The proceedings were initiated by JSC in the District Court of Jerusalem, after seven years of litigation before the Nablus Court. JSC sought an anti-suit injunction, instructing the Palestinian parties to put an end to the litigation they initiated before the Nablus court. Ultimately, the Jerusalem court issued the anti-suit injunction and, in doing so, also rejected the argument of forum non conveniens made on the part of the Palestinian litigants. The court anchored this holding in the proposition made in *Abu Attiya* that the forum non conveniens argument would not apply when the pending case implicates a significant Israeli element. The proceedings in *Hijalah* contain such an element given that JSC's shareholders and the hundreds of settlers who bought the land parcels from it were Israelis. The court also noted that the relations between Israel and the PT are not parallel to those as between two sovereign states, since the PT is controlled by Israel, is adjacent to Israel, and contains dozens of thousands of Israeli citizens as residents. Moreover, the court stressed the fact that the Israeli government authorized the establishment of a Jewish settlement on the area purchased by JSC and by so doing, surely did not intend that the rights of the settlers and the future of Jewish settlement—a problematic and sensitive matter for local Palestinian judges—be entrusted to Palestinian courts' judicial handling. This assessment was buttressed by the claim that under applicable Jordanian law, selling land to Israelis was considered equivalent to selling to enemy agents. No similar threat, the court observes, is eminent if litigation is to take place before an Israeli court, which the courts considered capable of handing the adjudication equitably and without bias.

Yet seemingly, the Palestinian litigant had an even more solid argument regarding why the Israeli court should refrain from handling this adjudication and abstain from granting the anti-suit injunction. JSC took an active part in the proceedings before the Nablus court for seven full years and initiated these proceeding before the Israeli courts only when the litigation before the Nablus court had terminated and the parties awaited the final judgment. The Jerusalem court was not moved, however. Rather, it adopted in full the four explanations provided by the JSC:

1. The Nablus court issued judgment against the JSC and other litigants without granting them the opportunity to be heard. Even though this judgment was vacated by the Ramallah Court of Appeal, the Nablus court was no longer impartial and the litigants would not receive a fair trial;

2. an assassination attempt was made on the attorney representing JSC;

3. the courthouse in Nablus was set on fire; and

4. in 1985, some years after the action was initiated before the Nablus court, the military commander issued a special order by which local courts in the PT were no longer authorized to adjudicate actions made regarding land subject to the process of first registration of title.[38] Following the issuance of this order, JSC petitioned the Nablus court to dismiss the action before it for lack of jurisdiction, but the Nablus court did not concede and up to the date of JSC's initiation of the proceedings before the Jerusalem court, it did not decide on the issue.

The court added that these allegations were properly substantiated by an affidavit filed by JSC's chief executive officer.

The *Hijalah* decision was truly remarkable. It shows the length to which an Israeli court is willing to go to in order to effectuate the general policy of control, particularly in the sphere of jurisdiction over land. Most noticeable in this respect is the great liberty the court took in depicting the local PT court as inefficient, biased, rigid and unaccommodating. Yet, when these same arguments were raised by Palestinian plaintiffs trying to sustain their cases before Israeli courts, there claims were summarily dismissed even when affidavit testimony was provided. The ease with which the court cites the Jordanian law that punishes by death the sale of land to an enemy party is telling as well. The decision affords no citation to this law, nor does it bring in any expert testimony in its regard. Furthermore, the court's exact statement here

38 The order is reproduced in Dinei ha-Tikhnun, ha-Bniya ve-ha-Mekarke'in be-Yehuda ve-ha-Shomron [Planning, Building and Land Law in Judea and Samaria] 548 (Aharon Mishnayot ed., 1996) (in Hebrew).

is unclear—is it indeed the case that this law, like many other Jordanian laws regarding real property, is applicable in the PT? But if so, how can this be the case when the PT is now effectively ruled by the IDF, and who exactly is the "enemy"? Or is it the case that this law is telling of a social practice ingrained in Palestinian society—and if so, how exactly did the court reach this conclusion? Perhaps the courthouse was set on fire—but who determined that the fire was related to this case in particular? Similarly, who determined that the attorney was assaulted because of this case and not some other matter? The other circumstances stated by the court showing the biased treatment of the Nablus court are also lacking. In fact, the Nablus court's rendering of judgment without hearing evidence can be accorded to the defendants' inaction in filing certain pleadings. Moreover, the court itself stated that the actions before the Nablus court were initiated before the IDF military commander issued a special order making it necessary to bring all such disputes before the special committee. How then is it that such an order is effective retroactively?

Not by coincidence, a prominent Israeli legal scholar has characterized *Hijalah* as a rather blunt example of the duality of the PT legal system: the Israeli legal system for the Jewish settlers, and a military occupation system for the local Palestinian population.[39] Yet when Israeli interests lie at the core of the litigation, this same duality is really a matter of control. Such is the case when a land dispute emerges between Jewish settlers and local Palestinians—the jurisdictional rules will be bent in order to accommodate the Israeli interests.

A further testament to this paradigmatic connection between Israeli control policy over land and jurisdictional capacity lies in the fact that when control over certain tracts of land became particularly important, the existing jurisdictional design was transformed, even dramatically, so as to accommodate it. This practice was applied regarding land and other property in the PT that was expropriated by the IDF, under the pretext that it was government property or deserted property—a measure responsible for much of the Israeli settlements and road system in the West Bank. As a judge in the District Court of Jerusalem had admitted, the first priority of the IDF military government was to arrange for handlings of property rights.[40] In the months following the 1967 Six-Day War, the IDF military

39 Amnon Rubinstein, *Yisra'el ve-ha-Shtakhim: Samkhuyot Shiput [Israel and the Territories: Judicial Powers]*, 14 IYUNEI MISHPAT 415, 456 (1989) (Hebrew). On the dual legal system that developed in the PT, *see generally* EYAL BENVENISTI, LEGAL DUALISM: THE ABSORPTION OF THE OCCUPIED TERRITORIES INTO ISRAEL 25 (1989); JOHN QUIGLEY, THE CASE FOR PALESTINE: AN INTERNATIONAL LAW PERSPECTIVE 180–81 (2d ed. 2005).

40 *See Kfar Gil'adi Quarries*, para. 30, Nevo Legal Database (by subscription).

commander enacted two important orders in this respect. The first was Order No. 59: Government Property (West Bank Region), 1967; and the second was Order No. 58: Deserted Property (Private Property) (West Bank Region), 1967.[41] Both of these enactments empowered an IDF-appointed official to take possession of property and conduct transactions in respect thereof. These enactments also grant immunity from civil adjudication for officials taking possession of nongovernment property as long as they acted in "good faith."[42] Another important measure regarded the power of the IDF military commander to expropriate land for what was deemed a "public cause." Interestingly, the law used by the IDF military government for taking land from the local Palestinian population for a public cause was a Jordanian enactment that existed in the laws of the West Bank before Israeli occupation. This was the Land Law—Acquisition for Public Cause (No. 2), 1953. This law granted the Jordanian government the power to expropriate land and also relegated the process of contesting the action or the proposed compensation for the taking before the local courts. According to Order 321: Land Law (Acquisition for Public Cause) (Judea and Samaria), 1969, the powers of expropriation previously held by the Jordanian government under the 1953 Jordanian law was now transferred to an organ appointed by the IDF. Order 172: Appeals Committee (West Bank Region), 1968 grants the IDF-appointed Appeals Committee exclusive jurisdiction over all matter related to expropriated land and claims regarding compensation following expropriation. Another important enactment that preceded both of these was Order 164: Local Courts (Standing of IDF Organs) (West Bank Region), 1967, which granted immunity for all IDF organs from the jurisdiction of local courts. Collectively, the schemes in all these enactments uncover how the Appeals Committee received exclusive jurisdiction to deal with actions relating to the expropriation of West Bank land by the IDF for a public cause. The laws also stipulated that as a subordinate of the IDF military commander, the Committee has recommendation capacities only and no power to order a certain act or refrain from action.

All of this is a matter of local West Bank law. If any local West Bank court is seized with a civil action regarding the expropriation of land, it is devoid of any jurisdictional capacity to deal with it, given the jurisdictional immunity of IDF organs and the exclusive jurisdiction of the Appeals Committee. One can only speculate what

41 Note that in the immediate aftermath of the 1967 Six-Day War, official IDF orders referred to the West Bank as such, literally (*Ha-Gadah ha-Ma'aravit*, in Hebrew), and not as Judea and Samaria (*Yehuda ve-ha-Shomron*, in Hebrew). These later terms will soon become the accepted official terminology.

42 *Kfar Gil'adi Quarries*, paras. 43–44, 47, Nevo Legal Database (by subscription).

an Israeli court would do if it were seized with a civil action, say for the payment of adequate compensation, in light of an IDF expropriation order granted by the authority conferred in the 1953 Jordanian law. This court would most probably conclude that it has personal jurisdiction authority over the named defendant (whether it is the State of Israel or the IDF) given the power to serve the defendant with process. In light of *Bassilious* and its progeny, the *Moçambique* rule cannot be applied to restrict an Israeli court's jurisdictional capacity in an action that deals with PT land. More importantly, all of the IDF orders that gave rise to the depicted jurisdictional design have no application in Israel and therefore the Israeli court has no formal obligation to follow any of them. So just as a regular Israeli court of general jurisdiction can adjudicate a commercial dispute that originated in a foreign jurisdiction because it has sufficient personal jurisdiction over the parties (irrespective of the fact that were the dispute to be adjudicated in that foreign jurisdiction, it would need to be adjudicated before the commercial court there)—one could logically conclude the same regarding an Israeli court's power to deal with the civil action over expropriated West Bank land. Indeed, none would argue that because matters of marriage and divorce of Jews in Israel are within the exclusively jurisdiction of rabbinical courts, if a couple were to litigate their divorce in some foreign country, that country would necessarily need to defer its existing jurisdictional capacity to the Israeli rabbinical court. Yet nonetheless, Israeli courts concluded that the exclusive jurisdiction of the Appeals Committee in the West Bank denies them the jurisdictional capacity to deal with all matters that fall within this jurisdictional authority.[43] Essentially, the Israeli courts defer to the dictates of the IDF military commander as representing Israeli policy, to which they are also committed. It is no wonder, then, that in the two cases in which the Israeli courts dismissed the actions dealing with expropriation of West Bank land for lack of jurisdiction on the pretext that local law deems the jurisdiction of the local Appeals Committee there as exclusive, the adjudication deals with a public act on part of the military commander.[44]

3. Jurisdiction over PT Land in the Post-Oslo Period

The jurisdiction of Israeli courts over PT land in the post-Oslo period seems to be much more accommodating of local Palestinian interests. One major indication

43 *See* CC (Jer) 2543/08 Hamamrah v. Ma'atz—National Roads Company (Aug. 8, 2009), Nevo Legal Database (by subscription); Originating Summons (Jer) 1537/85 Salameh v. State of Israel, PM 5747(2) 253 (1986). This latter decision was affirmed by the Israeli Supreme Court when leave for appealing this preliminary jurisdiction was denied. *See* LA 617/86 Salameh v. State of Israel (Dec. 1, 1986, unreported).

44 *Hamamrah*, para. 17, Nevo Legal Database (by subscription); *Salameh*, PM 5747(2) at 257–58.

of this policy shift is the Interim Agreement. In spite of its restrictive approach in the sphere of jurisdiction, the Interim Agreement was rather relaxed as it summarily granted a Palestinian court jurisdiction over an Israeli party when the subject-matter of the action was real property located in the "territory"—supposedly Areas A and B.[45]

One court decision seems to be even more accommodating: that of the District Court of Jerusalem in *Kahati v. Al-Afifi*.[46] The dispute in that case concerned property rights over a piece of land located in Area C, near the historic hill of Nabi Samuel. The plaintiffs were Israelis claiming that they had lawfully acquired the land from the original Palestinian owners—a claim disputed by the latter. The Israeli party sought a declaratory judgment asserting their rights from the Israeli court.

Greatly to the surprise of the plaintiffs, the court disposed of the claim on forum non conveniens grounds, notwithstanding the arguments made by the plaintiffs questioning the objectivity of a Palestinian court in dealing with land disputes between Israeli settlers and local Palestinian owners, an argument that the same court had embraced some years earlier in the *Hijala* case.[47] The court observed that in light of the Interim Agreement and the Israeli legislation that followed, the local Palestinian courts of the West Bank are to be regarded as a legitimate and qualified tribunal for adjudicating land disputes, including those to which an Israeli is a party. The land in dispute in this case was located in Area C, and thus not under the direct authority of the PA; yet in light of the new legal reality, Israelis should not take offense at being forced to litigate their claims over land situated in the West Bank before a local Palestinian court, which should be considered a possible recourse even regarding land in Area C. The court also took into account that the Israeli parties claimed to have intentionally invested their money in a transaction for the purchase of land outside of Israel, and so they should also have expected that such a dispute regarding the land purchase be litigated in the local courts of the jurisdiction where the land is situated.

How representative is the *Kahati* decision, and can it be considered as a substantial break from the general trend? To a large extent, it certainly is a break, with the Israeli court willing to concede much more than what the Interim Agreement

45 Israeli-Palestinian Interim Agreement on the West Bank and the Gaza Strip, Sept. 28, 1995, Annex IV, Article III, 36 I.L.M. 557 (1995).

46 CC (Jer) 1820/96 (Sept. 12, 1998), Nevo Legal Database (by subscription).

47 *See supra* text accompanying notes 36-39.

requires. If other Israeli courts were to follow its course, it just might be that local land disputes between Palestinians and Jewish settlers in the West Bank will need to be resolved by the local Palestinian courts. Yet I doubt whether an Israeli court would be willing to take this position in light the current state of relations between Israel and the PA. The *Kahati* decision was rendered back in 1998, in the heydays of the Oslo Peace Process and two years before the *Al-Aqsa Intifada*.

C. Jurisdiction over Matters of Personal Status

For centuries now, religion has governed matters of family law in the Middle East.[48] Depending on the country and the specific period of time, the religious community of the parties would have jurisdiction over issues including marriage and divorce, alimony, inheritance, custody, legitimation, and adoption of children, among others. The jurisdictional scheme that made this power possible was the Ottoman *millet* system.[49] The Ottoman Empire, after all, ruled many parts of the Middle East for some four hundred years (1517–1917) and resultantly left its footprints on many aspects of life, including the local legal system.[50]

The Turkish word *millet* (*millah* in Arabic) means religion, nation, community, or rite.[51] Effectively, the *millet* was a system that empowered the religious community that was accorded official recognition from the central Ottoman government (Sublime Porte) with judicial powers over its members.[52] At first, these powers were wide-ranging, making the *millet* responsible for the collection of taxes from among its members, applying punishment measures to discipline the members, and endowing the *millet* with legislative and judicial jurisdiction over its members

48 *See generally* HERBERT J. LIEBESNY, THE LAW OF THE NEAR AND MIDDLE EAST (1975). In recent years, however, there has been movement towards unifying family law under one national jurisdiction, with the exception of Lebanon and Israel. *See* CHIBLI MALLAT, INTRODUCTION TO MIDDLE EASTERN LAW 364 (2007).

49 Benjamin Braude & Bernard Lewis, *Introduction, in* CHRISTIANS AND JEWS IN THE OTTOMAN EMPIRE 1, 12 (Benjamin Braude & Bernard Lewis eds., 1982).

50 It is important to note, however, the jurisdictional designs by which religious communities were accorded jurisdiction over their members in the empires that ruled the region before the Ottomans. A significant example is the Byzantine Empire. *See* ANDREW SHARF, BYZANTINE JEWRY FROM JUSTINIAN TO THE FOURTH CRUSADE (1971).

51 Kamel S. Abu Jaber, *The Millet System in the Nineteenth-Century Ottoman Empire*, 57 THE MUSLIM WORLD 212, 212 (1967).

52 *See* Benjamin Braude, *Foundation Myths of the Millet System, in* CHRISTIANS AND JEWS IN THE OTTOMAN EMPIRE, *supra* note 49, at 69, 69–70 (regarding the reasons why such a jurisdictional authority was granted).

in family law matters.[53] In effect, the *millet* was a state within a state, given that it also worked to preserve its own language, culture and educational institutions.[54]

Another important feature of the Ottoman Empire legal system—perhaps the most important of all—was the official status of Islamic law and *Shari'a* courts in the Empire.[55] Islamic law was the major source of law in the Ottoman Empire: "in fact, the Ottomans went further than any prior Muslim regime in establishing the sole authority of the *Seriat* [*Shari'a*] and its exponents."[56] This meant that all matters that did not fall under the jurisdiction of the *millets* fell under the jurisdiction of the *Shari'a* court, which in turn applied Islamic law.[57]

Over the course of time, especially in the wake of the reforms that took place in the nineteenth century (commonly referred to as the *Tanzimat*), the jurisdiction of all religious courts was restricted to family law matters.[58] Territorial codes were compiled and applied by civil courts (*Nizamiya*) to all Ottoman subjects.[59]

In 1917, during the final stages of World War I, Palestine fell under British military control, and five years later, in 1922, British rule over the country was consolidated

---

53 Abu Jaber, *supra* note 51, at 215–16.

54 *Id.* at 215.

55 *See* June Starr, Law as a Metaphor: From Islamic Courts to the Palace of Justice 5 (1992). *See also* Joseph Schacht, An Introduction to Islamic law 89 (1964). In fact, the *millet* system itself was also instructed by the Islamic legal doctrine of affording protection to the People of the Book (*Ahl Al Kittab*) or the Protected People (*Ahl Al Dhimma*), such as Jews and Christians. As followers of a revealed religion who believe in a prophet and possess a scripture, Jews and Christians were allowed under Islam to continue practicing their religion and to maintain certain autonomy over their subjects. This by no means meant that Jews and Christians had an equal status with Muslim subjects; in fact, they had to pay a fixed poll tax called *Jizya* and a land tax, *Khuraj*, in exchange for the protection provided by the Muslim state. *See* C. E. Bosworth, *The Concept of Dhimmi in Early Islam, in* Christians and Jews in the Ottoman Empire, *supra* note 49, at 37, 38–39.

56 Bernard Lewis, The Emergence of Modern Turkey 40 (1961). *See also* Ebulula Mardin, *Development of the Shari'a under the Ottoman Empire, in* Law in the Middle East 279, 282–83 (Majid Khadduri & Herbert J. Liebesney eds., 1955).

57 The primary exceptions to this general rule were the capitulation agreements signed between the Ottoman Empire and major European powers, including Russia. These agreements granted immunity from the jurisdiction of the Shari'a courts to the subjects of these foreign powers, relegating them to their consular courts. In proceedings of a mixed nature, i.e., those between protected foreign subjects and local Muslims, mixed courts were established for adjudication. *See* Herbert J. Liebesney, *The Development of Western Judicial Privileges, in* Law in the Middle East, *supra* note 56, at 309.

58 Robert H. Eisenman, Islamic Law in Palestine and Israel 25 (1978).

59 *See* Starr, *supra* note 55, at 30. Some of these codes were taken from continental legal systems, but others, namely the civil code called the *majalla*, were a codification of Islamic law on the issues regulated. *See* S. S. Onar, *The Majalla, in* Law in the Middle East, *supra* note 56, at 292.

under a civilian government in the form of the British Mandate over Palestine.[60] The governing structure changed significantly with this new administration. In light of the 1917 Belfour Declaration promising the creation of a national home for the Jewish people in Palestine, Jewish-Palestinian relations also took a sharp turn for the worse, triggering what came to be defined as the Arab-Israeli conflict. Yet all the while, the basic structure of the Ottoman *millet* system continued to exist under the auspices of the British Mandate.[61] The Palestinian Order-in-Council, 1922 (POC, 1922)—a semi-constitutional document enacted after the establishment of the British Mandate—provided specific provisions regulating the jurisdiction of all three major religious authorities:[62] The Muslim *Shari'a* (which from now on could not possess any jurisdictional power over non-Muslims),[63] the Christian ecclesiastical authority,[64] and the Jewish rabbinate.[65]

The same basic structure of the *millet* system as regulated by the British Mandate also managed to survive after the creation of the State of Israel in 1948,[66] as Israel itself preserved many sections of the POC, notwithstanding its independence.[67]

In total, 14 different religious communities are recognized in Israel today: the Jewish community with its rabbinical courts are relevant for 5,999,600 forming 75.1 per cent of a total population of 7,984,500;[68] the Muslim community with its *Shari'a* courts maintain jurisdiction over 17.4 % (1,387,500) of the Israeli population;[69] the Druze community with its Druze courts are relevant for 1.5% (120,000)

---

60 *See* BERNARD WASSERSTEIN, THE BRITISH IN PALESTINE: THE MANDATORY GOVERNMENT AND ARAB-JEWISH CONFLICT, 1917–1929 (2d ed. 1991).

61 *See* FREDERIC M. GOADBY, INTERNATIONAL AND INTERRELIGIOUS PRIVATE LAW IN PALESTINE 114–20 (1926).

62 Palestine Order in Council, 1922, 3 THE LAWS OF PALESTINE 2569, art. 47–66 (Robert Harry Drayton compiler, rev. ed. 1933). *See also* EDOARDO VITTA, THE CONFLICT OF LAWS IN MATTERS OF PERSONAL STATUS IN PALESTINE 6–8 (1947).

63 POC, 1922, art. 52

64 *Id.* art. 54.

65 *Id.* art. 53.

66 MARTIN EDELMAN, COURTS, POLITICS, AND CULTURE IN ISRAEL 48–99 (1994).

67 *See* Josh Goodman, *Divine Judgment: Judicial Review of Religious Legal Systems in India and Israel*, 32 HASTINGS INT'L & COMP. L. REV. 477, 490–91 (2009); Issac S. Shiloh, *Marriage and Divorce in Israel*, 5 ISR. L. REV. 479 (1970); U. Yadin, *Reception and Rejection of English Law in Israel*, 11 INT'L & COMP. L. Q. 59 (1962); R. Gottschalk, *Personal Status and Religious Law in Israel*, 4 INT'L L. Q. 454, 454–55 (1951).

68 CENTRAL BUREAU OF STATISTICS, STATISTICAL ABSTRACT OF ISRAEL NO. 64 Table 2.1 (2013), available online at http://www.cbs.gov.il/reader/shnatonenew_site.htm [hereinafter CBS STATISTICAL ABSTRACT].

69 *Id.* at Table 2.2.

of the Israeli population; and ten Christian communities each with its ecclesiastical courts govern 1.6% (130,000) of the Israeli population.[70] The smallest is the Baha'i community, which is not specifically listed in the official statistics and whose number does not exceed a couple of thousands. As in Ottoman times, each of these recognized religious communities has exclusive jurisdiction to prescribe and adjudicate in matters of marriage and divorce among their respective members.[71] This exclusive jurisdictional authority carries special weight, as marriage and divorces that take place in Israel between members of the recognized religious communities cannot take the form of a civil ceremony, given the absence of a territorial law governing these matters.[72] Moreover, the prescriptive and jurisdictional capacity of the religious communities can be even broader, including matters of alimony, maintenance, custody, matrimonial property, inheritance, and adoption under these courts' respective concurrent jurisdiction. Such jurisdictional capacity is established when matters such as alimony, maintenance, custody of children, and patrimonial property arise incidentally to a divorce proceeding or if the concerned parties consent to the jurisdictional authority of the relevant religious courts. In absence of such consent, the competent court is a civil court, today the Court of Family Affairs.

A similar regime governs in the West Bank. After this part of mandatory Palestine became part of Jordan, laws of this kingdom recognizing the jurisdictional authority of the recognized religious communities there (the Muslim and four different Christian communities) were applied to the West Bank.[73] Regarding such issues in the Gaza Strip, nothing has really changed since the times of the British Mandate, given that the POC continues to apply there in matters of family law as previously.[74] When Israel occupied the Golan Heights, it found no religious courts operating there. In order to provide the local population, at the time exclusively Druze, with recourse to a judicial body to adjudicate matters of family law,

70 *See* CBS STATISTICAL ABSTRACT, *supra* note 68, atTable 2.2.

71 *See generally* Michael M. Karayanni, *The Separate Nature of the Religious Accommodations for the Palestinian-Arab Minority in Israel*, 5 NW. U. J. INT'L HUM. RTS. 41 (2006).

72 *See* Yoram Shachar, *History and Sources of Israeli Law*, *in* INTRODUCTION TO THE LAW OF ISRAEL 1, 3 (Amos Shapira & Karen C. DeWitt-Arar eds., 1995)

73 Ya'akov Meron, *The Religious Courts in the Administered Territories*, *in* 1 MILITARY GOVERNMENT IN THE TERRITORIES ADMINISTERED BY ISRAEL: THE LEGAL ASPECTS 353, 353–55 (Meir Shamgar ed., 1982). *See also* Aharon Layis, *Ha-Mimsad HaDati Ha-Muslmi Ba-Gada Ha-Ma'ravit Ba-Tkufa Ha-Yardinit* [*The Islamic Religious Establishment in the West Bank during the Jordanian Period*], *in* E'SER SHNOT SHILTON YISRAELI BI-YIHUDA VE-YEHUDA U-SHOMRON [TEN YEARS OF ISRAELI RULE IN JUDEA AND SAMARIA] 13 (Rafi Yisraeli ed., 1981) (Hebrew).

74 Meron, *supra* note 73, at 354.

the IDF military commander issued an order in 1970 establishing a Druze Court of First Instance and a Druze Court of Appeals.[75]

Conflict of laws issues that were directly tied to the Israeli-Palestinian (Arab) conflict and involved religious courts generally related to the Palestinian-Arab religious courts operating from East Jerusalem. Since this part of the city became an integral part of Israel, all institutions in East Jerusalem were now expected to operate in accordance with the Israeli legislation, in terms of both court administration and the definition of the courts' jurisdictional authority. However, the Palestinian religious courts operating from East Jerusalem did not cooperate with Israeli legislation, but rather chose to continue operating under the guidance of Jordanian law.[76] Eventually, this practice gave rise to a major jurisdictional conflict: how can a court siting in what was now considered Israel conduct its business according to the laws of a foreign country that until 1995 was considered to be Israel's enemy?[77] This next section presents an analysis of the evolution of the Israeli establishment's attitude regarding the jurisdictional authority of East Jerusalem religious courts—particularly the attitude of the Israeli Supreme Court.

1. East Jerusalem Religious Courts and the Institutional Policy of Control

It did not take long for the defiant attitude of the East Jerusalem religious court to draw the attention of the Israeli authorities, who ultimately called upon the Israeli Supreme Court to take a stand on the issue. At first, the Supreme Court issued a controlling reaction, claiming that *Shari'a* and ecclesiastical courts operating from East Jerusalem needed to abide by Israeli law—otherwise Israeli authorities would not recognize their judgments. At a later stage, this attitude took a sharp turn towards accommodation, as Israeli authorities and courts came to recognize *Shari'a* and ecclesiastical court judgments rendered in East Jerusalem according to Jordanian law, at least when the litigants were Palestinian residents of the West Bank. This turn begs the question of whether this attitude is exceptional, or is rather one that comports with a structural policy that Israeli authorities adopted in dealing with religious communities. But let us start from the beginning.

---

75 IDF (Golan Heights) Order no. 238, Regarding Druze Religious Courts, December 30, 1970.

76 *See* David Farhi, *Ha-Mo'atsa ha-Muslmit be-Mizrakh Yerushalayim u-ve-Yehuda u-Shomron Le'akhar Milkhemet Sheshet ha-Yamim [The Muslim Council in East Jerusalem and in Judea and Samaria After the Six-Day War]*, 28 Ha-Mizrakh ha-Hadash 3, 6–8 (1979) (Hebrew).

77 *See* Chaim I. Goldwater, *Religious Tribunals with a Dual Capacity*, 12 Isr. L. Rev. 114, 117 (1977).

Soon after occupying East Jerusalem, Israel commenced its quest to stress its control by demanding that East Jerusalem religious courts (particularly *Shari'a* courts) abide by Israeli law. On the eve of the 1967 Six-Day War, a *Shari'a* Court of first instance was operating in East Jerusalem, pursuant to Jordanian legislation.[78] Additionally, two *qadis* representing the West Bank were appointed to the *Shari'a* Court of Appeals, located in Jordan.[79] The application of Israeli law, jurisdiction, and administration to East Jerusalem shortly after the war was almost at once translated into restricting the operation of the East Jerusalem *Shari'a* court under the pre-1967 Jordanian law. On July 11, 1967, the Israeli Minister of Religions notified senior *Shari'a* officials that effective immediately, the Shari'a court system in East Jerusalem would come under the administration of the Israeli *Shari'a* court system and would be subjected to the jurisdiction of the Israeli *Shari'a* Court of Appeals.[80] Beyond disconnecting the East Jerusalem *Shari'a* court from the rest of the West Bank, this announcement entailed the appointment of *qadis* to the *Shari'a* courts according to Israeli law, including the need to pledge allegiance to the State of Israel following an official appointment by the president of Israel.[81] This also meant that the *Shari'a qadi* would receive their salaries from the Israeli treasury and all revenues from fees were to be transferred to the Israeli government. Another major implication was that the Israeli government would also oversee the administration of the vast Muslim religious endowments (*waqf* [singular], *awqaf* [plural]).

This policy of control was rapidly reflected in a major holding of the Israeli Supreme Court regarding a Christian ecclesiastical court operating in East Jerusalem, in *Hanzalis v. The Court of the Greek-Orthodox Patriarchate*.[82] The decedent was a Greek-Orthodox Christian domiciled in East Jerusalem and a national of Greece. She signed a will in December 1967, just over a year before her death in January 1968, according to which certain real property located in Jericho of the West Bank was to be transferred to her brother. The decedent's brother petitioned the Greek-Orthodox court in East Jerusalem to probate the will, but her widower objected, arguing that in accordance with the Israeli law now applicable to East Jerusalem, that court lacked jurisdiction since he did not consent to its concurrent jurisdictional authority. The Greek-Orthodox religious court approved of its

78 Yitzhak Reiter, *Irgun Inyaney ha-Dat shel ha-Muslimim be-Yerushalayim 1967–2001* [*The Organization of the Religious Affairs of Muslims in Jerusalem 1967–2001*], *in* HA-IR HA-ATIKA [THE OLD CITY] 173, 181 (Ruth Lapidoth ed., 2002) (Hebrew).

79 *Id.*

80 *Id.* at 177.

81 *Id.*

82 23(1) PD 260 (1970), annotated in 5 ISR. L. REV. 120 (1970).

own jurisdiction. It assumed that because the conflict involved residents of East Jerusalem and focused on land situated in the West Bank, the court could effectuate a probate action in accordance with the law in effect in the West Bank, rather than that of the State of Israel. The widower challenged this holding in a petition filed before the Israeli Supreme Court in its capacity as the High Court of Justice. Given the fact that this was a case of first impression and had a bearing on public interest, the Court asked the Office of the State Attorney General to afford its opinion. Surprisingly, the position this office took was the same as that taken by the Greek-Orthodox church itself: that the religious courts of East Jerusalem operate in accordance with the doctrine of double capacity, meaning that in the sphere of inheritance they can simultaneously operate under Israeli law and West Bank law, depending on where the disputed property is located.

The Supreme Court disagreed, by a vote of two Justices to one, with one of the Justices in the majority characterizing this double capacity argument as sophisticated but superficial.[83] The majority quite clearly noted that its guiding principle is the need for control. Justice Moshe Zilberg held that as a result of the application of Israeli law to East Jerusalem in June of 1967 (over a year before the Greek-Orthodox court was called upon to adjudicate this case), the Greek-Orthodox court was now instructed to follow the laws of Israel exclusively.[84] For it is hard to comprehend, Justice Zilberg went on to proclaim, "how a court can be the servant of two masters."[85] The other Justice in the majority, Benjamin Halevy, was even more adamant about the strict control principle. He categorically held that as a result of the application of Israeli law in East Jerusalem, "united Jerusalem is an integral part of the State of Israel."[86] He then held that courts operating from the territory of one sovereign must only follow the jurisdictional rules of that sovereign (unless explicitly permitted to act otherwise).[87] The minority Justice, Alfred Witkon, found no difficulty in characterizing the operation of the Greek-Orthodox court as falling under Jordanian law, and as such even excluded from the jurisdiction of the High Court of Justice as the ultimate administrative court of Israel, since it was not operating in this case as an Israeli court.[88]

---

83 *Id.* at 267.

84 *Id.*

85 *Id.*

86 *Id.* at 269.

87 *Id.* at 274.

88 *Id.* at 279. For a critique of the majority opinion that sides with the minority opinion of Justice Witkon, *see* Amos Shapira, *Shiput Yisraeli u-Shiput Zar bi-Kfifa Ahat—ha-Anomaliya shel Beit ha-Din ha-Yevani ha-Ortodoksi be-Yerushalayim [Israeli Jurisdiction and Foreign Jurisdiction in One—The Anomaly of the Greek-Orthodox Court in Jerusalem]*, 25 HA-PRAKLIT 456 (1969) (Hebrew).

A strong linkage clearly exists between Israel's general policy of territorial control and the design of jurisdictional authority. This connection is not exceptional; this policy of control significantly influenced the design of Israeli courts' personal jurisdiction, certainly regarding jurisdiction over PT real property. Yet unlike the overall design of personal jurisdiction—where the Israeli courts sought control but did not wish to bear the burden of the local community's litigation—the initial approach regarding the Palestinian religious courts was somewhat different. In light of Israel's strong quest to strengthen its hold over East Jerusalem, Israel was willing to take on complete jurisdictional authority, along with the associated burdens.

2. From Control to Accommodation

Eventually, however, Israel's policy of control regarding East Jerusalem religious courts took a sharp turn. The local Palestinian religious establishment was not ready to acquiesce to the official Israeli policy and showed outright civil disobedience. On July 24, 1967, a group of 22 Muslim religious figures convened and proclaimed themselves to be the Supreme Muslim Authority (*Al Haia'h Al Eslamia Al U'lia*).[89] In a letter sent to the IDF military commander of the West Bank, this body stated that the annexation of East Jerusalem is illegal, and in effect this part of the city remains an integral part of Jordan.[90] The council also stated that it is essential that Muslims handle their own institutions and that Islam does not accept the handling of Muslim affairs by non-Muslims. Consequently, this body continued the operation of the local *Shari'a* court of East Jerusalem in accordance with the pre-1967 Jordanian law and even appointed one of its members to operate as an appeals court over the judgments of the *Shari'a* court of East Jerusalem and the West Bank.[91]

In later stages, the Supreme Muslim Authority also tried to establish itself as a political body but ultimately failed. However, the legal defiance succeeded: the *Shari'a* court of East Jerusalem extended its jurisdiction, once again according to Jordanian law, to more than 20 West Bank villages.[92] Moreover, in 1976,

89 *See* Ido Shahar, Falastinim be-Beit Din Yisra'eli: Tarbut, Shlitta ve-Hitnagdut be-Beit ha-Din ha-Shara'i be-Ma'arav Yerushalayim [Palestinians before an Israeli Court: Culture, Control and Resistance in the *Shari'a* Court of West Jerusalem] 37–38 (M.A. Thesis, Hebrew University of Jerusalem, 2000) (Hebrew).

90 Farhi, *supra* note 76, at 6. Note that the defiant attitude was evidenced from the person this letter was addressed to: the IDF military commander of the West Bank, rather than the Israeli government itself.

91 Reiter, *supra* note 78, at 179.

92 *Id.* at 182.

Jordan enacted a law recognizing the existence of the *Shari'a* Court of Appeal in East Jerusalem and its jurisdiction over the entire West Bank.[93] Given Israel's official stance, Israeli authorities were not willing to enforce or recognize any of the East Jerusalem *Shari'a* court judgments.[94] However, this reaction was insignificant. A voluntary channel of judicial assistance developed between the East Jerusalem *Shari'a* court and the Israeli *Shari'a* court with jurisdiction over Jerusalem, which was located in Jaffa until 1987 and from then on in West Jerusalem. Accordingly, the Israeli *Shari'a* court recognized East Jerusalem judgments and then submitted them to Israeli authorities as Israeli *Shari'a* court judgments.[95]

The Israeli establishment acquiesced and did nothing substantial in order to prevent this judicial cooperation or to stop the East Jerusalem *Shari'a* court system from conducting its affairs in accordance with Jordanian legislation.[96] Control gave way to a policy of accommodation. Evidence of this shift in policy went much further than this acquiescence. In 1976, the Israeli Supreme Court handed down *Nassar v. Court of the Gregorian-Armenian Community*,[97] in which the Court ultimately adopted the double capacity doctrine it rejected in *Hanzalis*. After a short marriage that lasted 15 months, a Palestinian Armenian couple who lived in Biet Hanina, a suburb of East Jerusalem, decided to separate and eventually divorce. Custody over the couple's only child was granted to the wife, who meanwhile had moved back to live with her family in Ramallah. The wife's parents sought to establish a substantially meaningful relationship with their grandchild and asked the Gregorian-Armenian court operating from East Jerusalem to grant them an adoption order. Operating under Jordanian law, which recognized this court's power to grant such an order, the court issued the adoption order. The husband-father, who was not even notified of the adoption proceedings before the Gregorian-Armenian court, filed a petition before the Israeli Supreme Court in its capacity as the High Court of Justice asking that it declare that this religious court was incompetent to issue the adoption order. His underlying rationale was that Israeli law requires that the adopters be domiciled in Israel in order for any Israeli court—whether civil or religious—to be competent to deal with

93 *Id.*

94 Farhi, *supra* note 76, at 12.

95 YITZHAK REITER, ISLAMIC INSTITUTIONS IN JERUSALEM: PALESTINIAN MUSLIM ADMINISTRATION UNDER JORDANIAN AND ISRAELI RULE 15 (1997).

96 Farhi, *supra* note 76, at 7–8.

97 30(2) PD 44 (1976).

an adoption order.[98] This connection was absent in the present case, since the adopting grandparents lived in the West Bank. Moreover, the father argued that the adoption proceedings were deficient since he was never notified of them, thereby denying him a basic natural justice right. In spite of these seemingly powerful arguments, the Israeli Supreme Court denied the petition. The Court found nothing repugnant to Israeli territorial sovereignty in permitting courts in East Jerusalem to continue operating under Jordanian legislation when the proceeding concerns West Bank residents.[99] The Court did distinguish this case from that in *Hanzalis* by the fact that in *Hanzalis*, a civil court in Jerusalem was competent to deal with the action, whereas in the present case no such court could establish jurisdiction. Therefore, if the Gregorian-Armenian court were not found competent to deal with this adoption proceeding under the relevant Jordanian legislation, no court in Israel would have such jurisdiction.[100] What helped the Court to adopt the double capacity argument in this case was that it found no explicit legislative instruction on how to deal with local East Jerusalem religious courts—while explicit provisions existed regarding how it should address local East Jerusalem civil courts.[101]

Eventually, in 1999, the double capacity doctrine was applied to the *Shari'a* courts as well, in *Sal'it ha-Adomim Quarry Ltd. v. Ibrahim*.[102] Sal'it ha-Adomim was an Israeli corporation that operated a quarry near the West Bank village of Anata, located just outside of Jerusalem, and which had trespassed into an adjacent lot of land. When the plaintiffs filed a civil claim against Sal'it ha-Adomim based on their title as declared in a probate order by the East Jerusalem *Shari'a* court, the defendant argued that the probate order had no effect given that it was rendered by the *Shari'a* court of East Jerusalem according to its capacity under Jordanian law. Like in *Nassar*, the Israeli Supreme Court held that in this case, the *Shari'a* court was acting in its capacity under Jordanian law—which it is entitled to do. From here onward, the probation order of the East Jerusalem *Shari'a* court was

98 *See* Adoption of Children Law, 5720-1960, 14 LSI 93 (1960), sec. 25 (in force at the time of the decision). An identical provision is contained in sec. 28 of Adoption of Children Law, 5741-1981, 35 LSI 360 (1980–81), which replaced the 1960 Law.

99 *See* Philip L. Culbertson, *The Anglican Family Court in Israel and the West Bank*, 23 J. Church & State. 285, 307 (1981) (noting the apparent contradiction between the Court's decision in *Nassir* and its earlier position in *Hanzalis*).

100 *Nassar*, 30(2) PD at 47.

101 *Id.* at 49.

102 53(3) PD 247 (1999).

considered as a foreign order subject to the ordinary rule dealing with the recognition of foreign judgments.

3. The Policy of Accommodation—A Real Change of Heart?

Underlying the policy of accommodation is a long-standing Israeli policy of tolerance towards the non-Jewish religious communities that fell under Israeli control. According to this policy, the jurisdiction accorded to the Palestinian-Arab religious communities—first in Israel itself, and after 1967 in the PT—was perceived by Israeli institutions as an act of tolerance that Israel is committed to. Hence, the Israeli establishment was much more willing to grant recognition and powers to the Palestinian-Arab community when considering these religious communities as independent communities from one another and from the state, as opposed to its reserved (if not hostile) attitude when it came granting recognition and powers to the same community as one national unit. As I have identified elsewhere, from the point of view of group rights, Palestinian religious communities operating in Israel have enjoyed "thick" rights but the Palestinian minority as one national unit has enjoyed "thin" rights only.[103] Indeed, Israel tends to take special pride in how, as a Jewish state, it deals with its non-Jewish religious communities—against the backdrop of jurisdiction afforded to the Jewish rabbinical courts being perceived as a sort of a necessity and to some, a coercive and illiberal measure.[104]

A most telling piece of evidence of this policy of accommodation is a report published by the Information Department of the Israeli Ministry of Foreign Affairs in 1961.[105] Evidently, this report is a public relations initiative that sought to document "the efforts made during the past thirteen years to integrate the Arab population of Israel into the economic, social and political life of the new State."[106] In a separate chapter on "Religion," the report takes special pride in maintaining the jurisdictional authority of the Palestinian-Arab religious communities:

> Conformably with the injunctions of their faith, the law vests in the religious communities authority in matters of personal status...In fact, the

103 Michael M. Karayanni, *Two Concepts of Group Rights for the Palestinian-Arab Minority under Israel's Constitutional Definition as a "Jewish and Democratic" State*, 10 I-Con. 304 (2012).

104 Haim H. Cohn, *Religious Freedom and Religious Coercion in the State of Israel*, *in* Israel Among the Nations 79, 94 (Alfred E. Kellermann et al. eds., 1998).

105 Israeli Ministry for Foreign Affairs, Information Department, The Arabs in Israel (1961).

106 *Id.* at 49.

> Moslem and Christian religious courts have jurisdictional powers exceeding those of the Jewish rabbinical courts...This state of religious judicial autonomy continues to be maintained in Israel; lately, indeed, it has been extended to the Druze community, and Druze religious courts are now being established. At the same time, an entirely different process has been taking place in some of the neighboring Arab countries. In Egypt, for instance, sharia courts and the courts of other religious communities were abolished in 1956, and their powers transferred to civil courts.[107]

Clearly, this description hides the coercive and undemocratic nature of the jurisdiction ascribed to the Palestinian-Arab religious communities, while highlighting the fact that Israel's archenemy at the time, Egypt, abolished the jurisdiction of all religious courts there. Indeed, Israel took special pride in its stance towards the Palestinian-Arab religious communities, in its willingness to grant them such wide jurisdictional authority that at the time was even wider than that accorded to the Jewish rabbinical courts. This accommodating policy reached a certain climax in a 1955 Israeli Supreme Court case, *Jaday v. President of the Execution Office.*[108] A member of the Greek Catholic Melkite wanted to appeal a decision rendered by this community's ecclesiastical court, and did so before a panel of an appeals court appointed by the community's patriarch, located in Lebanon. The basic claim was that the composition as well as the legality of the appellate body contradicts Israeli law, given that the jurisdiction lies in a person present in a country that Israel considers an enemy state. From the perspective of administrative law, the argument was a particularly powerful one. If the Greek Catholic Melkite ecclesiastical court of appeals is governed by an entity beyond the jurisdictional reach of the Israeli courts, and more importantly beyond the ability of any Israeli authority to investigate and procure evidence in relation to that entity's execution of its powers, then how can Israel possibly be willing to credit it with full official powers over its subjects? In the *Jaday* case, however, the Israeli Supreme Court was willing to recognize the authority of Greek Catholic Melkite Lebanese patriarch over Israeli subjects, just as in the post-1967 Six-Day War era, the Court was willing to recognize the jurisdiction of East Jerusalem religious courts in accordance to Jordanian legislation.

At the same time as the *Jaday* decision was rendered, the Palestinian minority living inside of Israel was subject, as a national minority, to a military government

107 *Id.* at 17.

108 9 PD 135 (1955).

that ruled over it for 18 years (1948–1966).[109] This Military Administration maintained full control over the daily lives of the Palestinian-Arab minority, in a manner very similar to the military government in the PT. The military governor could restrict movement to and from any area in Palestinian-Arab towns and villages—all of which were declared "security zones"; special permits were required to move into and out of these zones, and according to emergency regulations inherited from the British Mandate, the Military Governor could banish individuals and force them to live only in designated areas.[110] Hence, evidently, the Israeli government would oppose any measure of autonomy or self-rule for the Palestinian-Arab minority, which was considered to be nourishing a national identity that could threaten Israel's unity.[111] The accommodating nature of Israeli policy towards the Palestinian-Arab religious communities is clearly discernible in contrast to the policy of strict control. Yet concurrently, when Palestinian-Arab citizens of Israel needed a special permit to visit a neighboring village or attend a university, they were nonetheless subject to the jurisdictional authority of a religious entity that no doubt nourished and sustained their religious identity, which at times even was found to function from beyond Israeli boarders and from a country Israel considered to be its enemy.

Another contrast that highlights Israel's accommodating policy towards minority religions is evident in the differing judicial attitudes adopted by the Israeli Supreme Court when interpreting the subject-matter jurisdiction of minority religious courts and the subject-matter jurisdiction of the rabbinical courts. A leading expert on Israeli family law, Professor Pinhas Shifman, has noted how the Israeli Supreme Court took a much more conservative approach that restricted the jurisdiction of the rabbinical courts, in comparison to its more accommodating approach that broadened the jurisdiction of the non-Jewish religious courts.[112] To exemplify this difference, Shifman compares two Supreme Court decisions rendered by the same panel of judges within a span of one year.

---

109 IAN LUSTICK, ARABS IN THE JEWISH STATE: ISRAEL'S CONTROL OF A NATIONAL MINORITY (1980).

110 *See* Suhaila Haddad et al., *Minorities in Containment: The Arabs of Israel*, in THE POLITICAL ROLE OF MINORITY GROUPS IN THE MIDDLE EAST 76, 84 (R. D. McLurin ed., 1979).

111 *See* CHARLES S. LIEBMAN & ELIEZER DON-YEHIYA, CIVIL RELIGION IN ISRAEL: TRADITIONAL JUDAISM AND POLITICAL CULTURE IN THE JEWISH STATE 165 (1983) ("Israeli encouragement of an Arab national identity, including a measure of Arab autonomy, is fraught with the danger of turning the population into agents of enemy countries, of encouraging them to demand territorial separation from Israeli and unification with a neighboring state"); Rebecca Kook, *Dilemmas of Ethnic Minorities in Democracies: The Effects of Peace on the Palestinians in Israel*, 23 POL. & SOC'Y 309, 312 (1995).

112 PINHAS SHIFMAN, DINEI HA-MISHPAKHA BE-YISRAEL [FAMILY LAW IN ISRAEL] 364–65 (2d ed. 1995) (Hebrew).

The first case dealt with the subject-matter jurisdiction of the Israeli Druze courts regarding residents of the Golan Heights: *Khattar v. The Druze Religious Court of Haifa*.[113] This case involved an action between a Druze couple, residents of the Golan Heights, filed before the Druze Religious Court of Haifa at a time when the Golan Heights were still considered by Israeli law to be occupied territory, and thus outside the official state borders.[114] The proceedings were initiated by the wife against the husband, asking the Druze Religious Court of Haifa to issue an order officially dissolving her marriage, as well as granting her possession of the house she had lived in during her marriage and payment of alimony and compensation—benefits she was entitled to from her husband according to Druze family law. The wife prevailed, both in the Druze Religious Court of First Instance and the Druze Religious Court of Appeal. The husband then petitioned the Supreme Court, arguing that the Druze courts in Israel lacked jurisdiction. He argued for lack of jurisdiction either because (1) the couple were not residents or citizens of Israel; or (2) the Druze Religious Court lacked jurisdictional competence to deal with matrimonial property rights between Druze couples, even if the determination of such rights happen to be ancillary to a divorce proceeding that such a court is fully competent to deal with.

On the surface, the husband's arguments were well founded in the Druze Religious Courts Law of 1962.[115] Section 4 of this law provides that "matters of marriage and divorce of Druze in Israel, who are citizens or residents of the state, shall be under the exclusive jurisdiction of the [Druze religious] court...." As noted above, the couple was neither citizens nor residents of the State of Israel, thus making the court's territorial jurisdiction over them questionable. Justice Berinzon, who delivered the Court's judgment, did not take cognizance of this apparent jurisdictional flaw, since when the husband filed his appeal before the Druze Religious Court of Appeal he stated that both he and his wife were Israeli citizens. Though such an admission is clearly insufficient to grant the couple the official status of Israeli citizens, Justice Berinzon was nonetheless prepared to take such an admission as binding as far as the litigants were concerned. Given that Israeli procedural law has traditionally been extremely formalistic when dealing with issues pertaining to the subject-matter jurisdiction and territorial competence of courts,

113 HCJ 409/72 Khattar v. Druze Religious Court of Haifa, 27(1) PD 449 (1987).

114 The laws of the State of Israel were applied to the Golan Heights only in 1981 after the enactment of the Golan Heights Law, 5742-1981, 36 LSI 7 (1981–82) *reprinted in* 21 ILM 163 (1982). This law sparked a discussion among scholars as to whether it also formally annexed the Golan Heights to Israel, thus transforming it into an Israeli territory for all matters. *See* Chapter One, Section C.

115 Druze Religious Courts Law, 5723-1962, 17 LSI 27 (1962–63).

this court's attitude can certainly be considered a conceptual stretch.[116] Another stretch was the manner in which the Court addressed the Druze religious court's competence to deal with matrimonial property and monetary disputes that arise in an ancillary manner through a divorce action.

In this context, it is worth mentioning that the Rabbinical Courts Jurisdiction (Marriage and Divorce) Law, 1953,[117] the model statute for the Druze Religious Courts Law, 1962, provided in section 3 that the rabbinical court, when seized with a divorce action between Jews, possesses exclusive jurisdiction to adjudicate all such matters that are considered ancillary to a divorce proceeding, including the alimony and maintenance entitlements of the wife and children. Such a provision was absent in the Druze Religious Courts Law, 1962. This absence significantly strengthened the husband's argument regarding the Druze religious court's lack of subject-matter jurisdiction over the wife's request for possession of the house and the other monetary entitlements.

Though Justice Berinzon acknowledged the merit of the husband's stance on this issue, he was not prepared to rule against the Druze court's jurisdiction. First, Justice Berinzon noted that the husband did not raise his argument about lack of subject-matter jurisdiction in the petition before the Druze religious court, and thus should be barred from raising the argument at this stage. This represents a further stretch of the existing practice, since courts in Israel have allowed litigants to raise subject-matter jurisdiction for the first time upon appeal. This decision—in its nature and in its exemplary use—signifies an extremely accommodating position by the Supreme Court towards a minority religious community institution.[118]

The decision Professor Shifman mentions in contrast is that of *Kahanof v. Regional Rabbinical Court of Tel-Aviv*.[119] The proceedings there involved a Jewish couple who performed a civil marriage in France and two years later emigrated from France to Israel and became Israeli citizens and residents. Some two decades later, the husband filed a divorce action in the rabbinical court. The wife contested the

---

116 *See, e.g.*, HCJ 6103/93 Levy v. Regional Rabbanical Court, Ma'ale Adumim, 48(4) PD 591 (1994).

117 Rabbinical Courts Jurisdiction (Marriage and Divorce) Law, 5713-1953, 7 LSI 139 (1952–53).

118 *See also* Yizhak Kahan, *Shipput Rabani ve-Shipput Hiloni* [*Rabbinic Jurisdiction and Secular Jurisdiction in Israel*], 7 DINÉ ISR. 205, 208 (1976) (in Hebrew). Yizhak Kahan was a Supreme Court Justice who ultimately became president of the Israel Supreme Court.

119 HCJ 3/73 Kahanof v. Regional Rabbinical Court of Tel-Aviv, 29(1) PD 449 (1974).

jurisdiction of the rabbinical court, arguing that Jewish law does not recognize civil marriages and thus would not afford the wife any monetary entitlement against her husband. The wife based her argument on Section 1 of the Rabbinical Courts Jurisdiction (Marriage and Divorce) Law of 1953, according to which, "matters of marriage and divorce of Jews in Israel, who are citizens or residents of the state, shall be under the exclusive jurisdiction of the rabbinical courts...." She argued that the term "in Israel" refers to all items that precede it. In other words, if the rabbinical court is to have jurisdiction in matters of marriage and divorce of Jews in Israel, the marriage as well as the divorce must be found to have taken place in Israel. Since in the present case the marriage took place abroad, the rabbinical court thus lacked the jurisdictional competence to address the divorce proceeding.

Justice Berinzon, who delivered the Supreme Court's opinion, rejected this argument, affirming the rabbinical court's position that it was fully competent to deal with the divorce proceeding. The Supreme Court held that the term "in Israel" can relate only to the term "divorce" of Jews instead of both "marriage and divorce" of Jews. Because the divorce proceeding was initiated between Jews who were Israeli citizens or residents, the rabbinical court was considered jurisdictionally competent in the action, despite the fact that the marriage itself was celebrated outside of Israel. However, Justice Berinzon issued an *obiter dicta* regarding the way that civil courts should relate to the jurisdiction of the rabbinical courts, which is more relevant to the present discussion. He observed that the rabbinical courts operate in essence outside the realm of the ordinary civil court, and thus their jurisdiction should be construed in a limited fashion. To emphasize this point, he said that if the court has two interpretational options—one enhancing jurisdiction and the other limiting it—it is this latter option that the court must choose. Justice Berinzon went on to add that it is an obligation of the courts to limit the jurisdiction of the rabbinical courts as much as possible in terms of the relevant statute. Nonetheless, he explained that it is impossible in the present case to limit the jurisdiction of the rabbinical court, given the semantic formation of Section 1 of the Rabbinical Courts Jurisdiction Law.

Though this *obiter dicta* in *Kahanof* was criticized,[120] much of its substance influenced the attitude of courts in a number of later decisions. As several scholars

120 Pinhas Shifman, *Samkhut Beit-Din Rabani be-Nisu'in ve-Gerushin she-Ne'erkhu Mikhuts le-Yisrael [Jurisdiction of Rabbinical Courts over Marriage and Divorce Effected Abroad]*, 6 Mishpatim 372 (1975) (Hebrew).

have noted, through instruments of judicial activism, the Supreme Court in Israel has worked consistently to limit the jurisdiction of the rabbinical courts as much as possible.[121] The approach taken in the *Khattar* decision was also exemplary. Regarding the Druze religious court's subject-matter jurisdiction to deal with matters ancillary to a divorce proceeding, it was ultimately held that the court possesses such jurisdiction, notwithstanding the absence of any specific provision granting Druze religious courts ancillary jurisdiction.[122] This contrast demonstrates the disparate attitude the Supreme Court expressed in dealing with the jurisdiction of the different religious courts. While it tended to restrict the rabbinical court's jurisdictional authority, it tended to enhance the Druze religious court's jurisdictional authority.

Though this overall accommodating policy towards the Palestinian religious communities is quite evident, and no doubt also underlies Israel's attitude towards the Palestinian religious courts operating from East Jerusalem, the motivations behind it are less clear. A set of overlapping motivations seem to be involved. One important motivation is based in the lasting legacy of the Ottoman *millet* system, namely the social code or even nomos it embodied, according to which local subjects should not mingle across religious lines in matters of family relations.[123] A subject's religious community was seen as the primarily social realm in which individuals interacted.[124] A second important motivation is more political in nature and goes to the heart of the Israeli-Palestinian (Arab) conflict. A salient feature of this conflict is the conditional relationship created between the recognition accorded to the national character of the sovereign national entity and its obligation to respect the status and jurisdiction of minority religions, especially in matters of family law. This conditioning was evident in the historic Balfour

121 *See* ASHER COHEN & BERNARD SUSSER, MI-HASHLAMA LE-HASLAMA: HA-SHESA HA-HILONI-DATI BE-FETAKH HA-ME'A HA-ESRIM VE-AHAT [FROM ACCOMMODATION TO ESCALATION: THE SECULAR-RELIGIOUS DIVIDE AT THE OUTSET OF THE 21ST CENTURY] 97–106 (2003) (Hebrew). *See also* Gidon Sapir, *Religion and State in Israel: The Case for Reevaluation and Constitutional Entrenchment*, 22 HASTINGS INT'L & COMP. L. REV. 617 (1999); Gerald M. Steinberg, *Interpretations of Jewish Tradition on Democracy, Land, and Peace*, 43 J. CHURCH & STATE 93, 98–101 (2001).

122 *See* HCJ 642/82 Safadi v. Druze Appellate Court, 37(3) PD 381 (1983); HCJ 208/88 Fakhr Al Din v. Druze Appellate Court, 43(2) PD 760 (1989); HCJ 6193/98 Kadour (Halabi) v. Shiekh Na'eem Hino—Qadi Madhab of the Druze Religious Court in Acre, 52(2) PD 625 (1999). These precedents were later overruled in HCJ 9611/00 Bader (Mari'ee) v. Mari'ee, 58(4) PD 256 (2004).

123 *See* Michael M. Karayanni, *In the Best Interests of the Group: Religious Matching under Israeli Adoption Law*, 3 BERKELEY J. MIDDLE EASTERN & ISLAMIC L. 1, 40–41 (2010).

124 *See* BRUCE MASTERS, CHRISTIAN AND JEWS IN THE OTTOMAN ARAB WORLD: THE ROOTS OF SECTARIANISM 39, 189 (2001).

Declaration (1917), in which Great Britain gave its historic promise to establish a national home for the Jewish people in Palestine. Although the document's text is short, it specifically conditioned this promise on it "being clearly understood that nothing shall be done which may prejudice the civil and religious rights of existing non-Jewish communities in Palestine." As the British Mandate over Palestine was established in 1922 following the 1920 San Remo Conference, the articles of the Mandate as determined by the League of Nations maintained that in addition to the promise in the Balfour declaration, which was incorporated into the document,[125] Article 9 of this same document made clear that "[r]espect for the personal status of the various peoples and communities and for their religious interests shall be fully guaranteed." Finally, UN Resolution 181 (1947), which envisioned a two-state solution to the local conflict—one Jewish and one Arab—clarified that in each of the established states, "[t]he family law and personal status of the various minorities and their religious interests, including endowments, shall be respected."[126]

In light of this conditional relationship between the character of the national sovereign and the recognition that must be accorded to minority religions, the Israeli establishment, including the courts, were ready to be especially accommodating in the sphere of minority religions. After all, Israeli was now fully in control of East Jerusalem and, as the years went by, worked to considerably expand its frontiers. In accordance with the traditional notion of conditioning, it felt bound to balance this control by being more accommodating to the religious minorities.

Finally, a potential third motivation behind this accommodating policy cannot be ruled out—a motivation based on control. As I have already indicated earlier, the Israeli establishment traditionally conceived of the Palestinian-Arab minority that resided inside Israel as a security threat. Therefore, various instruments of control were maintained in order to contain this threat, including fragmentation. This strategy was based on the notion that the more the establishment manages to fragment the Palestinian-Arab minority, the better it is able to control it. One resource that proved to be an effective facilitator of fragmentation was the existing religious communities—they indeed do divide the Palestinian-Arab minority

125 The Palestine Mandate, Preamble, *available at* http://avalon.law.yale.edu/20th_century/palmanda.asp.

126 Article 4 of the Partition Plan was specifically titled "Religious Minorities." *See* Partition Plan with Economic Union, annexed to Resolution Adopted on the Report of the Ad Hoc Committee on the Palestinian Question: Future Government of Palestine, G.A. Res. 181(II), U.N. Doc. A/RES/181(II) (Nov. 29, 1947), chap. 2, art. 4.

into different religious communities, each with a supposedly distinct identity.[127] The recognition of religious jurisdiction through accommodating policy facilitates control by maintaining the religious distinctions within the Palestinian-Arab community now in the PT and the Golan Heights and in the process also seeks to foster a religious identity that will necessarily weaken one uniting national identity.[128]

D. Sovereign Immunity for the Palestinian Authority

When recognized, sovereign immunity restricts the ability of local courts to adjudicate a civil claim filed against the foreign entity sued in the particular civil claim. Unlike the restrictions that were discussed earlier in this chapter regarding real property and family law, the identity of the defendant, rather than the subject-matter of litigation, underlies the jurisdictional restriction. In this section, I address the manner in which Israeli courts and ultimately the Israeli Knesset sought to treat the claim of sovereign immunity when raised by the PA.

Most likely, no other issue so vividly surfaced in the Israeli establishment's use of a legal doctrine in promoting its own policies as the foreign sovereign immunity claim raised by the PA. I arrive at this conclusion on the basis of the principal finding of this section, showing the complete politicization of the process whereby sovereign immunity was essentially denied to the PA.

The discussion that follows is divided into three subsections. First, I provide a descriptive analysis of the law on foreign sovereign immunity generally and the manner in which the law was incorporated in the Israeli legal system. Next, I survey the major decisions given by Israeli courts in which the foreign sovereign immunity of the PA was raised as a preliminary jurisdictional restriction. Last,

127 In this respect, it is worth noting that the Ottoman *millet* system has also been perceived as a mechanism of conservatism, as the *millets* preserved the separate religious identities of local subjects that overshadowed the development of a secular Ottoman citizenship. *See* Roderic H. Davison, *The Millets as Agents of Change in the Nineteenth Century Ottoman Empire, in* Christians and Jews in the Ottoman Empire, *supra* note 49, at 319, 333; Kemal H. Karpat, *Millets and Nationality: The Roots of the Incongruity of Nation and State in the Post-Ottoman Era, in* Christians and Jews in the Ottoman Empire, *supra* note 49, at 141, 147 (noting how the *millet* system was one important mechanism that prevented the fusion of various ethnic groups into one larger political unit.)

128 Some have also contended that by maintaining the jurisdiction of the religious communities, Israel also maintains patriarchy, thereby further facilitating state control, given patriarchy's community-weakening characteristics. *See* Karayanni *supra* note 71, at 60–64.

I offer a critical analysis of the current Israeli law that essentially denies the PA sovereign immunity.

1. Foreign Sovereign Immunity

Almost all discussions on foreign sovereign immunity start by depicting the traditional governing doctrine of absolute immunity: foreign states are absolutely immune from the jurisdiction of local courts, regardless of the issue. A number of considerations have been offered as the rationale behind this doctrine of absolute immunity. First among them is the principle of equality among sovereign states (*par in parem non habet imperium*).[129] According to this principle, jurisdiction over an entity assumes a form of obedience or subordination. Since states are presumed to be equal it thus follows that they cannot come under the jurisdiction of one another. A second consideration, which is occasionally presented as complementary to the principle of equality, is that of comity among nations. Given their equal and dominant stature in the sphere of international relations, states should refrain from adjudicating claims that will lead them to pass judgment on the actions of one another. Abstaining from handling such adjudication—so the argument continues—is beneficial to international "intercourse."[130] A third consideration focuses on the effectiveness of the prospected judgment. Since states cannot enforce their judgments on one another, why bother adjudicating a claim against a foreign state?

Another important ingredient of the doctrine of absolute immunity is its assumed source: customary international law. As a result, the accordance of sovereign immunity to foreign states needs no special enactment on behalf of the local forum—its attribution to customary international law is sufficient to make it part of the municipal law of each state worldwide.

Serious doubts were raised as to whether these considerations support the existence of an absolute immunity for foreign sovereigns. Some have contended that to the extent that this principle exists in international law, it supports the proposition that sovereign states have an equal capacity for rights.[131] Since this capacity for equal rights can exist irrespective of whether sovereign states come under one

129 Manuel R. García-Mora, *The Doctrine of Sovereign Immunity of Foreign States and its Recent Modifications*, 42 Va. L. Rev. 335, 336 (1956); Hazel Fox, The Law of State Immunity 57–58 (2008).

130 *See* Lee M. Caplan, *State Immunity, Human Rights, and* Jus Cogens: *A Critique of the Normative Hierarchy Theory*, 97 Am. J. Int'l L. 741, 749 (2003).

131 *Id.* at 752.

another's adjudicative jurisdiction, then equality among them cannot be a consideration for immunity, certainly not in its absolute form.[132]

Considerations of comity do not necessarily favor a doctrine of absolute immunity. To the contrary, comity can also be taken as instructing states to respect the duties conferred upon them and the jurisdiction of other states, rather than to defy them.[133]

Likewise, as the jurisdiction of local courts expanded to include instances where the defendant was absent from the forum state, effectiveness was no longer a measure for determining the adequacy of adjudicative authority in general. As such, why does it remain necessary to consider effectiveness in adjudicating cases against foreign states?

Revealing the unsound nature of the ideals behind the doctrine of absolute sovereign immunity was a major force behind its transformation. The increasing role that states played in the sphere of international commercial activities further facilitated such change. A basic sense of justice demanded that if states conduct commercial transactions like any other private entity, then they should not be immune from adjudication, as no other private entity is. Moreover, states realized that in order to be able to effectively engage in international commercial activities, it is in their own best interest to give up some of their immunity—for not many private parties will want to conduct business with entities that consider themselves to be above the law.

The revision of the doctrine of foreign sovereign immunity in common law countries took place towards the mid-twentieth century, with the introduction of the restrictive theory.[134] Under this new doctrine, a state is entitled to immunity only when the adjudication concerns a public act (*jure imperii*) committed by the state or on its behalf, but not regarding a private or commercial activity (*jure gestionis*).

Though the divide between private-commercial activities on the one hand and public acts on the other hand seems to work well in theory, the actual classification of different acts of the state proved to be problematic in a number of instances. To assist courts in this respect, an interesting practice developed in the United States.

---

132 *Id.* at 751–53.

133 *Id.* at 754–55.

134 *Id.* at 743.

Following the issuance of the historic Tate Letter (1952),[135] in which the United States adopted the restrictive theory, the U.S. Department of State, pursuant to the letter itself, was the institution that parties tuned to in order to classify the conduct of the foreign state.[136] This practice was by no means innovative, given that recourse to the U.S. Department of State was controlling even when the absolute immunity doctrine was in force.[137] However, in the pre-restrictive theory period, the task of the executive branch was limited in nature to determining whether the entity claiming sovereign immunity was sufficiently sovereign or not.[138] With the adoption of the restrictive theory, the executive branch's role became much more judicial in nature. The State Department needed to decide on the specific nature of the activity for which the claim against the foreign entity is brought—an act that required it to consider evidence, to adopt standards for the classification of the act, and to outline the procedure by which recourse to the State Department must be made.[139] This practice was quite unsatisfactory, since the State Department is ill-equipped to perform such functions.[140] But the more serious deficiency was that the State Department, as part of the executive branch, was subject to political pressure, which at times led to a corpus of contradictory results.[141]

Ultimately, Congress enacted the Foreign Sovereign Immunities Act of 1976 (FSIA).[142] Besides dealing with a whole score of matters regarding foreign

135 Letter from Jack B. Tate, Acting Legal Adviser of the U.S. Dep't of State, to Acting Attorney General Philip B. Perlman (May 19, 1952), reprinted in 26 DEP'T ST. BULL. 984 (1952). *See also* William A. Dobrovir, *A Gloss on the* Tate Letter's *Restrictive Theory of Sovereign Immunity*, 54 VA. L. REV. 1 (1968).

136 *See* GARY BORN & PETER B. RUTLEDGE, INTERNATIONAL CIVIL LITIGATION IN UNITED STATES COURTS 221–22 (4th ed. 2007).

137 *See* Republic of Mexico v. Hoffman, 324 U.S. 30, 35–36 (1945) ("it is . . . not for the courts to deny an immunity which our government has seen fit to allow, or to allow an immunity on new grounds which the government has not seen fit to recognize"); Ex Parte Republic of Peru, 318 U.S. 578, 589 (1943) (holding that a determination of immunity on the part of the U.S. State Department "must be accepted by the courts as a conclusive determination by the political arm of the government that the continued retention of the vessel interferes with the proper conduct of our foreign relations"). It should be noted, however, that the United States Supreme Court did not always take the position that the State Department view on whether sovereign immunity should be accorded is controlling. *See* BORN & RUTLEDGE, *supra* note 136, at 220 (citing the litigation that culminated in Berizzi Brothers Co. v. The Pesaro, 271 U.S. 562 (1926)).

138 Such as in the case of *Hoffman*, 324 U.S. 30, where immunity was claimed regarding the operation of a vessel in freight by a private Mexican company, when the vessel itself was owned by the Mexican government.

139 BORN & RUTLEDGE, *supra* note 136, at 221–22.

140 *See* Jessup, *Has the Supreme Court Abdicated One of Its Functions?*, 40 AM. J. INT'L L. 168 (1946); Michael H. Cardozo, *Judicial Deference to State Department Suggestions*, 48 CORNELL L.Q. 461 (1963).

141 BORN & RUTLEDGE, *supra* note 136, at 222.

142 28 U.S.C. §§ 1604–1611 (2006).

sovereign immunity including service of process, enforcement of judgments, and others, one major attribution of this enactment is the deferral of the decision on sovereign immunity back to the judiciary.[143] This improvement was explicitly intended to distance the decision on sovereign immunity from any political considerations subjecting it to objective standards with full procedural transparency.

2. Foreign Sovereign Immunity under Israeli Law

For decades, Israeli law on foreign sovereign immunity was inexplicit. Only in 1997 did the Israeli Supreme Court have its say on the matter. This happened in *Her Majesty the Queen in Right of Canada v. Adelson*.[144] After the Canadian ambassador's lease for his place of residence terminated and his request for extension was denied, the landlord filed a civil claim asking for a declaratory judgment of eviction and in due course for the payment of rent. Canada, the formal lessee and defendant, contested the propriety of jurisdiction over it based on foreign sovereign immunity. Ultimately, the Israeli Supreme Court denied Canada's immunity. After the Court officially adopted the restrictive theory, it classified the subject matter of litigation as a private-commercial act, thereby deeming immunity for Canada unnecessary. Given the general worldwide trend of applying the restrictive theory, this outcome was predictable. The interesting parts in the decision are those in which the Court identifies the rationales behind the doctrine of foreign sovereign immunity. In a characteristic line of reasoning, the president of the Court at the time, Aharon Barak, held that the limits of doctrines need to be determined in accordance with the causes they were intended to serve.[145] Upon investigation of the existing rationales, he admitted their shortcomings. Neither equality nor comity commands a theory of sovereign immunity, not even a restrictive one.[146] If it were up to him, Barak proceeded to proclaim, he would have fashioned a rule that foreign states, like the local sovereign, should come under the jurisdiction of local courts rather than enjoy such immunity. However, given the current state of customary international law, the Court has no option but to follow the restrictive theory of foreign sovereign immunity. Ultimately, the Court's main challenge is to draw a proper balance between two competing interests: the rule of law on the one hand, and on the other hand the interest of the

143 BORN & RUTLEDGE, *supra* note 136, at 222.

144 LCA 7094/94, 51(1) PD 625 (1997).

145 *Id.* at 651.

146 *Id.* at 652.

foreign state to pursue its political policies without the threat of judicial review by another state.[147]

The restrictive theory as adopted in *Adelson* went on to dominate Israeli law on foreign sovereign immunity.[148] Like in many other countries, Israeli courts became concerned with classifying the activity as one of a private-commercial nature or one of a public nature.[149] Finally, the Knesset adopted the Foreign States Immunity Law, 2008 (FSIL),[150] which offers a comprehensive scheme on the subject.[151] As expected, this law follows the restrictive theory and adopts a list of exceptions to the basic principle of immunity accorded to foreign sovereigns. Another important provision in FSIL is the one dealing with the possibility of granting immunity to "a political entity which is not a foreign state." As we shall see later on, this provision was generally understood as regulating the possible accordance of sovereign immunity to the PA. The most striking element of this provision is the complete politicization of this latter process, as opposed to FSIL's dependence on the judiciary in all other matters. But in order to fully comprehend the innovation of FSIL, we first need to turn to Israeli law on PA sovereign immunity as it developed prior to this enactment.

3. The PA's Entitlement to Sovereign Immunity before Israeli Courts

In the wake of the Second *Intifada* (2000–2005), scores of civil claims were filed before Israeli courts against the PA, at times naming senior Palestinian officials as additional defendants. In most of these actions, Israeli citizens sought monetary compensation based on the theory that the PA was directly or indirectly responsible for acts of violence and terror that left people dead or injured or property damaged. The PA asked that these civil claims be summarily dismissed, given its entitlement to sovereign immunity. The question this defense raised—whether the PA is a foreign sovereign entity entitled to immunity—caught Israeli courts off-guard. The Oslo Accords with their detailed Interim Agreement on matters of jurisdiction said nothing about the immunity of the PA. And as we have just seen, the guiding Israeli Supreme Court precedent on foreign sovereign immunity,

147 *Id.*

148 *See* Einhorn, *supra* note 24, at 328–32.

149 *Id.*

150 SH No. 2189 p. 76.

151 *See* Einhorn, *supra* note 24, at 325–28.

Adelson, did not offer much in terms of the justifications for the modern doctrine of foreign sovereign immunity.

Given that a fairly large number of civil actions against the PA were pending before the District Court of Jerusalem, the president of that court took the initiative of partially consolidating these into some preliminary questions, the first among which was the PA's entitlement to sovereign immunity. These consolidated actions were assigned to a special panel of three judges in *Noritz v. Palestinian Authority*.[152] The panel handed down a split decision. The majority, Judges Moshe Gal and Miriam Mizrahi, held that in the case of a semi-state such as the PA, the question regarding sovereign immunity should be deferred to the executive branch, namely the Israeli Ministry of Foreign Affairs, which is to determine whether immunity is warranted in each and every particular case.[153] The majority essentially empowered the Israeli Ministry of Foreign Affairs to determine the entitlement of immunity, rather than just whether the PA has the status of a foreign state. Interestingly, the majority judges note that the acts implicated in the claims filed against the PA are all seemingly of a private-commercial nature and therefore do not give rise to immunity under the now-applicable restrictive theory.[154] This holding ultimately makes it unnecessary to take a stand on whether the PA is entitled to sovereign immunity, for even if it is entitled, that immunity would not cover the alleged acts taken on the PA's behalf. On the surface, it would seem odd if a semi-sovereign entity would emerge with greater immunity than that accorded to full foreign sovereign states. It seems that the majority judges sensed that their holding is to be construed as rather principled and instructive for cases in general, including those in which the PA might be engaged in public acts; thus, it exceeded the scope of the issues at hand, adopting a holding for all cases.

An interesting discussion took place in *Noritz* about whether the PA does indeed qualify as a sovereign state. This discussion was guided by the 1933 Montevideo Convention on Rights and Duties of States, namely the four conditions indicated therein for a foreign entity to qualify as a foreign state. These conditions are: (1) a permanent population; (2) a defined territory; (3) a government; and (4) the capacity to enter into relations with other states.[155] The majority in *Noritz*, which

152 CC (Jer) 2538/00 Noritz v. Palestinian Authority, PM 5762(2) 776 (2003).

153 *Id.* at 807–08.

154 *Id.* at 797.

155 Montevideo Convention on Rights and Duties of States art. 1, Dec. 26, 1933, 165. L.N.T.S. 19 (1933)

was willing to recognize the immunity of the PA only following affirmation by the Minister of Foreign Affairs through the provision of a special certificate, was of the opinion that these four conditions are irrelevant to the decision regarding entitlement to immunity in a local judicial proceeding. They considered the primary relevance of these conditions to be in the realm of international relations: to help a state form a position on whether another foreign entity qualifies as a foreign state—but not for local courts facing the same question. Complete reliance on the executive branch, as the majority made explicit, is especially called for in such cases as this, where the status of the PA is the subject of much controversy within the Israeli public. This situation should distance the court from taking a position and lead it to defer completely to the Israeli government's decision. But the most striking part of this majority opinion is how the judges refine their holding, stating that obtaining a certificate from the minister is particularly necessary regarding foreign entities that are not full sovereigns.[156] Nowhere in the decision, however, do the judges clarify according to which standards they determine full and partial sovereignty, and given their previous stance on the need for total deferral to the executive branch, it is also unclear why such a characterization would be necessary.

The minority judge, Moshe Drori, was of the opinion that the judiciary and not the executive branch is responsible for deciding the question of foreign sovereign immunity, irrespective of whether the foreign entity who is seeking immunity is a full- or semi-state.[157] Judge Drori referred to the four conditions of the Montevideo Convention and concluded that the PA cannot qualify as a state.[158] In terms of having a government, he highlights the limited authority that was granted to the PA under the Oslo Accords. First of all, the PA only has such powers that were transferred to it from the IDF military government and that later authority is still the one with all residual powers. Under the Oslo Accords, the PA does not have jurisdiction over Israeli citizens, it is not responsible for the external security of the PT, and, more importantly, the IDF still controls who enters and who exits from the PT.[159] Given that the PA is not in control of a continuous strip of land and is also unable, per the Oslo Accords, to establish diplomatic and consular relations with foreign nations, Judge Drori concluded that the PA did not satisfy three of the essential conditions under the Montevideo Convention: it lacks a sovereign government, a territory, and the capacity to establish relations with other foreign states. At best,

156 *Noritz*, PM 5762(2) at 817.

157 *Id.* at 832, 835.

158 *Id.* at 841–52.

159 *Id.* at 844–49.

the PA is an entity with expansive administrative autonomy in the territories under its control.[160] The one condition that the PA probably satisfies is that of having a permanent population, given the existence of a substantial Palestinian community under its control, but even that is doubt, according to Judge Drori, given the fact that it lacks the power to grant entry and residency permits.[161]

Two peculiar positions stand out from this minority opinion. The first is the willingness to have the judiciary decide on whether a foreign entity is a foreign state (let alone if it is entitled to sovereign immunity, given the nature of its actions) without the need to defer to the executive branch, and supposedly irrespective of the position the executive branch might have on the subject. Perhaps Judge Drori did not conjecture the odd position his opinion would push the State of Israel into, at least internationally, when its Ministry of Foreign Affairs relates to a foreign entity as a foreign state but its court does not, or vice versa. The second peculiar position in Judge Drori's opinion is his willingness to downplay the sovereign attributes of the PA by stressing how incapable it is of controlling entrance and exit from the territories under its jurisdiction, noting that the territory it commands is discontinuous and its inability to deal with external security matters. Yet he proceeds to assess—unnecessarily for the conclusion he reached—that none of this can potentially downplay the PA's exclusive liability regarding acts of terror and hostilities that originated from the territories under its control.

Some discussion emerged in jurisdictions worldwide on whether the PA should be viewed as a sovereign state,[162] partly for the sake of deciding whether the PA is entitled to claim sovereign immunity.[163] The general tendency is to deny the PA the status of a sovereign state and, as a result, to deny sovereign immunity.[164] Two American courts have explicitly taken this view.[165]

---

160 *Id.* at 851.

161 *Id.* at 844–45.

162 *See* Justus R. Weiner, *An Analysis of the Oslo II Agreement in Light of the Expectations of Shimon Peres and Mahmoud Abbas*, 17 MICH. J. INT'L L. 667, 685–90 (1996); Omar M. Dajani, *Stalled Between Seasons: The International Legal Status of Palestine During the Interim Period*, 26 DENV. J. INT'L L. & POL'Y 27 (1997); Kathryn M. McKinney, *The Legal Effects of the Israeli-PLO Declaration of Principles: Steps towards Statehood for Palestine*, 18 SEATTLE U. L. REV. 93, 95–98 (1994).

163 *See* Katherine Reece Thomas, *Non-Recognition, Personality and Capacity: The Palestine Liberation Organization and the Palestinian Authority in English Law*, 29 ANGLO-AM. L. REV. 228 (2000).

164 *Id.* at 244. *See also* Celia Wasserstein Fassberg, *Israel and the Palestinian Authority: Jurisdiction and Legal Assistance*, 28 ISR. L. REV. 318, 320 n.7 (1994).

165 Unger v. Palestine Liberation Organization, 402 F.3d 274 (1st Cir. 2005), *cert. denied*, 126 S. Ct. 715 (2005); Knox v. Palestinian Liberation Organization, 306 F. Supp. 2d 424 (S.D.N.Y. 2004).

4. A Bold Step in Favor of PA Sovereign Immunity, and Its Rebuttal

The judgment in *Noritz* was rendered in 2003. Three years later, in 2006, another judgment was rendered in the same District Court of Jerusalem, this time granting the PA full sovereign immunity. This progression transpired in Judge Boaz Okun's decision in *Agudat Midreshet Alon Moreh v. State of Israel*.[166] The plaintiff in this action was an organization that obtained a judgment from an Israeli court against a Palestinian party who allegedly defaulted on a land sale contract. The land was located in Area A and purchased by the plaintiff for the purpose of settling Israelis in the PT. The plaintiff was unable to execute the judgment and blamed this on the ineffective judgment enforcement mechanism that existed between Israel and the PA. After the PA was named as a defendant for its alleged inaction to enforce the judgment, it moved to have the action against it summarily dismissed on sovereign immunity grounds. This time the court granted its motion.

In terms of the restrictive theory, the action or more accurately the inaction on which the claim is based is of a decisively public nature. But once again: is the PA a foreign state for foreign sovereign immunity purposes? Relying on the various Israel-PLO agreements, especially the Interim Agreement, the court concluded that the PA possesses sufficient sovereign attributes (exclusive control over a territory, a police force, elected government bodies, international status) that entitle it to sovereign status and immunity, although the court admitted that the PA has not attained the status of a fully independent state.[167] According to the court, sovereign immunity is to be determined under a functional analysis that examines the actual sovereign functions possessed by the implicated entity.[168] Moreover, Judge Okun considered it unfair that in terms of responsibilities, the PA is often held on par with independent sovereign states, but when it comes to rights, it is denied those that states are entitled to.[169]

Judge Okun's decision was short-lived. On appeal, the Supreme Court vacated it, holding that the majority decision in *Noritz* is controlling for this case as well.[170]

166 MPC (Jer) 1008/06 (Apr. 23, 2006), Nevo Legal Database (by subscription).

167 *Id.* paras. 9–12.

168 *Id.* para 11.

169 *Id.* para 10.

170 CA 5093/06 Agudat Midreshet Alon Moreh v. State of Israel, para. 13 (Aug. 6, 2008), Nevo Legal Database (by subscription). It is important to note that the PA appealed the decision in *Norits* to the Supreme Court. However, on appeal, the PA did not argue against the majority holding on the need to obtain a certificate from the Israeli Minister of Foreign Affairs to the effect that it is entitled to sovereign immunity.

What this meant was that the decision on whether the PA is entitled to sovereign immunity is contingent on the providing of a certificate from the Israeli Minister of Foreign Affairs for each of the pending actions, which determines whether the PA is entitled to immunity or not. As far as my research has revealed, there was not one instance in which a certificate was issued by the Israeli Minister of Foreign Affairs recognizing the sovereign immunity of the PA. In all the cases in which the certificate was sought, the Ministry flatly denied immunity for the PA. No reasons were afforded. The text usually read as follows: "I... inform the honorable court that the PA and/or the Palestinian National Council do not have immunity from jurisdiction in this case."[171]

5. A New Israeli Law on Foreign Sovereign Immunity

The majority decision in *Noritz* was consolidated further in 2008, when the Knesset enacted a comprehensive law on foreign sovereign immunity—FSIL. A separate provision (Section 20) provides that in the case of an application for immunity by "a political entity which is not a foreign state," it is up to the Israeli Minister of Foreign Affairs to prescribe immunity, and in such a case the minister will need to issue a special order to that effect. But this is not all. Before considering whether to issue the order, the Minister of Foreign Affairs is required to first consult with the State of Israel's Attorney General and also to have the entire Israeli government approve of it. On top of all that, the Knesset Constitution and Law Committee also needs to approve of the order. So in essence, the recognition of immunity for the PA requires the approval of two political bodies—the Israeli government and the Knesset Constitution and Law Committee—with the judiciary having no say on the matter. Interestingly, in order to deny this foreign entity sovereign immunity, the Minister of Foreign Affairs does not need the approval or the advice of any other party—the Minister can make that decision independently.

As prescribed in FSIL, Section 20, immunity granted under this provision must conform with the limits set in FSIL for sovereign immunity generally. What this means is that the "political entity which is not a foreign state" upon the rendering of the order as stipulated in FSIL, Section 20, will be entitled to the immunity

With the office of the State Attorney General backing this holding, it effectively became the formal holding on the subject. *See* LCA 4060/03 Palestinian Authority v. Dayan (July 17, 2007), Nevo Legal Database (by subscription).

171 *See, e.g.*, CC 4071-02 (Jer) Ploni v. Palestinian Authority, para. 441 (Oct. 15, 2012), Nevo Legal Database (by subscription).

that regular foreign sovereign states are entitled to under the restrictive theory as adopted in this law—no more and no less. However, there seems to be one basic distinction in the immunity granted to a "political entity which is not a foreign state" if and when an order is made to that effect under FSIL, Section 20, and the immunity that regular foreign states are entitled to under FSIL generally. The immunity prescribed under FSIL, Section 20 is made in the order itself, i.e., in the order issued by the Minster of Foreign Affairs and approved by the Israeli government and the Knesset Constitution and Law Committee. Since this order is the act that grants the immunity and yet it must confirm with the restrictive theory as adopted in FSIL, it follows that these organs are the ones bestowed with the power to determine the nature of the act and the extent to which the foreign body deserves immunity. This state of being resembles the practice existing in the United States in the period between the Tate Letter and the enactment of a federal law on foreign sovereign immunity in 1976, when the U.S. State Department performed the function of characterizing the act that is the subject of litigation and determining if the foreign state is entitled to immunity or not. In the Israeli context, this function is to be performed in a joint action by the executive branch and the Knesset Constitution and Law Committee. On the other hand, when an ordinary foreign sovereign state is claiming sovereign immunity, the function of characterizing the act and deciding the extent of immunity under FSIL lies fully and exclusively in the hands of the Israeli judiciary.

6. In the Final Analysis—Politics Override the Judiciary

Neither the Israeli courts nor the Knesset convincingly rationalized in any direct way this politicization of the process of granting foreign sovereign immunity to the PA. This void becomes particularly intriguing, given the overwhelming tendency in other legal systems—particularly those that Israeli courts looked into when devising the appropriate local standard on foreign sovereign immunity—to distance the executive branch, let alone the legislative branch, from the decision whether the foreign entity deserves foreign sovereign immunity in the particular case at hand. If any power is reserved to a non-judicial body, it is usually the power of determining whether the foreign entity is a state or not, but not if that entity (even if not a fully recognized state) should be granted immunity under the circumstances—and if so to what extent. The *Noritz* majority based its deference to the executive branch on the contention that the status of the PA is a subject of controversy within the Israeli public. Likewise, it can be argued that if the status of PA is as such, than why not call for the input of the Israeli Knesset? But this is like adding insult to injury; courts in Israel, like those of many other countries, have been constantly drawn into matters of public debate. Thus, for example, the courts have decided on issues pertaining to the definition of who is a Jew,[172] whether there should be restrictions on transportation on the Sabbath,[173] the recognition of same-sex marriage celebrated abroad,[174] and the disqualification of lists of candidates because of their political agendas.[175]

The legislative history of FSIL was more elaborate. This enactment was in large part derived from the work of a committee of experts appointed by the Ministry of Justice in order to produce a model law on foreign sovereign immunity for Israel.[176] Four academics and representatives of the government, one of whom was the legal advisor of the Ministry of Foreign Affairs, comprised this committee. Initially, the committee was of the opinion that the question of whether a foreign entity qualifies as a state or not is a legal one that should be answered by the judiciary rather than be determined by a certificate of executive branch.[177] However, in the model bill annexed to the committee report, the committee seems to have retracted its position deferring to the executive branch the decision on whether a foreign entity which is not a state is entitled to immunity.[178]

It is interesting to note that the Knesset deliberations on FSIL do afford more insight into why the grant of immunity to a foreign non-state entity should be the result of a joint action of the executive and legislative branches. When the FSIL bill was first introduced to the Knesset, Section 21 required only the production of a certificate from the Minister of Foreign Affairs (granted after consultation with the Attorney General and the approval of the government) that recognizes the immunity of the non-state foreign entity for immunity to be accorded by the court.[179] This bill, in its original form, managed to pass the first hurdle in the

---

172 For a review of the jurisprudence, *see* 1 AMNON RUBINSTEIN & BARAK MEDINA, HA-MISHPAT HA-HUKATI SHEL MEDINAT YISRA'EL [THE CONSTITUTIONAL LAW OF THE STATE OF ISRAEL] 398–409 (6th ed. 2005) (Hebrew).

173 HCJ 5016/96 Horev v. Minister of Transport, 51(4) PD 1 (1997).

174 HCJ 3045/05 Ben-Ari v. Director of Population Registry (Nov. 21, 2006), Nevo legal database (by subscription).

175 *See* 2 RUBINSTEIN & MEDINA, *supra* note 172, at 587–642.

176 STATE OF ISRAEL, MINISTRY OF JUSTICE & FOREIGN MINISTRY, HA-VA'ADA HA-TSIBURIT LE-HAKHANAT HOK HASINUT MEDINOT ZAROT: MISMAKHEI HA-VA'ADA [THE PUBLIC COMMITTEE ON DRAFTING THE FOREIGN STATES IMMUNITY LAW: THE COMMITTEE PAPERS] (2005) (Hebrew) [hereinafter COMMITTEE ON THE FOREIGN STATES IMMUNITY LAW].

177 *Id.* at 6–7.

178 *Id.* at 149.

179 Draft Foreign States Immunity Law, 5768-2008, HH (Gov't) 357, p. 334.

legislation process, the first reading, and was then referred for further deliberation in order to prepare it for the second and third readings, to the Knesset committee with the appropriate portfolio, which in this case was determined to be the Constitution and Law Committee. It has become a common practice in the deliberations of the various Knesset committees to hear out representatives of different stakeholders from the government, academia, and interest groups and lobbyists. In these deliberations, that it was argued that Section 21 is inadequate. The first to raise the issue was an attorney appearing on behalf of an NGO: The Legal Forum for the Land of Israel, which was established as an advocacy group on behalf of Jewish settlers who were evicted by the Israeli government in 2005 from the Gaza Strip and "Northern Samaria," better known as the Israeli Disengagement.[180] When presenting himself and later presenting his views, this representative was rather candid about two things: that he came before the committee for the sole interest of presenting a view regarding Section 21 of the bill,[181] and that he like everyone else took it that the primary importance of this section is to regulate the possible grant of immunity to the PA.[182] In substance, the primary argument he made is that the power of granting immunity to such a body should rest only in the hands of the executive branch but that another branch of government, like a Knesset committee or the court, should also have its say on the matter.[183] The point was immediately picked up by the chairman of the committee, who added that the grant of immunity should indeed be subject to a measure of a check and balance between the branches of government.[184] Following a practice that has evolved during his tenure as chairman, he proposed that his committee also approve of the grant of immunity for a non-state foreign entity.[185] Ultimately, this proposition was incorporated into Section 21, and in a later session in which only one committee member took part—the chairman himself—the amendment to the bill was approved.[186] Shortly afterwards, the bill was brought back to the Knesset floor for the final second and third readings on November 5, 2008, and Section 21 with its necessary two-branch approval procedure for granting

---

180 For this NGO's agenda, see http://www.haforum.org.il/newsite/about-us.asp.

181 Protocol No. 647, Constitution and Law Committee, Sept. 2, 2008, p. 3, *available at* http://www.knesset.gov.il/protocols/data/rtf/huka/2008-09-02-01.rtf.

182 *Id.* at 68.

183 *Id.*

184 *Id.* at 69–70.

185 *Id.*

186 Protocol No. 670, Constitution and Law Committee, Oct. 27, 2008, p. 28, *available at* http://www.knesset.gov.il/protocols/data/rtf/huka/2008-10-27.rtf.

immunity to a non-state foreign entity was enacted into law. The bill was unanimously approved—17 Knesset members voted in favor, with no abstentions or objections.

What stands out from this legislative process is that the rationale behind the multiple-hurdle process in FSIL, Section 21, is the concern that the executive brach will be too quick to grant sovereign immunity to a non-state foreign entity such as the PA. In order to balance any hastiness from the executive branch or prevent it from being overwhelmingly politically motivated, the bill provided that the Knesset Constitution and Law Committee, as an arm of another branch of government, should also approve of the grant of sovereign immunity to any such entity in question. What is particularly curious about the outcome is that no one seemed to be bothered by the fact that the Knesset Constitution and Law Committee, an inherently political body, can also be motivated by political concerns when asked to confirm the order of the Minister of Foreign Affairs. As things stand today, this committee can essentially veto any order issued by the Minister of Foreign Affairs that accords the PA immunity, and is free to do so on the basis of its members' political agenda.

7. The Functional Approach to the PA's Sovereign Immunity

Israel could have followed another path on this matter—that of functionalism. The committee of experts appointed by the Israeli Minster of Justice for the purpose of producing a model sovereign immunity law for Israel did relate to the possible grant of immunity to a foreign entity that has not attained full statehood. This committee had recommended that courts should follow a functional approach on this matter, rather than a formal one that grants immunity only if the foreign entity has attained statehood.[187] What lies at the heart of the suggested functional approach is that the grant of immunity must be derived from the objectives it is set to serve.[188] However, the committee report does not disclose what these objective are—at least not those that support the modern doctrine of foreign sovereign immunity. In the following, I discuss this functional approach to foreign sovereign immunity and observe that even when the subject of foreign sovereign immunity is analyzed from a functional perspective, the doctrine can be evenly susceptible to political interests.

---

187 Committee on the Foreign States Immunity Law, *supra* note 176, at 6–7.

188 *Id.*

As already indicated, the first step towards pursuing a functional analysis of the doctrine of foreign sovereign immunity is to establish the objectives that this doctrine seeks to attain. The doctrine can be functional only when the standards set for its applicability make it possible to achieve these objectives. As I have observed earlier, the traditional notion under which sovereign immunity is dictated by the principle of equality between states is not so convincing anymore. The primary objective of modern sovereign immunity is that of practical courtesy.[189] The judicial scrutiny of the public acts of one foreign entity by another can give rise to tensions and disrupt relations among them. One can thus argue that under this objective, the fact that a certain entity did not attain full statehood but only a partial one should not affect the decision regarding its sovereign immunity one way or another. What matters is the existence of a vital or meaningful sphere of international relations between these two entities. Given that such a sphere does indeed exist between the State of Israel and the PA, and that the relations between them can be strained or disrupted if one passes judgment on the public acts of the other, then the functional approach to sovereign immunity can very well justify granting sovereign immunity to the PA. Indeed, the existing body of jurisprudence on foreign sovereign immunity does include a number of cases where foreign entities that have not attained full statehood were granted sovereign immunity.[190] Thus, one scholar has noted that international law does not prohibit the grant of immunity to semi-independent states, just as it does not oblige states to grant immunity in such cases.[191] As a matter of fact, the Australian law on foreign sovereign immunity explicitly recognizes that a separate territory can also be granted sovereign immunity.[192]

This conclusion can be strengthened further from the inner logic that dictated the development of the modern restrictive theory of foreign sovereign immunity. Under the same rationale that foreign states that act as private parties should not be immune in a way that no other private party is when a claim is filed before a local court,[193] reason allows that if a foreign entity is accorded substantial governmental powers over a population and a territory and is expected to apply these powers like no other private party can, then it should be accorded the sovereign immunity.

189 Caplan, *supra* note 130, at 748.

190 Fox, *supra* note 129, at 424.

191 *Id.* at 423.

192 *See* Gavan Griffith, *Foreign Sovereign Immunity in Australia, in* 2 ESTUDIOS EN HOMENAJE A JORGE BARRERA GRAF 837, 842–43 (1989).

193 *See, e.g.*, García-Mora, *supra* note 129, at 344.

But a functional approach to the sovereign immunity of the PA, especially when considered by Israeli courts and other branches of government, implicates one other important aspect. The Palestinian nation and more recently the PA have constantly worked to gain international recognition of statehood.[194] Israel has constantly opposed these efforts.[195] In the post-Oslo period, the official Israeli position was that Palestinian statehood is a subject for the parties to negotiate and not for the Palestinians to unilaterally pursue. One can reasonably suspect that a grant of sovereign immunity by Israeli courts to the PA can curtail the Israeli efforts against Palestinian statehood, irrespective of whether the Palestinian claim of statehood is justified or not. In terms of global politics, such an act by Israeli courts can have far-reaching implications. If an Israeli court were to concede to the sovereign immunity claim of the PA, this act would not be considered just like a concession made by any other state. Rather, it would be a concession on the part of the Palestinians' main adversary; should it come to pass, other states would most probably just follow suit. The legislative history of FSIL's enactment provides evidence that such a consideration indeed influenced the design of sovereign immunity under that enactment. When discussing the propriety of granting sovereign immunity to foreign entities that have not yet attained full statehood (which participants understood to refer primarily to the PA), the chairman of the Knesset Constitution and Law Committee cautioned about the international implications of the grant of immunity in such cases.[196] As the chairman of the committee made explicitly clear, such a grant of immunity can very well indicate the *de jure* recognition of statehood.[197] This in turn corroborates yet further, in his view, why an arm of the Knesset, such as this committee, should also have a say on the subject, rather than depending exclusively on the executive branch.[198]

From the perspective of Israeli interests, these latter contentions can also take the form of a functional approach to sovereign immunity. The sphere of international relations that takes center stage here is not that between the immediate parties—in this case Israel and the PA. Rather, it is the sphere of international relations in general, and to be accurate, the ramification of the Israeli action in favor of sovereign immunity for the PA for the international community at large. If this

---

194 *See* Adam G. Yoffie, Comment, *The Palestine Problem: The Search for Statehood and the Benefit of International Law*, 36 YALE J. INT'L L. 497, 497 (2011). *See also* Chapter One, Section I(3).

195 Yoffie, *supra* note 194 at 505.

196 Protocol No. 647, *supra* note 181, at 73.

197 *Id.*

198 *Id.*

notion indeed underlay the FSIL scheme, then once again politics did dictate the outcome of the jurisdictional inquiry.

E. Summary

This chapter demonstrates once again how Israeli jurisdictional doctrines were particularly receptive to institutional policy concerns in PT-related civil disputes. Territorial control was central in devising Israeli courts' jurisdiction over PT land. It was also demonstrated here that as these interests became especially potent, an Israeli court was ready to issue an anti-suit injunction to prevent a PT court from adjudicating a local land dispute. On the other hand, when in the wake of the Oslo Accords Israeli interests in controlling land that was under the jurisdiction of the PA eased to some extent, so did the Israeli courts' willingness to let go of litigation over such land, even when an Israeli litigant was involved.

The case of jurisdiction over family law matters was the most accommodating of all. Israel simply acquiesced to the existing design, even when the jurisdictional authority of religious courts in East Jerusalem undermined Israel's territorial sovereignty over this part of the city. In spite of the initial position taken by the Israeli Supreme Court, these courts were permitted to continue operating under Jordanian laws as if nothing had happened there. Later on, a jurisdictional doctrine known as that of "double capacity" was adopted by the Court itself. A closer look at the jurisdictional design in family law matters also reveals that in some respects, this design was driven by an institutional policy of control. Maintaining the existing religious courts also maintained the division between the religious communities. In turn, these rifts make it easier for the establishment to better control this group.

The most intimate relationship between institutional policies and a jurisdictional policy was discernible in the sphere of foreign sovereign immunity. Though foreign legal systems and the new Israeli law have taken substantial leaps forward in limiting the role of political considerations in the granting of foreign sovereign immunity, this was not the case in terms of the Israeli experience with the PA. Today, an arm of the Israeli Knesset is required to approve of the grant of sovereign immunity to the PA, beyond the approval of the Israeli executive branch and the Attorney General.

CHAPTER 4

Choice of Law

Contents

Introduction

This chapter offers an analysis of the choice of law doctrines that developed in Israel over the years regarding Palestinian Territories (PT)-related disputes. The discussion that follows is divided into five main sections. The first focuses on legislative designs made by the IDF as well as the Israeli legislature and courts, by which norms were extended to apply to Israeli settlers living in the PT. The extraterritorial application of Israeli law in this fashion obviated much of the choice of law inquiry in PT civil litigation among Israeli settlers. The two following sections in this chapter deal with the choice of law doctrine that developed when no extraterritorial application of Israeli legislation took place. This discussion will concentrate on two such disputes that will be dealt with respectively: torts and contracts (with a special emphasis on employment relations). The two remaining sections highlight the importance of general priciples of equality and fairness in the choice of law evaluation.

A. Choosing the Law through Legislative Designs

It is widely acknowledged that the choice of law inquiry can be minimized if legislatures were to define the scope of their enactments, yet legislatures seldom do that. In most cases, norms are enacted without giving much thought to whether they should apply only to acts taking place in a certain territory or to a certain category of persons and corporations, and if so, whether their application need be exclusive. Ultimately, courts end up with the task of determining the scope of local and foreign legislation. If the competing norms happen to be in conflict, courts need to develop choice of law rules in order to choose which norm is controlling. The most frustrating part of this situation is that when scholars try to help out by developing choice of law rules that will ultimately help courts fulfill their obligation and reach definite resolutions of cases before them, some scholars find themselves being labeled "learned but eccentric professors who theorize about mysterious matters in a strange and incomprehensible jargon."[1]

With this in mind, one could, in a sense, compliment the Israeli efforts to undertake the painstaking job of defining the application of so many Israeli enactments regarding PT-related disputes. The resultant embroidery was clear, at least when perceived from a certain distance; it is that of a modern-day *millet* system. Israeli settlers living in the PT, the Israeli *millet*, are governed by one system of law, namely Israeli law, and the indigenous Palestinian population, the Palestinian *millet*, is governed by another system of law: the local law as preserved and amended.[2] Truthfully, in some cases, Palestinians sought to apply Israeli law and

1 William L. Prosser, *Interstate Publication*, 51 Mich. L. Rev. 959, 971 (1953).

2 Orna Ben-Naftali, Aeyal M. Gross & Keren Michaeli, *Illegal Occupation: Framing the Occupied Palestinian Territory*, 23 Berkeley J. Int'l L. 515, 584 (2005) (commenting that the legal reality in the PT consists of "separate legal systems operating concurrently . . . effectively dividing the population along ethnic lines. Jewish settlers are extra-territorially subject to Israeli law, whereas the Palestinians are subject to the military orders and local law.")

won, and Israelis—even the Israeli establishment—have sought to benefit from local PT norms (especially in cases of takings of real property) and succeeded in doing so. But these were the exceptions, and as far as Israel was concerned, most of these exceptions were allowed since ultimately, they also served a specific Israeli interest.

In one of the first scholarly works on Israeli policies in the PT, Eyal Benvenisti called this reality "legal dualism," given that two systems of law apply to Israelis and Palestinians living the PT.[3] This classification, of course, bears much truth. But as I will reveal in the following sections, the guiding norms in this respect went beyond the identification of two systems of laws that operated in the PT. The system also developed norms to guide courts in mixed Israeli-Palestinian cases. I will show that when such disputes emerged, the predominant tendency was to turn to Israeli law, just like when during the Ottoman Empire Islamic *Shari'a* courts applying the *Shari'a* itself had the residual jurisdiction authority in disputes between local subjects who belonged to different *millets*. The superior status of Israeli interests and Israeli law as the law of the hegemon was controlling, thereby making the existing reality more complex than just that of legal dualism.

1. Importing Israeli Law: PT Military Orders

The orders of the IDF military commander in the PT not only have the force of primary legislation there, but also, in terms of hierarchy, they supersede any existing pre-occupation law. So any local PT enactment that is designed to apply to all those who live in the PT or regards acts that take place in the region will no longer apply if by virtue of an IDF military commander's order, some other norm is meant to apply to a certain category of people.[4]

The primary design through which Israeli law was imported into the PT for the purpose of governing Israeli settlers was that of local government.[5] Local government bodies in Israeli settlements were categorized into two types: regional councils in the rural areas, and municipal councils in urban centers. In the orders governing both these bodies, the IDF military commander accorded himself the

3 Eyal Benvenisti, Legal Dualism: The Absorption of the Occupied Territories into Israel 3–4 (1989).

4 Eyal Benvenisti, The International Law of Occupation 236 (2d ed. 2012) [hereinafter Benvenisti, International Law of Occupation].

5 *See* Amir Paz-Fuchs & Yaël Ronen, *Occupational Hazards*, 30 Berkeley J. Int'l L. 580, 600 (2012).

power to determine rules governing the constituents.[6] Thereafter, Israeli enactments were adopted on a wholesale basis in respect to these residents, all of whom were, of course, Israeli settlers.[7] These enactments were divided among twelve categories: welfare, statistics, personal status, education, health, labor, agriculture, condominiums, environmental protection, consumer protection and commerce, communications, and religion.[8] To make things less complicated, the military orders provided that in case any of these enactments are amended in Israel, then the amendment will automatically apply in these local government units without the need to amend the military order.[9] Furthermore, if under any of the stipulated enactments, administrative agencies were empowered to perform certain functions (such as supervision or licensing), these powers cover settlements as well.[10] Operating within this local government regime was a court system that was also established by a military order in 1983: the Court of Local Affairs. In Israel, this court would normally deal with disputes between residents and their respective municipality. In the settlements, however, the judicial functions of these courts were extended much beyond this, to deal with disputes under the laws that were imported into the settlements. Additionally, these courts had the power of a small-claims court handling small-scale civil disputes of all types. Eventually, a special appeals court was established for these courts as well.[11]

2. Exporting Israeli Law: Extraterritorial Application of Israeli Legislation

Another method by which Israeli law was extended to settlements in the PT was by defining the scope of Israeli legislation so that the specific enactment will be applicable to Israelis who reside in the PT. Major pieces of legislation in the sphere of criminal law, taxes, elections to the Knesset, national insurance, and conscription were applied to Israelis in the PT. A special definition of "Israelis" was adopted for the purpose of determining the extraterritorial application of Israeli legislation. An "Israeli" included "also a person whose place of residence is the Area [the West Bank or Gaza Strip] and who is an Israeli citizen, or who is entitled to

6 Order on the Administration of Regional Councils (Judea and Samaria) (No. 783), 5739-1979, K.M.Z.M. 45, 88 (1980); Order on the Administration of Municipal Councils (Judea and Samaria) (No. 892), 5741-1981, K.M.Z.M. 48, 864 (1982).

7 *See* Paz-Fuchs & Ronen, *supra* note 5, at 601.

8 Benvenisti, International Law of Occupation, *supra* note 4, at 236.

9 *Id.*

10 *Id.* 236–37.

11 *Id.* at 237.

immigrate to Israel under the Law of Return, 1950...."[12] So in principle, the definition includes the Jewish residents of the PT and relatives of Jews who might not be Jewish themselves, but it certainly excludes the local Palestinian population.

Yet further efforts were made in this regard as well. Courts have also played their role in extending the application of Israeli legislation to Israeli settlers through various methods of judicial construction.[13] A prominent case in this regard is *Eden v. Eden*.[14] A Jewish Israeli couple who married in Israel left the country to live in the United States. Following the marriage's apparent failure, the wife together with the couple's four children came back to Israel. The husband did not approve of the wife's return to Israel, certainly not with the children. When the husband came back to Israel looking for his children, he found them living with their mother in an Israeli settlement in the Gaza Strip. The husband then initiated proceedings to have the children returned to the United States under Israel's Hague Convention Law (Return of Abducted Children), 1991, the objective of which is to give effect in Israel to the Convention of October 25, 1980 on the Civil Aspects of International Child Abduction.[15] The basic question was whether this Israeli enactment was applicable to children held beyond Israeli borders, namely in an Israeli settlement in the Gaza Strip. The Israeli Supreme Court gave an affirmative answer. The Court reasoned that the central purpose of the Israeli enactment was to give effect to the rules outlined in the Hague Abduction Convention, by which children who are wrongfully removed from one country should be returned there unless one of the specified exceptions apply. The Court held that Israel's commitment to enforce this principle would be frustrated if children held in an Israeli PT settlement were considered beyond the reach of the Israeli enactment. So in order to fulfill the purpose of the Israeli enactment, as well as that of the Hague Abduction Convention, what matters is whether Israel has effective control over the territory in which the children are held, such as in the case of PT Israeli settlements.[16] This decision provides strong support to the proposition that when an Israeli court identifies a powerful Israeli interest, and this interest is better served when Israeli law is applied extra-territorially to the PT, then by virtue of statutory interpretation, Israeli legislation will be extended to apply there.

---

12 Benvenisti, International Law of Occupation, *supra* note 4, at 234 n.187.

13 *See* Paz-Fuchs & Ronen, *supra* note 5, at 602–03.

14 CA 6056/93, 51(4) PD 197 (1997).

15 SH No. 1355, p. 148.

16 *Eden*, 51(4) PD at 201.

3. Settlements as "Israeli Enclaves"

The aggregate effect of importing Israeli law into the PT by a host of Military Orders and its export by the extraterritorial application of Israeli enactments created the Israeli *millet* in the PT. Israelis, largely defined as such based on national-ethnic lines, living in the PT are governed by Israeli law as if they were living in Israel itself. Therefore, in terms of the identity of the governing norms, PT Israeli settlements were in fact not much different from East Jerusalem and the Golan Heights.[17] It is not surprising, therefore, that scholarly articles, as well as Israeli court decisions, have commonly referred to the Israeli settlements as "Israeli enclaves."[18]

This state of affairs spared Israeli courts from the need to deal with a whole range of choice of law issues, particularly where the dispute involved Israeli settlers or Israeli parties generally. In all such cases, Israeli law was regarded as governing, to the extent that the choice of law question in such cases could be perceived as a non-issue. Given the political-nationalistic agenda behind the Israeli settlement project, an Israeli settler would not even consider the option of *not* applying Israeli law, whether he or she were litigating the case against another Israeli settler or against an Israeli government agency. By virtue of raising such an argument or suggesting that the intra-settlers dispute is not governed by Israeli law, a settler litigant would essentially undermine the authority by which his/her own status and rights became possible. But at times, the reality of maximizing self-interests seemed to be much more powerful than any political agenda. Indeed, on certain occasions, Israeli settlers did try to argue that the PT are beyond the reach of Israeli law, when the argument was self-serving. The judgment in *Eden* is one example. Another one is *KPA Pladot Kiryat Arba Ltd. v. State of Israel.*[19] In that case, six individuals and a firm, all of which were based in the West Bank settlement of Kiryat Arba, were indicted before an Israeli court with income tax-related offences, mainly for their failure to file their annual tax reports with the Israeli Tax Authority. The defendants raised a host of preliminary arguments in order to have all of the indictments summarily dismissed. They argued that they are not obliged to file any annual tax report, given that they do not reside in Israel and because international law restricts Israel from levying taxes on individuals residing in what their own attorney termed

---

17 *See supra*, Chapter One, Parts B–C.

18 This term is a translation of the Hebrew term *muvla'ot Yisraeliyot*, coined by Amnon Rubinstein in the late 1980s. *See* Amnon Rubinstein, *Yisra'el ve-ha-Shtakhim: Samkhuyot Shiput* [*Israel and the Territories: Judicial Powers*], 14 IYUNEI MISHPAT 415, 456 (1989) (Hebrew). The Israeli Supreme Court adopted this term in CA 1432/03 Yanon Manufacturing and Marketing of Foodstuffs Ltd. v. Qara'an, 59(1) PD 345, 379 (2004) (*per* E. Rivlin, J.).

19 CA 123/83, 38(1) PD 813 (1984).

as "occupied territories" no less![20] The Court rejected the argument, showing that like many other Israeli enactments, Israeli income tax law has also been extended to Israelis residing in the PT. Given the wording of the Israeli tax law that explicitly taxes income generated by Israelis in the PT and which the court cited verbatim,[21] it was hard to imagine that the Court could have reached any other conclusion. What is more important about this decision and that in *Eden*, in which the letter of the law was less forthright but was extended to the PT nonetheless, is that they guided courts in resolving the choice of law inquiry in an Israeli- PT related dispute in favor of Israeli law.[22] In cases involving Israeli settlers, Israeli law was conceived as being the only law applicable to the controversy, thereby denying the very fact that a conflict exists among different potentially governing laws. Using the terminology developed within the governmental interest analysis approach, these cases presented a "false conflict," since only Israeli law was considered to have an interest in disputes among Israeli settlers. The main reason for this determination was the identity of the involved litigants. One Israeli magistrate court judge was rather candid about this. In *Bitton v. Helman*,[23] the plaintiff was a real estate agent working in the Israeli settlement of Ma'ale Adumim who claimed his fees from the defendant after having allegedly brokered the sale of a home in that settlement. The defendant argued that the sale took place irrespective of the any efforts put forth by the plaintiff. Additionally, she argued that the plaintiff could make the claim, given that Israeli law that regulates the operation of sale agents require registration and other forms of licensing that the plaintiff had not fulfilled. The plaintiff then replied that this Israeli law did not apply in Ma'ale Adumim, given that it is a West Bank settlement. The judge of the Magistrate Court in Jerusalem dismissed these arguments. He reasoned that in almost all spheres of life, Israeli settlers are guided by Israeli law and their relation with the local Jordanian law "is nothing more than an abstract proposition devoid from any real implication (with the exception of land ownership law)."[24] He then went on to hold that given the reality in the PT, it is justified that Israeli law generally applies on a personal basis to all Israelis who reside there.

Applying one's law on a personal rather than on a territorial basis is exactly how the Ottoman *millet* system operated during the reign of the Ottoman Empire.

---

20 *Id.* at 819.

21 *Id.*

22 *See* BENVENISTI, INTERNATIONAL LAW OF OCCUPATION, *supra* note 4, at 238 ("The jurisprudence of the Israel courts in choice of law issues also constituted the extension").

23 CC (Jer) 6718/05 at 7 (Feb. 27, 2006), Nevo Legal Database (by subscription). I owe the reference to this decision to Paz-Fuchs & Ronen, *supra* note 5, at 603.

24 CC (Jer) 6718/05, *Bitton* at 7.

Although locals were governed by one sovereign, the laws that governed their actions could differ given their religious affiliation. However, during the Ottoman times, at least in the nineteenth century and onward, the *millet* system was operational in the realm of family law, with territorial laws introduced to govern other relations. The system of laws governing Israeli settlers in the PT is of much wider application, including both civil and public law, all in addition to the long-standing *millet* system in matters of family law.

In terms of the choice of law inquiry, this modern-day *millet* design had far-reaching implications beyond defining the governing laws in intra-Israeli *millet* affairs in the PT. This same design automatically created another *millet*—the Palestinian one. Indeed, when Palestinians brought their mutual civil disputes before the Israeli courts, the jurisdictional design created in the PT had a powerful signaling effect, saying that in such an instance, the Israeli court should apply local PT law rather than Israeli law. As we have already seen in Chapter Two and as I will further clarify in the following sections, Israel managed to maintain the Palestinian *millet* by means of the forum non conveniens doctrine, which effectively operated as a choice of law rule.

The hard cases were those of a mixed nature, i.e., Israeli-Palestinian civil disputes. In the past, like in late-nineteenth-century Egypt, mixed cases between locals and foreigners were referred to mixed courts.[25] However, no such institute was established in Israel. What developed was a peculiar body of choice of law rules of a mixed character—some were overtly protective of Israeli interests, while others were more considerate of Palestinian interests. The two following sections dealing with choice of law in torts and contracts (employment relations) will focus on these mixed disputes, as well as on Palestinian-Palestinian disputes that were brought before Israeli courts.

B. Choice of Law in Torts

1. Introduction

Like in many other common law jurisdictions, the Israeli choice of law rule for torts has undergone some genuine reforms over the years. In general, one can point to three different approaches that developed gradually. The initial basis was

25 *See, e.g.*, MARK S.W. HOYLE, MIXED COURTS OF EGYPT (1991).

the English rule that demonstrated an obvious bias for the law of the forum as the governing law. A second source was the most significant contacts test modeled after the American Restatement (Second) on the Conflict of Laws. The third system to be applied is the current approach that follows the *lex loci delicti* rule, with the exception that if the underlying dispute is significantly connected to another jurisdiction then the law of that jurisdiction applies. Ultimately, all three approaches have been followed regarding PT-related disputes. The discussion that follows will relate to each of these approaches separately, and in doing so will try to highlight to the fullest extent possible the policy consideration that stood at the basis of each approach.

2. The English Rule

Faithful to their English law heritage in the sphere of conflicts, Israeli courts commenced their practice with the English rule as prescribed in *Phillips v. Eyre*.[26] According to the formula articulated in this landmark English decision from 1870, a claim based on a tort committed in a foreign jurisdiction can be filed in the local court if the act on which the claim is based is (1) actionable according to the local law of the forum (*lex fori*); and (2) unjustifiable according to the local law where the tort was committed (*lex loci delicti commissi*). Initially, some questions loomed as to whether this is a jurisdictional rule instructing English courts regarding their competence to deal with foreign torts.[27] However, it was soon clarified that these two conditions do form English law's basic choice of law rule for foreign torts, given that if both of these conditions are satisfied, then the court is supposed to apply its own law as the governing law.[28] In due course, the *Phillips v. Eyre* rule underwent a major modification in the wake of the House of Lords' 1969 decision in *Boys v. Chaplin*.[29] Though the Law Lords did not seem to have any clear majority in favor of a particular holding, it was commonly believed that as a result of the decision, the English choice of law rule in torts was that of double actionability. From that point on, the action on which the claim for the foreign tort is based needs also be actionable (not just unjustifiable) according to the *lex loci delicti* rule. Once this second prong is satisfied, the English forum could apply its own law. The main reason for this modification is the need

26 (1870) 6 Q.B.D. 1.

27 *See* Peter Handford, *Edward John Eyre and the Conflict of Laws*, 32 Melbourne U. L. Rev. 822, 823–24 (2008).

28 *Id.* at 823 n.9.

29 [1971] A.C. 356 (H.L.).

to control forum shopping. If the act on which the claim is based must only be unjustifiable in the country in which it took place, say because it is considered a criminal act but does not form a civil cause of action, then an English forum with proper personal jurisdiction over the defendant will be especially sought after by the plaintiff when the action is also actionable under English law.[30] Additionally, the *Boys v. Chaplin* ruling was believed to contain an exception. If the claim as brought before the English court is not actionable according to the *lex loci delicti*, then English law can still govern—as long as it has the most significant contact to the underlying dispute.[31]

The Israeli Supreme Court adopted the English choice of law rule in torts in 1954.[32] This Court did not have a chance to consider reformulating the rule in light of *Boys v. Chaplin*. Lower courts, however, did consider the issue and eventually adopted what was considered as guiding in the House of Lords' decision.[33]

a. Applying the English Rule in an All-Israeli Dispute

The application of the English choice of law rule in torts presented no real challenge for Israeli courts when both the plaintiff and the defendant were Israelis. After all, the English rule as articulated before and after *Boys v. Chaplin* sought to apply the *lex fori* if and when the two prongs of the rule are met. As we have observed from the discussion on the extraterritorial application of Israeli norms to acts taking place in the PT, the approach adopted by courts clearly favored ruling in favor of the extraterritorial application, when the concerned parties were all Israelis. In other words, the English choice of law rule was perfectly aligned with what would become the dominant approach in terms of applying Israeli law when all of the concerned parties in a PT-related dispute are Israelis.

---

30 The case that is commonly cited in order to show the potential for forum shopping of the *Phillips v. Eyre* rule is Machado v. Fontes, [1897] 2 Q.B. 231 (C.A.). An action based on a libel committed in Brazil was filed in England. Under Brazilian law at the time, libel was a crime but did not form a cause for a civil action. Under English law, libel was actionable. Given these attributes, the *Phillips v. Eyre* rule was satisfied and the English court applied its own law. The case drew much criticism, given that the plaintiff used the English forum in a clear act of forum shopping, for England had no real connection to the underlying libel dispute.

31 *See* 2 Dicey, Morris & Collins, The Conflict of Laws 2201 (Lord Collins of Mapesbury general ed., 15th ed. 2012).

32 *See* CA 180/51 Goldkorn v. Wissotzky, 8 PD 262, 266 (1954). The Court reaffirmed its commitment to the English rule some 13 years later in CA 98/67 Liebherr v. Gazit & Shaham Building Co. Ltd., 21(2) PD 243, 249 (1967).

33 *See* CA 178/71 (TA) Grossman v. Mekorot Mayim, Development Works Co. Ltd., PM 5736(1) 386, 391 (1975); CC (BS) 151/80 Kaplan v. Gabbay, PM 5742(2) 290 (1982).

Israeli courts faced a dilemma when applying the English rule to an all-Israeli foreign tort litigation when one of the two prongs of the English rule, especially the second, was not satisfied. Would the Israeli court be prepared to dismiss the claim if it happens to be perfectly actionable according to Israeli law? A review of the relevant cases leads me to conclude that the answer was clearly in the negative. Israeli courts always managed to find a good excuse as to why Israeli law should still apply, notwithstanding the fact that they may be unable to determine the exact position of the *lex loci delicti* rule in respect to the pending claim. This situation, in turn, substantiates yet further the assessment that when Israelis are involved, Israeli law will apply even if the action took place in the PT.

The first indication for this situation came back in 1958, in *Blau v. State of Israel*,[34] some nine years before the Six-Day War. In the aftermath of the 1956 Suez War (Crisis), Israel occupied the Sinai Peninsula for a period of five months (November 1956–March 1957). During this period, a group of three Israelis who were touring the Sharm al-Shiekh resort town in Sinai were injured in a road-traffic accident, while riding in an IDF vehicle driven by an IDF soldier. One of the injured passengers filed a civil action before an Israeli court, claiming damages for his injuries from the State of Israel based on the theory of *respondeat superior*. Given that the alleged accident took place outside of Israel in what the court considered an occupied territory, it turned to the then-applicable English choice of law rule that required proof of the act being unjustifiable under the *lex loci delicti*. The relevant law was deemed to be that of Egypt, for under the principles of belligerent occupation, the local law of the occupied territory rather than the law of the occupying force continues to apply. However, the plaintiff, who carried the burden of proof regarding the two prongs of the English rule, easily passed the first (the negligent driving of an IDF soldier was apparently actionable under Israeli law, and Israeli law supposedly recognized the principle of *respondeat superior*) but failed to offer up-to-date evidence regarding the second. The best he could do was to provide expert testimony as to the state of Egyptian law in 1948. The expert on Egyptian law was an Israeli who practiced law in Egypt until he immigrated to Israel shortly after the state's establishment. According to this testimony, the accident was assumed to be an unjustifiable act under Egyptian law.[35] The State of Israel mounted a forceful defense against the claim. First, it argued that the second prong was not sufficiently proven, given

34 CC (Haifa) 440/58, 22 PM 41 (1958).

35 *Id.* at 44.

that the expert testimony did not provide any proof about Egyptian law recognizing the principle of *respondeat superior*. The court dismissed this argument, explaining that the English rule at the time only demanded that the action be unjustified under the *lex loci delicti*, but not necessarily actionable.[36] Second, the defendant argued that the expert testimony should be dismissed because it did not provide evidence as to the state of Egyptian law on the date of the accident. The court dismissed this argument as well. In its place, it applied the common law presumption that the particular foreign law is the same as local law.[37] In fact, the court sensed that applying this presumption in the context of the English choice of law rule in torts is problematic. Practically, the presumption, certainly if applied regularly, would abolish the second limb of the rule. Nonetheless, the court justified the application of the presumption in light of the state of relations between Egypt and Israel, under which collecting up-to-date materials concerning Egyptian law is difficult; the court noted that the plaintiff did the best he could to provide some evidence in respect of that law.[38] As a result, Israeli law was deemed as the governing law.

Two other district court judgments affirmed this approach. These holdings also dealt with an all-Israeli litigation concerning a tort that took place in the Sinai Peninsula, but this time after this territory's second occupation in the 1967 Six-Day War.[39] Once again, no proper proof was offered regarding Egyptian law as the *lex loci delicti*. Yet this failure did not bring these two courts to summarily dismiss the action, as they should have once the plaintiff does not satisfy his burden. Moreover, both courts were of the opinion that no need exists to even refer to the presumption that the foreign law is the same as the local law. In light of the fact that all parties to the litigation are Israelis, even if the claim is not actionable according to the *lex loci delicti*, this fact pattern provided the suitable situation for applying the now-acceptable exception under *Boys v. Chaplin*. Party expectations, as well as the lack of any interest on part of Egypt to have its laws apply to such parties when its territory is being occupied by Israel, make Israeli law the one with the most significant contact.

36 *Id.*

37 *Id.* at 45.

38 *Id.*

39 *See Kaplan*, PM 5742(2) 290; Summons (Jer) 1329/84 Kupat Holim of the General Federation of Laborers in the Land of Israel v. Neveh Midbar Sharm al-Sheikh Ltd. (in Liquidation), PM 5745(2) 412 (1984).

In yet a third opinion (*Abu Itta*) that will be discussed below, Judge Dalia Dorner, while serving on the District Court of Jerusalem (later to become a Justice on the Supreme Court), summed up the situation in the most candid way possible:

> It appears that when all of the involved parties to a wrong that occurred in the Administered Territories [i.e., PT] belong to the same group of the population, the approach discernible from Israeli judgments regarding the forum for adjudication and choice of law is clear and straight forward: the matter should be adjudicated in the parties' home forum and in accordance with the local law there.[40]

b. Applying the English Rule in an All-Palestinian Dispute

So courts are now speaking frankly about different groups of people that are governed by different laws if the wrong that takes place in the PT involves one specific group. So far, I have demonstrated this situation regarding wrongs involving Israelis. But what about choice of law inquiries by Israeli courts when the wrong committed in the PT involves only Palestinians? If Israeli courts were to apply the English rule, the result would have been somewhat different from what Judge Dorner indicated. As noted before, if the two prongs of the English rule are satisfied, the court is supposed to apply the *lex fori*. So in a case filed in an Israeli court where all parties are Palestinians, the governing law is deemed to be that of Israel, rather than that of the PT. Moreover, when the Israeli choice of law rule for torts was still the English rule, there would have been no problem establishing personal jurisdiction in an all-Palestinian dispute brought before the Israeli court. The *Al-Khir* holding requiring only the personal service of process was applicable in all PT-related personal actions.[41] More importantly, given that torts were governed in Israel by the Civil Wrong Ordinance, if the action was actionable under this enactment, then it would almost certainly be actionable under local PT law. The reason was simple. This same ordinance is a legacy from the British Mandate and as such, it was also absorbed into both the local law of the West Bank and the Gaza Strip.

Though all-Palestinian tort claims were often filed before Israeli courts, I could not find one Israeli court decision in which the English choice of law rule in torts was applied. This is not surprising. Should Israeli courts have applied this rule, the

40 CC (Jer) 910/82 National Insurance Institute v. Abu Itta, PM 5748(2) 133, 142 (1988).

41 LCA 55/71 Al-Khir & Sons Co. v. Van Der Hurst Fruit Import, 25(2) PD 13 (1971). See *supra* Chapter Two, Part C.1.a.

outcome would have yielded Israeli law as the governing law—a result that defies the *millet* paradigm according to which Palestinians should be governed by local PT law. The reason why no choice of law inquiry was undertaken by Israeli courts regarding an all-Palestinian tort litigation was that courts did not have a chance to reach that stage. As soon as access to Israeli courts was provided to Palestinians, the forum non conveniens doctrine was made available to Israeli courts and applied regularly in all-Palestinian tort litigation.[42] This doctrine made it possible to decline the acquired jurisdictional authority at an early stage of the adjudication, thus making application of the existing choice of law rule unnecessary.

The most interesting part of the use of the forum non conveniens doctrine in an all-Palestinian dispute involved turning the doctrine into a choice of law rule rather than just a jurisdictional doctrine. Ultimately, when all the parties were Palestinians, normative considerations—such as the most suitable forum in which to apply the governing norms—became instrumental in determining the natural forum for litigation. This strong normative quest became evident shortly after Palestinians were provided unhindered access to Israeli courts following the 1979 venue amendment.[43] The Israeli Supreme Court approved of this course in *Salhat v. Municipality of Nablus*.[44] Maher Salhat, a Palestinian minor who was 15 years old at the time of the accident at issue, was a resident of a village in the vicinity of the West Bank city of Nablus. While visiting his aunt, Maher climbed up an electricity post, came in contact with a high velocity cable, and suffered severe personal injuries as a result of the electric shock. Given that the Municipality of Nablus was in charge of maintaining the electric network in the area, Maher named it as a defendant and claimed entitlement to damages. At first, proceedings were taken in the name of Maher before the local PT courts and IDF authorities, but later these were terminated and a civil action was filed in the District Court of Jerusalem. As expected, the action was stayed on forum non conveniens grounds—for all the parties were Palestinians and the place of the wrong was in the PT. On appeal, the Supreme Court affirmed. After stressing the fact that the claim against the defendant is based on its alleged negligence and its failure to abide by some statutory obligations, the president of the Supreme Court at the time, Meir Shamgar, went on to explain that the norms governing these

---

42 *See* CA 300/84 Abu Attiya v. Arabtisi, 39(1) PD 365 (1985); CA 588/83 Al-Rayis v. Arab Insurance Co. Ltd., 38(3) P.D. 495 (1984); CA 489/85 Salahat v. Municipality of Nablus, 42(1) PD 497 (1988); Summons (Jer) 1410/83 Arab Insurance Company v. Khader, PM 5744(2) 172 (1984); Originating Summons (Jer) 748/82 Jabbour v. Hanitan, PM 5743(1) 499 (1982).

43 *See Khader*, PM 5744(2) at 175; *Jabbour*, PM 5743(1) at 507.

44 CA 489/85, 42(1) PD 497 (1988).

claims have a strong local element.[45] Therefore, he concluded, it was appropriate that these norms that are also influenced by local conditions of life as well as public interests "be determined and assessed by local courts."[46]

What emerges from this mode of application of the forum non conveniens doctrine is obvious: the quest to achieve what is predetermined to be the appropriate normative outcome of the whole adjudicative procedure, rather than just adjusting the jurisdictional assessment. Accordingly, disputes are believed to be better handled by the forum that will apply the proper norms. If at some point in the conflict's analysis, scholars believed that first one needs to determine the proper forum for adjudication and then identify that fourm's law as the proper law that should govern the case,[47] the course just identified purports to do the exact opposite. It identifies what should be the proper law to govern the case and then deems the forum of that law as the proper forum for adjudication. As I have demonstrated elsewhere, this course of action is by no means special to Israel. Different courts in other jurisdictions have also taken into consideration the normative interests of the competing forums in order to determine the most appropriate forum in which to adjudicate the dispute.[48] The Israeli course stands out, perhaps, in that it identified the proper law that should govern the case independently from the applicable choice of law rule at the time. Supposedly, if a forum is to identify the proper law that should govern the dispute, then it should at least consult the rules that were entrusted by the forum to identify this law—the relevant choice of law rules. Yet such consideration never took place. The reason for this, in my assessment, is quite clear. If Israeli courts were to defer to the existing choice of law rules in torts at the time, they would have found them to refer to Israeli law as the governing law. This law was not the one deemed proper when all the parties were Palestinians seeking to litigate a PT tort dispute in Israel. As we have seen, Judge Dorner was rather candid about this. So essentially, courts in Israel sought to rectify this undesirable result by placing in motion a jurisdictional instrument—the forum non conveniens doctrine—in order to achieve what was predetermined to be the appropriate normative result.

---

45 *Id.* at 504.

46 *Id.*

47 *See* Albert A. Ehrenzweig, *A Proper Law in a Proper Forum: A "Restatement" of the* "Lex Fori" *Approach*, 18 OKLA. L. REV. 340 (1965).

48 MICHAEL KARAYANNI, FORUM NON CONVENIENS IN THE MODERN AGE 82–86 (2004). As I also argue, this normative calculation within the forum non conveniens doctrine will become much more dominant in the future. *Id.* at 212–29.

One Israeli Supreme Court Justice sought to rectify this tension between the existing choice of law rule in torts and the forum non conveniens doctrine by proposing to adopt a new choice of law rule in torts modeled on the American Law Institutes Restatement (Second) of Conflict of Laws, which identifies the law with the most significant contact with the underlying dispute as the governing law. This course was followed in *Abu Attiya v. Arabtisi*.[49] Like all of the cases discussed above, this case also dealt with an alleged wrong that took place in the PT (a factory in Ramallah where the plaintiff was employed and injured in a work-related accident) and was between a Palestinian plaintiff and a Palestinian defendant (who also happened to be insured by an insurance company with a branch in Jerusalem). The main judgment of the Court was handed down by Justice Strassberg-Cohen, who, as already indicated, favored the American "most significant contacts" test as the choice of law rule in torts. After also adopting the modern American approach on forum non conveniens, which takes into consideration choice of law as one factor, the newly-adopted choice of law rule identifies PT law as the governing law. So if the forum non conveniens doctrine seeks to identify the natural forum for litigation while taking into consideration public and private factors, the fact that the dispute will be governed by PT law favors litigation in the PT rather than in Israel. Yet Justice Strassberg-Cohen's opinion on this matter did not convince the other two Justices. Aharon Barak identified the choice of law consideration as a public factor, hence doubting whether courts should consider any public factors when making a decision on forum non conveniens.[50] In any event, Aharon Barak thought that in this specific case, no definite position needs to be taken on this subject, nor on the complicated issue of the choice of law rule in torts.[51] However, just before making these observations, Justice Barak himself reasoned that the appropriate forum in this case is in the PT. He made this assessment based on party expectations, maintaining that

> no meaningful connection exists between the underlying dispute and Israel. The reasonable expectations of all the parties is to have this dispute litigated in Judea and Samaria [i.e., the West Bank] and according to the law applicable there. This law is the law that has determined, according to party expectations, the level or risk they faced, the amount of premium payments and the expected level of compensation.[52]

49 39(1) PD 365.

50 *Id.* at 386.

51 *Id.*

52 *Id.* 385–86.

The third Justice of the panel sided with this holding of Justice Barak rather than that of Justice Strassburg-Cohen.[53]

With all due respect, it is hard to see how the considerations enumerated by Justice Barak are anything but normative. He is also saying that it is proper to have the adjudication held in the PT, because this will bring to the proper resolution of the dispute in terms of the rights and duties of the parties. Justice Strassberg-Cohen sought to identify this normative outcome by reference to what she deemed to be the proper choice of law rules, and Justice Barak by reference to normative considerations, irrespective of the existing choice of law rule.

If we are to consider Justice Barak's opinion alongside the decisions that were discussed above, my conclusion is that the forum non conveniens doctrine as applied in a wrong committed in the PT among all-Palestinian parties is considerably normative in character. The Court assembled its own normative consideration without specific reference to the existing choice of law rules in order to assure that the adjudication takes place in the PT. In this respect, the forum non conveniens doctrine functioned as a "detour" to the English choice of rule in torts which, if applied, would have pointed to Israeli law rather than PT law. Yet as we have seen in the previous section, when all of the concerned parties were Israelis, the court applied different exceptions in order to make sure that the English rule applies to the underlying dispute and hence to have Israeli law govern. This proves once again how candid Judge Dorner was when she commented that Israelis involved in civil wrongs committed in the PT were supposed to litigate their disputes in an Israeli forum and in accordance with Israeli law, while Palestinians' mutual local tort actions are supposed to be litigated in the PT and in accordance with PT law. Choice of law and jurisdictional rules have all been mended in order to achieve this aim. Referring back to the basic argument of this chapter that choice of law in the PT was motivated by the *millet* paradigm, it is safe to say that the forum non conveniens doctrine was instrumental in creating the Palestinian *millet* in the 1980s, which lasted until the creation of the Palestinian Authority (PA).

c. Mixed Israeli-Palestinian Tort Litigation

So far, the civil *millet* paradigm dominated the choice of law inquiry in PT related torts. When all the parties were Israelis, Israeli law governed and when all parties were Palestinians, local PT law governed. By definition, this *millet* paradigm does

53 *Id.* at 387.

not apply to mixed Israeli-Palestinian disputes, irrespective of who is suing whom. In the past, when the *millet* system was in effect in the Ottoman Empire, mixed disputes, at least when they implicated a foreign subject, were assigned in some places to mixed courts.[54] However, when all the subjects were locals, it was *Shari'a* courts and *Shari'a* law that maintained the residual jurisdictional authority.[55] No mixed courts were ever established to adjudicate mixed Israeli-Palestinian disputes, neither before the Oslo Accords nor after. Yet since Israeli law and Israeli courts were considered to be hegemonic when the PT were under total Israeli control, Israeli courts and Israeli law were considered to be the appropriate forum and the governing law, respectively.

The leading adjudication on this issue involves the Abu Itta factory in the West Bank town of Beit Sahour. In 1977 Yehezkel Ya'akobi, a resident of Israel, drove his truck from Israel to the Abu Itta factory in order to pick up a load of mattresses manufactured there and bring them back to Israel. The load was not ready when he arrived, so he took a nap on one of the mattresses that had been laid down in the factory. Welders were also working at the time in the factory. Apparently, a spark generated by this welding activity caused the fire that broke out in the factory and Mr. Ya'akobi lost his life as a result. His widow and dependent children filed a civil claim in the District Court of Jerusalem, claiming damages from the factory owner, Nicola Abu Itta, and the welders that were working in the factory—all of whom were residents of the West Bank (the welders were from the nearby town of Beit Jalla).[56] In the first round of litigation, the defendants tried to have the action dismissed for lack of jurisdiction and alternatively to be stayed, given that Israel was the inappropriate forum. These objections to litigating the case in Israel were all dismissed. Based on the *Al Khir* progeny, jurisdiction was found to be sufficiently established by virtue of service of process on the defendants in the West Bank. The court also did not find a sufficient basis for staying the action. At the time, the standards for a discretional stay were a bit more stringent than those of forum non conveniens, requiring the defendant to prove, among other issues, that the filing of the action in the local forum was oppressive or vexatious.[57] As

---

54 *See supra* Chapter Three, Part C.

55 *See* Edoardo Vitta, The Conflict of Laws in Matters of Personal Status in Palestine 103–04 (1947). Moreover, at the time some non-Muslim communities applied the Shari'a in order to gain more legitimacy in the eye of the Ottoman Empire, at least when the issue at hand did not implicate "vital interests of the community." *See* Frederic M. Goadby, International and Inter-Religious Private Law in Palestine 134 (1926).

56 CC 274/77 (Jerusalem) Ya'akobi v. Abu Itta (1980, unreported) (on file with the author).

57 *See supra* Chapter Two, Part C.2.

opposed to the obvious contacts of the defendants and the incident to the West Bank, the court stresses the following contacts to Israel: the plaintiffs are all residents of Israel; evidence and witnesses relevant for the proof of damages are in Israel; all defendants are residents of Beit Sahour and Beit Jalla townships, which are minutes away from the Jerusalem court; and no apparent hardships would prevent the defendants from bringing their witnesses to Jerusalem, nor would any special expenses be incurred in this respect. Therefore, the court found the filing of the action before the Israeli court to be neither vexatious nor oppressive. The Palestinian defendants appealed this decision to the Supreme Court, but to no avail.[58] The Court backed the lower court's decision on all counts and proceeded to highlight two additional considerations. First, the defendants did not come before the Israeli courts as residents and citizens of a foreign sovereign state. The IDF was in control of the West Bank, and thus there can be no actual infringement on the sovereignty of another state if this case is adjudicated in Israel. Second, although the West Bank was not annexed to Israel, the "reality of life" is such that this territory has become economically integrated with the State of Israel. The court noted the extensive commercial activities between residents of both sides, open transportation, and labor relations as testaments to this notion.

This round of litigation did not deal with the choice of law question—whether Israeli or local West Bank law (which the Court assume to be Jordanian) should govern. Towards the end of its decision, the Court noted that this choice of law inquiry is the sole serious legal question to be decided in this adjudication. When the litigation was reinitiated in the District Court of Jerusalem, the parties settled and agreed that the governing law between them was Jordanian. Given that the accident was work-related, the deceased dependents were already receiving certain benefits from the Israeli National Insurance Institute (NII); hence, the parties stipulated that their agreement regarding the governing law was not binding on the NII.

A short while afterwards, the NII filed a subrogation claim against the original defendants—the West Bank factory owner and the welders—to compensate it for the benefits it paid the deceased's dependents.[59] This action was based on Israeli law, as it recognized the entitlement of NII for such compensation from the tort-feasor. However, expert testimony on the applicable law in the PT (the original British Mandate Civil Wrong Ordinance) provided that no such subrogation

58 CA 425/81 Abu Itta v. Ya'akobi (1981, unreported) (on file with the author).

59 *Abu Itta*, PM 5748(2) 133.

right existed under this law.[60] Another expert testimony provided that local PT law would refer the parties to the foreign law if this law was recognized in a subrogation claim—a kind of *renvoi*.[61]

Judge Dalia Dorner was assigned the case. In the judgment she rendered (which I have referred to earlier),[62] she dismissed the need to decide upon the exact content of PT law, since she was of the opinion that this case was governed by Israeli law.[63] Judge Dorner's reasoning was fully policy-oriented. She adopted all of the considerations already stated in the jurisdictional inquiry in this same dispute as guiding in terms of choice of law.[64] Consequently, given that no foreign sovereign existed in the PT under IDF control, and the integrated relations of economy and daily life between Israel and the PT, it was reasonable to assume that Israelis who enter the PT should not expect to be governed by local law, nor should local Palestinians coming in contact with an Israeli expect to be governed by local law but rather by Israeli law. Why so? Because the PT "is only in theory under foreign sovereignty, but in reality is under Israeli control."[65] Given Israeli control, Israeli law and not local PT law governs. Local Palestinian residents should therefore adjust to the reality now created, at least when they come in contact with Israelis, and not the other way around. So if in the sphere of jurisdiction, this ruling notion became evident by making all those present in the PT come under Israeli jurisdiction by virtue of service of Israeli process and in the context of the forum non conveniens doctrine to decide in favor of the Israeli forum whenever the case implicates an Israeli element, the same was held in the sphere of choice of law as well. The existence of an Israeli element, in itself, makes Israeli law applicable.

I must add here that this conclusion is not just a theorizing effort on my part. Judge Dorner, whose rather candid approach was already noted before, makes it perfectly clear that the existing approach in the sphere of jurisdiction "is applicable for the purposes of choice of law."[66] Given these policy considerations, both public policy and reference to the *Boys v. Chaplin* exception point to Israeli law as the governing law. Indeed, under *Boys v. Chaplin*, if the act is not actionable under the *lex loci delicti*, the forum can still apply its law if it has the most significant contacts with

60 *Id.* at 137.

61 *Id.* at 137–38.

62 *See supra* Chapter Four, Part B.2.a.

63 *Abu Itta*, PM 5748(2) at 138.

64 *Id.* at 144.

65 *Id.* (citing her own decision in *Kaplan*, PM 5742(2) at 297).

66 *Abu Itta*, PM 5748(2) at 144.

the case. In light of the above, Judge Dorner evidently believe that Israel, rather than the PT, was the jurisdiction with the most significant contacts.

3. The Adoption of the Most Significant Contacts Approach

The traditional English choice of law rule for torts was not satisfactory, even in England itself. No wonder that as time went by, even after the rule's modification in *Boys v. Chaplin*, it was made subject to yet an additional exception.[67] Ultimately, the rule was abolished by Part III of the Private International Law (Miscellaneous Provisions) Act 1995.[68] This new enactment held the *lex loci delicti* as the governing law in torts but allowed the application of another law when that law was substantially more appropriate under the specific circumstance of the case. This English dissatisfaction with England's own choice of law rule for torts was sensed in Israel as well. On two different occasions in the first half of the 1980s, two Israeli Supreme Court Justices wrote lengthy opinions supporting the adoption of the most significant contacts test of the Restatement (Second) of the Conflict of Laws. The first was Justice Miriam Ben-Porath in *Klausner v. Berkovitz*,[69] and the second was Justice Strassberg-Cohen in *Abu Attia v. Arabtisi*.[70] These two Justices stressed the American approach's elasticity and the fact that it affords the court sufficient latitude to choose the most appropriate law as the governing law, in contrast to the rigidness and uncertainty that came to plague the English rule. Another important factor that helped these two Justices to adopt this approach was the fact that as of 1980, Israeli courts became freed from any legal obligation to resort to English common law in the case of a legal lacuna. Until that year, courts were governed by Article 46 of the British Mandate Order in Council, which directed local courts to look into English common law precedents when they could not find direction in local law in order to solve a particular legal question.[71] But this article was abolished in the Foundations Law, 1980, in which the "heritage of

---

67 *See* Red Sea Insurance Co. Ltd. v. Bouygues S.A. [1994] 3 All E.R. 749 (P.C.) (holding that the law of the forum where the wrong was committed can be applied if it has the most significant relationship, even if the action is not actionable according to the law of the forum).

68 Yet, in defamation cases the traditional English common law rules still apply. *See* CHESHIRE, NORTH & FAWCETT, PRIVATE INTERNATIONAL LAW 767–68 (James Fawcett & Janeen M. Carruthers eds., 14th ed. 2008).

69 CA 750/79, 37(4) PD 449, 459 (1983).

70 CA300/84, 38(1) PD 365, 381 (1985).

71 *See generally* A. LEVONTIN & H. GOLDWATER, KLALEI BREIRAT HA-DIN BE-YISRA'EL VE-HA-SIMAN 46 LE-DVAR HA-MELEKH [CHOICE OF LAW RULES IN ISRAEL AND ARTICLE 46 OF THE ORDER-IN-COUNCIL] (1974) (Hebrew).

Israel" was now identified as the residual source of guidance.[72] However, in both of these cases, the other Justices were speculative about the propriety of adopting this new choice of law rule for torts in Israel, given that a different course of action existed for the proper resolution of each case.

For some considerable time, the Israeli Supreme Court did not need to take a definite stand on whether to adopt this new choice of law in a torts approach regarding PT-related litigation. I suspect that the primary reason for this situation was that the existent *millet* paradigm did most of the work in this regard. Israelis (settlers or others) who sought to litigate their mutual tort disputes had free access to Israeli courts and were presumed to accept the applicability of Israeli law, whereas Palestinian litigants seeking to litigate their mutual tort disputes in Israel were directed back to the PT via stays of the Israeli action on forum non conveniens grounds. Regarding the Palestinian *millet*, an important decision was handed down in 1993 that demonstrated once again how the forum non conveniens doctrine assumed a normative function, effectively operating as a choice of law rule. This was the case of *Abu Jahla v. East Jerusalem Electric Co.*,[73] which I already discussed in Chapter Two. Beyond the fact that this case was an all-Palestinian dispute dealing with a tort allegedly committed in the PT, critical here was also the defendant company's headquarters location in East Jerusalem, a region that by now Israel considered it to be an integral part of the State of Israel. It is important to note that the defendant company—known in the English translation of its name in Arabic as the Jerusalem District Electric Company (JDEC)—provided an important public utility to the Palestinian population of East Jerusalem and to large parts of the West Bank and was hence "a symbol of Palestinian independence in East Jerusalem."[74] Some have suggested that the interaction between Israeli authorities and JDEC also became a microcosm of the conflict between Israel and the two main Palestinian factions at the time, namely pro-Jordanians and Palestinian nationalists.[75] In light of this context, Israeli courts could have taken a position that would stress Israeli control over East Jerusalem and thus maintain its jurisdictional authority instead of staying the proceedings on forum non conveniens grounds. Additionally, the JDEC headquarters is in fact located just a few blocks away from the Jerusalem court in which the case was originally

72 Foundations of Law, 5740-1980, 34 LSI 181 sec. 1 (1979–80).

73 CA 2705/91, 48(1) PD 554 (1993).

74 Bill Hutman & Amir Cheshin, *Living Together and Apart in Jerusalem: Lessons Learned*, in JERUSALEM: A CITY AND ITS FUTURE 401, 417 (Marshal J. Breger & Ora Ahimeir eds., 2002).

75 JEHUDA LUKACS, ISRAEL, JORDAN AND THE PEACE PROCESS 84 (1997).

filed. If the plaintiff, who was a resident of the West Bank, was ready to incur the inconvenience of litigating this case in Jerusalem, this willingness was evident by virtue of his filing the case there instead of at a local PT court; so the situation was appropriately set for the Israeli court to proceed to judgment. Surprisingly, or rather not surprisingly, the Israeli Supreme Court stayed the proceedings. In the holding of the president of the Court at the time, Meir Shamgar, of note here is the passage relating to the reasonable expectations of the parties concerning the proper forum for adjudication:

> [T]he standard that guided the actions of the respondent [JDEC] in the territories since its establishment is the standard that directed its action in the matter before us. According to this standard, it calculated its steps, took (or failed to take) the proper precautionary measures, and also determined the price for its services.... Accordingly it would not be legally proper... to judge its action in an ex post manner according to another standard.[76]

Immediately afterwards, President Shamgar added that it might well be the case that the PT court and the Israeli court would both apply the same law to this adjudication. However, since liability under both of these laws would depend on the applicable standards, it was best that the forum more acquainted with the standard at the site of the accident determine them.[77]

These pronouncements are all normative in nature. The Court was not primarily concerned about litigation convenience per se, or about the procedural ease of applying the particular law, given that the law might be identical in substance irrespective of where litigation is actually held. The primary concern of the Court involved the identity and judicial knowledge of the forum that was best situated to determine the standard of care according to which the defendant's action should be evaluated. Supposedly, the Court emphasized the place of the wrong as controlling in this respect. But we have seen already (and will still observe in the upcoming discussion) how this factor plays no significant role in a PT-related civil wrong; the *Abu Itta* litigation provides evidence for that. In fact, what is controlling in such cases is the fact that all of the concerned parties are Palestinians.

The formal adoption of the most significant contacts approach as a choice of law rule in torts came in 1997 in *Al Tarifi v. Salaymeh*.[78] The plaintiff was a Palestinian

---

76 *Abu Jahla*, 48(1) PD at 578.

77 *Id.*

78 CA 5118/92, 50(3) PD 407 (1997).

resident of East Jerusalem who held Israeli citizenship and an Israeli national ID. Consequently, he was treated as an Israeli plaintiff. When the plaintiff was barely 13 years old, he entered the premises of a nearby quarry, climbed up a pile of gravel, touched an electricity cable that belonged to JDEC, and suffered personal injuries as a result of an electric shock. When the plaintiff became an adult, he filed a civil claim in the District Court of Jerusalem for damages against JDEC and the company that operated the quarry. At first, the defendants tried to stay the proceedings on forum non conveniens grounds. They failed. They also tried to argue for the application of local PT law, according to which the plaintiff would be entitled to less damages than he would be if the action were governed by Israel law. They also failed in this respect. On appeal, the Israeli Supreme Court affirmed. What is particularly interesting about the Court's decision is that it officially adopts the most significant contacts test as the guiding choice of law rule in torts. For in identifying the applicable choice of law rule, the Court specifically refers to two previous opinions: that of Justice Ben-Porath in *Klausner* and that of Justice Strassberg-Cohen in *Abu Attiya*. Given the identity of the plaintiff and the fact that one of the defendants, JDEC, was a firm incorporated in Jerusalem (and at this point this incorporation was not merely a formality, as it was in *Abu Jahla*) and the accident took place near Jerusalem (if not within the municipal boarders of Jerusalem),[79] the Court concluded that Israel was the jurisdiction with the most significant contacts.

The adoption of this new choice of law rule in torts did not change the trend identified already when Israeli courts followed the English choice of law rule. To the contrary, the most significant contacts test, with its elastic approach, provided the rule that Israeli courts were effectively following before. Regarding litigation involving only Israeli parties, the courts would be able to conclude, as they actually did, that Israel is the jurisdiction with the most significant contacts; and if all of the parties are Palestinians, then the PT would be identified as the appropriate jurisdiction. In mixed cases, *Al Tarifi* provides an indication that in such a case, like before, Israeli law would govern (even though this case does not clearly support this proposition, in light of the fact that the accident took place just outside the municipal boarders of Jerusalem). The lower courts as well understood this to be the delineation. An important case in this respect is that of *Ben-Or Tsa'atsu'im Ltd. v. Sultan*,[80] a decision rendered by the magistrate court of Petah Tikva. The plaintiff-respondent, a Palestinian resident of the West Bank,

79 *Id.* at 413.

80 MPC (Petah-Tikva Magistrate Ct.) 1308/00, PM 5760(3) 628 (2000).

was injured in a work-related accident that occurred in a business operated by an Israeli-incorporated company in a West Bank settlement. An Israeli insurance company was named as an additional defendant, having issued the policy that covered the employer's liability for work-related accidents. Notably, this insurance policy stipulated that coverage of injury to residents of the West Bank would be provided in accordance to employer liability under West Bank law. By filing the claim before an Israeli forum, the Palestinian plaintiff hoped to have his claim adjudicated in Israel and, as was made explicit in the plea filed on his behalf, he also opted for the application of Israeli law. The Israeli defendants, on the other hand, asked the court to dismiss the case on forum non conveniens grounds, and alternatively, were the court to adjudicate the claim on the merits, to do so in accordance with West Bank law. In an interlocutory judgment, the court responded to both arguments, holding on the one hand that there was no room for applying the forum non conveniens doctrine, and on the other that the applicable law was that of the West Bank. On the issue of the forum non conveniens, the court noted the holding of Justice Barak in *Abu-Attiya*, according to which a court in a PT-related civil action is to refrain from staying the proceedings when a significant Israeli factor exists. The court stressed that the defendants' Israeli nationality created the necessary significant Israeli contact, notwithstanding the Israeli defendants' attempt to dismiss the Israeli forum as inappropriate. The court observed that the determining factor was the reasonable expectations of the Israeli defendants before the accident. Had they been asked where they would prefer litigation with a Palestinian resident of the West Bank to be conducted, they would have pointed to the Israeli forum.

Another important holding in this interlocutory judgment concerns the choice of law inquiry. Building once again on the putative expectations of the parties and on the most significant contacts test as articulated in *Abu-Attiya*, the court concluded that the applicable law is that of the West Bank. In terms of policy, the court explicitly noted two major considerations. First and foremost was the fact that in articulating the law governing in the PT, Israeli authorities had clarified that West Bank law was applicable, including in the sphere of work-related injuries of local residents, which the court could not merely disregard. Second, given that the insurance policy covered the employer's liability only to the extent that was determined according to West Bank law, it would have been unfair to the employer if he were to be held liable in accordance with Israeli law. Concerned that the decision would be seen as implying discrimination against Palestinian workers employed in PT settlements, the court noted that it did not discern a normative scheme of this sort in the PT, since labor law in the West Bank did not differentiate between Israeli and local employers, or between Israeli and local employees. But if such a differentiation were made, it should not be taken to impose on the employer a law that he did not expect to have applied to him. Moreover, local West Bank law did not necessarily undermine the interests of local Palestinian employees since, under that law, the employer carries a non-fault liability toward the employee in work-related accidents, whereas under Israeli law the employee must prove negligence by the employer for the latter to be liable in torts.

These choice of law policy concerns were by no means isolated. They were echoed in at least two other judgments with a similar fact pattern: a Palestinian plaintiff injured in a work-related accident filed a tort claim based on Israeli law before an Israeli court against an Israeli-incorporated defendant operating a business in a West Bank settlement, who had acquired an insurance policy in Israel for its work-related liability. One of these judgments was issued by the Tel-Aviv District Court in *Aryeh Insurance Co. v. Nuzhah*,[81] and the second by the magistrate court of Kfar-Saba in *Muhammad v. Yakir, Co-operative Society for Communal Settlement Ltd.*[82] In both of these cases, the court emphasized the fact that according to IDF orders, the local law in the West Bank, inasmuch as it has not been changed or altered by other military orders or applicable Israeli legislation, was meant to govern activities taking place in the West Bank—a legislative intent that Israeli courts must take into consideration when undertaking a choice of law inquiry.[83] In addition, in both judgments, the courts found that West Bank law was to apply also in terms of the most significant contacts test, which was taken

---

81 LA (TA) 200680/98 (Jan. 1, 1998), Nevo Legal Database (by subscription).

82 CC (Kfar-Saba Magistrates' Ct.) 5777/99 (Mar. 22, 2001), Nevo Legal Database (by subscription).

83 At first glance, the case of CA (TA) 1269/85 Amsalem v. Levy, PM 5753(1) 232 (1993), seems to be exceptional. Here, the plaintiff was a resident of Israel who was injured in a road accident during work while in an Israeli settlement in the West Bank. The defendant insurance company was also an Israeli corporation. The case presented no choice of law question in terms of the defendant's liability, for PT law was identical in this regard with that of Israeli law. The choice of law question only arose regarding whether certain sums should be deducted from the compensation the plaintiff was entitled to—a deduction mandated by Israeli law but not by PT law. Ultimately, the court ruled that the applicable law was that of the PT. This conclusion seems to contradict the trend uncovered so far, under which when all parties are Israelis, the courts would apply Israeli law. However, investigation of the reasoning afforded by the court in this case uncovers that the court sustained the prevailing tendency rather than negating it. For the court made clear that this position was taken because Israel controls the PT and can legislate there as it sees fit (*id.* at 243); and since Israel had so far refrained from applying the same standards of deductions from personal injury compensation in PT road accidents in which Israelis were injured, the court should not circumvent this implicit norm. *Id.*

to be the choice of law rule in torts. An additional point raised in favor of West Bank law was that of party expectations.

The Kfar-Saba Magistrate Court in *Muhammad* further elaborated upon other policy concerns, especially the concern that Palestinian and Israeli workers might be governed by different laws even if injured in the same accident. First, the court argued, it is not at all certain that different laws would be applicable in such a case, for the Israeli worker might also be governed by West Bank law. The court acknowledged that in a case involving two Israeli settlers, Israeli rather than West Bank law could potentially govern their relation, either because both parties would willingly opt for Israeli law or on the basis of their presumed expectations. In either case, this outcome would be the exception rather than the rule, for it builds on the implicit intent of both parties. To further stress that this was indeed an exception, the court referred to the intent of the Israeli legislature, the Knesset, to determine the identity of the injured party—an Israeli or a local Palestinian resident—as pivotal in determining whether an Israeli motorist should be liable under the Israeli no-fault liability scheme in Road Accident Victims Compensation Law, 1975.[84]

The observations made by the courts in these decisions, especially in *Ben-Or* and in *Muhammad*, imply that PT local law—namely the law in effect in the West Bank—applies equally to Israelis and Palestinians, even when the incident takes place in an Israeli settlement, and that in some respects, recourse to this law is advantageous. However, this position will soon be revealed as unsubstantiated. In spite of some modifications in PT law, whether in matters of torts or employment, this law was far less developed than Israeli law, and Israeli settlers or residents employed in Israeli settlements were generally presumed to be governed by Israeli law rather than PT law. It is no coincidence that in all three proceedings, the Palestinian plaintiffs argued for the application of Israeli law while the Israeli settler defendants sought the application of PT law. Above all, the courts seemed to be perfectly attuned to official Israeli policy and followed the *millet* paradigm, namely that local Palestinian residents shall remain governed by local PT norms and not by Israeli municipal law, which was meant to benefit only the Israeli settlers of the PT.

84 29 LSI 311 (1974–75). Section 2(A1) of this law, as amended, provides: "The driver of an Israeli vehicle is obliged to compensate an injured person who is an Israeli or foreign tourist [who under the law cannot be a Palestinian resident of the PT] and who suffered bodily injuries in an accident that occurred in the Ezor [Region] or the territories of the Palestinian Authority... and the accident is deemed to have happened in Israel."

4. The New *Lex Loci Delicti* Rule

This situation did not change much after the establishment of the PA, in the wake of the Oslo Peace Accords, until the Israeli Supreme Court sought to adopt a new choice of law rule in torts. This happened in an PT-related tort and eventually led the court to counter the trends identified in the preceding discussion. The case was that of *Yanon v. Qara'an*.[85] The plaintiff, Ms. Majdah Qara'an, a Palestinian resident of the West Bank city of Qalqiliya, was seriously injured in a work-related accident. Her employer was an Israeli-incorporated company that operated a factory in Alfei Menasheh, an Israeli settlement in the West Bank, which was also the site in which the accident took place. The plaintiff argued for the application of Israeli tort law, under which, if successful in her suit, she would have been entitled to the sum of 1.4 million New Israeli Shekels (NIS) (equivalent to approximately USD 390,000). The Israeli defendant argued for the application of Jordanian labor law as it existed in PT municipal law, under which the plaintiff would have been entitled to the sum of NIS 187,200 (equivalent to approximately USD 52,000) in compensation. In the District Court, the plaintiff won, proving that the accident was caused by the defendant's negligence.

The Supreme Court concluded that Israeli law should govern in this case. Given the fact that this outcome was a significant departure from the attitude evinced by courts in Israel thus far, the decision contains two major holdings: one regarding proper relations between choice of law rules and official Israeli policy towards the PT, and the other connected to the choice of law rule in torts. On the first issue, the Court, as represented by Justice Eliezer Rivlin, took the position that the official policy of maintaining a separate jurisdictional entity in the PT (proclaimed by IDF orders and public international law norms) does not mean that all events that take place in the PT are necessarily governed by PT law, even if the claimant happens to be a Palestinian resident of the PT. Israeli courts must identify the governing law in a choice of law inquiry.[86] To further stress the independent nature of Israeli choice of law rules, the Court observed that application of Israeli municipal law to an PT-related civil action does not and should not be construed to indicate that the PT have now become part of Israeli sovereign territory.[87] Essentially, the Court held that while public international law principles and IDF orders have worked to identify what PT municipal law is, in the case that such law comes into conflict with Israeli municipal law (or any other foreign law

85 *Yanon*, 59(1) PD 345.

86 *Id.* at 350, 358.

87 *Id.* at 357.

for that matter), it is up to the relevant choice of law rules of the forum undertaking the choice of law inquiry to determine the governing law. In retrospect, this holding terminates the long-standing symbiosis between Israeli official policy in maintaining a separate jurisdictional entity in the PT as far as the indigenous Palestinian population is concerned, and applicable Israeli conflict of laws policy in PT-related civil disputes.

Another important holding the Court made involves an articulation of a new choice of law rule for torts. After undertaking an extensive review of the different approaches in this respect, both in foreign legal systems and in previous Israeli decisions,[88] the Court opted for an approach very similar to that of the English Private International Law (Miscellaneous Provisions) Act 1995. The choice of law rule the Court ultimately adopted is that in torts, the law of the place where the tort was committed is the governing law. However, in rare circumstances, such as when the location in which the tort was committed is fortuitous, with no real or substantive connection to the act that was committed, the governing law is to be that of the state having the most substantial connection with the tort. In adopting this new choice of law rule in torts, the Supreme Court provided a number of theoretical and practical considerations. The rule serves the territorial principle, a guiding principle in private (and public) international law:[89] the interest of the state in regulating actions that take place within its territory,[90] which is based on the most objective connecting factor in a tort action, is a rule that provides for certainty[91] and predictability,[92] and in a sense also serves party expectations, as a multi-lateral rule that helps to deter parties from forum shopping.[93]

Before applying the new choice of law rule to the case at hand, the Court chose to highlight the unique status of Israeli settlements in the West Bank. The law regarded as the municipal law in the West Bank was Jordanian law, together with the amendments and additions made by the IDF military commander. However, this situation is dramatically different for Israeli Jewish residents who settled in the West Bank. Major sections of Israeli municipal law were made personally applicable to such residents, whether by defining Israeli municipal legislation

88 *Id.* at 358–69.

89 *Id.* at 373.

90 *Id.*

91 *Id.*

92 *Id.*

93 *Id.* at 373–74.

to be directly applicable to such residents or by virtue of military orders issued by the military commander, which incorporated Israeli municipal law into the municipal law of the West Bank but made it applicable only to the Israeli settlers residing there. As a result of this legal status of Israeli settlements, the court calls them "Israeli enclaves,"[94] for although they have not been officially annexed to Israel, this law, to a large extent, happens to be Israeli law.

At this point, the Court could easily have applied the choice of law rule it had just formulated to determine that the law that should govern Ms. Qara'an's claim is Israeli law, for the tort took place in a Jewish settlement, i.e., an "Israeli enclave," and therefore the tort effectively took place in Israel. Interestingly, however, the Court did not take this course. Instead, it went out of its way to apply Israeli law through the exception. For as a result of the same legal reality, in such "Israeli enclaves," the connection between the act giving rise to Ms. Qara'an's claim and Jordanian law is essentially fortuitous.[95] Moreover, the exceptional state of the law governing in Israeli settlements made it necessary, in the Court's opinion, to apply the exception to the rule.[96] This lead the Court to identify Israeli law as the governing law—a law that in the Court's assessment has the most significant contact to the case at hand.[97] In taking this position, the Court also emphasizes that it has done so not because Israeli law happens to be the law that works to the advantage of the plaintiff. The Court clarified that although the "better law" approach can be acceptable to some, in its judgment it is unfitting to choose between laws depending on their content, except when the foreign law is held to contradict the forum's public policy.[98]

5. Choice of Law Rules in Tort—Conclusions

The relatively high number of civil claims filed before Israeli courts in relation to PT-related wrongs proved to be particularly challenging for Israeli courts. In essence, these types of claims helped to reform Israeli choice of law rules in torts throughout the years. This section also demonstrates how courts turned to the forum non conveniens doctrine in order to adjust the choice of law calculation, at least when Israeli law would have been identified as the governing law in an

94 *Id.* at 379

95 *Id.* at 379–80.

96 *Id.* at 379.

97 *Id.* at 380.

98 *Id.* at 380–81.

all-Palestinian dispute. In this sense, the forum non conveniens doctrine was an escape device not much different from the traditional escape devices (mainly classification and public policy) that courts resorted to in order to avoid the dictates of a rigid choice of law rule. However, in the Israel-PT context, the forum non conveniens doctrine itself was transformed in order to refer to what Israeli courts identified as guiding normative concerns. This is somewhat different from the escape devices applied about a century ago in order to avoid the result dictated by the traditional choice of law rule. Israeli courts had also applied classification and public policy considerations at the time in a mechanical fashion. Courts have been rather candid about the normative objectives that they sought to achieve through the use of the forum non conveniens doctrine in modern-day Israeli jurisprudence, at least in the context of PT-related litigation.

C. Choice of Law in Contracts

Unlike the choice of law rule for torts, the choice of law rule for contracts witnessed no dramatic changes since its importation from English common law. This rule sought to apply the "proper law of the contract." If the parties were considered to have evinced an explicit or implicit intention that a certain law will govern their relationship, then this law was deemed to be the proper law of the contract, at least in such spheres in which the subjective expectations of the parties were of significance. Otherwise, the proper law of the contract was held to be that of the jurisdiction with the most significant contacts to the contractual relationship.

In this section, I analyze the trends that can be identified from the application of this rule in PT-related contracts, with special emphasis on employment relations. The reason why I chose to limit this analysis to employment relations is an empirical one—of all other contractual relations, this was the sphere that drew the most considerable litigation before Israeli courts, ultimately yielding two major Israeli Supreme Court judgments that are worth highlighting. I submit from the outset that these two decisions do not offer any new approaches compared to the ones already identified. To the contrary—they only substantiates the civil *millet* paradigm. In an all-Israeli dispute, the courts have assumed that the contractual relationship is governed by Israeli law; in an all-Palestinian dispute, they assumed that local PT law governed; and in mixed disputes, they identified Israeli law to be the proper law of the contract. But before I go into the details of these cases, some introductory remarks on Palestinian labor in the service of Israeli employers are in order.

1. Palestinians Working for Israelis

For decades, Palestinians have depended on employment by Israelis. At one time, some two decades into the occupation of the PT, over 50% of the Palestinian workforce was working in Israel.[99] The relatively high wages that Israeli employers were willing to pay unskilled and semi-skilled Palestinian workers was the primary reason for this dependence. In turn, PT residents experienced a significant rise in the standard of living as the years went by.[100] However, certain circumstances hampered Palestinian employment in Israel. First, Israelis employing Palestinians were required to make certain deductions for the Israeli National Insurance Institute (NII) fund equal to those they had to make for Israeli employees, even though Palestinian workers (as opposed to Israeli workers) could not claim NII benefits.[101] These deductions were implemented in an attempt to prevent Israeli employers from preferring Palestinian workers over Israelis.[102] Second, although the Israeli economy heavily depended on Palestinian labor, no overall scheme governing Israeli employment of Palestinians was ever articulated. Palestinian workers working inside Israel needed to get an appropriate permit from the IDF authorities, and these permits could be revoked or suspended depending on Israeli security concerns. Hence, during the clashes that commenced in the First *Intifada* and the suicide bombing of the Second *Intifada*, unemployment in the PT soared up to 50%.[103]

As to the substantive labor law applicable in the PT, the dominant opinion was that this law was relatively developed.[104] Yet, an entire range of entitlements and benefits was missing. The latter included collective labor rights, such as the right to form a union and the right to strike.[105] Additionally, a disparity existed in entitlements to minimum wage, compensation for delay in payment of wages, and pay in lieu of annual leave—workers were entitled to more benefits under Israeli law than under local PT law.[106] Hence, it was just a matter of time until Palestinians employed by Israeli employers would demand full benefits under Israeli law. The leading case in this respect is *Amutat Kav la-Oved v. National Labor Court in Jerusalem*.[107]

---

99 Paz-Fuchs & Ronen, *supra* note 5, at 580–81.

100 Benvenisti, International Law of Occupation, *supra* note 4, at 226.

101 *Id.* at 227.

102 *Id.*

103 Paz-Fuchs & Ronen, *supra* note 5, at 581.

104 *Id.* at 586.

105 *Id.*

106 *Id.* at 587–88.

107 HCJ 566/03 (Oct. 10 2007), Nevo Legal Database (by subscription).

The proceeding dealt with a cluster of claims filed on behalf of Palestinian residents of the West Bank employed in Israeli settlements in the West Bank. Five of the employers were Israeli-registered corporations that operated in the West Bank, and the sixth was the local municipality of Giv'at Ze'ev—a West Bank settlement near Jerusalem. At issue was whether the Palestinian plaintiffs were entitled to work-related benefits guaranteed under Israeli law, such as the right to a minimum wage, or only to the benefits provided by West Bank local law, which would entitle the Palestinian plaintiffs to much less. The plaintiffs were represented by Kav la-Oved, a non-profit non-governmental organization that protects the rights of disadvantaged workers in Israel.[108] Kav la-Oved argued for the application of Israeli law, while the Israeli defendants argued for the application of West Bank local law as relevant for the Palestinians. Notably, the office of the Israeli Attorney General, who also took part in the proceedings before the Supreme Court, sided with the defendants. In the view of the Attorney General's representative, Palestinian workers employed in the West Bank are to be governed by West Bank local law, even when employed by Israeli entities operating there. On a more principled level, the representative of the Attorney General's office argued that Israel had intentionally refrained from applying Israeli law to all of the West Bank, and what Israel as a sovereign state had refrained from doing cannot be achieved through the operation of choice of law rules applied by the courts.[109]

Before reaching the Israeli Supreme Court, the claims filed by the plaintiffs regarding their entitlement for work-related benefits under Israeli law were adjudicated first in the Regional Labor Court, and thereafter, on appeal, in the National Labor Court. According to standard procedure under Israeli law, the labor court hierarchy is entrusted with dealing with work-related claims.[110] However, the Israeli Supreme Court, sitting in its capacity as the High Court of Justice, has judicial powers to oversee the activities of various governmental bodies, including special tribunals such as the labor court, and to intervene in their judgments under appropriate and pre-defined circumstances. Interestingly, the two labor courts that dealt with these consolidated claims arrived at different conclusions regarding the governing law. The Regional Labor Court decided that the governing law

108 http://www.kavlaoved.org.il/en/.

109 For an extended analysis of the brief submitted on behalf of the Israeli Attorney General, see Tobias Kelly, *Jurisdictional Politics in the Occupied West Bank: Territory, Community, and Economic Dependency in the Formation of Legal Subjects*, 31 LAW & SOCIAL INQ. 39, 65–66 (2006).

110 *See* Ruth Ben-Israel, *Labor Law*, *in* INTRODUCTION TO THE LAW OF ISRAEL 213, 216–17 (Amos Shapira & Keren C. DeWitt-Arar eds., 1995).

was Israeli law. On appeal before the National Labor Court, however, this decision was vacated, and it was held that West Bank law was applicable. Nonetheless, this court added that certain Israeli law provisions could be applied if public policy considerations deem such application necessary. Therefore, the National Labor Court decided to remand the case back to the Regional Labor Court in order to decide whether it was necessary from a public policy perspective to apply certain Israeli law provisions in any of the claims. This latter decision was challenged in the Israeli Supreme Court in its capacity as the High Court of Justice. And indeed, this challenge ultimately proved to be successful. The Israeli Supreme Court deemed the choice of law analyses of the National Labor Court to be both erroneous and unjust.

Aware of the fundamental nature of the petition, the Supreme Court convened in a panel of nine justices, instead of the usual three. Once again, Justice Rivlin, now deputy president of the Court, gave the leading decision. As in *Qara'an*, the Court made an essential distinction between the identity and different tiers of law that exist in the PT and Israeli choice of law rules. The Court once again held that maintaining the PT as a separate jurisdictional entity cannot prevent Israeli courts from applying Israeli choice of law rules to identify Israeli law as the governing law in a particular civil dispute related in one way or another to the PT.

In terms of the choice of law rule relevant for the pending claims, the Court made two fundamental observations. First, the Court identified the Israeli choice of law rule for contracts, since an employment relationship is essentially a contractual relationship, albeit of a special kind. The position the Court took here is not different from the one it took in the previous decision, holding that in the absence of an indication by the parties as to which law should govern their contractual relationship, the court will choose the law with the most significant contact to the contractual relationship as the proper law of the contract.

In employment relations, the Court further notes, it is necessary to take cognizance of special policy considerations and mandatory norms, notwithstanding any specific contractual stipulation to the contrary. One such policy consideration the Court emphasized was that of equality among workers. Employees performing the same job should be entitled to the same wage and the same work benefits, whether they are men, women, parents, non-parents, Jews, Muslims, Israelis, or Palestinians. The influence of the principle of equality on the choice of law process can also be attained, according to the Court, through reference to guiding principles such as public policy and the basic tenets of the legal order.

Applying these considerations to the case at hand led the Court to identify Israeli law as the governing law. First, the Court pointed out, no indication existed in the employment contracts as to the law the parties perceived to be the governing law of the employment relationship. True, if the place of employment were to be the determinative nexus for identifying the governing law, then that law would need to be the municipal law of the West Bank. But such a territorial nexus cannot be the controlling issue; the most significant contact test requires that other important contacts be examined, as does the reality of what the Court once again called "Israeli enclaves" in the PT. In such territories, a number of legal orders exist depending on the personal identity of the party, as we too have seen. Israeli citizens—settlers—are governed by a different set of laws than the ones governing Palestinian residents. The legal nature of these "Israeli enclaves" themselves therefore diminishes the significance of territorial connections, whilst increasing the weight of other connections in the overall assessment of the most significant contacts. The Court set out the following important contacts: the currency in which the wages were paid, which was New Israeli Shekels; the documents relating to the employment, all written in Hebrew; and the holidays and days of rest for the employees, which were those in effect in Israel. The Court also noted that income tax and other taxes were usually paid to the Israeli authorities.

In addition, the Court stressed the general policy of labor law, whereby one body of law should be applied to different workers doing the same job. A distinction between Palestinian workers and Israeli workers in this respect is unjustified and, from a choice of law vantage point, intolerable in employment contracts. For such choice of law rules must also represent the basic notions of justice accepted by Israeli society and the "family of nations" and prevent employment discrimination on the basis of national or ethnic affinity. Therefore, the Court concluded, the applicable law is Israeli law. The Court stressed that in applying Israeli law in this specific case, no consideration was given to which law provides more benefits to the employees.

2. Choice of Law in All-Palestinian Employment Relations

The course taken by the Israeli Supreme Court in an all-Palestinian employment relationship was a different one. Like in tort cases, such a relationship was held to be subject to local PT law. The leading case on this is *A. Dynamica Holdings 2002 Ltd. v. Civil Administration for Judea and Samaria Region*.[111] The Civil Administration

111 HCJ 1234/10 (July 21, 2010), Nevo Legal Database (by subscription).

authority in the West Bank sought to outsource the operations of unloading and loading of goods across checkpoints for security purposes. One of these checkpoints was in Betunia, in the West Bank. The Civil Administration publicized a tender and a local Palestinian operator that sought to employ local Palestinian employees was declared the winner. An Israeli company, A. Dynamica, which had lost, petitioned the Israeli Supreme Court, arguing that the Palestinian operator won unjustly. The petitioner claimed that the Palestinian employer did not intend to pay his employees all the benefits that are owed to them under Israeli law but rather the lesser benefits required under West Bank law. A. Dynamica was obliged to offer work-related benefits under Israeli law, and therefore its offer was necessarily higher. The Court dismissed the petition. Utilizing the proper law of the contract analysis as articulated in the *Amutat Kav la-Oved* decision, it identified local West Bank law as the governing law between a Palestinian employer and a Palestinian employee. Since the employment would take place in the West Bank, the Court ruled that no grounds existed to conclude that the parties would have any law in mind in terms of governing their employment relationship other than local West Bank law. Therefore, it was reasoned that the Palestinian employer was perfectly within the terms of the tender when he submitted his offer.

So once again, we see that the *millet* paradigm was controlling within the realm of choice of law in contracts as it was in the realm of torts.

D. On Equal Treatment and the Choice of Law Process

The two Israeli Supreme Court decisions in *Qara'an* and *Amutat Kav la-Oved* express particular concern with the issue of equality between Palestinians and Israelis who are either injured or employed together in an Israeli settlement. The Court was rather explicit about this in *Amutat Kav La-Oved*, when it clarified that the prospects of having a Palestinian worker in the PT governed by PT municipal law and an Israeli worker in the same workplace governed by Israeli law contradicts basic notions of justice and public policy. This concern about equality resonated also in the holdings of lower courts. One judgment that stands out in this regard is *Ashkanta v. Az-Rom Metal Works Ltd.*[112] In that case, Palestinian workers from the Gaza Strip claimed benefits under Israeli law from their Israeli employer after their employment at the Erez Industrial Park came to an end

112 LabC (BS) 2142/06 (Feb. 13, 2008), Nevo Legal Database (by subscription).

following the 2005 Israeli disengagement from the Gaza Strip.[113] After admitting that two systems of law govern in the PT—Israeli law regarding Jewish settlers and local PT law for Palestinians,[114] the Regional Labor Court of Bear Sheva goes on to say that

> [t]he application of two legal systems to employees that work together for one employer, will bring to unlawful discrimination that labor choice of law rules are not supposed to legitimate. It is impossible to accept a pattern of employment that is based on a distinction that builds on the ethnic and national affinity of the employees.[115]

Building on the principle of equality in order to direct the choice of law analysis is of course admirable. In this respect, the well-intentioned course of analysis taken in *Amutat Kav La-Oved* and *Ashkanta* is clearly apparent. However, when considering this course of analysis in the context of Israeli policies toward the PT generally, it is hard not to see how pretentious it really is. As Israeli courts have clarified on a number of occasions, and most recently in *A. Dynamica* and *Ashkanta*, the general legal design in the PT was specifically aimed to differentiate between Israelis and Palestinians when it came to the governing norms, notwithstanding the fact that they all happen to live in one jurisdictional entity. Additionally, in Israel itself, the law explicitly differentiates between local citizens based on their religious affiliation. The clearest example is Israeli law on marriage and divorce; depending on their religious affiliation, Israeli citizens can be subject to different sets of norms in such matters.[116] No wonder that in *Amutat Kav La-Oved*, the Office of the Attorney General of the State of Israel backed the decision of the National Labor Court that accepted the proposition whereby Palestinian and Israelis working in the same workplace can nevertheless be governed by different norms.[117]

Moreover, the Israeli Supreme Court's insistence in *Amutat Kav la-Oved* that it was choosing between PT and Israeli law irrespective of the content of these

113 The Erez Industrial Park was established back in the 1970s in order to employ Palestinians from the Gaza Strip. The overwhelming majority of the businesses that operated in this zone were either owned by Israeli entities or subcontractors of Israeli entities. In the wake of the Oslo Peace Process, when this industrial zone was at the height of its operation, some 4,500 Palestinians and 500 Israelis were employed there. *Id.* para. 3.

114 *Id.* para. 14.

115 *Id.* para. 15.

116 *See, e.g.*, Menashe Shava, *Connecting Factors in Matters of Personal Status in Israel*, 5 TEL-AVIV U. STUD. IN L. 144 (1982); ARIEL BIN-NUN, THE LAW OF THE STATE OF ISRAEL: AN INTRODUCTION 23 (1990).

117 *Amutat Kav la-Oved*, para. 9; *See* Kelly, *supra* note 109, at 65–66.

laws, let alone the substantive and material consequences of their application, is also unconvincing. The underlying assumption in *Amutat Kav la-Oved* proves the contrary. The Court's attention to such notions as "public policy" and "notions of justice of Israeli society" would hardly have been put forward if PT law were as beneficial to employees as Israeli law is. We should also note in this respect that the claims in *Amutat Kav la-Oved* were of a general nature, whereby the Court was asked to decide whether Israeli or PT employment law should govern, rather than this or that specific norm in this or that particular labor statute. However, given the Court's use of norms pertaining to public policy and to basic notions of justice of Israeli society, it must have assumed what it was trying to deny—namely, that PT law was not merely different from Israeli law, but far less developed, and if applied to Palestinian plaintiffs such as those in *Qara'an* and *Amutat Kav la-Oved*, would produce severe injustice.[118] If this assessment is accurate, and I see no other way to understand the Court's analysis, then much of what has been presumed in previous decisions about Palestinian plaintiffs not necessarily being disadvantaged when governed by PT tort or employment law should also be rejected from now on. Similarly, the previous guiding assumption that Israelis working in Israeli settlements might also be found to be governed by PT tort and employment law was also rejected by the Court, for if this were the case, the Court would hardly need to discuss the value of equality: why should it if Palestinian and Israeli employees working in the PT are presumed to be governed by the same PT norms? Indeed, as Tobias Kelly notes, "[t]erritorial jurisdiction in the [West Bank] was reduced to effective personal jurisdiction by the unequal distribution of political and military resources."[119]

However, since I believe that justice was served in both *Qara'an* and *Amutat Kav la-Oved*, though unsupported as yet by the policies as articulated by the Court, I would like to suggest here an alternative argument in support of the Court's choice of law analysis. Essentially, I argue, the primary support for the Court's analysis lies in the notion of fairness in the choice of law process. Though this notion is largely marginal in modern choice of law analysis, long stranded between the notion of vested territorial rights and a consequentialist interest analysis approach, I do believe that it provides important tools in guiding choice of law analysis, especially in the context of military occupation.

118 *See* Kelly, *supra* note 109, at 59.

119 *Id.* at 60.

E. The Principle of Fairness in the Choice of Law Process

One major division in the choice of law methodology of the past century or so is that between the territorial paradigm and the state interest-policy paradigm. The territorial paradigm seeks to identify the governing law for a legal relationship by identifying the major territorial event in that relationship and thereafter applying the law of the place where that event took place to govern the relationship if and when a choice of law controversy arises. In this context, each relationship is presumed to have a "seat" in a jurisdiction that is deemed to have the central territorial connection to the relationship at hand.[120] And since according to traditional territorial thinking, the law of one state cannot travel across state lines, it was resolved that what is effectuated when a foreign law is identified as the governing law is not the law of the place where the act occurred, but rather the rights vested by this law in the litigants who are now before the court. The interest-policy paradigm, on the other hand, seeks to resolve the choice of law inquiry by investigating the normative interests and policies of the laws concerned and, after identifying such interests and policies, asks whether in light of the specific circumstances of the case, those interests and policies are to be implemented. The dominant factor making state interests and policies converge was found to be the domicile of the concerned parties. Discussion regarding these two paradigms has resulted in some scholars theorizing about the issue of fairness in the choice of law process.[121] Some contend that a choice of law inquiry should also be concerned with achieving a result that is considered to be fair. This fairness standard, as we shall see, is derived from a set of considerations that lie outside any specific choice of law paradigm and is primarily concerned with preventing unfair results.

This fairness approach is deontological in substance and seeks to limit the results that the choice of law inquiry could produce, based on the rights that litigants are perceived to possess.[122] These rights are adjudicative ones designed to impose limits on state authority and to protect individuals "from being forced to sacrifice for the good of society as a whole."[123] This logic differentiates the fairness approach from the consequentialist approach, for according to the latter, rules are

120 Eugene F. Scoles et al., Conflict of Laws 48 (4th ed. 2004).

121 Two major articles stand out in this regard: Lea Brilmayer, *Rights, Fairness, and Choice-of-Law*, 98 Yale L.J. 1277 (1989); Terry S. Kogan, *Toward a Jurisprudence of Choice-of-Law: The Propriety of Fairness over Comity*, 62 N.Y.U. L. Rev. 651 (1987).

122 Brilmayer, *supra* note 121, at 1278.

123 *Id.*

evaluated by the desirability of their consequences rather than their compatibility with the pre-existing rights of the parties.[124] However, the fairness approach is not a vested rights approach in the traditional territorial sense either. Rights within the fairness paradigm are not meant to identify the law that should be applied, but rather are primarily concerned with providing limits on the application of state law to litigants.[125] So while vested rights theory sought to design rights in a horizontal manner—defining the rights litigants had against one another—the fairness theory of rights is vertical in nature, designed to define the rights the individual litigant has against the state whose law is considered for application.[126] Additionally, the fairness paradigm is anchored in considerations of political legitimacy rather than rigid territorial notions, inquiring, instead, into whether the application of the laws of a certain state is fair.[127]

Thus, the question arises regarding the criteria for determining the fairness of an application of a particular state law, which, ultimately, are deeply rooted in principles of political fairness.[128] One major factor in this respect is consent.[129] Politically, it is considered just and fair to coerce an individual or entity to follow the laws of a particular state when that individual has consented (explicitly or implicitly) to the application of such laws.[130] A second factor in identifying such criteria involves the availability of a political process for the individual litigant burdened with the application of the particular state law to influence the shape and design of such a law.[131] In most cases, the availability of such a political process is dependent on the individual litigant's domicile or citizenship in the state whose law is identified as the governing law.[132] A third factor in assessing the fairness of applying a particular law is that of territoriality. Individuals present in the territory of a certain state anticipate that their actions will be governed by local norms.[133] However, this territorial connection between the state and the individual foreign to the territorial unit needs to be purposeful in order to "assure a minimal level of individual control over the legal norms to which the individual

---

124 *Id.* at 1285.

125 *Id.* at 1291–92.

126 *Id.* at 1295.

127 *Id.* at 1295; Kogan, *supra* note 121, at 656, 694.

128 Brilmayer, *supra* note 121, at 1295.

129 *Id.* at 1298; Kogan, *supra* note 121, at 573.

130 Brilmayer, *supra* note 121, at 1298.

131 Kogan, *supra* note 121, at 699.

132 Brilmayer, *supra* note 121, at 1299–1300.

133 *Id.* at 1303.

will be subjected."[134] A fourth factor is that of mutuality,[135] whereby a substantive rule should not be applied to an individual's detriment unless that individual would be eligible to receive the benefits of the rule if the tables were turned.[136]

Applying this notion of choice of law fairness to the inquiries undertaken in *Qara'an* and *Amutat Kav la-Oved* lends substantial policy support to the results reached in both of these decisions. Indeed, in a choice between Israeli and PT law, when the defendant is an Israeli settler or an Israeli entity operating in the PT, and the plaintiff is a Palestinian who seeks the application of Israeli law, it is fair and just to have Israeli law govern the claim rather than PT law. In terms of the first factor, in neither case was it established that the Palestinian plaintiff consented to the application of PT law. In terms of the second factor, which in my opinion is especially relevant in a choice of law inquiry in the context of occupation, it is fairer to have the Israeli defendant burdened by the application of Israeli law rather than the Palestinian plaintiff burdened by the application of PT law. Throughout the period of occupation, the Palestinian residents of the PT had no meaningful political process by which local residents could mobilize to influence government and shape the governing law.[137] As George Bisharat has noted in his comprehensive sociological study on Palestinian lawyers working in the context of Israeli occupation in the West Bank, "Israeli occupation introduced an alien regime to the West Bank,"[138] and local institutions such as the police and courts, even when operated by local Palestinian officials, were "recognized as mere shells of their former selves, possessing no power independent of the military government...."[139] On the other hand, Israeli settlers or other entities operating businesses in the PT were afforded full access to the political process that determines government in the PT.[140] Therefore, it should be generally held unfair to have Palestinian litigants burdened by a law produced by a government whose

---

134 *Id.* at 1307.

135 *Id.* at 1308. Kogan articulates a similar principle under the heading of "benefaction." Kogan, *supra* note 121, at 674.

136 Brilmayer, *supra* note 121, at 1312.

137 *See* Iris Canor, *Yisra'el ve-ha-Shtahim: Al Mishpat Beinle'umi Prati, Mishpat Beinle'umi Pumbi, u-Ma -she-Beinehem* [*Israel and the Territories: The Interplay between Private International Law and Public International Law*], 8 MISHPAT U-MIMSHAL 551, 584 (2005); Guy Mundlak, *Power-Breaking or Power-Entrenching Law? The Regulation of Palestinian Workers in Israel*, 20 COMP. LAB. L. & POL'Y J. 569, 593 (2000).

138 GEORGE E. BISHARAT, PALESTINIAN LAWYERS AND ISRAELI RULE: LAW AND DISORDER IN THE WEST BANK 68 (1989).

139 *Id.*

140 Ben-Naftali, Gross & Michaeli, *supra* note 2, at 585.

formation they have no political power to influence, whereas the Israeli settlers and other entities operating in Israeli settlements in the PT did have such political influence over their governing laws. Arguably, it can be asserted that since local civil law in the PT was absorbed by the IDF military government from the pre-existing legal system in the PT, then this law is the product of a political process of some sort. This assertion is unpersuasive, however, given the prolonged state of occupation in the PT. In over three decades of occupation, the local law has not been modified to any major extent, and the minor changes that did occur were those introduced by Israel and not the result of a political process by those governed by local law. It is also important to note that the local Palestinian population in the PT seemed to cease identifying itself with the local legal system and its institutions after the latter came under the control of an occupying power. It is no surprise that immediately after the 1967 Six-Day War, the vast majority of judges resigned their posts,[141] and a considerable number of Palestinian lawyers went on strike.[142] Interacting with local legal institutions—so it was perceived—would give legitimacy to Israeli actions.[143]

The two other factors pertaining to fairness also seem to buttress this conclusion. Given the fact that settlements are generally governed by Israeli law, the territoriality principle seems to back the application of Israeli law regarding actions occurring there. The mutuality factor also affords support to such a conclusion. Throughout the settlement project in the PT, the norms and designs articulated by the military government and the Israeli government have worked to accommodate to the utmost the interests of the settlers in the PT, while denying or circumventing those of the local Palestinian population. Therefore, it is just and fair that settler entities also be held accountable according to Israeli law standards when claims are filed against them by local Palestinian plaintiffs.

I have been able to locate this choice of law methodology based on fairness only in one Israeli judgment: the Magistrate Court of Tel-Aviv's decision in *Muhammadah v. Yehoshu'a*.[144] The fact pattern in this case was the same as in most of the previously discussed cases. The plaintiff was a Palestinian from the West Bank who was injured in a work-related accident while employed in a business operated by

---

141 ISRAEL NATIONAL SECTION OF THE INTERNATIONAL COMMISSION OF JURISTS, THE RULE OF LAW IN THE AREAS ADMINISTERED BY ISRAEL 23 (1981).

142 BISHARAT, *supra* note 138, at 67.

143 RAJA SHEHADEH & JONATHAN KUTTAB, THE WEST BANK AND THE RULE OF LAW 45–46 (1980).

144 CC (TA Magistrates' Ct.) 83875/95 (Apr. 15, 1998, unreported).

an Israeli settler entity that had also acquired insurance from an Israeli insurance company to cover its liability for work-related accidents. The plaintiff sought to have his claim governed by Israeli law, but the defendants argued for the application of West Bank law. The court ruled in favor of the plaintiff. In his judgment, Judge Boaz Okun, who preceded the Israeli Supreme Court in referring to notions of public policy and justice, concluded that in cases such as that of the present plaintiff, West Bank law cannot be applied if the plaintiff does not opt for its application. For Judge Okun observed that in the context of the PT, the local residents "do not live in a legal system that they developed. They are subject to the instructions of the military commander." In light of this basic observation, Judge Okun concluded that the regular rules of choice of law between those of two sovereign nations are not applicable in the context of a PT civil action in which a Palestinian is the plaintiff. Interestingly, Judge Okun cites in this respect the *Abu-Attiya* judgment, in which it was indeed stated that the relations between Israel and the PT are not as those between two sovereign nations. But instead of such a relation leading to the dominance of Israeli interests in conflict of law inquiries, a methodology the *Abu-Attiya* decision was taken to represent, Okun sought to diminish such Israeli law dominance precisely because of the state of occupation.

Notably, resorting to the standards of choice of law fairness, either in general or in the context of occupation in particular, still falls short of applying the "better law" approach, regarding which the Court in *Qara'an* seemed to have some reservations. The fairness factors, as indicated before, are still within the confines of "the spatially best solution" rather than "the materially best solution" methodology.[145] These factors seek to identify the jurisdiction whose laws it would be unfair to apply, rather than the substantive norms—the choice of which would undermine fair treatment of the parties involved.

Nonetheless, and in spite of the Court's reservations about the "better law" approach, I think that such reservations are to a large extent irrelevant in the sphere of occupation, especially when the choice of law inquiry is undertaken by the courts of the occupying power and the occupation is of a prolonged nature.

Indeed, as David Cavers observed in his seminal 1933 essay, in a choice of law inquiry "the court is not idly choosing a law: it is determining a controversy. How can it choose wisely without considering how the choice will affect the

---

145 *See* SCOLES ET AL., *supra* note 120, at 48.

controversy?"[146] Later on in the twentieth century, evaluation of the "materially best solution" (as opposed to the spatially best solution) was perceived to be legitimate in the choice of law inquiry, along the lines of a "look before you leap" approach.[147] Robert A. Leflar has produced a list of "choice influencing considerations." In addition to considerations such as predictability of results, maintenance of inter-state and international order, simplification of the judicial task, and the advancement of the forum's governmental interests, it is also necessary to consider the better rule of law.[148] In due course, this better law consideration, even when taken as only one among a list of other considerations, has drawn criticism as well as support.[149] The criticism seems to be based on the concern that a forum using a better law approach will effectuate an institutional bias towards its own law.[150] It has also been observed that courts will generally be unable to evaluate the nature and virtue of foreign law, given their own legal background.[151] Additionally, one could argue that from a separation of powers point of view, a court goes beyond its judicial tasks when it evaluates the substantive nature of the competing norms. If the norms in conflict are the output of a legislative process, then courts should generally refrain from evaluating the substantive value of the norms. But it is questionable whether these worries apply regarding Israeli-PT relations. After all, it was the Israeli Supreme Court itself that has emphasized throughout the years of occupation that the relations between these jurisdictions are not identical to those among two sovereign states, since the PT are controlled by an Israeli organ and devoid of any foreign sovereignty. In the preceding chapters, we saw how this underlying perception worked to afford Israeli courts more leeway in asserting their jurisdictional power regarding PT present defendants. In fact, this same perception has also worked to influence the Supreme Court itself when determining the status of military orders issued by the IDF military commander in the PT as either "foreign" or "domestic" law, with the predominant approach considering such orders as "domestic."[152] Arguably, therefore, if Israel has created such an intimate relationship with the PT legal system—issuing over 1,200 military orders regulating almost all spheres of life in the PT during the

146 David Cavers, *A Critique of the Choice-of-Law Problem*, 47 Harv. L. Rev. 173, 189 (1933).

147 *See* Gerhard Kegel, *Paternal Home and Dream Home: Traditional Conflict of Laws and American Reformers* 27 Am. J. Comp. L. 615, 616 (1979). *See also* Symeon C. Symeonides, The American Choice-of-Law Revolution: Past, Present and Future 25–26 (2006).

148 *See* Robert A Leflar, *Choice-Influencing Considerations in Conflicts Law*, 41 NYU L. Rev. 267, 282 (1966).

149 Scoles et al., *supra* note 120, at 53.

150 *Id.*

151 *Id.* at 53 n. 10.

152 *See* CA 6860/01 Hamadah v. Israeli Pool for Vehicle Insurance, 57(3) PD 8, 22–23 (2003).

first two decades of the Israeli occupation only[153]—why then should Israeli courts refrain from evaluating the nature and substance of PT law, at least to the same extent as local Israeli norms are evaluated when they come in conflict with each other? In this vein, therefore, it should be legitimate for Israeli courts to consider the underdeveloped state of law in the PT and the interest of injured and grieved plaintiffs to recover full compensation when claiming their rights.[154]

At this stage, it would be relevant to consider the possible ramifications of the establishment of the PA on the present and future application of the *Qara'an* and *Amutat Kav la-Oved*. This question becomes even more appropriate in light of the fairness analysis afforded here to buttress the Court's approach in both these decisions. The PA is a legislative entity with wide jurisdiction capacity in matters of local civil law. Possibly, it can work to reform the current system and adapt to the wishes of the local Palestinian community in both the West Bank and the Gaza Strip.[155] And the more independence the PA gains, the more meaningful the local political process will become from the perspective of the local community. In fact, so extensive are the ramifications of this new reality that they exceed the scope of this chapter and deserve a study of their own. And although this reality seems to be evolving in a different direction at present, and will probably continue to do so in the foreseeable future, occupation undoubtedly presents choice of law theory with a challenge that has not been fully answered.

---

153 *See* Raja Shehadeh, *The Legislative Stages of the Israeli Military Occupation, in* International Law and the Administration of Occupied Territories: Two Decades of Israeli Occupation of the West Bank and Gaza Strip 151, 152 (Emma Playfair ed., 1992). The total number of military orders has since risen to over 1,700. *See* the website of the IDF MAG Corps, http://www.mag.idf.il/801-he/Patzar.aspx.

154 *See* Luther L. McDougal III, *Toward Application of the Best Rule of Law in Choice-of-Law Cases* 35 Mercer L. Rev. 483 (1984); Scoles et al., *supra* note 120, at 57.

155 *See, e.g.*, Eyal Benvenisti, *The Israeli-Palestinian Declaration of Principles: A Framework for Future Settlement* 4 Eur. J. Int'l L. 542, 549 (1993); David L. Schulman, *The Israel-PLO Accords on the Declaration of Principles on Interim Self-Government Arrangements: The First Step Towards Palestinian Self-Determination*, 7 Emory Int'l L. Rev. 793 (1993); Raja Shehadeh, *Questions of Jurisdiction: A Legal Analysis of the Gaza-Jericho Agreement*, 23 J. Palestine Stud. 18, 22–23 (1994); Justus R. Weiner, *Co-Existence Without Conflict: The Implementation of Legal Structure for Israeli-Palestinian Cooperation Pursuant to the Interim Peace Agreements*, 26 Brook J. Int'l L. 591 (2000).

CHAPTER 5

Judgments and Access to Justice

Contents

Introduction

The conflict of laws issues that have been discussed and analyzed so far—jurisdictional issues and choice of law—dealt with particular disputes. This chapter discusses additional conflict of laws topics of a broader scope: namely, the enforcement of PT judgments in Israel and access to justice rights for Palestinian plaintiffs as a fundamental constitutional right.

A. PT Judgments in Israel

1. Introducing the General Framework

Clearly, recognition and enforcement of judgments is a central theme in the conflict of laws. Discussion of this topic usually focuses on the conditions articulated by the municipal law of the particular forum that make it possible to recognize or even enforce a foreign judgment. It is widely accepted that in the absence of a particular treaty instructing otherwise, a foreign judgment has no effect locally unless it is granted recognition by the local legal system.[1] When the judgment-creditor seeks to enforce the foreign judgment, he or she will ordinarily utilize a special procedure that exists in the local legal system by which the foreign judgment is entered into the local legal system. This process essentially transforms the judgment into a local one. The traditional common law procedure for enforcement of a foreign judgment involves filing an ordinary civil claim based on a cause of action formed by the foreign judgment itself (rather than on the original cause of action on which this foreign judgment was based). If the judgment-creditor, who now becomes the plaintiff, succeeds in establishing the conditions for enforcement as set by the local legal system, then as already indicated, the foreign judgment becomes a local judgment and is enforceable as such. Yet dealing with foreign judgments need not only take the form of enforcement. In some cases, there is simply nothing to enforce—for example, in the case of judgments that declare a person's entitlement to a certain right, or declare a person's status. Additionally, at times the foreign judgment is referred to as *res judicata* in order to prevent the local court from re-litigating what has already been litigated in a foreign forum. Here as well, the court is only asked to recognize the effect of the foreign judgment rather than enforcing it.

Under English common law, the conditions of enforcement and recognition are almost the same. The judgment needs to be final and rendered by a jurisdictionally competent court. The defendant can prevent the foreign judgment from being enforced or recognized on the basis that it was obtained by fraud, that he or she

1 *See* CHESHIRE, NORTH & FAWCETT, PRIVATE INTERNATIONAL LAW 514 (James Fawcett & Janeen M. Carruthers eds., 14th ed. 2008); 1 DICEY, MORRIS & COLLINS, THE CONFLICT OF LAWS 664 (Lord Collins of Mapesbury general ed., 15th ed. 2012).

was not offered a fair process in the rendering court, or that the judgment itself is contrary to public policy. Moreover, under English law, for a foreign judgment to be enforceable it needs to be monetary in nature; i.e., it must establish a debt in favor of the winning party.

These conditions are of a general nature and over the years, volumes of commentaries have been written about their application and meaning. Of note here is that these rules, like many other English common law rules, were also absorbed into local Israeli law and guided local courts even before the establishment of the State of Israel, during the period of the British Mandate. Another important attribute of the English common law rules on the enforcement of judgments is the theory on which the rules were based—the *obligatio* theory.[2] This theory assumes that the foreign judgment creates a debt that the judgment creditor seeks to collect through its enforcement.

In 1958, the Knesset enacted what seemed to be a comprehensive set of rules for the enforcement of foreign judgments: the Foreign Judgments Enforcement Law, 1958 (FJEL).[3] In many respects, this new Israeli enactment was a genuine departure from the English common law approach. First, FJEL is guided by the comity theory of enforcement rather than by the *obligatio* theory. Hence, the foreign judgment is conceived as a sovereign act by the foreign state and as such is worthy of enforcement. Evidence for this conceptualization lies in Section 4(a) of FJEL, which requires the existence of reciprocity in enforcement between the foreign state in which the judgment was rendered and the State of Israel. So if the rendering state does not enforce Israeli judgments, Israeli courts are not supposed to enforce the judgments of that state, irrespective of whether the foreign proceedings were fair, producing what seems to be a sensible and balanced final judgment. An enforcement design that is guided by the *obligatio* theory would have cared less about whether the foreign judgment is rendered by a state that is willing to enforce local judgments. Indeed, under English common law rules, reciprocity was not a pre-condition for enforcement.

FJEL departed from the common law rules in some other important matters. Whereas under the traditional common law approach, the defendant who objects to enforcement is expected to prove that the judgment stands against public policy, under FJEL, the party seeking enforcement must prove that the judgment can

2 *See* Adams v. Cape Industries Plc. [1990] Ch. 433 (C.A.).

3 12 LSI 82 (1957–1958).

be enforced under local law and is not contradictory to public policy. Another adjustment is the time frame in which the foreign judgment can be enforced. FJEL stipulates a time limit of five years on enforcement, while under the traditional rules the time limit is that of the ordinary statute of limitations on causes of action, which in Israel is seven years from the time the cause of action (in such cases, the rendering of the foreign judgment) arose.

In terms of the procedure required for enforcement, FJEL envisioned a special petition to that effect. This procedure is regulated today in the Israeli Rules of Civil Procedure, 1984, instead of as an ordinary civil claim of which the foreign judgment is a cause of action.[4]

Finally, FJEL did not seek to regulate the direct recognition of judgments in general. The only provision dealing with recognition of foreign judgments is Section 11 of FJEL. Subsection (a) provides that recognition can be made to a foreign judgment issued by foreign states that Israel has treaties with, in accordance with the provision of this section and the specific treaties. Subsection (b) provides that recognition of a foreign judgment can be made in an incidental manner within an existing legal proceeding, under conditions mandated by "law and justice."[5] The exact meaning of this term as a pre-condition for incidental recognition was unclear for some considerable time after the enactment of FJEL, and to some extent up to the present. One important Supreme Court holding resolved that the term "law" in the mentioned pre-condition cannot be the regular conditions set for the enforcement of judgments under FJEL. The Court maintained that recognition of a foreign judgment is something more limited than the enforcement of judgment (which always includes recognition) and therefore the pre-conditions for recognition need be more limited as well.[6] As to the conditions under the law, the Court understood these to be the conditions of recognition of foreign judgment under the English common law.

The more difficult question is the one concerning the direct recognition of foreign judgments in Israel. Since FJEL did not regulate this matter, it has been assumed that English common law still governs.[7] However, in a curious holding, the Court

4 KT 4685, 2290, Part 27.

5 12 LSI 82, sec. 11.

6 CA 499/79 Ben Dayan v. A.D.S. International Ltd., 38(2) PD 99 (1984).

7 Celia Wasserstein-Fassberg, Psakim Zarim ba-Mishpat ha-Yisra'eli: Ha-Din ve-Hegyono [Foreign Judgments in Israeli Law: Deconstruction and Reconstruction] 34 (1996) (Hebrew).

held that direct recognition of foreign judgment can only take place under FJEL, Section 11(a), i.e., when there is a treaty to that effect between the State of Israel and the state in which the judgment was rendered.[8] This holding drew much criticism—even by the Supreme Court itself in later judgments.[9] The main reason for this criticism is that Israel has only four treaties on mutual recognition of judgments (with Austria, Germany, Great Britain, and Spain), and hence direct recognition of judgment is a very rare event. One judge of the District Court of Tel-Aviv held that the Supreme Court holding in this respect should be limited to issues of family law and exclude those dealing with insolvency proceedings.[10] However, in attempting to identify the conditions for recognition, this same judge turned to those of enforcement under FJEL rather than English common law, which were taken to be guiding for incidental recognition.[11] Additionally, as the Supreme Court itself suggested, the problem of not having a general track for the direct recognition of foreign judgments can be overcome by having the court make the right or the status that is the subject of the foreign judgment be the right or status claimed in a civil claim. When the local court must determine if the right or the status exists, then it will be required to incidentally recognize the foreign judgment.[12] Though this might be an easy way out of the quandary, it is not the most efficient way, for incidental recognition is assumed to be valid only for the proceedings in question and not for all other possible proceedings—as would have been the case if direct recognition were possible.[13]

Overall, Israeli law reveals much discomfort today over the issue of enforcement and recognition of foreign judgments. The existing law is fraught with multiple proceedings that sometimes overlap and sometime contradict each other.[14] This state leaves much to be desired in terms of the logic behind the different mechanisms. As I will observe in detail later on, the current reality left its imprint of confusion and disorder on the manner in which Israeli courts should deal with PT judgments.

---

8 CA 970/93 Attorney General v. Agam, 48(1) PD 561 (1995).

9 *See* CA 4525/08 Oil Refineries Ltd. v. New Hampshire Insurance Co. (December 15, 2010), Nevo Legal Database (by subscription) (*per* E. Arbel, J.); CA 3441/01 Ploni v. Plonit, 58(3) PD 1, 10–11 (2004) (*per* A. Barak, C.J.).

10 CELIA WASSERSTEIN FASSBERG, MISHPAT BEINLE'UIMI PRATI [PRIVATE INTERNATIONAL LAW] 518 (2013) (Hebrew).

11 *Id.*

12 *See Agam*, 48(1) PD at 568–69.

13 WASSERSTEIN FASSBERG, *supra* note 10, at 517.

14 *Id.* at 489.

2. FJEL: An Exclusive Mechanism of Enforcement?

The text of FJEL creates a strong impression that the Knesset's intention was to introduce a comprehensive and exclusive mechanism for the enforcement of foreign judgments in Israel. FJEL, Section 2, for example, provides that "a foreign judgment shall not be enforced in Israel but in accordance to this law." The Israeli Supreme Court, however, has held otherwise. It perceived FJEL as offering an expedient mechanism of enforcement that a judgment-creditor can utilize if he or she desires. Yet a judgment-creditor is also at liberty to seek to enforce the judgment through the English common law's traditional mechanism of filing a civil claim for which the foreign judgment serves as the cause of action.[15] Additionally, the Court accepted the English common law rule that the original cause of action does not necessarily merge in the foreign judgment. Therefore, the judgment-creditor can also choose to start litigation in Israel in accordance with the original cause of action that served the foreign judgement. In other words under the traditional English rule the cause of action does not merge in the foreign judgment.[16]

It is questionable whether the Israeli Supreme Court appreciated the possible implications of these holdings. The Court must have assumed that a judgment-creditor would normally turn to the more expedient course of enforcement under FJEL—why wouldn't it, if it is interested in a prompt enforcement of the judgment? Choosing the English common law course of enforcement demands the initiation of a regular civil claim, with the burdensome adjudication process that such a claim entails. But rapidly, the Arab-Israeli conflict would once again challenge prevalent assessments, including those of the Israeli Supreme Court itself.

In *Ovadia v. Cohen*,[17] an Israeli court was asked to enforce a judgment rendered by a court in Morocco. The original dispute was between two Jewish litigants who lived in Morocco and operated a business together. Ultimately one of them, the judgment-creditor, immigrated to France and the other one, the judgment-debtor, immigrated to Israel. When the judgment was rendered, the judgment-creditor was already in Israel but was represented by a local counsel in Morocco. At the time, and to a certain extent up to the present, Israel and Morocco had no diplomatic relations. Therefore, if reciprocity is a condition for enforcement—as indeed it is under FJEL—then this action was supposed to be summarily dismissed.

15 CA 423/63 Rosenbaum v. Guli, 18 PD 374 (1964).

16 CA 101/63 Winter v. Kovacz, 17 PD 2032 (1963).

17 CA 221/78, 33(1) PD 293 (1979).

Given the state of relations between Morocco and Israel at the time, it was safe to assume that Morocco would not enforce an Israeli judgment and thus Israel is supposed to do the same and not enforce the Moroccan judgment. Moreover, the judgment-debtor argued that this judgment should not be enforced given that it was rendered against a Jew in a "hostile" country, especially as both litigants have since left that country. The Israeli Supreme Court dismissed all of these arguments and declared the judgment enforceable. The Court noted the fact that this was a civil action that relied on the foreign judgment as its cause of action, and filed in accordance with the English common law mechanism of enforcement that still exists under Israeli law.[18] Given that the English rules do not require reciprocity, no reciprocity was held to be necessary here either. According to the Court, a just and fair proceeding between Jewish litigants can take place even in a hostile regime that abhors Israel.[19] For anti-Jewish sentiments to be relevant as a defense, concrete evidence of mistreatment must to be provided rather than just making general allegations about the character of the regime in Morocco, as the case was here.

Interestingly, the Court in *Ovadia* perceived the English common law option of enforcement being based on FJEL, Section 11(b). According to this law, when the civil action is based on a foreign judgment as its cause of action, the local Israeli court is asked to enforce the debt created while incidentally recognizing the foreign judgment. However, when the English course of enforcement was originally offered by the Court as an alternative mode of enforcement, it was taken to exist beyond the realm of FJEL.

The end result is that Israeli law on foreign judgments offers two alternative paths for the enforcement of foreign judgments. The first is the English common law path, by which a civil claim in which the foreign judgment and the debt created by it constitute the cause of action. The second option involves filing a petition for enforcement under FJEL. The existence of two paths is grounds for process shopping, since the conditions of enforcement can differ between FJEL and English common law. I have already alluded to some major differences, such as reciprocity—a necessary condition under FJEL but not under English common law. On the other hand, enforcement under FJEL can be advantageous, given that it is relatively more expedient as it is regulated by a special set of procedural rules rather than by the general set that deals with a civil claim and all that it entails in terms of pleadings, pre-trial motions, discovery, etc. Additionally,

18 *Id.* at 295.

19 *Id.*

FJEL is available for the enforcement of non-monetary foreign judgments (such as those that include injunction relief), while the English common law route is not.

I chose to highlight this feature of Israeli conflicts on judgments because there is one other important implication of maintaining the English common law path of enforcement. The possibility to enforce Palestinian Authority (PA) judgments today in Israel under FJEL is seriously doubtful. These judgments are not considered to be those of a "foreign state," nor is there any reciprocity today with the PA. This, in turn, raises the question of whether PA judgments can be enforced under the English common law path of enforcement. I will deal with this question in a later stage in this chapter.

3. The Enforcement of PT Judgments in Israel

It is essential to distinguish between two phases when discussing the enforcement of PT judgments in Israel: the pre-Oslo and the post-Oslo period. The primary reason for this distinction lies in the fact that different sets of rules governed in each of the periods.

a. Enforcement of PT Judgments in the Pre-Oslo Accords Period

The enforcement of PT judgments in Israel has always been the subject of a separate set of rules, different from both FJEL and the English common law claim of enforcement. As the following discussion will clarify, this special enforcement path was much more expedient than the one offered by FJEL and much less complicated in terms of the conditions the judgment-creditor needed to establish in order to enforce the foreign judgment, whether under FJEL or English common law.

The first set of rules that regulated the enforcement of PT judgments in Israel was issued by the Israeli Minister of Justice in November 1969. These included Emergency Order (Territories Administered by Israel Defense Force—Judicial Assistance), 1969 (the "1969 Order").[20] According to these rules, a civil judgment rendered by a civil court in the PT (which is not a religious court) is enforceable in Israel as if it were a local Israeli judgment.[21] What this means

20 KT 2842, 459.

21 *Id.* sec. 3(a).

is that the judgment-creditor can go directly to the Israeli Execution Officer and ask that the judgment be enforced, without the need to seek approval by an Israeli court.[22] The exception to enforcement is when the Attorney General of the State of Israel intervenes in the proceedings before the Execution Officer, stating that the judgment might undermine the sovereignty of the State of Israel, forms a risk to security, or contradicts rules of public policy.[23] In such a case, the Execution Office is expected to abstain from enforcement. Some seven years later, this order was superseded by Emergency Order (Judea and Samaria—Judicial Assistance) (No. 2), 1976 (the "1976 Order").[24] This new enactment did not change much in terms of the procedure and conditions that existed in the 1969 Order. It seems that this new set of rules was needed in order to enumerate new judicial bodies now operating in the PT, such as the rabbinical court and the administrative appeals committees—the judgments of which were now regarded as PT judgments.[25] It is important to add that the facilitation of enforcement across the Green Line moved in both directions. The IDF military commander in the PT issued a set of rules by which Israeli judgments were enforceable in the PT as if they were local judgments. This procedure was set in the same month of November 1969, in a special order on judicial assistance.[26] If the Israeli judgment was certified by the IDF judicial officer in charge of legal matter and did not contradict public policy, it was to be recognized in the PT and enforced through the local execution office.

Given Israel's total occupation of the PT at the time, it comes as no surprise that the IDF military commander sought to guarantee unhindered recognition and enforcement of Israeli judgments in the PT. Just like Israeli personal jurisdiction, authority was made available over all those present in the PT, so it was then pronounced that Israeli judgments shall be recognized and enforced in the PT as local judgments were. What was surprising, though, was the Israeli willingness to be more or less equally accommodating regarding PT judgments that parties sought to enforce in Israel. After all, the PT formed a separate jurisdictional entity that operated under a different regime of procedural and substantive law—part of which was enacted by countries that Israel was at war with.

22 *Id.* sec. 3(b).

23 *Id.* sec. 4(a).

24 KT 3529, 1670.

25 *Id.* sec. 1.

26 Judicial Assistance Order (Judea and Samaria) (No. 348), 5729-1969, K.M.Z.M. 20, 694 (1970).

However, this accommodation of PT judgments can also be explained by Israel's control over the PT. First of all, one should recall that the jurisdiction of PT courts in matters that were conceived to be in the vital interest of Israel was restricted. This was the case in claims and petitions filed against different IDF agencies regarding takings and land surveys, for example.[27] Second, in other disputes in which a vital Israeli interest was discernible, an Israeli court could also issue an anti-suit injunction and prevent the PT adjudication from taking place. One Israeli court indeed did so even when the PT adjudication was well into the resolution of the claim.[28]

b. Enforcement in the Post-Oslo Accords Period

The judicial assistance apparatus in the Interim Agreement envisioned a mechanism of mutual enforcement of Israeli and PA civil judgments.[29] The Interim Agreement makes it apparent that the designed path of enforcement is supposed to be efficient and direct, as the only two pre-conditions appearing there are: (1) the court that rendered the judgment had the judicial capacity to do so; and (2) enforcement is not contrary to public policy. The Interim Agreement also instructed each party to consider the judgment of the other party as if rendered by its own local courts. Accordingly, no recourse to a local court is necessary for the purpose of enforcing the judgment.[30] As already outlined in Chapter Two, the Interim Agreement's provisions on judicial assistance were enacted in Israel in Emergency Order (Judea and Samaria and the Gaza Strip—Jurisdiction over Crimes and Legal Assistance) (the Territories of the Palestinian Council—Judicial Assistance in Civil Matters), 1999 (the "1999 Emergency Order").[31] This enactment became possible by virtue of the Law for the Extension of Emergency Regulations (Judea and Samaria—Jurisdiction over Criminal Offences and Legal Assistance), 1967, as amended in 1996 (LEER, 1996).[32] In terms of the pre-conditions for enforcement, the 1999 Emergency Order was faithful to the letter of the Interim Agreement. Section 6 of this enactment provides that the PA judgment is to be

---

27 *See supra* Chapter One, Part E.4; Chapter Three, Part B.2.

28 Summons (Jer.) 2967/87 Hijalah v. Judea and Samaria Company (JSC) (1988, unreported); *see supra* Chapter Three, Part B.2.

29 Israeli-Palestinian Interim Agreement on the West Bank and the Gaza Strip, Sept. 28, 1995, Annex IV, Art. IV, 36 I.L.M. 557 (1995).

30 *Id.* Annex IV, Art. IV, Sec. 3 ("The execution offices under the responsibility of each side shall execute such judgments as if rendered by their own judicial organs.")

31 KT 5947, 278.

32 22 LSI 20 (1967–68). The relevant 1996 amendments were published in SH No. 1556, p. 34.

regarded as if rendered by an Israeli court and is enforceable if the PA court that rendered it was jurisdictionally competent to do so under PA law and the judgment otherwise complies with Annex IV, Section III of the Interim Agreement. If so, then enforcement can be performed directly by Israel's Execution Office. However, the 1999 Emergency Order added two gate-keeping functions that can stay or even inhibit enforcement. First, it granted to the Attorney General of the State of Israel the power to declare the judgment unenforceable on the grounds that it undermines the State of Israel's sovereignty, security, public policy, or other vital interest.[33] One should note here that even though the Execution Office performs a number of judicial functions in the process of executing judgments, it does not have the capacity to decide on this manner, but must defer to the decision of the Attorney General. Another gate-keeping function is that accorded to the Judicial Assistance Officer, who was granted the powers of handling judicial assistance functions under the Interim Agreement. Section 6(b) of the 1999 Emergency Order instructs the judgment creditor of a PA judgment to first file the request for enforcement, with all the necessary documentation, with the Israeli Judicial Assistance Officer. This official is then instructed to check if all the pre-conditions for enforcement are satisfied and if so, to authorize the judgment for enforcement by the Execution Office. Only then would the PA judgment be enforced like any other Israeli judgment—but as noted, the Attorney General can intervene to prevent enforcement.

The enforcement mechanism of the 1999 Emergency Order was short lived. Soon afterwards, in the year 2000, the *Al-Aqsa Intifada* broke out, bringing cooperation between Israel and the PA to a halt—at least in the sphere of judicial assistance. Though reciprocity was not indicated in the Interim Agreement or in the 1999 Emergency Order as a pre-condition for enforcement, it was nonetheless taken that the overall judicial assistance apparatus between Israel and the PA is built on the judicial cooperation of both parties. So if no judicial cooperation is possible under the current conditions—a circumstance that has not changed since 2000—the enforcement mechanism as regulated in the 1999 Emergency Order is effectively blocked. In order to stress the reciprocal nature of the 1999 Emergency Order, the Israeli Minister of Justice issued explicit instructions not to enforce PA judgments. It appears that in the sphere of judicial assistance, generally there exists yet one additional gate-keeping function: that of the Israeli Minister of Justice. Under LEER, 1996, by virtue of which the 1999 Emergency Order was enacted, the Israeli Minister of Justice can instruct that a judicial assistance function not

33 1999 Emergency Order, sections 6(f)–(g).

be performed in either a certain matter or generally, if and when the PA is not reciprocating by performing the judicial assistance function requested by Israeli authorities.[34] In accordance with this power, the Israeli Minister of Justice issued instructions by which PA judgments are not to be enforced under the judicial assistance mechanism of the 1999 Emergency Order. This became public in the Supreme Court judgment of *Massalha v. Palestine International Bank*.[35] A Palestinian Bank based in Ramallah filed a civil action against the defendant, Muhsen Massalha, an Israeli citizen. The bank claimed that it was entitled to monetary relief from the defendant based on a set of credit agreements drawn in Ramallah and governed by PA law. The defendant asked that the proceedings be stayed based on forum non conveniens. Though the magistrate court granted the petition, this judgment was overruled by the district court. The Supreme Court, after being asked to grant leave for an additional appeal, denied the petition for such a leave. In justifying its stand, the Court noted that according to a letter provided by the Israeli Judicial Assistance Officer, the Israeli Minster of Justice had issued instructions by which no PA judgments were to be enforced in Israel in accordance with LEER, 1996, Section 13(d). This in turn, led the Court to the conclusion that if the Israeli proceedings are stayed, then the plaintiff bank will be in a tough position, for it would need to file the claim before a PA court—only to realize that the judgment would be ineffective given that it must be enforced in Israel—the place of residence and citizenship of the defendant and supposedly where his assets were held.

So under the current circumstances, there is no possibility of enforcement of PA judgments under the 1999 Emergency Order. The question that arises is whether alternative paths exist, such as under FJEL or even under English common law. One can conceivably argue that no such alternative path exists. The 1999 Emergency Order is certainly an enactment that is specifically designed for the enforcement of PA judgments and as such, can be perceived as the exclusive path of enforcement. However, I doubt whether this argument will stand, given the evolution of Israeli law on the enforcement of foreign judgments. It suffices to recall here that when FJEL was enacted, it did contain a provision explicitly providing for its exclusivity.[36] Yet, the Israeli Supreme Court held that such a provision does not exclude enforcement under the traditional English common law, making it possible for a plaintiff to choose between the two paths. One can thus

34 LEER, 1996, sec. 13(d).

35 LCA 3608/10 (June 29, 2010), Nevo Legal Database (by subscription).

36 FJEL, sec. 2.

argue that the same holding applies regarding the 1999 Emergency Order, even more so given that this enactment does not even include any explicit language suggesting its exclusivity. In terms of substance, it can also be argued here that the intention of the 1999 Emergency Order was to provide an expedient path of enforcement, given the special relations that were constructed in the Oslo Peace Accords. If these accords are no longer operational in the sphere of judicial assistance, then one might argue that no shortcuts to enforcement are now available; but the possibility of enforcement cannot be denied altogether if it exists through some other alternative mechanism.

The two possible alternative paths that come to mind are the general paths for the enforcement of judgments. The first is that under FJEL. Yet given the current state of relations between Israel and the PA, it is questionable whether this path is realistic. The Israeli Supreme Court had a chance to comment on this issue in *Massalha*. First, it noted that the definition of a foreign judgment under this law requires that it be rendered by a court in a "foreign state."[37] In light of the fact that the PA has not yet attained statehood, at least from the point of view of the State of Israel, there are "serious doubts," according to the Court, whether this condition can be satisfied.[38] Second (and this seems to be the more serious impediment to enforcement under FJEL of a PA judgment), the Court noted the absence of reciprocity—a crucial pre-condition under FJEL.

Other than the path of enforcement under FJEL, the Israeli Supreme Court in *Massalha* did not mention or recall that enforcement of a PA judgment could still be possible under yet a third path. As already indicated, the English common law mechanism of filing a civil claim for the enforcement of a foreign judgment was held as still being available under Israeli conflict of laws rules on judgment, notwithstanding FJEL. As noted above, by the same token it can be argued the English common law path of enforcement is also available notwithstanding the 1999 Emergency Order. The fact that no reciprocity in the enforcement of judgments exists between Israel and the PA should not preclude enforcement under

37 LCA 3608/10 *Massalha*, para. 9.

38 The Court here refers to another decision by an Israeli district court. This is Originating Summons (Jer) 4332/05 Mustafa v. Zaid (April 29, 2007) Nevo Legal Database (by subscription). Ultimately, the PA judgment was enforced in these proceedings under FJEL. However, this enforcement was based on the fact that the judgment-debtor did not show up to respond to the petition for enforcement notwithstanding the fact that he was duly summoned to do so. In the course of making his decision, the presiding judge in this case did indicate concern over whether the PA judgment satisfied the definition of a foreign judgment under FJEL. Yet given that the petition of enforcement was not contested, he did not find it necessary to take a definite stand on the matter.

English common law rules that do not require reciprocity. In fact, the Israeli Supreme Court itself made this rather explicit in *Ovadia*, when it ordered the enforcement of a Moroccan judgment despite its assumption that no reciprocity in the enforcement of judgment existed at the time between Israel and Morocco.[39]

As to the question of whether under English common law local courts can enforce or recognize judgments of foreign entities that are not internationally recognized as a foreign state or whose existence as a foreign sovereign state is disputed by the local forum, the answer seems to be in the affirmative.[40] What is controlling is not the *de jure* recognition or status of the foreign entity, but rather the fact that it has *de facto* control as a government and the judgment that is the subject of enforcement or recognition deals with a private right or an everyday occurrence.[41] The basic motivation behind this holding is that private parties litigating private disputes should not suffer the backlash of an international dispute when the litigation that took place seems to be fair and ordinary. The most direct authority to this effect is that of the Hong Kong Court of Final Appeal in *Chen Li Hung v. Ting Lei Miao*.[42] Here, Hong Kong, now a special administrative region of the People's Republic of China (the legal system of which still adheres to the principles of English common law), was instructed to recognize a decree rendered in a bankruptcy proceedings that took place in Taiwan. Notably, this recognition was ordered by Hong Kong's highest court of appeal, notwithstanding the fact that as far as China is concerned, Taiwan is part of China. Moreover, China regards the existing government in Taiwan as unlawful. Yet the Hong Kong court was not dissuaded from recognition. As one of the judges held:

> In my judgment, the Taiwanese Bankruptcy Order is to be given effect by the Hong Kong court. The rights thereunder are plainly private. By the general nature and particular circumstances of those rights, giving effect to them accords with the interest of justice, the dictates of common sense and the needs of law and order.[43]

Actually, one need not look as far as Hong Kong in order to conclude that PA judgments have enough intrinsic value to be enforceable under the English common law mechanism. On a previous occasion, the Israeli Supreme Court assumed

39 *Ovadia*, 33(1) PD at 294–95.

40 *See* 2 Dicey, Morris & Collins, *supra* note 1, at 1382–83.

41 *Id. See* Carl Zeiss Stiftung v. Rayner & Keeler Ltd. (No. 2) [1967] 1 AC 853, 954 (*per* Lord Wilberforce).

42 [2000] 1 HKC 461.

43 *Id.* at 474.

as a matter of course that a Shari'a court judgment rendered in East Jerusalem in accordance with Jordanian law and in a litigation that concerned West Bank Palestinian litigants was worthy of recognition under FJEL, Section 11(b).[44] The incidental recognition of PT judgments was also accorded to regular PT courts, both before and after the Oslo Accords.[45] This stand is telling. If FJEL Section 11(b) recognition is governed by FJEL's definitions as to what constitutes a foreign judgment, then what the Israeli courts are essentially holding in these cases is that the PA is a foreign state for the purpose of FJEL. It would be a serious anomaly if the PA is considered a foreign state for the purpose of incidental recognition under FJEL, Section 11(b) but not so for the purpose of enforcement under the English common law mechanism or even under FJEL itself, for that matter. On a more principled level, my colleague Celia Fassberg has argued that the conflict of laws, as a discipline, is less interested about whether the foreign entity has gained international recognition under public international law standard.[46] Rather, this field of law focuses on the fact that there are different legal systems that are identified as separate from each other, irrespective of whether they are considered to belong to independent sovereign states or not.[47] Accordingly, the fact that the PA is a separate legal system with a court system that like any other legal system conducts litigation and produces judgments that are intended to resolve the pending conflict is prima facie sufficient to render these judgments as potentially enforceable.

In conclusion, it seems that PT judgments rendered by PA courts after the Oslo Accords are enforceable under the English common law path of enforcement. As we shall see in the following discussion, a clear trend of enforceability is apparent regarding the recognition of PT judgments.

4. On the Recognition of PT Judgments

As indicated before, Israeli conflict rules on the recognition of foreign judgments are in a state of disorder. It is unclear whether direct recognition of foreign judgments is still possible. In any case, Israeli law sanctions the incidental recognition of foreign judgments when filing an action based on the right vindicated in the foreign judgment. Yet uncertainty as to the conditions for recognition always

44 CA 1227/97 Sal'it ha-Adomim Quarry Ltd. v. Ibrahim, 53(3) PD 247, 251 (1999).

45 *See infra* Chapter Five, Part A.4.

46 WASSERSTEIN FASSBERG, *supra* note 10, at 498–99.

47 *Id.* at 499.

exists. Are these conditions the same as the ones articulated under English common law, or are they those deemed necessary for the purpose of enforcement under FJEL?

In spite of this state of confusion, one course of action was rather consistent and clear: Israeli courts recognized the judgments rendered in the PT both before the Oslo Accords and after as if they are those of a foreign state. In fact, Israeli courts were so eager in granting this recognition that they overlooked explicit provisions in an Israeli enactment that would have rendered recognition in the particular case impossible.

The first case in which such recognition was accorded was that of *Bassilious—The Coptic Bishop of the Holy Seat of Jerusalem and the Near East v. Adila.*[48] The case dealt with a dispute over the rights in certain real property located in the West Bank city of Jericho in the pre-Oslo period. The Coptic Bishop filed a civil suit before an Israeli court asking that he should be declared as the holder of property rights in the Jericho land. The defendants argued that this action should be dismissed, given that the local courts in Ramallah had already conducted adjudication on the issue of the parties' rights and dismissed the claims of the Coptic Bishop. In other words, the defendant sought to argue that the Ramallah judgment is *res judicata* in this Israeli action. This argument made it necessary to confront the question of whether the Israeli court should incidentally recognize the Ramallah judgment. When this question reached the Israeli Supreme Court, it was held that the Ramallah judgment was entitled to incidental recognition under FJEL, Section 11(b).[49] The primary question that concerned the Court in this respect was how to interpret the term "law and justice" as a pre-condition for incidental recognition under this provision. No reservation was indicated in the decision about the fact that the PT judgment at the time did not qualify as one rendered in a "foreign state." In this respect, the PT judgment was regarded as any other judgment of a foreign state, even though the PT at the time were under full Israeli occupation and the IDF military commander was the sole and ultimate sovereign there.

The *Bassilious* judgment was handed down in 1990. Some three years earlier, the Israeli Supreme Court had a chance to relate to the propriety of recognizing a PT judgment in *Battarsa v. Ayash.*[50] The Israeli adjudication started here when Moussa

48 54(4) PD 397 (1990).

49 *Id.* at 404–05.

50 LCA 383/86, 41(2) PD 100 (1987).

Ayash sought an attachment order over real property located in the West Bank city of Bethlehem from the District Court of Jerusalem. This preliminary relief was justified in order to facilitate the collection of an alleged debt that Ayash claimed from the defendant. Following this attachment order, a petition was filed for its lifting by apparently two Palestinian residents of the West Bank who had been declared the lawful owners of this real property by the local PT courts. The Israeli Supreme Court ordered that the attachment order be lifted, in light of the PT judgment. Apparently, this recognition should have been arranged through FJEL, Section 11(b) as a clear case of incidental recognition. However, the Court did not take this route but rather ruled that in the 1976 Order, "a judgment of a judicial body in the Region is to be executed in Israel as if it was a judgment rendered in Israel. . . ." Seemingly, turning to this order is mistaken. Clearly, this enactment is concerned with the enforcement—but not the recognition—of PT judgments. Given the clear distinction in Israeli conflicts rules on judgments between recognition and enforcement, it seems that the Court did not correctly identify what was at issue in the pending case, nor the law that was governing. Probably this is why this case was not even mentioned in *Bassilious*, which was rendered only a few years after.

The Israeli Supreme Court had the chance to set the record straight in *Sal'it ha-Adomim Quarry Ltd. v. Ibrahim*.[51] The case dealt with a land dispute between a corporation operating a quarry in the West Bank and local Palestinian residents who claimed ownership of land occupied by the quarry. Eventually, the Palestinian residents filed a civil claim against the Israeli corporation asking, among other things, the payment of rent for the unlawful use of their land. In order to prove their property rights, the Palestinian residents-plaintiffs presented a Shari's court judgment by which they were considered to be the legal heirs to the land that was occupied by the quarry. Though the Shari'a court operated from East Jerusalem, the Israeli Supreme Court regarded it as PT court operating under PT law. So once again, the case presented a proceeding in which the PT judgment was supposed to be incidentally recognized, and the Court ultimately granted this recognition. But instead of determining the proper course for the incidental recognition of this PT judgment, the Court held that the following two mechanisms are available: either the process under FJEL, Section 11(b) (as ordered in *Bassilious*), or the one under the 1976 Order (as held in *Battarsa*).[52] It is worth noting here that this second course of incidental recognition is problematic not only because it is designed to tend to the enforcement of judgments rather than

51 *Sal'it ha-Adomim*, 53(3) PD 247.

52 *Id.* at 251.

their recognition, but also because of the fact that the 1976 Order, in Section 1, has precluded judgments rendered by religious courts from its scope! Yet, like in *Battarsa* and *Bassilious*, the Court seemed to be equally determined to grant recognition to the PA judgment, all notwithstanding the doubts about this judgment not being that of a foreign state or about the applicability of the 1976 Order.

This same attitude was evident also in a judgment granted in the post-Oslo period. *Abu Hajla v. Custodian for Absentee Property*[53] involved a dispute over the property rights in the estate of a Palestinian who an Israeli official—the Custodian for Absentee Property—declared to be an absent owner under an Israel's Absentee Property Law, 1953. Upon this declaration, the property of such a person is taken over by this state official, who then can deal with it as a state entitlement. The cause for this declaration was that the property was located in Israel but the decedent had moved in 1952 to live in the West Bank and for that reason was found to be an absentee under the law. In an effort to defeat the claims of the Custodian for Absentee Property, the Palestinian heirs to the decedent were supposed to first establish that they had rights in the estate as legal heirs. In this vein, they produced a judgment rendered by the Shari'a court operating in the PA in which they were declared to be as such. The Custodian argued that this judgment was invalid given that Israeli law does not recognize this PA Shari'a court. The president of the District Court of the Center, Hila Gerstel, dismissed the argument. She held that incidental recognition of this judgment was possible under FJEL, Section 11(b), and that under the circumstances, there was no reason to not grant incidental recognition to this PA judgment under the terms of the "law and justice." It seems that she would have also awarded incidental recognition under the 1999 Emergency Order, but did not do so given the fact that at present, no reciprocity in judicial cooperation exists between the PA and the State of Israel. This District Court overlooked the fact that the 1999 Order on judicial cooperation, like the 1976 one, is also concerned with the enforcement of judgments rather than recognition,[54] as well as the fact that FJEL itself requires as a general rule that reciprocity be present as a condition for enforcement and hence incidental recognition. The only way to justify this holding is by assuming a proposition that the court did not clarify—that the conditions of incidental recognition under FJEL, Section 11(b) is under the traditional rules of English common law that do not require reciprocity. This suggestion, of course, was also made on previous occasions.[55]

---

53 Originating Summons (CT) 52974-02-11 (November 11, 2012), Nevo Legal Database (by subscription).

54 1999 Order, sec. 6.

55 *Ovadia*, 33(1) PD at 294–95. *See supra* Chapter Five, Part A.3.

If anything can be said about the ensuing discussion, it is that Israeli courts were determined to grant incidental recognition to PT judgment both before and after the Oslo Accords, and in taking this position they largely followed a teleological course of analysis. The wording or the design of the enactments that the Israeli courts resorted to in order to provide this incidental recognition did not matter as much as did the quest to grant recognition. If any principled conclusion is to be drawn from this discussion, it is no doubt the one Celia Fassberg has alluded to before: that conflict of law is about interaction between legal systems rather than between internationally recognized sovereign and independent states that qualify as such under standards of public international law. The experience of Israeli courts on the incidental recognition of PT judgments in the period before and after the Oslo Accords is powerful evidence for this proposition. What remains to be determined is whether Israeli courts will be willing to take the same stand in the sphere of the enforcement of PT judgments as rendered today by PA courts, either in accordance with FJEL or under the traditional English common law path for enforcement of foreign judgments.

B. Israeli Access to Justice Principles and Palestinian Plaintiffs

The issue of Palestinian plaintiffs' access to justice rights should supposedly open a discussion of the sort undertaken in this book. Logically, the conception of whether the plaintiff (or the group of persons to which the plaintiff belongs) is entitled to access to justice rights before local courts is of such a fundamental nature that it deserves to be addressed first, rather than last. I decided to include this discussion in the last chapter of the book, however, given the nature of the analysis I seek to offer regarding the access to justice rights of Palestinian plaintiffs before Israeli courts. As will be revealed, this analysis builds on the trends and attributes already identified in the spheres of jurisdiction and choice of law and takes this discussion one step further by showing how important these trends have become in defining the actual access to justice rights accorded to Palestinian plaintiffs today.[56]

My main objective here is to highlight the two major hurdles that Palestinian plaintiffs face today in seeking to litigate their PT-related civil claims before

56 For an analysis of the access to justice standard that Israeli courts have applied regarding Palestinian plaintiffs in light of constitutional and international civil litigation standards, *see* Michael Karayanni, *Access to Justice Ascends to International Civil Litigation: The Case of Palestinian Plaintiffs before Israeli Courts*, 33 CIVIL JUSTICE Q. 43 (2014).

Israeli courts. By doing so, I also aim to emphasize how notions of control and separation already embedded in the evolution of jurisdictional and choice of law doctrines have become instrumental in shaping the actual access to justice rights of Palestinian plaintiffs in Israeli courts. Before proceeding, however, I will provide a brief overview of the status of access to justice rights under international law norms, especially those pertaining to belligerent occupation, as well as under the guiding principles of Israeli law.

1. Access to Justice under International Law

Much controversy has revolved around the question of whether the law of international belligerent occupation affords subjects of an occupied territory access to the courts of the belligerent occupant.[57] While common law countries have not tended to recognize any such right, continental systems took a different position that essentially accepted such a right.[58] The immediate cause of this controversy was Section 23(h) of the Hague Convention of 1907, considered to represent customary international law. The section prohibits the belligerent occupant "to declare abolished, suspended, or inadmissible in a court of law the rights and actions of the nationals of the hostile party...." Common law countries read this article as providing an instruction directed at the military commander of the belligerent occupant rather than the courts of the belligerent occupant, under the understanding that the military commander shall not issue a command that embodies such a declaration. Continental systems, on the other hand, maintained that this provision offers a positive right of access to courts of the belligerent occupant.[59] No definite resolution exists to this long-standing controversy, though there seems to be a clear trend in common law systems to afford more access to those considered affiliated in one way or another to a foreign enemy state.[60] Additionally, Francesco Francioni recently submitted a powerful claim that access to justice comprises a recognized human right under public international law.[61] However, these approaches acknowledging the existence of access to justice rights under international law have thus far not taken the discussion much further than the recognition of the right as a matter of principle.

---

57 GERHARD VON GLAHN, THE OCCUPATION OF ENEMY TERRITORY 108–09 (1957),

58 *See* James W. Garner, *Treatment of Enemy Aliens*, 13 AM. J. INT'L L. 22, 24–29 (1919).

59 *Id.*

60 Karen Knop, *Citizenship, Public and Private*, 71 LAW & CONTEMP. PROBS. 309, 321–22 (2008).

61 Francesco Francioni, *The Rights of Access to Justice under Customary International Law*, *in* ACCESS TO JUSTICE AS A HUMAN RIGHT 1, 42 (Francesco Francioni ed., 2007).

On the other hand, a number of international conventions have been conscious of the interests behind access to justice rights and thus worked to transform the principle into specific rights: first the 1954 Hague Convention on Civil Procedure,[62] then the 1980 Convention on International Access to Justice.[63] Yet these conventions represent consensual international law only, and as such compel the contracting states in their mutual relations but create no further obligations.

The absence of any real guidance in international law norms—both in general and within specific references pertaining to belligerent occupation in particular—explains why Israeli courts have permitted themselves a great deal of latitude in articulating the access to justice rights of Palestinian plaintiffs. Hence, it is not surprising that in fashioning these rights, Israeli courts tended not to reference public international law. This omission is uncharacteristic of the handling of Israeli institutions and courts of PT matters which, as we have seen in Chapter One, were from the start overtly conscious, though not necessarily convincing, of international law norms.

2. Access to Justice under Israeli Jurisprudence

Axiomatically, access to justice is a principle of constitutional significance in Israel today.[64] This fact is somewhat surprising, given that Israel has no formal

62 286 U.N.T.S. 265 (May 14, 1954).

63 19 I.L.M. 1505 (October 25, 1980).

64 HCJ 2171/06 Cohen v. Chairman of the Knesset, para. 19 (August 29, 2011), Nevo Legal Database (by subscription); LCA 993/06 State of Israel v. Dirani, paras. 22–25 (July 18, 2011), Nevo Legal Database (by subscription); HCJ 9198/02 Physicians Union of Israel v. Attorney General, para. 51 (October 2, 2008), Nevo Legal Database (by subscription); CA 1480/04 Malibu Israel Ltd. v. State of Israel (September 17, 2006), Nevo Legal Database (by subscription); CA 6805/99 Talmud Torah v. Local Council for Zoning and Planning in Jerusalem, 57(5) PD 433, 444–45 (2003); LCA 7608/99 Loki Bitzu'a Proyektim (Bniya) 1989 Ltd. v. Mitzpeh Kinneret 1995 Ltd., 56(5) PD 156, 163–64 (2002); LCA 2808/00 Shufersal Ltd. v. Niv, 54(2) PD 845, 848 (2000). Major works on access to justice rights can be found in ACCESS TO JUSTICE AS A HUMAN RIGHT (Francesco Francioni ed., 2007); ACCESS TO JUSTICE FOR A NEW CENTURY: THE WAY FORWARD (Julia Bass, W. A. Bogart & Fredrick H. Zemans eds., 2005); DEBORAH L. RHODE, ACCESS TO JUSTICE (2004); REFORM OF CIVIL PROCEDURE: ESSAYS ON "ACCESS TO JUSTICE" (A. A. S. Zuckerman & Ross Cranston eds., 1995); SIR HARRY WOOLF, ACCESS TO JUSTICE: FINAL REPORT TO THE LORD CHANCELLOR ON THE CIVIL JUSTICE SYSTEM IN ENGLAND AND WALES (1996); ACCESS TO JUSTICE AND THE WELFARE STATE (Mauro Cappelletti ed., 1979). Access to justice rights gained international recognition after World War II and since then became a basic concept in the law of procedure. *See* MAURO CAPPELLETTI, THE JUDICIAL PROCESS IN COMPARATIVE PERSPECTIVE 237–38 (1989); Simon Roberts, *Litigation and Settlement, in* REFORM OF CIVIL PROCEDURE: ESSAYS ON "ACCESS TO JUSTICE," *id.* at 447, 448.

constitution. The following legal construct has made this characterization possible: an individual's civil cause of action is considered to be a property right as well as an attribute of human dignity. Both the right to property and the right to human dignity are protected rights under Israel's Basic Law: Human Dignity and Liberty (BLHDL).[65] Since this law affords Israeli courts the power of judicial review over Knesset legislation, and for that reason was considered to be part of the Israeli constitutional revolution, rights protected under the BLHDL commonly became referred to as constitutional rights. Indeed, as we shall see later on, parts of a Knesset legislation that unduly infringed upon the access to justice rights of Palestinian plaintiffs were held invalid based on BLHDL judicial review powers. Moreover, on one occasion, the Israeli Supreme Court opined that the access to justice right has ultra-constitutional status. According to this view, access to justice is central to the ability of the judiciary to fulfill its function as a branch of government.[66] In a democracy that seeks to guarantee the functioning of its judiciary, safeguarding access to courts is imperative. So as a matter of principle, Israeli law recognizes the prominence of access to justice rights. Arguably, therefore, Palestinian plaintiffs coming before a competent, jurisdictional Israeli court should be entitled to adjudicate their claim and to enforce their rights. However, the situation proved to be otherwise.

3. Restricting Access to Justice Rights of Palestinian Plaintiffs

a. Restricting Access to Justice Rights through Jurisdictional Doctrines

The discussion in Chapter Two provided a vivid picture of how Palestinian plaintiffs were restricted from adjudicating their civil claims before Israeli courts, especially when the named defendants were also Palestinian residents of the PT. Though the Israeli courts would have been fully competent to adjudicate such claims on their merits based solely on the fact that the defendant was properly served with the court process, they nonetheless abstained from doing so. The judicial tool that made this abstention possible was the forum non conveniens doctrine. In this sense, the doctrine functioned to control the stream of litigation

---

65 S.H. 1391 (1992).

66 CA 733/95 Arpel Aluminum Corp. v. Kalil Industries Corp., 51(3) PD 577, 590–91, 629 (1997) (*per* M. Cheshin, J.). *See also* Frank I. Michelman, *The Supreme Court and Litigation Access Fees: The Right to Protect One's Rights—Part I*, 1973 DUKE L.J. 1153, 1172; John Leubsdorf, *Constitutional Civil Procedure*, 63 TEX. L. REV. 579, 597 (1984); Mauro Cappelletti & Bryant Garth, *Access to Justice and the Welfare State: An Introduction*, *in* ACCESS TO JUSTICE AND THE WELFARE STATE, *supra* note 64, at 1, 13; Deborah L. Rhode, *Access to Justice*, 69 FORDHAM L. REV. 1785, 1799 (2001).

into Israeli courts; when all of the concerned parties were Palestinians, the doctrine worked to divert the flow of PT-related litigation back to the PT. This was the case before the Oslo Accords, and it certainly remains the situation in the post-Oslo period. On the other hand, when all of the concerned parties were Israeli settlers in the PT, the plaintiff was provided with unhindered access to Israeli courts, even though the claim was based on events that took place solely in the PT. Courts precluded the application of the forum non conveniens doctrine in such cases, given the safety valve implanted in the doctrine; the Israeli Supreme Court had instructed that if a "significant Israeli element" was involved in a case then proceedings are not supposed to be stayed on forum non conveniens grounds.[67] In this sense, the access to justice standard functioned to stream litigation into and out of Israeli courts, just as it had directed the choice of law inquiry. When the litigation was of a mixed Israeli-Palestinian character, the tendency was and essentially still is to have the dispute litigated before an Israeli court. As observed before, this trend is also in line with Israel's control policy, whereby the proper default rule is to defer to hegemonic interests.

In the period after the *Al-Aqsa Intifada* that broke out in 2000, two other restrictions on the access to justice rights of Palestinian plaintiffs emerged. The first involved conditioning litigation before an Israeli court upon the provision of a security bond. Palestinian plaintiffs were asked to provide the Israeli courts a guarantee that secures the payment of court expenses to defendants that prevail in the adjudication. The imposition of security bonds flourished, even when adjudication before the Israeli court was deemed appropriate. The second limitation involved restricting the ability of Palestinian plaintiffs to file civil claims against the State of Israel or any of its agencies regarding damages incurred as a result of IDF operations.

b. Conditioning Litigation upon the Deposit of Security Bonds

Under Israeli law, the prevailing party in a civil action is entitled to receive compensation for its litigation expenses from the losing party.[68] In this respect, the trial court has broad discretion in determining the actual sum of compensation

67 *See supra* Chapter Two, Part C.2.

68 Stephen Goldstein, *The Influence of Constitutional Principles on Civil Procedure in Israel*, 17 ISR. L. REV. 467, 496 (1982); Stephen Goldstein & Elisheva HaCohen, *Israel*, *in* 3 INTERNATIONAL ENCYCLOPEDIA OF LAWS: CIVIL PROCEDURE 67, 93 (Piet Taelman ed., 1994). On the different rules of taxing costs, *see* Hein Kötz, *Public Interest Litigation: A Comparative Survey*, *in* ACCESS TO JUSTICE AND THE WELFARE STATE, *supra* note 64, at 85, 90.

to be levied on the losing party and can certainly take into consideration whether the prevailing party was also responsible for unnecessary litigation.[69] If for some reason the trial court doubts the ability of the plaintiff (and only that of the plaintiff) to actually pay the litigation costs of the defendant (should the latter prevail), then under an explicit provision in the Israeli Rules of Civil Procedure (Rule 519),[70] the court can order the plaintiff to provide a security bond guaranteeing the actual payment of court expenses. Should the plaintiff not comply with this condition, the court is then empowered to dismiss the claim altogether.

Ordering the plaintiff to provide such a security bond is an exceptional procedure precisely because it might hinder the plaintiff's access to justice rights.[71] Yet, if there are strong indications that the plaintiff might not comply with a final judgment in favor of the defendant or that some special hardships might make the enforcement of such a final judgment complicated, ordering the provision of the security bond lies within the trial court's powers. The common example for such cases is when the plaintiff happens to be a foreigner.

Shortly following the Oslo Peace Accords, it became common practice to condition the actual adjudication of civil claims filed by Palestinian plaintiffs upon the plaintiff's deposit of a security bond, especially in claims filed against the State of Israel as a result of injuries or damages sustained from an IDF operation in the West Bank or the Gaza Strip.

The guiding Israeli Supreme Court decision in this respect is that of *State of Israel v. Ibrahim*.[72] Family dependents of a Palestinian resident of the Gaza Strip who was shot dead by the IDF filed a civil claim for damages before a court in Haifa. The named defendant was the State of Israel, which asked that the plaintiffs be required to provide a security bond guaranteeing the payments of its litigation costs (should the claim fail, of course). In arguing for this need, the state emphasized the fact that enforcement of Israeli judgments in the Gaza Strip had become impossible.[73] The trial court denied the motion, stressing that the defendant in this case is not a private entity but rather a public one. This judgment was reversed in the appeal filed before the Israeli Supreme Court. Although the Court

69 Goldstein & HaCohen, *supra* note 68, at 93.

70 Rules of Civil Procedure, 1984, Rule 519, KT 4685, 2220 (hereinafter RCP, 1984).

71 Dudi Schwartz, Seder Din Ezrahi: Hidushim, Tahalikhim u-Megamot [Civil Procedure: Developments, Processes and Trends] 112 (2007) (Hebrew).

72 LCA 2146/04, 58(5) PD 865 (2004).

73 *Id.* at 867.

(represented by Justice Grunis) recognized the right of access to justice as providing constitutional standing,[74] it ordered the plaintiffs to provide a security bond in the amount of 9,000 NIS (2,516 USD according to the July 29, 2013 exchange of rate: 1 USD=3.5770 NIS).[75] In its decision, the Court noted that access to justice is not an absolute right; the Court viewed access to justice, like other fundamental rights, as a right that needs to be balanced against other concerns.[76] The state, whose budget is dependent on the public, was held entitled to protect its interests in recovering its litigation costs, though the state's identity might be taken as a factor in reducing the sum guaranteed through the security bond.[77]

Compared to a number of other cases in which Palestinian plaintiffs were ordered to deposit a security bond, the sum of 9,000 NIS is at the lower end of the spectrum.[78] At the higher end is the sum of 50,000 NIS (14,241 USD).[79] The more representative sums levied as security bonds on Palestinian plaintiffs today range between 15,000 NIS and 30,000 NIS (4,272 USD and 7,120 USD).[80] This practice

---

74 *Id.* at 868.

75 *Id.* at 870.

76 *Id.* at 868.

77 *Id.* at 870.

78 *See also* LA (Hi) 3206/08 State of Israel – Ministry of Defense v. El Hilou (July 9, 2008), Nevo Legal Database (by subscription) (bond set at 10,000 NIS); CC (Haifa Magistrate Ct.) 4527/08 State of Israel v. Barhum (October 28, 2008), Nevo Legal Database (by subscription) (bond for the sum of 7,000 NIS); CC (Nazareth Magistrate Ct.) 5867/07 State of Israel – Ministry of Defense v. Estate of Jalhoum (April 30, 2009), Nevo Legal Database (by subscription) (bond for the sum of 7,500 NIS); MPC (Jerusalem Magistrate Ct.) 3107/09 State of Israel – Ministry of Defense v. Khashan (May 4, 2009), Nevo Legal Database (by subscription) (bond set at 10,000 NIS); CC (Nazareth Magistrate Ct.) 13212-11-08 State of Israel v. Abd el-Aziz (March 18, 2010), Nevo Legal Database (by subscription) (bond for the sum of 10,000 NIS).

79 *See* LA (Hi) 3206/08 *El Hilou*, at para. 5, where the State of Israel explicitly argued that bonds range today between 15,000 and 50,000 NIS. In a rather exceptional case, the plaintiffs, sons of Palestinian Authority President Mahmud Abbas, were ordered to place a bond of 80,000 NIS; *see* MPC (Jer) 2572/08 Abbas v. Israel Broadcasting Authority (June 30, 2008), Nevo Legal Database (by subscription).

80 *See, e.g.*, LCA 10514/04 Abu Ragila v. Israeli Vehicle Insurance Pool (December 13, 2004), Nevo Legal Database (by subscription) (15,000 NIS); MPC (Jer) 7284/07 State of Israel – Ministry of Defense v. Elmasri (March 13, 2008), Nevo Legal Database (by subscription) (25,000 NIS); MPC (Hi) 1873/08 State of Israel – Ministry of Defense v. Hajaj (April 24, 2008), Nevo Legal Database (by subscription) (30,000 NIS); LA (Hi) 3026/08 State of Israel – Ministry of Defense v. Abu Ara (April 29, 2008), Nevo Legal Database (by subscription) (18,000 NIS); MPC (Jer) 3298/08 State of Israel v. Estate of Al Sa'er (September 15, 2008), Nevo Legal Database (by subscription) (25,000 NIS); MPC (Beersheba Magistrate Ct.) 3363/08 State of Israel v. Estate of Majdalawi (September 2, 2008), Nevo Legal Database (by subscription) (20,000 NIS); LCA 8998/08 Al Zafar General Contracting v. State of Israel (November 23, 2008), Nevo Legal Database (by subscription) (15,000 NIS); LCA 8274/08 State of Israel v. Masri Gabon Company Ltd. (April 6, 2009), Nevo Legal Database (by subscription) (20,000 NIS); LCA 8206/08 Elbashiti v. State of Israel (May 6, 2009), Nevo Legal Database (by subscription) (20,000 NIS, reduced on

imposes a particularly heavy burden on Palestinian plaintiffs, given their relatively low standard of living. One survey indicates that the average monthly income of a Palestinian family is 1,771 NIS (504 USD).[81] To deposit even the lower sums of security bonds, an average Palestinian family would need to pay the equivalent of some six months' income.

Notably, Palestinian plaintiffs have not been singled out vis-à-vis other foreign plaintiffs in the practice of levying these security bonds. Generally, foreign plaintiffs were treated just the same. At this point, then, one might ask: if the purpose of security bonds is to ensure the payment of court expenses, then why should foreign plaintiffs—Palestinian or otherwise—be treated differently from local Israeli plaintiffs? In all cases, the losing plaintiff would have to pay for the litigation costs of the defendant, whether he or she is a local or foreigner. The main reason for this different treatment lies in the assumed complexities that would arise if and when the plaintiff is reluctant to pay the court expenses as mandated. In

---

appeal from the 40,000 NIS set by the trial court); CC (Jer) 7204/05 State of Israel – Ministry of Defense v. Estate of Kamal (September 9, 2009), Nevo Legal Database (by subscription) (20,000 NIS); CC (Hi) 128/07 State of Israel v. Estate of Abu Shamla (October 29, 2009), Nevo Legal Database (by subscription) (15,000 NIS); MPC (Jer) 7615/08 State of Israel – Ministry of Defense v. Su'arka (October 14, 2009), Nevo Legal Database (by subscription) (20,000 NIS); MPC (Jerusalem Magistrate Ct.) 6697/09 State of Israel v. Al Harimi (November 25, 2009), Nevo Legal Database (by subscription) (20,000 NIS); CC (Jerusalem Magistrate Ct.) 19985/08 Ahmad v. State of Israel – Ministry of Defense (November 15, 2009), Nevo Legal Database (by subscription) (20,000 NIS); CC (Jer) 1858/07 Estate of Amru v. State of Israel (January 13, 2010), Nevo Legal Database (by subscription) (15,000 NIS); CC (Hi) State of Israel v. Abu-Fada (January 17, 2010), Nevo Legal Database (by subscription) (18,000 NIS); MPC (Na) 2686/09 State of Israel v. Heirs of Ra'ed (February 10, 2010), Nevo Legal Database (by subscription) (30,000 NIS); CC (BS) 4608/09 State of Israel v. Nabaheen (April 28, 2010), Nevo Legal Database (by subscription) (20,000 NIS); LCA 7160/11 Estate of Abd Elda'im v. State of Israel (November 13, 2011), Nevo Legal Database (by subscription) (20,000 NIS); LCA 8066/11 Estate of Aju v. State of Israel – Ministry of Defense (November 21, 2011), Nevo Legal Database (by subscription) (15,000 NIS, reduced on appeal from 20,000 NIS); LCA 9148/11 Estate of Abu Halima v. State of Israel – Ministry of Defense (July 5, 2012), Nevo Legal Database (by subscription) (sums of 15,000-20,000 NIS for different plaintiffs). *Cf.* MPC (Hi) State of Israel – Ministry of Defense v. Estate of Ghaben (November 24, 2008), Nevo Legal Database (by subscription) (bond set at 70,000 NIS in a suit brought by 25 plaintiffs); LCA 1007/08 Estate of Jaliya v. State of Israel (January 31, 2010), Nevo Legal Database (by subscription) (bond of 35,000 NIS levied on 21 plaintiffs from two families; the sum was reduced on appeal from the 75,000 NIS set by the trial court); LCA 3124/08 Hamad v. State of Israel (August 3, 2008), Nevo Legal Database (by subscription) (bond of 50,000 NIS confirmed on appeal by the Supreme Court; A. Grunis, J., in an obiter dictum, remarking that the sum set by the trial court might be excessive); MPC (Jer) 12591/08 State of Israel – Ministry of Defense v. Estate of Qaraja (December 21, 2008), Nevo Legal Database (by subscription) (bond set at 40,000 NIS); MPC (Na) 1563/09 State of Israel v. Heirs of Salem (August 23, 2009), Nevo Legal Database (by subscription) (bond for the sum of 35,000 NIS).

81 DWRC – Democracy and Workers' Rights Center, Overview of Current Economic Conditions in Palestine (2006).

the case of a local plaintiff, the defendant can turn directly to the local Execution Office and initiate the enforcement of the judgment—a prospect that in and of itself can be an incentive for immediate compliance with the court order. When the plaintiff is a foreigner, however, enforcement of the court order for the payment of litigation expenses assumedly must be performed in the plaintiff's home country, which generally requires initiation of another proceeding in that country in order to enforce the judgment there. Given that this logic applies to enforcement of judgments in the PA against Palestinian plaintiffs (even more forcefully so, given the current state of judicial assistance between Israel and the PA), then it is seemingly justified to treat Palestinian plaintiffs like any other foreign plaintiff when they seek to litigate their cases before Israeli courts.

Yet in light of the current design of jurisdictional authority of PA courts as outlined in the Oslo Accords, the Palestinian plaintiff should not be treated like any other foreign plaintiff, and certainly not so when seeking to file a claim against the State of Israel or any of its organs. The Oslo Accords, namely the Interim Agreement, significantly restricted the ability of Palestinian plaintiffs to file civil claims against Israeli parties in PA courts and precluded this possibility altogether when the defendant is the State of Israel or any of its organs. For the PA court to be able to adjudicate the claim, the dispute must involve a business that the Israeli party operated in the PA or land situated there. Alternately, the Israeli party must explicitly submit in writing to the jurisdiction of the PA courts. This same agreement provides a flat immunity to the State of Israel and any of its organs from the jurisdiction of the PA courts. Article III of Annex IV of the Interim Agreement is quite clear on this, as it states: "[t]he jurisdiction of the Palestinian courts and judicial authorities does not cover actions against the State of Israel including its statutory entities, organs and agents." Given that these restrictions are beneficial to Israeli entities and were apparently insisted upon by the Israeli side, it is probable that Israel's quest, if at all, is to drive Palestinian plaintiffs into Israeli courts in claims filed against Israeli entities. But if this is the intention (matched by no other in terms of plaintiffs coming from other foreign jurisdictions), then procedural fairness seems to demand that the Palestinian plaintiff not be treated like any other foreign plaintiff in this regard. Therefore, levying of these security bonds on Palestinian plaintiffs forms a rather severe restriction on their access to justice rights.

Moreover, courts' assessments of the sums they required plaintiffs to post through security bonds seem to be ignorant of the personal economic abilities of the plaintiffs. As a matter of black letter law, Israeli courts are supposed to consider the financial ability of the claimant when ordering the deposit of security bonds.[82] In practice, however, a score of cases in which security bonds were ordered show that courts made very little effort in inquiring into the financial ability of the claimant.[83] Take, for example, the case of *State of Israel – Ministry of Defense v. Abu Ma'tek*.[84] According to the claim, on an April morning in 2008, as a mother and six of her children were having breakfast in their Beit Hannoun home in the Gaza Strip, a missile fired from an Israeli aircraft killed the mother and four of the children. The two children that survived were injured. The plaintiffs, who effectively were the two injured children, the mother's husband and the mother's parents,[85] filed this civil action alleging the commission of various torts on the part of the State of Israel. Upon a motion made by the state, the plaintiffs were ordered to provide a bond in the amount of 12,000 NIS (3,355 USD) as a pre-condition for litigation. In issuing the order, the court took cognizance of two considerations: the fact that this claim had a slim chance of success given the immunity enjoyed by the state when sued regarding a military operation, and the inability to enforce an Israeli judgment in the Gaza Strip should it tax the plaintiffs with costs, given the current conditions. Nowhere in the judgment does the court refer to the financial status of the plaintiffs.

Another illustrative case is that of *Khatib v. State of Israel – Ministry of Defense*.[86] The plaintiff had previously filed a claim and was ordered to provide a bond in the amount of 15,000 NIS. This action was dismissed without prejudice. The plaintiff then refiled the same action and was prepared to deposit a bond in that sum. However, the court, upon the request of the State of Israel, raised the sum to 22,500 NIS (6,290 USD), citing the trend of courts in Israel to raise the sum of bonds in such actions. Once again, the court was indifferent to the plaintiff's ability to provide a bond of this sum, referring solely to considerations of enforcement and the slim chances of success.

---

82 *See Ibrahim*, 58(5) PD at 869; LCA 3607/00 State of Israel v. Barash (January 10, 2000), Nevo Legal Database (by subscription).

83 *See* LA (Hi) 3206/08 *El Hilou*; CC (Hadera Magistrate Ct.) 20571-05-10 State of Israel – Ministry of Defense v. Qadous (March 21, 2011), Nevo Legal Database (by subscription); CC (Haifa Magistrate Ct.) 13931-07 State of Israel v. Estate of Makhimer (January 20, 2010), Nevo Legal Database (by subscription). One notable exception in this regard is the judgment of Judge Zvi Zilbertal, who later became a Justice of the Israeli Supreme Court, in LCA (Jer) 308/08 State of Israel v. Sabbah (February 26, 2008), Nevo Legal Database (by subscription). Here, the court relieved the plaintiffs from providing the bond, noting among other factors that the first plaintiff was employed as a driver in the municipality of the West Bank city of Jenin with a monthly income of 1,200 NIS.

84 CC (Hertzliya Magistrate Ct.) 16517-04-10 (Oct. 18, 2011), Nevo Legal Database (by subscription).

85 The claim named the five decedent family members as plaintiffs.

86 CC (Hadera Magistrate Ct.) 27614-09-10 (September 18, 2011), Nevo Legal Database (by subscription).

c. Restricting Access to Justice by Limiting State Responsibility for Damages Resulting from IDF Operations

Damages suffered by Palestinians as a result of IDF operations in the PT were the subject of numerous civil claims filed by Palestinian plaintiffs before Israeli courts.[87] The main argument the State of Israel raised against such claims was the principle of state immunity, as defined in Section 5 of the Civil Wrongs (Liability of the State) Law, 1952 (CWSR).[88] This section, in its original format, spoke only generally of immunity against actions filed as a result of combatant military action, but did not define what such an action consists of. The definition of combatant military action became especially critical during the First *Intifada*, given that the personal injuries and property damage caused by the IDF in the PT did not take place within the context of a conventional war, but rather occurred over the course of suppressing and containing an uprising of the indigenous Palestinian community. These suppression and containment initiatives necessitated frequent policing activities on the part of the IDF, namely arresting suspects, conducting searches and seizures, and the like. Given the indeterminate nature of the provision on policing activities, lower courts were in disagreement as to whether such activities entitled the State of Israel to claim immunity. The Israel Supreme Court took a stand on the matter in *Odeh v. State of Israel*.[89] In that case, upon the arrival of IDF soldiers (some in civilian clothes and the others in IDF uniforms) in a civilian car with a local West Bank license plate, two Palestinian youngsters started to run away. Some of the soldiers fired shots at the fleeing youngsters. The soldiers' fire killed one of these youngsters, Sou'od Bani Odeh, and injured the other, Jamal Qassem. After civil claims regarding this incident were filed, the State of Israel claimed that they should be dismissed based on state immunity. The president of the Supreme Court, Aharon Barak, on behalf of a panel of nine justices, denied immunity. Under the circumstances, the action taken by the soldiers was held to be one of "policing" and not part of a combatant military action. No fighting took place before the firing, nor were the soldiers threatened before the actual firing. The *Odeh* judgment seemed to signify a considerable step towards recognizing the right of Palestinians to bring what were called "*Intifada* claims" before Israeli courts, especially since many of the operations of the IDF during the First *Intifada* involved policing activities. As the Court indicated in the *Odeh* ruling

87 Assaf Ya'acov, *Hasinut Tahat Esh: Hasinut ha-Medina Beshel Nezek she-Nigram Ketotsa'a mi-"Pe'ula Milhamtit"* [*Immunity under Fire: State Immunity for Damage Caused by "Combat Action"*], 33 MISHPATIM 107, 178 (2003) (Hebrew).

88 6 LSI 147 (1951–52).

89 CA 5964/92, 66(4) PD 1 (2002).

itself, according to the submission of the state, at the time over 900 *Intifada* claims were pending before Israeli courts and some 30 appeals were pending before the Supreme Court itself.[90] Nonetheless, the *Odeh* decision was not as significant as it seems. First, it took the Court some 10 years to render its judgment.[91] The case dragged on while the Knesset was expected to enact appropriate legislation on the matter. Since no legislation was forthcoming, the Court ultimately had no choice but to decide the matter.[92]

The long delay was no doubt a great burden to the plaintiffs in *Odeh*. But a greater burden to Palestinian plaintiffs was the further curtailment of access to justice before Israeli courts in two major amendments to the CWSR that the Knesset managed to pass. The first amendment was made in 2002, some three months after *Odeh*. This amendment, known as CWSR Amendment No. 4, provided a much more detailed definition of "combatant military operation," which included all actions taken while fighting terrorism, hostilities, and uprising. Even if the action does not fall under this broad definition of a combatant military operation, CWSR Amendment No. 4 includes a series of conditions for adjudication: appropriate notice is to be given to the Israeli authorities within 60 days of the date of the incident; the statute of limitation on such actions is reduced to two years instead of the regular seven; and the evidence rule of *res ipsa loquitur* was made inapplicable in such claims. Three years later, in 2005, another series of conditions were enacted, restricting yet further the ability to file a civil action related to an activity of the IDF that is not entitled to immunity as a "combatant military operation." This further limitation was accomplished in CWSR Amendment No. 7. The main feature of this detailed amendment is that it absolves the state of any responsibility in torts towards those deemed to be citizens of an enemy state or members of a terror organization. Additionally, CWSR Amendment No. 7 grants total immunity to the state in torts for actions undertaken on its behalf in what is defined as a "conflict zone" (*ezor imut*, in Hebrew). The most striking feature of this amendment is that it authorizes the Minister of Defense to define a "conflict zone" retroactively, as far back as September 29, 2000 (when the *Al-Aqsa Intifada* erupted).[93] CWSR Amendment No. 7 also provides that the Minister of Defense shall appoint a committee that will

90 *Id.* at 4.

91 The judgment of the court of first instance, the District Court in Nazareth, was handed down on October 30, 1992, and the Supreme Court judgment was handed down on March 20, 2002.

92 Ya'acov, *supra* note 87, at 168.

93 This part of the amendment was declared to be void, given that it unduly restricts the access to justice rights of Palestinian plaintiffs. *See* discussion in the next section.

be authorized to permit the payment of compensation notwithstanding the general exemption from liability now granted.

The latest restrictions on access to justice rights regarding damages and injuries suffered from an IDF-related operation are found in CWSR, Amendment No. 8, passed in 2012.[94] The objective here was to broaden yet further the definition of a "military operation." In the past, for the operation to be considered as such, a threat to life or a bodily injury needed to have been proven. As of now, the operation must only be proven to be of a belligerent nature given all of the relevant circumstances, including its objective, its geographical location, or the threat created towards the force undertaking the operation. Following this amendment, the defense of immunity under CWSR is to be regarded as a preliminary matter and the court is instructed to decide on the defense immediately afterwards, instead of deferring the judgment to some latter part of the proceedings. Finally, venue in such actions filed against the State of Israel for IDF-related activities was restricted to only two districts: that of Jerusalem and that of the South.

These amendments form additional restrictions on the access to justice rights of Palestinian plaintiffs. As noted before, Palestinian plaintiffs have no recourse to their own home forum when seeking to file a civil claim against the State of Israel or any of its organs, even if the military operation took place in PA territory. A Palestinian plaintiff can resort to some third country with his or her civil claim against the State of Israel for the damages suffered as a result of the IDF military operation. But even then, realistically, such claims will most likely be summarily dismissed on foreign sovereign immunity grounds.[95] IDF operations are evidently activities of a public nature (*jure gestionis*). Hence, Palestinian plaintiffs have only one realistic option for litigating a claim: to turn to the Israeli courts. But when they do so, they are now faced with a number of new limitations on the liability of the State of Israel—all in addition to the security bonds they need to provide just to initiate the litigation.

4. Conceptualizing the Access to Justice Doctrine

These developments demonstrate once again the interdependence between conflicts, doctrines and politics. As relations between Israel and the PA became more

---

94 SH No. 2370 at 522.

95 *See* Belhas v. Ya'alon, 515 F.3d 1279 (D.C. Cir. 2008); Doe I v. State of Israel, 400 F. Supp. 2d 86 (D.D.C. 2005). *See also* Adam N. Schupack, *The Arab-Israeli Conflict and Civil Litigation Against Terrorism*, 60 DUKE L.J. 207, 229–30 (2010); Graham Ogilvy, Belhas v. Ya'alon: *The Case for a* Jus Cogens *Exception to the Sovereign Immunities Act*, 8 J. INT'L BUS. & L. 169 (2009).

strained, the Israeli legislature initiated more severe restrictions on access to justice rights. Yet in a recent case, a new trend is discernable.

Shortly after CWSR Amendment No. 7 came into effect, a petition was filed to the Supreme Court in its capacity as the High Court of Justice challenging the amendment's constitutionality. The petitioners were a group of human rights organizations and various plaintiffs that sustained injuries from actions taken by Israeli security forces in the PT during the *Al-Aqsa Intifada*. The Court's judgment in *Adalah, The Legal Center for Arab Minority Rights in Israel v. Minister of Defense*[96] highlighted one civil case in particular. On the evening of October 11, 2002, Ms. Abu Hajlah was sitting with her husband and son on the balcony of their Nablus home. Shots were fired from an IDF jeep that had just pulled over in a nearby street. As a result, Ms. Abu Hajlah was killed and her husband and son were injured. The civil claim that followed was blocked, based on the newly enacted CWSR Amendment No. 7. Operating under his new powers, the Minister of Defense issued an order in 2006 designating the area of Nablus between June 2002 and March 2003 as a "conflict zone."

The basic argument in the petition was that CWSR Amendment No. 7 encroached on Palestinian plaintiffs' right of access to justice guaranteed under BLHDL. But do these plaintiffs enjoy the protection of this Israeli enactment? Four propositions were offered in this regard: (1) BLHDL is applicable, since CWSR Amendment No. 7 works to abolish rights inside of Israel and in court proceeding initiated in Israel itself; (2) CWSR Amendment No. 7 applies according to its own terms to Palestinian as well as Israeli claimants; (3) BLHDL applies in the PT, since it applies to actions undertaken by any Israeli authority, wherever it operates; and (4) BLHDL applies to Palestinian residents of the PT in light of the fact that the PT are under Israeli belligerent occupation. President Barak, who authored the leading opinion, resolved the question in a very special way. He held that civil claims filed by the Palestinian plaintiffs were all filed in Israeli courts and in accordance with Israeli municipal law.[97] This standing is enough to implicate Israeli constitutional norms that seek to guarantee access to justice. Hence, whenever a claim is filed before an Israeli court and that claim is governed by Israeli law, then the plaintiff is supposedly entitled to Israeli constitutional norms pertaining to access to justice rights. Ultimately, Barak, with the total agreement

96 HCJ 8276/05 (December 12, 2006), Nevo Legal Database (by subscription).

97 *Id.* paras. 22–23.

of seven other justices, concluded that the part of CWSR Amendment No. 7 that grants total immunity in conflict zones unduly infringes on Palestinian plaintiffs' right of access to justice and is thus null and void.

In his concurring opinion, Justice Grunis sought to clarify that no link necessarily exists between a claim's status as governed by Israeli law and the availability of the constitutional rights to a plaintiff who files a claim before Israeli courts. So even if Israeli choice of law rules point to Israeli law as the governing law, it is still necessary to determine whether constitutional norms such as those in BLHDL apply in an extraterritorial manner. However, since the State of Israel did not raise the question of whether BLHLD applies to Palestinian plaintiffs, Grunis concurred with Barak's conclusion.

This decision yields great potential to change some of the basic paradigms that directed Israeli courts in addressing conflicts issues in the context of the Israeli-Palestinian conflict. Some can argue that the Court's invalidation of primary Knesset legislation was only partial, since it applies only to the provision by which the Israeli Minister of Defense can declare a certain region to be a "combat region" retroactively, and not to the other restrictions. But even so, the Supreme Court's invalidation of Knesset legislation is quite a rare occurrence in Israel. It remains to be seen whether the sense of justice expressed in this action will come to dominate.

Bibliography

Sakr Abu Fakhr, *Voices from the Golan*, 29 J. PALESTINE STUD. 5 (2000).

Kamel S. Abu Jaber, *The Millet System in the Nineteenth-Century Ottoman Empire*, 57 THE MUSLIM WORLD 212 (1967).

ACCESS TO JUSTICE AS A HUMAN RIGHT (Francesco Francioni ed., 2007).

ACCESS TO JUSTICE FOR A NEW CENTURY: THE WAY FORWARD (Julia Bass, W. A. Bogart & Fredrick H. Zemans eds., 2005).

ACCESS TO JUSTICE AND THE WELFARE STATE (Mauro Cappelletti ed., 1979).

Agora: ICJ Advisory Opinion on Construction of a Wall in the Occupied Palestinian Territory, 99 AM. J. INT'L L. 1 (2005).

Michael Akehurst, *The Arab-Israeli Conflict and International Law*, 5 NEW ZEALAND UNIVERSITIES L. REV. 231 (1973).

Michael Akehurst, *Jurisdiction in International Law*, 46 BRIT. Y.B. INT'L L. 145 (1972–73).

Susan Akram & Michael Lynck, *The Wall and the Law: A Tale of Two Judgments*, 24 NETH. Q. HUM. RTS. 61 (2006).

EITAN Y. ALIMI, ISRAELI POLITICS AND THE FIRST PALESTINIAN INTIFADA: POLITICAL OPPORTUNITIES, FRAMING PROCESSES AND CONTENTIOUS POLITICS (2007).

Yigal Allon, *Israel: The Case for Defensible Borders*, 55 FOREIGN AFF. 38 (1976).

Mark Angehr, Comment, *The International Court of Justice's Advisory Jurisdiction and the Review of Security Council and General Assembly Resolutions*, 103 NW. U. L. REV. 1007 (2009).

THE ARAB-ISRAELI ACCORDS: LEGAL PERSPECTIVES (Eugene Cotran, Chibli Mallat & David Stott eds., 1996).

Fr. Robert J. Araujo, S. J., *Implementation of the ICJ Advisory Opinion—Legal Consequences of the Construction of a Wall in the Occupied Palestinian Territory: Fences [Do Not] Make Good Neighbors?*, 22 B.U. INT'L L.J. 349 (2004).

Mahnoush H. Arsanjani, *United Nations Competence in the West Bank and the Gaza Strip*, 31 INT'L & COMP. L.Q. 426 (1982).

Daphne Barak-Erez, *Israel: The Security Barrier—Between International Law, Constitutional Law, and Domestic Judicial Review*, 4 INT'L J. CONST. L. 540 (2006).

Charles Bryan Baron, *The International Legal Status of Jerusalem*, 8 TOURO INT'L L. REV. 1 (1998).

Yaacov Bar-Siman-Tov & Kobi Michael, *The Israeli Disengagement Plan as a Conflict Management Strategy*, *in* THE ISRAELI-PALESTINIAN CONFLICT: FROM CONFLICT RESOLUTION TO CONFLICT MANAGEMENT 261 (Yaacov Bar-Siman-Tov ed., 2007).

Nissim Bar-Yaacov, *The Applicability of the Laws of War to Judea and Samaria (The West Bank) and the Gaza Strip*, 24 ISR. L. REV. 485 (1990).

Pieter H. F. Bekker, Comment, *World Court's Ruling Regarding Israel's West Bank Barrier and the Primacy of International Law: An Insider's Perspective*, 38 CORNELL INT'L L.J. 553 (2005).

Ruth Ben-Israel, *Labor Law*, *in* INTRODUCTION TO THE LAW OF ISRAEL 213 (Amos Shapira & Keren C. DeWitt-Arar eds., 1995).

Orna Ben-Naftali, Aeyal M. Gross & Keren Michaeli, *Illegal Occupation: Framing the Occupied Palestinian Territory*, 23 BERKELEY J. INT'L L. 515 (2005).

Daniel Benoliel & Ronen Perry, *Israel, Palestine, and the ICC*, 32 MICH. J. INT'L L. 73 (2010).

EYAL BENVENISTI, THE INTERNATIONAL LAW OF OCCUPATION (2d ed., 2012).

Eyal Benvenisti, *The Israeli-Palestinian Declaration of Principles: A Framework for Future Settlement*, 4 EUR. J. INT'L L. 542 (1993).

Eyal Benvenisti, *Judicial Review of Administrative Action in the Territories Occupied in 1967*, *in* PUBLIC LAW IN ISRAEL 371 (Itzhak Zamir & Allen Zysblat eds., 1996).

EYAL BENVENISTI, LEGAL DUALISM: THE ABSORPTION OF THE OCCUPIED TERRITORIES INTO ISRAEL (1989).

Eyal Benvenisti, *Responsibility for the Protection of Human Rights under the Interim Israeli-Palestinian Agreements*, 28 ISR. L. REV. 297 (1994).

Eyal Benvenisti & Eyal Zamir, *Private Claims to Property Rights in the Future Israeli-Palestinian Settlement*, 89 AM. J. INT'L L. 295 (1995).

MERON BENVENISTI, THE WEST BANK DATA PROJECT: A SURVEY OF ISRAEL'S POLICIES (1984).

Marilyn J. Berliner, *Palestinian Arab Self-Determination and Israeli Settlements on the West Bank: An Analysis of Their Legality Under International Law*, 8 LOY. L.A. INT'L & COMP. L.J. 551 (1986).

John Bies, Comment, *Conditioning Forum Non Conveniens*, 67 U. CHI. L. REV. 498 (2000).

ARIEL BIN-NUN, THE LAW OF THE STATE OF ISRAEL: AN INTRODUCTION (1990).

GEORGE E. BISHARAT, PALESTINIAN LAWYERS AND ISRAELI RULE: LAW AND DISORDER IN THE WEST BANK (1989).

George E. Bisharat, *Peace and the Political Imperative of Legal Reform in Palestine*, 31 CASE W. RES. J. INT'L L. 253 (1999).

Yehuda Z. Blum, *From Camp David to Oslo*, 28 ISR. L. REV. 211 (1994).

Yehuda Z. Blum, *The Missing Reversioner: Reflections on the Status of Judea and Samaria*, 3 ISR. L. REV. 279 (1968).

William W. Blume, *Place of Trial of Civil Cases*, 48 MICH. L. REV. 1 (1949).

Patrick J. Borchers, *The Problem with General Jurisdiction*, 2001 U. CHI. LEGAL F. 119 (2001).

GARY BORN & PETER B. RUTLEDGE, INTERNATIONAL CIVIL LITIGATION IN UNITED STATES COURTS (4th ed. 2007).

C. E. Bosworth, *The Concept of Dhimmi in Early Islam*, *in* CHRISTIANS AND JEWS IN THE OTTOMAN EMPIRE 37 (Benjamin Braude & Bernard Lewis eds., 1982).

Francis A. Boyle, *The Creation of the State of Palestine*, 1 EUR. J. INT'L L. 301 (1990).
Baruch Bracha, *Hamtsa'at Mismakhim la-Shtakhim ha-Mukhzakim*, [*Service of Documents to the Administered Territories*], 4 MISHPATIM 119 (1972).
RONALD A. BRAND & SCOTT R. JABLONSKI, FORUM NON CONVENIENS (2007).
Benjamin Braude, *Foundation Myths of the Millet System*, *in* CHRISTIANS AND JEWS IN THE OTTOMAN EMPIRE 69 (Benjamin Braude & Bernard Lewis eds., 1982).
Benjamin Braude & Bernard Lewis, *Introduction*, *in* CHRISTIANS AND JEWS IN THE OTTOMAN EMPIRE 1 (Benjamin Braude & Bernard Lewis eds., 1982).
Irus Braverman, *Powers of Illegality: House Demolition and Resistance in East Jerusalem*, 32 LAW & SOC. INQ. 333 (2007).
David L. Breau, *The World Court's Advisory Function: "Not Legally Well-Founded,"* 14 U. MIAMI INT'L & COMP. L. REV. 185 (2006).
LEA BRILMAYER, CONFLICT OF LAWS (2d ed. 1995).
Lea Brilmayer, *Consent, Contract, and Territory*, 74 MINN. L. REV. 1 (1989).
Lea Brilmayer, *How Contacts Count: Due Process Limitations on State Court Jurisdiction*, 1980 SUP. CT. REV. 77.
Lea Brilmayer, *Rights, Fairness, and Choice-of-Law*, 98 YALE L. J. 1277 (1989).
Lea Brilmayer et al., *A General Look at General Jurisdiction*, 66 TEX. L. REV. 721 (1988).
NATHAN J. BROWN, PALESTINIAN POLITICS AFTER THE OSLO ACCORDS (2003).
IAN BROWNLIE, PRINCIPLES OF PUBLIC INTERNATIONAL LAW (6th ed., 2003).
Michelle Burgis, *Discourses of Division: Law, Politics and the ICJ Advisory Opinion on the Legal Consequences of the Construction of a Wall in the Occupied Palestinian Territory*, 7 CHINESE J. INT'L L. 33 (2008).
Yaron Butovsky, *Law of Belligerent Occupation: Israeli Practice and Judicial Decisions Affecting the West Bank*, 21 CAN. Y.B. INT'L L. 217 (1983).
Iris Canor, *Yisra'el ve-ha-Shtahim: Al Mishpat Beinle'umi Prati, Mishpat Beinle'umi Pumbi, u-Ma she-Beinehem* [*Israel and the Territories: The Interplay between Private International Law and Public International Law*], 8 MISHPAT U-MIMSHAL 551 (2005).
Lee M. Caplan, *State Immunity, Human Rights, and* Jus Cogens: *A Critique of the Normative Hierarchy Theory*, 97 AM. J. INT'L L. 741 (2003).
Robert A. Caplen, Note, *Mending the "Fence": How Treatment of Israeli Palestinian Conflict by the International Court of Justice at the Hague Has Redefined the Doctrine of Self-Defense*, 57 FLA. L. REV. 717 (2005).
Robert A. Caplen, *Rule of "Disengagement": Relating the Establishment of Palestinian Gaza to Israel's Right of Exercise Self-Defense as Interpreted by the International Court of Justice at the Hague*, 18 FLA. J. INT'L L. 679 (2006).
Richard B. Cappalli, *Locke as the Key: A Unifying and Coherent Theory of* In Personam *Jurisdiction*, 43 CASE W. RES. L. REV. 97 (1992).
MAURO CAPPELLETTI, THE JUDICIAL PROCESS IN COMPARATIVE PERSPECTIVE (1989).
Mauro Cappelletti & Bryant Garth, *Access to Justice and the Welfare State: An Introduction*, *in* ACCESS TO JUSTICE AND THE WELFARE STATE 1 (Mauro Cappelletti ed., 1979).

Michael H. Cardozo, *Judicial Deference to State Department Suggestions: Recognition of Prerogative or Abdication to Usurper?*, 48 CORNELL L.Q. 461 (1963).

Robert C. Cassad, *Jurisdiction in Civil Actions at the End of the Twentieth Century:* Forum Conveniens *and* Forum Non Conveniens, 7 TUL. J. INT'L & COMP. L. 91 (1999).

Antonio Cassese, *The Israel-PLO Agreement and Self-Determination*, 4 EUR. J. INT'L L. 564 (1993).

Antonio Cassese, *Legal Considerations on the International Status of Jerusalem*, 3 PALESTINE Y.B. INT'L L. 13 (1986).

J.-G. CASTEL, CANADIAN CONFLICT OF LAWS (3d ed. 1994).

HENRY CATTAN, PALESTINE AND INTERNATIONAL LAW: LEGAL ASPECTS OF THE ARAB-ISRAELI CONFLICT (1973).

David Cavers, *A Critique of the Choice-of-Law Problem*, 47 HARV. L. REV. 173 (1933).

CENTRAL BUREAU OF STATISTICS, STATISTICAL ABSTRACT OF ISRAEL NO. 64 (2013), *available at* http://www.cbs.gov.il/reader/shnatonenew_site.htm.

CHESHIRE, NORTH & FAWCETT, PRIVATE INTERNATIONAL LAW (James Fawcett & Janeen M. Carruthers eds., 14th ed. 2008).

Noam Chomsky, *The Intifada and the Peace Process*, 14 FLETCHER F. WORLD. AFF. 345 (1990).

Brice M. Clagett & O. Thomas Johnson, *May Israel as a Belligerent Occupant Lawfully Exploit Previously Unexploited Oil Resources of the Gulf of Suez?*, 72 AM. J. INT'L L. 558 (1978).

Kevin M. Clermont & John R. B. Palmer, *Exorbitant Jurisdiction*, 58 ME. L. REV. 474 (2006).

ASHER COHEN & BERNARD SUSSER, MI-HASHLAMA LE-HASLAMA: HA-SHESA HA-HILONI-DATI BE-FETAKH HA-ME'A HA-ESRIM VE-AHAT [FROM ACCOMMODATION TO ESCALATION: THE SECULAR-RELIGIOUS DIVIDE AT THE OUTSET OF THE 21ST CENTURY] (2003).

ESTHER R. COHEN, HUMAN RIGHTS IN THE ISRAELI-OCCUPIED TERRITORIES, 1967–1982 (1985).

Esther Rosalind Cohen, *Justice for Occupied Territory? The Israeli High Court of Justice Paradigm*, 24 COLUM. J. TRANSNAT'L L. 471 (1986).

Haim H. Cohn, *Forward*, *in* ISRAEL NATIONAL SECTION OF THE INTERNATIONAL COMMISSION OF JURISTS, THE RULE OF LAW IN THE AREAS ADMINISTERED BY ISRAEL vii (1981).

Haim H. Cohn, *Religious Freedom and Religious Coercion in the State of Israel*, *in* ISRAEL AMONG THE NATIONS 79 (Alfred E. Kellermann et al. eds., 1998).

J. G. COLLIER, CONFLICT OF LAWS (3d ed. 2001).

John Collins, Note, *Self-Determination in International Law: The Palestinians*, 12 CASE W. RES. J. INT'L L. 137 (1980).

LAWRENCE COLLINS, ESSAYS IN INTERNATIONAL LITIGATION AND THE CONFLICT OF LAWS (1994).

Catherine Cook & Adam Hanieh, *The Separation Barrier: Walling in People, Walling out Sovereignty*, *in* The Struggle for Sovereignty: Palestine and Israel, 1993–2005 338 (Joel Beinin & Rebecca L. Stein eds., 2006).

Zelman Cowen, *Transient Jurisdiction: A British View*, 9 J. Pub. L. 303 (1960).

James Crawford, *The Creation of the State of Palestine: Too Much Too Soon?*, 1 Eur. J. Int'l L. 307 (1990).

Antonio Crivellaro, *Oil Operations by a Belligerent Occupant: The Israel—Egypt Dispute*, 3 Italian Y.B. Int'l L. 171 (1977).

Philip L. Culbertson, *The Anglican Family Court in Israel and the West Bank*, 23 J. Church & St. 285 (1981).

Stephen L. Cummings, *International Mass Tort Litigation:* Forum Non Conveniens *and the Adequate Alternative Forum in Light of the Bhopal Disaster*, 16 Ga. J. Int'l & Comp. L. 109 (1986).

Omar M. Dajani, *Stalled between Seasons: The International Legal Status of Palestine During the Interim Period*, 26 Denv. J. Int'l L. & Pol'y 27 (1997).

Shane Darcy & John Reynolds, *"Otherwise Occupied": The Status of the Gaza Strip from the Perspective of International Humanitarian Law*, 15 J. Conflict & Security L. 211 (2010).

Roderic H. Davison, *The Millets as Agents of Change in the Nineteenth Century Ottoman Empire*, *in* Christians and Jews in the Ottoman Empire 319 (Benjamin Braude & Bernard Lewis eds., 1982).

Amin R. Dawwas, Tanaz' al-Qawanin fi Falastin [Conflict of Laws in Palestine] (2001).

Ronan E. Degnan, Livingston v. Jefferson—*A Freestanding Footnote*, 75 Cal. L. Rev. 115 (1987).

Joseph W. Dellapenna, *Exploring the Oslo Accords: Recipe for Peace or Footnote to History?*, 40 Alberta L. Rev. 525 (2002).

Alberto De Puy, *Bringing Down the Barrier: A Comparative Analysis of the ICJ Advisory Opinion and the High Court of Justice of Israel's Ruling on Israel's Construction of a Barrier in the Occupied Territories*, 13 Tul. J. Int'l & Com. L. 275 (2005).

L. I. De Winter, *Excessive Jurisdiction in Private International Law*, 17 Int'l & Comp. L.Q. 706 (1968).

Dicey, Morris & Collins, The Conflict of Laws (Lord Collins of Mapesbury ed., 15th ed. 2012).

Din ve-Heshbon ha-Va'ada le-Bdikat Mivne Batei ha-Mishpat ha-Regilim be-Yisrael [Report of the Committee to Overview the Structure of General Courts in Israel] (1997).

Din ve-Heshbon ha-Va'ada le-Bdikat ha-Mivne ve-ha-Samkhuyot shel Batei ha-Mishpat [Report of the Committee to Overview the Structure and the Powers of the Courts] (1980).

Dinei ha-Tikhnun, ha-Bniya ve-ha-Mekarke'in be-Yehuda ve-ha-Shomron [Planning, Building and Land Law in Judea and Samaria] (Aharon Mishnayot ed., 1996).

YORAM DINSTEIN, THE INTERNATIONAL LAW OF BELLIGERENT OCCUPATION (2009).

Yoram Dinstein, *The International Law of Belligerent Occupation and Human Rights*, 8 ISR. Y.B. HUM. RGTS 104 (1978).

Yoram Dinstein, *The Israel Supreme Court and the Law of Belligerent Occupation: Reunification of Families*, 18 ISR. Y.B. HUM. RTS. 173 (1988).

Yoram Dinstein, *The Legal Issues of "Para-War" and Peace in the Middle East*, 44 ST. JOHN'S L. REV. 466 (1970).

William A. Dobrovir, *A Gloss on the* Tate Letter's *Restrictive Theory of Sovereign Immunity*, 54 VA. L. REV. 1 (1968).

MOSHE DRORI, HA-HAKIKA BE-EZOR YEHUDA VE-HA-SHOMRON [THE LEGISLATION IN THE AREA OF JUDEA AND SAMARIA] (1975).

Moshe Drori, *The Legal System in Judea and Samaria: A Review of the Previous Decade with a Glance at the Future*, 8 ISR. Y.B. HUM. RTS. 144 (1978).

Ron Dudai, *The Wall, the Law and the Court: Reflections on the Beit Sourik Case in the Israeli Supreme Court*, 10 Y.B. ISLAMIC & MIDDLE E. L. 471 (2003–2004).

Michael Dumper, *Constructive Ambiguities? Jerusalem, International Law, and the Peace Process*, *in* INTERNATIONAL LAW AND THE ISRAELI-PALESTINIAN CONFLICT: A RIGHTS-BASED APPROACH TO MIDDLE EAST PEACE 113 (Susan M. Akram et al. eds., 2011).

DWRC—DEMOCRACY AND WORKERS' RIGHTS CENTER, OVERVIEW OF CURRENT ECONOMIC CONDITIONS IN PALESTINE (2006).

MARTIN EDELMAN, COURTS, POLITICS, AND CULTURE IN ISRAEL (1994).

ALBERT A. EHRENZWEIG, A TREATISE ON THE CONFLICT OF LAWS (1962).

TALIA EINHORN, PRIVATE INTERNATIONAL LAW IN ISRAEL (2d ed. 2012).

ROBERT H. EISENMAN, ISLAMIC LAW IN PALESTINE AND ISRAEL (1978).

Michael Eisner, *Jerusalem: An Analysis of Legal Claims and Political Realities*, 12 WIS. INT'L L.J. 221 (1993–94).

Khaled Elgindy, *Palestine Goes to the UN: Understanding the New Statehood Strategy*, 90 FOREIGN AFF. 102 (2011).

June F. Entman, *Abolishing Local Action Rules: A First Step toward Modernizing Jurisdiction and Venue in Tennessee*, 34 U. MEM. L. REV. 251 (2004).

Richard Falk, *International Law and the al-Aqsa Intifada*, 217 MIDDLE EAST REP. 16 (2000).

Richard Falk, *Some Legal Reflections on Prolonged Israeli Occupation of Gaza and the West Bank*, 2 J. REFUGEE STUD. 40 (1989).

Richard A. Falk & Burns H. Weston, *The Relevance of International Law to Israeli and Palestinian Rights in the West Bank and Gaza*, *in* INTERNATIONAL LAW AND THE ADMINISTRATION OF OCCUPIED TERRITORIES: TWO DECADES OF ISRAELI OCCUPATION OF THE WEST BANK AND GAZA STRIP 125 (Emma Playfair ed., 1992).

Carol Farhi, *On the Legal Status of the Gaza Strip*, *in* 1 MILITARY GOVERNMENT IN THE TERRITORIES ADMINISTERED BY ISRAEL 1967–1980: LEGAL ASPECTS 61 (Meir Shamgar ed., 1982).

David Farhi, *Ha-Mo'atsa ha-Muslimit be-Mizrakh Yerushalayim u-ve-Yehuda u-Shomron Le'ahar Milhemet Sheshet ha-Yamim* [*The Muslim Council in East Jerusalem and in Judea and Samaria after the Six-Day War*], 28 HA-MIZRAH HA-HADASH 3 (1979).

Ben-Zion Farhy, *Current Legal Trends in the Area Administered by Israel*, 113 MIL. L. REV. 47 (1986).

NATHAN FEINBERG, STUDIES IN INTERNATIONAL LAW WITH SPECIFIC REFERENCE TO THE ARAB-ISRAELI CONFLICT (1979).

Barry A. Feinstein & Justus Reid Weiner, *Israel's Security Barrier: An International Comparative Analysis and Legal Evaluation*, 37 GEO. WASH. INT'L L. REV. 309 (2005).

Richard Ford, *Law's Territory (A History of Jurisdiction)*, 97 MICH. L. REV. 843 (1999).

Forum, *Al ha-Reforma be-Ma'arekhet Batei ha-Mishpat* [*On the Reform in the Court System*], 8 MEHKAREY MISHPAT 9 (1990).

HAZEL FOX, THE LAW OF STATE IMMUNITY (2008).

Francesco Francioni, *The Rights of Access to Justice under Customary International Law*, *in* ACCESS TO JUSTICE AS A HUMAN RIGHT 1 (Francesco Francioni ed., 2007).

Mayer Gabay, *Legal Aspects of the Camp David Framework for Peace in Relation to the Autonomy Proposal*, *in* MODELS OF AUTONOMY 255 (Yoram Dinstein ed., 1981).

Michael Galchinsky, *The Jewish Settlements in the West Bank: International Law and Israeli Jurisprudence*, 9 ISR. STUD. 115 (2004).

Manuel R. García-Mora, *The Doctrine of Sovereign Immunity of Foreign States and Its Recent Modifications*, 42 VA. L. REV. 335 (1956).

James W. Garner, *Treatment of Enemy Aliens*, 13 AM. J. INT'L L. 22 (1919).

Shlomo Gazit, *Policy in the Administered Territories*, 1 ISR. Y.B. HUM. RTS. 278 (1971).

Allan Gerson, *Off-Shore Oil Exploration by a Belligerent Occupant: The Gulf of Suez Dispute*, 71 AM. J. INT'L L. 725 (1977).

Allan Gerson, *Trustee Occupant: The Legal Status of Israel's Presence in the West Bank*, 14 HARV. INT'L L. J. 1 (1973).

ALLAN GERSON, THE WEST BANK AND INTERNATIONAL LAW (1978).

FREDERIC M. GOADBY, INTERNATIONAL AND INTERRELIGIOUS PRIVATE LAW IN PALESTINE (1926).

Stephen Goldstein, *Civil Procedure*, *in* INTRODUCTION TO THE LAW OF ISRAEL 295 (Amos Shapira & Keren C. DeWitt-Arar eds., 1995).

Stephen Goldstein, *The Influence of Constitutional Principles on Civil Procedure in Israel*, 17 ISR. L. REV. 467 (1982).

Stephen Goldstein, *Israel*, *in* DECLINING JURISDICTION IN PRIVATE INTERNATIONAL LAW 259 (James J. Fawcett ed., 1995).

Stephen Goldstein, *Samkhut Shipput Beinle'umit Mevuseset al Tfisat ha-Nitba—Halakha le-Ma'ase ka-Yom* [*International Jurisdiction Based Solely on Service of Process—In Practice Today*], 10 MISHPATIM 409 (1980).

Stephen Goldstein & Elisheva HaCohen, *Israel*, *in* 3 INTERNATIONAL ENCYCLOPEDIA OF LAWS: CIVIL PROCEDURE 67 (Piet Taelman ed., 1994).

Chaim I. Goldwater, *Religious Tribunals with a Dual Capacity*, 12 ISR. L. REV. 114 (1977).
Davis P. Goodman, Note, *The Need for Fundamental Change in the Law of Belligerent Occupation*, 37 STAN. L. REV. 1573 (1985).
Josh Goodman, *Divine Judgment: Judicial Review of Religious Legal Systems in India and Israel*, 32 HASTINGS INT'L & COMP. L. REV. 477 (2009).
NEVE GORDON, ISRAEL'S OCCUPATION (2008).
GERSHOM GORENBERG, THE ACCIDENTAL EMPIRE: ISRAEL AND THE BIRTH OF THE SETTLEMENTS, 1967–1977 (2006).
R. Gottschalk, *Personal Status and Religious Law in Israel*, 4 INT'L L. Q. 454 (1951).
DORIS A. GRABER, THE DEVELOPMENT OF THE LAW OF BELLIGERENT OCCUPATION 1863–1914—A HISTORICAL SURVEY 37 (1949).
Gavan Griffith, *Foreign Sovereign Immunity in Australia*, *in* 2 ESTUDIOS EN HOMENAJE A JORGE BARRERA GRAF 837 (1989).
Aeyal M. Gross, *The* Construction of a Wall *Between The Hague and Jerusaelm: The Enforcement and Limits of Humanitarian Law and the Structure of Occupation*, 19 LEIDEN J. INT'L L. 393 (2006).
Leo Gross, *Voting in the Security Council and the PLO*, 70 AM. J. INT'L L. 470 (1976).
Mark I. Gruhin, *Jerusalem: Legal & Political Dimensions in a Search for Peace*, 12 CASE W. RES. J. INT'L L. 169 (1980).
Suhaila Haddad et al., *Minorities in Containment: The Arabs of Israel*, *in* THE POLITICAL ROLE OF MINORITY GROUPS IN THE MIDDLE EAST 76 (R. D. McLurin ed., 1979).
LISA HAJJAR, COURTING CONFLICT: THE ISRAELI MILITARY COURT SYSTEM IN THE WEST BANK AND GAZA (2005).
Usama Halabi, *Revoking Permanent Residency: A Legal Review of Israeli Policy*, 9 JERUSALEM Q.FILE 40 (2000).
Malvina Halberstem, *The Myth that Israel's Presence in Judea and Samaria is Comparable to Iraq's Presence in Kuwait*, 19 SYRACUSE J. INT'L L. & COM. 1 (1993).
Peter Handford, *Edward John Eyre and the Conflict of Laws*, 32 MELBOURNE U. L. REV. 822 (2008).
WILLIAM W. HARRIS, TAKING ROOT: ISRAELI SETTLEMENT IN THE WEST BANK, THE GOLAN AND GAZA-SINAI, 1967–1980 (1980).
Ellen L. Hayes, Forum Non Conveniens in *England, Australia and Japan: The Allocation of Jurisdiction in Transnational Litigation*, 1992 U. BRIT. COLUM. L. REV. 41.
David Herling, *The Court, the Ministry and the Law: Awad and the Withdrawal of East Jerusalem Residence Rights*, 33 ISR. L. REV. 67 (1999).
Moshe Hirsch, *The Impact of the Advisory Opinion on Israel's Future Policy: International Relations Perspective*, 1 J. INT'L L. & INT'L REL. 319 (2004–2005).
Moshe Hirsch, *The Legal Status of Jerusalem Following the ICJ Advisory Opinion on the Separation Barrier*, 38 ISR. L. REV. 298 (2005).
MENACHEM HOFNUNG, DEMOCRACY, LAW AND NATIONAL SECURITY IN ISRAEL (1996).
K. J. HOOD, CONFLICT OF LAWS WITHIN THE UK (2007).
MARK S.W. HOYLE, MIXED COURTS OF EGYPT (1991).

Hiba I. Husseini, *Challenges and Reforms in the Palestinian Authority*, 26 FORDHAM INT'L L.J. 500 (2003).

Bill Hutman & Amir Cheshin, *Living Together and Apart in Jerusalem: Lessons Learned*, *in* JERUSALEM: A CITY AND ITS FUTURE 401 (Marshal J. Breger & Ora Ahimeir eds., 2002).

Ardi Imseis, *Facts on the Ground: An Examination of Israeli Municipal Policy in East Jerusalem*, 15 AM. U. INT'L L. REV. 1039 (2000).

Ardi Imseis, *On the Fourth Geneva Convention and the Occupied Palestinian Territory*, 44 HARV. INT'L L. J. 65 (2003).

THE INTERNATIONAL COMMISSION OF JURISTS, THE CIVILIAN JUDICIAL SYSTEM IN THE WEST BANK AND GAZA: PRESENT AND FUTURE (Center for the Independence of Judges and Lawyers, 1994).

INTERNATIONAL LAW AND THE ADMINISTRATION OF OCCUPIED TERRITORIES: TWO DECADES OF ISRAELI OCCUPATION OF THE WEST BANK AND GAZA STRIP (Emma Playfair ed., 1992).

INTERNATIONAL LAW AND THE ISRAELI PALESTINIAN CONFLICT: A RIGHTS-BASED APPROACH TO MIDDLE EAST PEACE (Susan M. Akram et al. eds., 2011).

Israel Is Selling Lands in the Occupied Territories: Adalah Position Paper on the Privatization of the Lands of the Settlements on the Golan Heights and in East Jerusalem, 63 ADALAH'S NEWSLETTER (2009), *available at* http://www.adalah.org/features/land/Position_Paper_on_Land_Reform_and_EJ_and_GH_settlements_English_Final%5B1%5D.pdf.

ISRAEL NATIONAL SECTION OF THE INTERNATIONAL COMMISSION OF JURISTS, THE RULE OF LAW IN THE AREA ADMINISTERED BY ISRAEL (1981).

ISRAELI MINISTRY FOR FOREIGN AFFAIRS, INFORMATION DEPARTMENT, THE ARABS IN ISRAEL (1961).

George Ivezaj, *Oslo Breakdown: The Failing Israeli and Palestinian Peace Process*, 7 J. INT'L L. PRAC. 275 (1998).

Carey James, *Mere Words: The "Enemy Entity" Designation of the Gaza Strip*, 32 HASTINGS INT'L & COMP. L. REV. 643 (2009).

Philip C. Jessup, *Has the Supreme Court Abdicated One of Its Functions?*, 40 AM. J. INT'L L. 168 (1946).

W. Rupert Johnson, *The Mozambique Rule and the (Non) Jurisdiction of the Supreme Court of Western Australia over Foreign Land*, 31 U. W. AUST. L. REV. 266 (2003).

Friedrich K. Juenger, *The American Law of General Jurisdiction*, 2001 U. CHI. LEGAL F. 141 (2001).

Friedrich K. Juenger, *A Page of History*, 35 MERCER L. REV. 419 (1984).

Arie M. Kacowicz, *The Normative Dimension of International Relations and the Advisory Opinion of the ICJ on the Separation Barrier*, 38 ISR. L. REV. 348 (2005).

Yizhak Kahan, *Shipput Rabani ve-Shipput Hiloni* [*Rabbinic Jurisdiction and Secular Jurisdiction in Israel*], 7 DINNEI YISRA'EL 205 (1976).

O. KAHN-FREUND, GENERAL PROBLEMS OF PRIVATE INTERNATIONAL LAW (1976).

Marc S. Kaliser, *A Modern Day Exodus: International Human Rights Law and International Humanitarian Law Implications of Israel's Withdrawal from the Gaza Strip*, 17 IND. INT'L & COMP. L. REV. 187 (2007).

Michael M. Karayanni, *Access to Justice Ascends to International Civil Litigation: The Case of Palestinian Plaintiffs before Israeli Courts*, 33 CIVIL JUSTICE Q. 43 (2014).

Michael M. Karayanni, *In the Best Interests of the Group: Religious Matching under Israeli Adoption Law*, 3 BERKELEY J. MIDDLE EASTERN & ISLAMIC L. 1 (2010).

MICHAEL KARAYANNI, FORUM NON CONVENIENS IN THE MODERN AGE (2004).

Michael M. Karayanni, *The Separate Nature of the Religious Accommodations for the Palestinian-Arab Minority in Israel*, 5 NW. U. J. INT'L HUM. RTS. 41 (2006).

Michael M. Karayanni, *Two Concepts of Group Rights for the Palestinian-Arab Minority under Israel's Constitutional Definition as a "Jewish and Democratic" State*, 10 INT'L. J. CONST. L. 304 (2012).

Kemal H. Karpat, *Millets and Nationality: The Roots of the Incongruity of Nation and State in the Post-Ottoman Era*, *in* CHRISTIANS AND JEWS IN THE OTTOMAN EMPIRE 141 (Benjamin Braude & Bernard Lewis eds., 1982).

Anis F. Kassim, *Legal Systems and Developments in Palestine* 1 PALESTINE Y.B INT'L L. 19 (1984).

Anis F. Kassim, *The Palestine Liberation Organization's Claim to Status: A Juridical Analysis under International Law*, 9 DENV. J. INT'L L. & POL'Y 1 (1980).

Yadin Kaufmann, *Israel's Flexible Voters* 61 FOREIGN POL'Y 109 (1985–86).

Gerhard Kegel, *Paternal Home and Dream Home: Traditional Conflict of Laws and American Reformers* 27 AM. J. COMP. L. 615 (1979).

Tobias Kelly, *Jurisdictional Politics in the Occupied West Bank: Territory, Community, and Economic Dependency in the Formation of Legal Subjects*, 31 LAW & SOCIAL INQ. 39 (2006).

TOBIAS KELLY, LAW, VIOLENCE AND SOVEREIGNTY AMONG WEST BANK PALESTINIANS (2006).

Scott Kennedy, *The Druze of the Golan Heights: A Case of Non-Violent Resistance*, 13 J. PALESTINE STUD. 48 (1984).

Orde F. Kittrie, *More Process than Peace: Legitimacy, Compliance, and the Oslo Accords*, 101 MICH. L. REV. 1661 (2003).

Larry Kletter, Note, *The Sovereignty of Jerusalem in International Law*, 20 COLUM J. TRANSNAT'L L. 319 (1981).

Karen Knop, *Citizenship, Public and Private*, 71 LAW & CONTEMP. PROBS. 309 (2008).

Terry S. Kogan, *Toward a Jurisprudence of Choice-of-Law: The Propriety of Fairness over Comity*, 62 N.Y.U. L. REV. 651 (1987).

Rebecca Kook, *Dilemmas of Ethnic Minorities in Democracies: The Effects of Peace on the Palestinians in Israel*, 23 POL. & SOC'Y 309 (1995).

Hein Kötz, *Public Interest Litigation: A Comparative Survey*, *in* ACCESS TO JUSTICE AND THE WELFARE STATE 85 (Mauro Cappelletti ed., 1979).

DAVID KRETZMER, THE OCCUPATION OF JUSTICE: THE SUPREME COURT OF ISRAEL AND THE OCCUPIED TERRITORIES (2002).

JONATHAN KUTTAB & RAJA SHEHADEH, CIVILIAN ADMINISTRATION IN THE OCCUPIED WEST BANK: ANALYSIS OF ISRAELI MILITARY GOVERNMENT ORDER NO. 947 (1982).

Thomas S. Kuttner, *Israel and the West Bank: Aspects of the Law of Belligerent Occupation*, 7 ISR. Y.B. HUM. RTS. 166 (1977).

Bob Labes, Note, *The Law of Belligerent Occupation and the Legal Status of the Gaza Strip*, 9 MICH. Y.B. INT'L LEGAL STUD. 383 (1988).

Ruth Lapidoth, *International Law within the Israel Legal System*, 24 ISR. L. REV. 451 (1990).

ELIHU LAUTERPACHT, JERUSALEM AND THE HOLY PLACES (1968).

THE LAWS OF PALESTINE (Robert Harry Drayton compiler, revised ed. 1933).

Aharon Layish, *Ha-Mimsad ha-Dati ha-Muslimi ba-Gada Ha-Ma'aravit ba-Tkufa ha-Yardenit* [*The Islamic Religious Establishment in the West Bank During the Jordanian Period*], *in* ESER SHNOT SHILTON YISRA'ELI BE-YEHUDA U-SHOMRON [TEN YEARS OF ISRAELI RULE IN JUDEA AND SAMARIA] 13 (Rafi Yisraeli ed., 1981).

Stephen Lee, *Jurisdiction over Foreign Land: A Reappraisal*, 26 ANGLO-AM. L. REV. 273 (1997).

Stephen Lee, *Title to Foreign Real Property in Transnational Money Claims*, 32 COLUM. J. TRANSNAT'L L. 607 (1995).

ROBERT LEFLAR ET AL., AMERICAN CONFLICTS LAW (4th ed. 1986).

Robert A. Leflar, *Choice-Influencing Considerations in Conflicts Law*, 41 N.Y.U. L. REV. 267 (1966).

John Leubsdorf, *Constitutional Civil Procedure*, 63 TEX. L. REV. 579 (1984).

Alan Levine, *The Status of Sovereignty in East Jerusalem and the West Bank*, 5 N.Y.U. J. INT'L L. & POL. 485 (1972).

Evyatar Levine, *A Landmark on the Road to Legal Chaos: Recognition of the PLO as a Menace to World Public Order*, 10 DENV. J. INT'L L. & POL'Y 243 (1981).

A. LEVONTIN & H. GOLDWATER, KLALEI BREIRAT HA-DIN BE-YISRA'EL VE-HA-SIMAN 46 LE-DVAR HA-MELEKH [CHOICE OF LAW RULES IN ISRAEL AND ARTICLE 46 OF THE ORDER-IN-COUNCIL] (1974).

Nathan Levy, Jr., *Mesne Process in Personal Action at Common Law and the Power Doctrine*, 78 YALE L. J. 52 (1968).

BERNARD LEWIS, THE EMERGENCE OF MODERN TURKEY (1961).

Herbert J. Liebesny, *The Development of Western Judicial Privileges*, *in* LAW IN THE MIDDLE EAST 309 (Majid Khadduri & Herbert J. Liebesny eds., 1955).

HERBERT J. LIEBESNY, THE LAW OF THE NEAR AND MIDDLE EAST (1975).

CHARLES S. LIEBMAN & ELIEZER DON-YEHIYA, CIVIL RELIGION IN ISRAEL: TRADITIONAL JUDAISM AND POLITICAL CULTURE IN THE JEWISH STATE (1983).

Kurt Lipstein, *The General Principles of Private International Law*, 135 RECUEIL DES COURS 97 (1972-I).

JEHUDA LUKACS, ISRAEL, JORDAN AND THE PEACE PROCESS (1997).

IAN LUSTICK, ARABS IN THE JEWISH STATE: ISRAEL'S CONTROL OF A NATIONAL MINORITY (1980).

Ian S. Lustick, *Has Israel Annexed East Jerusalem?* 5 MIDDLE EAST POL'Y 34 (1997).

Harold G. Maier & Thomas R. McCoy, *A Unifying Theory for Judicial Jurisdiction and Choice of Law*, 39 AM. J. COMP. L. 249 (1991).

Peter Malanczuk, *Israel: Status, Territory and Occupied Territories*, *in* 2 ENCYCLOPEDIA OF PUBLIC INTERNATIONAL LAW 1468 (Rudolf Bernhardt ed., 1995).

Peter Malanczuk, *Some Basic Aspects of the Agreement between Israel and the PLO from the Perspective of International Law*, 7 EUR. J. INT'L L. 485 (1996).

CHIBLI MALLAT, INTRODUCTION TO MIDDLE EASTERN LAW (2007).

Sally V. Mallison & W. Thomas Mallison, *The Juridical Bases for Palestinian Self-Determination*, 1 PALESTINE Y.B. INT'L L. 36 (1984).

W. Thomas Mallison, Jr. & Sally V. Mallison, *A Juridical Analysis of the Israeli Settlements in the Occupied Territories*, 10 PALESTINE Y.B INT'L L. 1 (1998–99).

W. THOMAS MALLISON & SALLY V. MALLISON, THE PALESTINIAN PROBLEM IN INTERNATIONAL LAW AND WORLD ORDER (1986).

Andrew R. Malone, Comment, *Water Now: The Impact of Israel's Security Fence on Palestinian Water Rights and Agriculture in the West Bank*, 37 CASE W. RES. J. INT'L L. 639 (2005).

F. A. Mann, *The Doctrine of Jurisdiction in International Law*, 111 RECUEIL DES COURS 1 (1964-I).

Asher Maoz, *Application of Israeli Law to the Golan Heights Is Annexation*, 20 BROOK. J. INT'L L. 355 (1994).

Tayseer Mara'i & Usama R. Halabi, *Life under Occupation in the Golan Heights*, 22 J. PALESTINE STUD. 78 (1992).

Ebulula Mardin, *Development of the Shari'a under the Ottoman Empire*, *in* LAW IN THE MIDDLE EAST 279 (Majid Khadduri & Herbert J. Liebesny eds., 1955).

Mustafa Mari, *The Israeli Disengagement from the Gaza Strip: An End of Occupation?*, 8 Y.B. INT'L HUM. L. 356 (2005)

Charles F. Martel, *Give Peace a Chance: How Considering Peace Process Obligations Would Have Improved the Rulings of the International Court of Justice and the Israeli Supreme Court on the Israeli Security Barrier*, 17 DUKE J. COMP. & INT'L L. 305 (2007).

Abd El-Mahdi Massadeh, *The Structure of Public Administration in Jordan: A Constitutional and Administrative Law Perspective*, 14 ARAB L.Q. 91 (1999).

BRUCE MASTERS, CHRISTIAN AND JEWS IN THE OTTOMAN ARAB WORLD: THE ROOTS OF SECTARIANISM (2001).

DAVID MCCLEAN & KISCH BEEVERS, MORRIS ON THE CONFLICT OF LAWS (7th ed. 2009).

Luther L. McDougal III, *Toward Application of the Best Rule of Law in Choice-of-Law Cases*, 35 MERCER L REV. 483 (1984).

Kathryn M. McKinney, *The Legal Effects of the Israeli-PLO Declaration of Principles: Steps Toward Statehood for Palestine*, 18 SEATTLE U. L. REV. 93 (1994).

Katherine Meighan, Note, *The Israel-PLO Declaration of Principles: Prelude to Peace?*, 34 Va. J. Int'l L. 435 (1994).

Theodor Meron, *Applicability of Multilateral Conventions to Occupied Territories*, 72 Am. J. Int'l L. 542 (1978).

Theodor Meron, *West Bank and Gaza: Human Rights and Humanitarian Law in the Period of Transition*, 9 Isr. Y.B. Hum. Rts. 106 (1979).

Ya'akov Meron, *The Religious Courts in the Administered Territories*, *in* 1 Military Government in the Territories Administered by Israel: The Legal Aspects 353 (Meir Shamgar ed., 1982).

Frank I. Michelman, *The Supreme Court and Litigation Access Fees: The Right to Protect One's Rights—Part I*, 1973 Duke L.J. 1153.

Laurel E. Miller, Comment, *Forum Non Conveniens and State Control of Foreign Plaintiff Access to U.S. Courts in International Tort Actions*, 58 U. Chi. L. Rev. 1369 (1991).

Robert W. Miller, *The Formative Principles of Civil Procedure—I*, 18 Ill. L. Rev. 1 (1923).

Alex Mills, The Confluence of Public and Private International Law (2009).

Alex Mills, *The Private History of International Law*, 55 Int'l & Comp. L.Q. 1 (2006).

Robert H. Mnookin & Ehud Eiran, *Discord "Behind the Table": The Internal Conflict Among Israeli Jews Concerning the Future of Settlements in the West Bank and Gaza*, 1 J. Dispute Resolution 11 (2005).

Robert H. Mnookin, Ehud Eiran & Sreemat Mitter, *Barriers to Progress at the Negotiating Table: Internal Conflicts among Israelis and among Palestinians*, 6 Nev. L.J. 299, 311 (2006).

Keith C. Molkner, *Legal and Structural Hurdles to Achieving Political Stability and Economic Development in the Palestinian Territories*, 19 Fordham Int'l L.J. 1419 (1996).

Jonathan Molony, Michelle Stewart & Nancy Touhy-Hamill, From Settlement to Shelf: The Economic Occupation of the Syrian Golan (2009).

Peter J. Morgan III, Note, *Recent Israeli Security Measures under the Fourth Geneva Convention*, 3 Conn. J. Int'l L. 485 (1988).

C. G. J. Morse, *Not in the Public Interest?* Lubbe v. Cape Plc, 37 Tex. Int'l L.J. 541 (2002).

W. Müller-Freienfels, *Conflicts of Law and Constitutional Law*, 45 U. Chi. L. Rev. 598 (1978).

Guy Mundlak, *Power-Breaking or Power-Entrenching Law? The Regulation of Palestinian Workers in Israel*, 20 Comp. Lab. L. & Pol'y J. 569 (2000).

Kurt H. Nadelmann, Conflict of Laws: International and Interstate, Selected Essays (1972).

Kurt H. Nadelmann, *Jurisdictionally Improper Fora*, *in* XXth Century Comparative and Conflicts Law 321 (Kurt H. Nadelmann et al. eds., 1961).

Eli Nathan, *Israeli Civil Jurisdiction in the Administered Territories*, 13 Isr. Y.B. Hum. Rts. 90 (1983).

Eli Nathan, *The Power of Supervision of the High Court of Justice over Military Government*, *in* 1 MILITARY GOVERNMENT IN THE TERRITORIES ADMINISTERED BY ISRAEL 1967–1980: LEGAL ASPECTS 109 (Meir Shamgar ed., 1982).

Note, *Protection of Human Rights in Israeli-Occupied Territories*, 15 HARV. INT'L L.J. 470 (1974).

Arthur Nussbaum, *Jurisdiction and Foreign Judgments*, 41 COLUM. L. REV. 221 (1941).

ARTHUR NUSSBAUM, PRINCIPLES OF PRIVATE INTERNATIONAL LAW (1943).

Richard Ober, *Current Israeli Practices and Policies in the West Bank and the Gaza Strip: A Historical and Legal Analysis*, 10 B.C. THIRD WORLD L.J. 91 (1990).

William V. O'Brien, *The PLO in International Law*, 2 B.U. INT'L L.J. 349 (1984).

Graham Ogilvy, Belhas v. Ya'alon: *The Case for a* Jus Cogens *Exception to the Sovereign Immunities Act*, 8 J. INT'L BUS. & L. 169 (2009).

Wendy Olson, *UN Security Council Resolutions Regarding Deportations from Israeli Administered Territories: The Applicability of the Fourth Geneva Convention Relative to the Protection of Civilian Persons in Time of War*, 24 STAN. J. INT'L L. 611 (1988).

S. S. Onar, *The Majalla*, *in* LAW IN THE MIDDLE EAST 292 (Majid Khadduri & Herbert J. Liebesny eds., 1955).

Arie Pach, *Human Rights in the West Bank Military Courts*, 7 ISR. Y.B. HUM. RTS. 222 (1977).

Jordan J. Paust et al., *Report of ICJ Mission of Inquiry into the Military Court System in the Occupied West Bank and Gaza*, 14 HASTINGS INT'L & COMP. L. REV. 1 (1990).

Amir Paz-Fuchs & Yaël Ronen, *Occupational Hazards*, 30 BERKELEY J. INT'L L. 580 (2012).

Susan Power, *War, Invasion, Occupation? A Problem of Status on the Gaza Strip*, 12 TRINITY COLLEGE L. REV. 25 (2009).

James L. Prince, *The International Legal Implication of the November 1988 Palestinian Declaration of Statehood*, 25 STAN. J. INT'L L. 681 (1988–1989).

Antonin I. Pritetic, *Staking Claims against Foreign Defendants in Canada: Choice of Law and Jurisdictional Issues Arising From the In Personam Exception to the Mocambique Rule for Foreign Immovables*, 25 ADVOC. Q. 230 (2009).

William L. Prosser, *Interstate Publication*, 51 MICH. L. REV. 959 (1953).

Michael Pryles, *The Basis of Adjudicatory Competence in Private International Law*, 21 INT'L & COMP. L.Q. 61 (1972).

JOHN QUIGLEY, THE CASE FOR PALESTINE: AN INTERNATIONAL LAW PERSPECTIVE (2005).

John Quigley, *Judicial Autonomy in Palestine: Problems and Prospects*, 21 U. DAYTON L. REV. 697 (1996).

John Quigley, *Living in Legal Limbo: Israel's Settlers in Occupied Palestinian Territory*, 10 PACE INT'L L. REV. 1 (1998).

John Quigley, *Old Jerusalem: Whose to Govern*, 20 DENV. J. INT'L L. & POL'Y 145 (1991).

John Quigley, *Palestine Is a State: A Horse with Black and White Stripes Is a Zebra*, 32 MICH. J. INT'L L. 749 (2011).

John Quigley, The Statehood of Palestine: International Law in the Middle East Conflict (2010).

John Quigley, *Sovereignty in Jerusalem*, 45 Cath. U. L. Rev. 765 (1996).

Mazen Qupty, *The Application of International Law in the Occupied Territories as Reflected in the Judgments of the High Court of Justice in Israel*, *in* International Law and the Administration of Occupied Territories: Two Decades of Israeli Occupation of the West Bank and Gaza Strip 124 (Emma Playfair ed., 1992).

Reform of Civil Procedure: Essays on "Access to Justice" (A. A. S. Zuckerman & Ross Cranston eds., 1995).

Cheryl V. Reicin, *Preventive Detention, Curfews, Demolition of Houses, and Deportations: An Analysis of Measures Employed by Israel in the Administered Territories*, 8 Cardozo L. Rev. 515 (1987).

Mathias Reiman, *Domestic and International Conflicts in the United States and Western Europe*, *in* International Conflict of Laws for the Third Millennium: Essays in Honor of Friedrich K. Juenger 109 (Patrick J. Borchers & Joachim Zekoll eds., 2001).

Mathias Reiman, *A New Restatement—For the International Age*, 75 Ind. L. J. 575 (2000).

Yitzhak Reiter, *Irgun Inyanei ha-Dat shel ha-Muslimim be-Yerushalayim 1967–2001* [*The Organization of the Religious Affairs of Muslims in Jerusalem 1967–2001*], *in* ha-Ir ha-Atika [The Old City] 173 (Ruth Lapidoth ed., 2002).

Yitzhak Reiter, Islamic Institutions in Jerusalem: Palestinian Muslim Administration under Jordanian and Israeli Rule (1997).

Deborah L. Rhode, Access to Justice (2004).

Deborah L. Rhode, *Access to Justice*, 69 Fordham L. Rev. 1785 (2001).

Adam Roberts, *The Palestinians, the Uprising and International Law*, 2 J. Refugee Stud. 26 (1989).

Adam Roberts, *Prolonged Military Occupation: The Israeli-Occupied Territories since 1967*, 84 Am. J. Int'l L. 44 (1990).

Adam Roberts, *What Is a Military Occupation?*, 55 Brit. Y.B. Int'l L. 249 (1985).

Simon Roberts, *Litigation and Settlement*, *in* Reform of Civil Procedure: Essays on "Access to Justice" 447 (A. A. S. Zuckerman & Ross Cranston eds., 1995).

David W. Robertson & Paula K. Speck, *Access to State Courts in Transnational Personal Injury Cases: Forum Non Conveniens and Antisuit Injunctions*, 68 Tex. L. Rev. 937 (1990).

Yaël Ronen, *ICC Jurisdiction over Acts Committed in the Gaza Strip*, 8 J. Int'l Crim. Just. 3 (2010).

Meir Rosenne, *Development of Oil Resources in Sinai*, *in* 1 Military Government in the Territories Administered by Israel 1967–1980: Legal Aspects 335 (Meir Shamgar ed., 1982).

Shabtai Rosenne, *Directions for a Middle East Settlement—Some Underlying Legal Problems*, 33 Law & Contemp. Probs. 44 (1968).

Eugene Rostow, *Palestinian Self-Determination: Possible Futures for the Unallocated Territories of the Palestine Mandate*, 5 YALE STUD. IN WORLD PUB. ORDER 147 (1979).

CHERYL RUBENBERG, THE PALESTINIANS: IN SEARCH OF A JUST PEACE (2003).

Benjamin Rubin, *Disengagement from the Gaza Strip and Post-Occupation Duties*, 42 ISR. L. REV. 528 (2009).

Amnon Rubinstein, *The Changing Status of the "Territories" (West Bank and Gaza): From Escrow to Legal Mongrel*, 8 TEL-AVIV U. STUD. IN L. 59 (1988).

Amnon Rubinstein, *Yisra'el ve-ha-Shtakhim: Samkhuyot Shiput* [*Israel and the Territories: Judicial Powers*], 14 IYUNEI MISHPAT 415 (1989).

AMNON RUBINSTEIN & BARAK MEDINA, HA-MISHPAT HA-HUKATI SHEL MEDINAT YISRA'EL [THE CONSTITUTIONAL LAW OF THE STATE OF ISRAEL] (6th ed. 2005).

Robbie Sabel, *The International Court of Justice Decision on the Separation Barrier and the Green Line*, 38 ISR. L. REV. 316 (2005).

Elizabeth Samson, *Is Gaza Occupied?: Redefining the Status of Gaza under International Law*, 25 AM. U. INT'L L. REV. 915 (2010).

Jordie Saperia, *Jerusalem: Legal Status, Condominium and Middle East Peace*, 3 J. E. ASIA & INT'L L. 175 (2010).

Gidon Sapir, *Religion and State in Israel: The Case for Reevaluation and Constitutional Entrenchment*, 22 HASTINGS INT'L & COMP. L. REV. 617 (1999).

JOSEPH SCHACHT, AN INTRODUCTION TO ISLAMIC LAW (1964).

JEFFREY A. SCHOENBLUM, MULTISTATE AND MULTINATIONAL ESTATE PLANNING (2009).

David L. Schulman, *The Israel-PLO Accords on the Declaration of Principles on Interim Self-Government Arrangements: The First Step Toward Palestinian Self-Determination*, 7 EMORY INT'L L. REV. 793 (1993).

Adam N. Schupack, *The Arab-Israeli Conflict and Civil Litigation Against Terrorism*, 60 DUKE L.J. 207 (2010).

Rhona Schuz, *Controlling Forum-Shopping: The Impact of* MacShannon v. Rockware Glass Ltd., 35 INT'L & COMP. L.Q. 374 (1986).

DUDI SCHWARTZ, SEDER DIN EZRAHI: HIDUSHIM, TAHALIKHIM U-MEGAMOT [CIVIL PROCEDURE: DEVELOPMENTS, PROCESSES AND TRENDS] (2007).

Edmund H. Schwenk, *Legislative Power of the Military Occupant under Article 43, Hague Regulations*, 54 YALE L.J. 393 (1945).

Iain Scobbie, *An Intimate Disengagement: Israel's Withdrawal from Gaza, the Law of Occupation and of Self-Determination*, 11 Y.B. ISLAMIC & MIDDLE E. L. 3 (2003–2005).

Iain Scobbie, *Natural Resources and Belligerent Occupation: Perspectives from International Humanitarian and Human Rights Law*, *in* INTERNATIONAL LAW AND THE ISRAELI-PALESTINIAN CONFLICT: A RIGHTS-BASED APPROACH TO MIDDLE EAST PEACE 229 (Susan M. Akram et al. eds., 2011).

Eugene F. Scoles, *Interstate and International Distinctions in Conflict of Laws in the United States*, 54 CAL. L. REV. 1599 (1966).

EUGENE F. SCOLES ET AL., CONFLICT OF LAWS (4th ed. 2004).

Yoram Shachar, *History and Sources of Israeli Law*, *in* INTRODUCTION TO THE LAW OF ISRAEL 1 (Amos Shapira & Karen C. DeWitt-Arar eds., 1995).

GERSHON SHAFIR & YOAV PELED, BEING ISRAELI: THE DYNAMICS OF MULTIPLE CITIZENSHIP (2002).

Samirah Shah, *On the Road to Apartheid: The Bypass Road Network in the West Bank*, 29 COL. HUM. RGHTS L. REV. 221 (1997).

Ido Shahar, Falastinim be-Beit Din Yisra'eli: Tarbut, Shlita ve-Hitnagdut be-Beit ha-Din ha-Shara'i be-Ma'arav Yerushalayim [Palestinians before an Israeli Court: Culture, Control and Resistance in the *Shari'a* Court of West Jerusalem] (M.A. Thesis, Hebrew University of Jerusalem, 2000).

MICHAL SHAKED, MOSHE LANDAU, SHOFET [MOSHE LANDAU, JUDGE] (2012).

Meir Shamgar, *Legal Concepts and Problems of the Israeli Military Government—The Initial Stage*, *in* 1 MILITARY GOVERNMENT IN THE TERRITORIES ADMINISTERED BY ISRAEL 1967–1980: LEGAL ASPECTS 13 (Meir Shamgar ed., 1982).

Meir Shamgar, *The Observance of International Law in the Administered Territories*, 1 ISR. Y.B. HUM. RTS. 262 (1971).

Yuval Shany, *Faraway So Close: The Legal Status of Gaza after Israel's Disengagement*, 8 Y.B. HUMANITARIAN L. 369 (2005).

Yuval Shany, *The Law Applicable to the Non-Occupied Gaza: A Comment on* Bassiouni v. The Prime Minister of Israel, 42 ISR. L. REV. 101 (2009).

Amos Shapira, *Private International Law*, in INTRODUCTION TO THE LAW OF ISRAEL 361 (Amos Shapira & Karen C. DeWitt-Arar eds., 1995).

Amos Shapira, *Shiput Yisraeli u-Shiput Zar bi-Kfifa Ahat—ha-Anomaliya shel Beit ha-Din ha-Yevani ha-Ortodoksi be-Yerushalayim [Israeli Jurisdiction and Foreign Jurisdiction in One—The Anomaly of the Greek-Orthodox Court in Jerusalem]*, 25 HA-PRAKLIT 456 (1969).

ANDREW SHARF, BYZANTINE JEWRY FROM JUSTINIAN TO THE FOURTH CRUSADE (1971).

Menashe Shava, *Connecting Factors in Matters of Personal Status in Israel*, 5 TEL-AVIV U. STUD. IN L. 144 (1982).

MALCOLM N. SHAW, INTERNATIONAL LAW (6th ed. 2008).

Raja Shehadeh, *Can the Declaration of Principles Bring About a "Just and Lasting Peace?,"* 4 EUR. J. INT'L L. 555 (1993).

Raja Shehadeh, *The Gaza Occupation: Beginnings and Endings*, 14 PAL. Y.B. INT'L L. 13 (2006–2007).

Raja Shehadeh, *The Legislative Stages of the Israeli Military Occupation*, *in* INTERNATIONAL LAW AND THE ADMINISTRATION OF OCCUPIED TERRITORIES: TWO DECADES OF ISRAELI OCCUPATION OF THE WEST BANK AND GAZA STRIP 151 (Emma Playfair ed., 1992).

RAJA SHEHADEH, FROM OCCUPATION TO INTERIM ACCORDS: ISRAEL AND THE PALESTINIAN TERRITORIES (1997).

RAJA SHEHADEH, OCCUPIER'S LAW: ISRAEL AND THE WEST BANK (revised ed. 1985).

Raja Shehadeh, *Questions of Jurisdiction: A Legal Analysis of the Gaza-Jericho Agreement*, 23 J. PALESTINE STUD. 18 (1994).

RAJAH SHEHADEH, STRANGERS IN THE HOUSE: COMING OF AGE IN OCCUPIED PALESTINE (2002).

RAJA SHEHADEH & JONATHAN KUTTAB, THE WEST BANK AND THE RULE OF LAW (1980).

Leon Sheleff, *Application of Israeli Law to the Golan Heights Is Not Annexation*, 20 BROOK. J. INT'L L. 333 (1994).

PINHAS SHIFMAN, DINEI HA-MISHPAHA BE-YISRAEL [FAMILY LAW IN ISRAEL] (2d ed. 1995).

Pinhas Shifman, *Samkhut Beit-Din Rabani be-Nisu'in ve-Gerushin she-Ne'erkhu Mikhuts le-Yisrael [Jurisdiction of Rabbinical Courts over Marriage and Divorce Effected Abroad]*, 6 MISHPATIM 372 (1975).

Raja Shihadeh, *Can the Declaration of Principles Bring About a "Just and Lasting Peace"?*, 4 EUR. J. INT'L L. 555 (1993).

Ibrahim F. I. Shihata, I. Hadi Abushakra & Hans-Jürgen Gruss, *Legal Aspects of the World Bank's Assistance to the West Bank and the Gaza Strip*, 7 PAL. Y.B. INT'L L. 19 (1992–94).

Issac S. Shiloh, *Marriage and Divorce in Israel*, 5 ISR. L. REV. 479 (1970).

Joel Singer, *Aspects of Foreign Relations under the Israeli-Palestinian Agreements on Interim Self-Government Arrangements for the West Bank and Gaza*, 28 ISR. L. REV. 268 (1994).

Joel Singer, *The Establishment of a Civil Administration in the Areas Administered by Israel*, 12 ISR. Y.B. HUM. RTS. 259 (1982).

Jerome Slater, *Lost Opportunities for Peace in the Arab-Israeli Conflict: Israel and Syria (1948–2001)*, 27 INT'L SECURITY 79 (2002).

William R. Slomanson, *Palestinian Statehood: A Successionist Dialogue*, 8 MISKOLC J. INT'L L. 1 (2011).

Adam M. Smith, *Good Fences Make Good Neighbors?: The "Wall Decision" and the Troubling Rise of the ICJ as a Human Rights Court*, 18 HARV. HUM. RTS. J. 251 (2005).

Solon Solomon, *Occupied or Not: The Question of Gaza's Legal Status after the Israeli Disengagement*, 19 CARDOZO J. INT'L & COMP. L. 59 (2011).

JUNE STARR, LAW AS A METAPHOR: FROM ISLAMIC COURTS TO THE PALACE OF JUSTICE (1992).

STATE OF ISRAEL, MINISTRY OF JUSTICE & FOREIGN MINISTRY, HA-VA'ADA HA-TSIBURIT LE-HAKHANAT HOK HASINUT MEDINOT ZAROT: MISMAKHEI HA-VA'ADA [THE PUBLIC COMMITTEE ON DRAFTING THE FOREIGN STATES IMMUNITY LAW: THE COMMITTEE PAPERS] (2005).

Allan R. Stein, *The Meaning of "Essentially at Home" in* Goodyear Dunlop, 63 S. CAR. L. REV. 527 (2012).

YAEL STEIN, THE QUIET DEPORTATION: REVOCATION OF RESIDENCY OF EAST JERUSALEM PALESTINIANS (1997).

Gerald M. Steinberg, *Interpretations of Jewish Tradition on Democracy, Land, and Peace*, 43 J. CHURCH & STATE 93 (2001).

Milena Sterio, *The Gaza Strip: Israel, Its Foreign Policy, and the Goldstone Report*, 43 CASE W. RES. J. INT'L L. 229 (2010–2011).

JULIUS STONE, ISRAEL AND PALESTINE: ASSAULT ON THE LAW OF NATIONS (1981).

PETER STONE, EU PRIVATE INTERNATIONAL LAW: HARMONIZATION OF LAWS (2006).

JOSEPH STORY, COMMENTARIES ON THE CONFLICT OF LAWS, FOREIGN AND DOMESTIC (Boston, Hilliard, Gray, and Co., 1834).

JOSEPH STORY, COMMENTARIES ON THE CONFLICT OF LAWS, FOREIGN AND DOMESTIC (Boston, Hilliard, Gray & Co., 2d ed. 1841).

Andrew L. Strauss, *Beyond National Law: International Law of Personal Jurisdiction in Domestic Courts*, 36 HARV. INT'L L.J. 373 (1995).

JOHN STRAWSON, PARTITIONING PALESTINE: LEGAL FUNDAMENTALISM IN THE PALESTINIAN-ISRAELI CONFLICT 168 (2010).

SYMEON C. SYMEONIDES, THE AMERICAN CHOICE-OF-LAW REVOLUTION: PAST, PRESENT AND FUTURE (2006).

Ghada Talhami, *The Palestinian Perception of the Human Rights Issue*, 13 SYRACUSE J. INT'L L. & COM. 475 (1987).

MARK TESSLER, A HISTORY OF THE ISRAELI-PALESTINIAN CONFLICT 677 (2d ed. 2009).

Katherine Reece Thomas, *Non-Recognition, Personality and Capacity: The Palestine Liberation Organization and the Palestinian Authority in English Law*, 29 ANGLO-AM. L. REV. 228 (2000).

MICHAEL TILBURY ET AL., CONFLICT OF LAWS IN AUSTRALIA (2002).

Joseph B. Tulman, *The International Legal Status of Jerusalem*, 3 ASILS INT'L L.J. 39 (1979).

Mary Twitchell, *The Myth of General Jurisdiction*, 101 HARV. L. REV. 610 (1988).

EDOARDO VITTA, THE CONFLICT OF LAWS IN MATTERS OF PERSONAL STATUS IN PALESTINE (1947).

Christof von Dryander, *Jurisdiction in Civil and Commercial Matters under the German Code of Civil Procedure*, 16 INT'L LAW. 671 (1982).

GERHARD VON GLAHN, THE OCCUPATION OF ENEMY TERRITORY: A COMMENTARY ON THE LAW AND PRACTICE OF BELLIGERENT OCCUPATION (1957).

Bernd von Hoffmann, *The Europeanization of Private International Law*, in EUROPEAN PRIVATE INTERNATIONAL LAW 13 (Bernd von Hoffmann ed., 1998).

Arthur Taylor von Mehren, *Must Plaintiffs Seek out Defendants? The Contemporary Standing of Actor Sequitur Forum Rei*, 8 KING'S COLLEGE L.J. 23 (1997).

Arthur T. von Mehren & Donald Trautman, *Jurisdiction to Adjudicate: A Suggested Analysis*, 79 HARV. L. REV. 1121 (1966).

Martin Wählisch, *Beyond a Seat in the United Nations: Palestine's U.N. Membership and International Law*, 53 HARV. INT'L L.J. ONLINE 226 (2012).

BERNARD WASSERSTEIN, THE BRITISH IN PALESTINE: THE MANDATORY GOVERNMENT AND ARAB- JEWISH CONFLICT, 1917–1929 (2d ed. 1991).

Celia Wasserstein Fassberg, *Israel and the Palestinian Authority: Jurisdiction and Legal Assistance*, 28 ISR. L. REV. 318 (1994).

CELIA WASSERSTEIN FASSBERG, MISHPAT BEINLE'UIMI PRATI [PRIVATE INTERNATIONAL LAW] (2013).

CELIA WASSERSTEIN-FASSBERG, PSAKIM ZARIM BA-MISHPAT HA-YISRA'ELI: HA-DIN VE-HEGYONO [FOREIGN JUDGMENTS IN ISRAELI LAW: DECONSTRUCTION AND RECONSTRUCTION] (1996).

GEOFFREY R. WATSON, THE OSLO ACCORDS: INTERNATIONAL LAW AND THE ISRAELI-PALESTINIAN PEACE AGREEMENTS (2000).

Geoffrey R. Watson, *The "Wall" Decision in Legal and Political Context*, 99 AM. J. INT'L L. 6 (2005).

Ruth Wedgwood, *The ICJ Advisory Opinion on the Israeli Security Fence and the Limits of Self-Defense*, 99 AM. J. INT'L L. 52 (2005).

Joseph H. Weiler, *Israel and the Creation of a Palestinian State: The Art of the Impossible and the Possible*, 17 TEX. INT'L L.J. 287 (1982).

Joseph H. H. Weiler, *Israel, the Territories and International Law: When Doves are Hawks*, *in* ISRAEL AMONG THE NATIONS: INTERNATIONAL AND COMPARATIVE LAW PERSPECTIVES ON ISRAEL'S 50TH ANNIVERSARY 381 (Alfred E. Kellermann et al. eds, 1998).

Jill Allison Weiner, Comment, *Israel, Palestine and the Oslo Accords*, 23 FORDHAM INT'L L.J. 230 (1999).

Justus R. Weiner, *An Analysis of the Oslo II Agreement in Light of the Expectations of Shimon Peres and Mahmoud Abbas*, 17 MICH. J. INT'L L. 667 (1996).

Justus R. Weiner, *Co-Existence without Conflict: The Implementation of Legal Structure for Israeli-Palestinian Cooperation Pursuant to the Interim Peace Agreement*, 26 BROOK. J. INT'L L. 591 (2000).

Justus R. Weiner, *Hard Facts Meet Soft Law—The Israel-PLO Declaration of Principles and the Prospects for Peace: A Response to Katherine W. Meigham*, 35 VA. J. INT'L L. 931 (1995).

RUSSELL J. WEINTRAUB, COMMENTARY ON THE CONFLICT OF LAWS (4th ed. 2001).

B. Welling & E. A. Heakes, *Tort and Foreign Immovables Jurisdiction in Conflict of Laws*, 18 U. W. ONTARIO L. REV. 295 (1979–1980).

Michael J. Whincop, *Conflicts in the Cathedral: Towards a Theory of Property Rights in Private International Law*, 50 U. TORONTO L.J. 41 (2000).

William H. Wicker, *The Development of the Distinction Between Local and Transitory Actions*, 4 TENN. L. REV. 55 (1926).

Sarah Williams, *Has International Law Hit the Wall? An Analysis of International Law in Relation to Israel's Separation Barrier*, 24 BERKELEY J. INT'L L. 192 (2006).

SIR HARRY WOOLF, ACCESS TO JUSTICE: FINAL REPORT TO THE LORD CHANCELLOR ON THE CIVIL JUSTICE SYSTEM IN ENGLAND AND WALES (1996).

Quincy Wright, *The Middle East Problem*, 64 AM. J. INT'L L. 270 (1970).

Assaf Ya'acov, *Hasinut Tahat Esh: Hasinut ha-Medina Beshel Nezek she-Nigram Ketotsa'a mi-"Pe'ula Milhamtit" [Immunity under Fire: State Immunity for Damage Caused by "Combat Action"]*, 33 MISHPATIM 107 (2003).

U. Yadin, *Reception and Rejection of English Law in Israel*, 11 INT'L & COMP. L.Q. 59 (1962).

Yael Yishai, *Israeli Annexation of East Jerusalem and the Golan Heights: Factors and Processes*, 21 MIDDLE EASTERN STUD. 45 (1985).

Hessel E. Yntema, *The Historic Bases of Private International Law*, 2 AM. J. COMP. L. 297 (1953).

Adam G. Yoffie, Comment, *The Palestine Problem: The Search for Statehood and the Benefit of International Law*, 36 YALE J. INT'L L. 497 (2011).

Eyal Zisser, *June 1967: Israel's Capture of the Golan Heights*, 7 ISR. STUD. 168 (2002).

ADRIAN ZUCKERMAN, ZUCKERMAN ON CIVIL PROCEDURE (2d ed. 2006).

Index

C

D

U

V

W

Y

Z

www.ingramcontent.com/pod-product-compliance
Lightning Source LLC
LaVergne TN
LVHW062224200926
848484LV00006B/1473
9780199873715